PHILADELPHIA ACCESS

W9-BFI-468

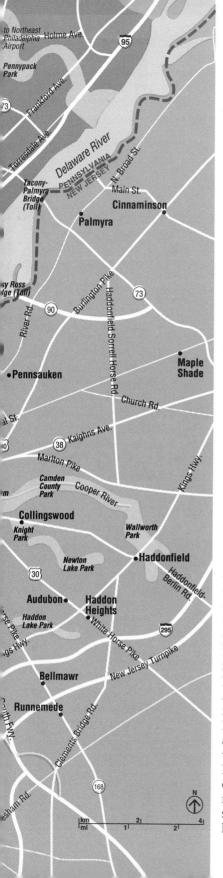

Orientation

Permit Philadelphians a moment of expansiveness. After years of hearing their city distinguished mainly for the Liberty Bell, cheesesteaks, brick streets, and rabid sports fans, civic pride is on the upswing as a result of a massive dose of revitalization. The $500 million **Pennsylvania Convention Center** officially opened in July of 1993, its debut heralded with a series of newspaper editorials instructing everyone to be on good behavior. (For Philadelphia's surly cabbies, this may mean charm school.) Meanwhile, **City Hall**, a stately granite and white marble monolith finished at the turn of the century, has seen its 584-foot-tall tower emerge from a face-lift that kept it under scaffolding for years. And **30th Street Station**, a beautiful early 20th-century train station, was recently restored to its Depression-era grandeur.

Tour operators who once considered Philadelphia a day-trip destination—catch the **Liberty Bell, Betsy Ross House, Rodin Museum, Philadelphia Museum of Art, Independence Hall** and get out before sundown—now urge visitors to spend a few leisurely days getting to know their city. **William Penn** designed Philadelphia with the pedestrian in mind and walking is still the best way to see this spirited metropolis. The town is laid out in quadrants, with City Hall at the center. Each of the four areas is arranged around a public square: **Franklin Square** near Independence Hall; **Washington Square** near Society Hill; **Rittenhouse Square**, west of Broad Street, and **Logan Circle**, with the recently refurbished **Swann Fountain**, at the Benjamin Franklin Parkway. Wander a few blocks from any of these tranquil greenswards to delve into Philadelphia's history. The past isn't confined to museums here, nor is it necessarily marked on your historic-sites map. You'll see it in the horse-and-buggy-size alleys; the

Old City factories converted to condos; the regal row houses flanking Rittenhouse Square; and at funky, down-home **Reading Terminal Market**, where you can stock up on Lancaster County produce, Amish baked goods, and Italian gourmet sauces.

In contrast to its blue-collar image, Philadelphia also has a reputation as a bastion of culture. The city is now developing an "Avenue of the Arts" corridor of buildings devoted to the performing arts near the **Academy of Music** on South Broad Street. And a renaissance that began in the late 1970s continues to produce new coffeehouses, bookstores, and restaurants for loyal patrons. Philadelphia has also shed its meat-and-potatoes tendencies in favor of culinary inventiveness, owing in part to the various ethnic groups that have settled in this city of neighborhoods. **Chinatown**, near the convention center, boasts a number of authentic (and inexpensive) Vietnamese and Thai restaurants as well as vegetarian diners and noodle shops. And if you search beyond the well-publicized trattorias of **South Philadelphia**, you'll find many menus that transcend the traditional tomato sauce.

Past the area that locals call **Center City** is **Fairmount Park**, a cool stretch of green popular for its bike and nature trails; the satellite neighborhoods of **University City**, where you'll find three college campuses and thousands of students; trendy **Manayunk**; ultraposh **Chestnut Hill**, home to the country's first cricket club; and the gaming halls of **Atlantic City. Kelly Drive** snakes along the **Schuylkill River**, offering ringside seats for rowing competitions as well as urban skyline vistas, while a host of nightclubs along the **Delaware River** have been known to inspire more than a few waterside pub crawls.

Many new attractions, particularly waterfront bars and dancehalls, wouldn't have had a prayer in what was a somewhat stodgy town 20 years ago. For decades Philadelphia lived in the shadow of Manhattan, just 90 miles to the north, and omnipresent history—such as **Christ Church**, where brass plaques mark the pews once occupied by **George Washington** and **Benjamin Franklin**—represented the city's only draw. A reverse trend is in progress, however, with New Yorkers (among others) discovering a place that's quieter, cleaner, less frantic . . . and full of possibility. And though the "City of Brotherly Love" may still feel a bit awkward in its new urbane role, no one will fault Philadelphians for a little self congratulation—the city has been modest for too long.

City Hall

Philadelphia International Airport (PHL)

Terminal Locations for Major Airlines

A American Airlines
American Eagle
Swissair
Lufthansa German Airlines
Air Jamaica
USAir (intl. arrivals only)
MAC (intl. arrivals only)
British Airways
Charters

B USAir (domestic depart)
USAir Express

C USAir (domestic/intl. depart)
Continental
Continental Express
Midwest Express

D MAC (depart only)
United

E TWA
TWA Express
Delta Air Lines
Delta Connection
Northwest
Northwest Airlink

Getting to Philadelphia

Area code 215 unless otherwise noted.

Philadelphia International Airport (PHL)
Located in southwest Philadelphia, eight miles from
Center City, the airport has direct flights to more than
a hundred national and international destinations. A
$1 billion renovation is in progress (to be completed
by 1997), so anticipate some inconveniences when
flying into or out of the airport. The Overseas
Terminal already has been replaced by a brand-new
facility, **Terminal A.** Be prepared to walk a lot (though
plans to install moving sidewalks in some areas are
in the works). If that's a problem, contact your airline
for courtesy cart service.

Driving to Center City from the airport, take Interstate
95 north and get off at Exit 17 (Central Philadelphia).
This puts you on the Vine Street Expressway
(Interstate 676), which has Center City exits for
Broad Street, 15th Street, and 21st Street.

Airlines

Air Jamaica	800/523.5585
Air Mobility Command	897.5640
American Airlines	800/443.7300
American Eagle	800/443.7300
British Airways	800/AIRWAYS
Continental	800/525.0280
Continental Express	800/525.0280
Delta Air Lines	800/221.1212
Delta Connection	800/221.1212
Midwest Express	800/452.2022
Northwest Airlines	800/225.2525
Northwest Airlink	800/225.2525
Swissair	800/221.4750
TWA	800/221.2000
TWA Express	800/221.2000
United	800/241.6522
USAir	563.8055
USAir Express	800/428.4322

Rental Cars

Alamo	800/327.9633
Avis	800/331.1212
Budget	800/527.0700
Dollar	800/562.7850
Hertz	800/654.3131

Airport Shuttles and **Limousines** listed below offer a
range of services, including drop-offs at the city's
major hotels and door-to-door service to the
suburbs. The fares start at about eight dollars per
person. Most of the shuttles run every 15 to 30
minutes; call ahead with flight information to make
reservations.

Airport Limelight Limousine Inc	342.5557
Dave's Best Limousine Service	288.1000
Deluxe Transportation Company	463.8787
Philadelphia Airport Shuttle	969.1818

Buses do not run directly downtown from the airport,
but you can take the No. 37 to Broad Street and
Snyder Avenue or the No. 68 to Broad Street and
Oregon Avenue, and then take the Broad Street subway northbound to City Hall. Bus No. 108 also leaves
from the airport for the 69th Street Terminal in Upper
Darby. Look for SEPTA bus stops outside baggage-
claim areas.

**Southeastern Pennsylvania Transportation
Authority (SEPTA)** is the best means of public
transportation to and from the airport; it runs a high-
speed rail line that picks up passengers at all five
airport terminals for nonstop service to three Center
City locations: **30th Street Station, Suburban
Station,** and **Market East Station.** The trains (which
are cleaner and faster than the subways) leave the
airport every 30 minutes from 6:10AM to 12:10AM.
(SEPTA claims the on-time rate falls in the 90th per-
centile, which sure beats most of the airlines.) Adult
fare is five dollars.

Taxis line up outside baggage-claim areas; be
prepared to part with at least $20 for a ride to
Center City.

Airport Emergencies	**937.6800**
General Information	937.6937
Lost and Found	936.6888
Paging	937.6937
Parking	492.2775
Police	937.6918
Transportation	937.6937
Traveler's Aid	365.6525
U.S. Customs Service	596.1972

Getting around Philadelphia

Bikes

Cycling in town is not for the faint-of-heart. With narrow streets, parked cars, and unsympathetic drivers, cyclists have a hard time getting around, particularly in Center City. But just beyond the downtown core, you'll find lots of options. By taking advantage of the new **Bike-On-Rail** permits offered by SEPTA and PATCO, you can bring your bike on board trains going all the way to Atlantic City.

West River and Kelly drives on each side of the **Schuylkill River** have more than nine miles of exclusive bike and jogging paths. On weekends in warmer months the drives close to through traffic during designated times. A bike map of the Delaware Valley, showing several hundred miles of suggested routes in the three-state area, can be purchased by writing to the **Bicycle Coalition of the Delaware Valley,** P.O. Box 8194, Philadelphia, PA 19101; or calling 242.9253.

Buses

For the most part, bus service here is clean, reliable, and safe. **SEPTA** operates a large fleet of buses and trolleys that feed into the rail and subway system, with several routes designed specifically with the tourist in mind. Starting from the **Society Hill/South Street** area, the No. 76 bus runs along **Chestnut Street** and the **Benjamin Franklin Parkway,** offering a panorama of the city and stops at all the museums. The No. 38 will take you from Center City down the Benjamin Franklin Parkway all the way to the **Philadelphia Zoo,** and the No. 42 connects Center City to the **Civic Center** and **University City**—home to the University of Pennsylvania and Drexel University.

Base fare on most routes is $1.50 and 40 cents for a transfer. Senior citizens ride free during off-peak hours and holidays; children under 12 pay 50 cents (have exact change; paper money is accepted). Discounted tokens and passes can be purchased at the SEPTA sales offices in the three Center City stations and in most Rite Aid drugstores.

Driving

With the recent completion of several highway projects, you no longer need to be an expert map reader to navigate Philadelphia. Interstate 95 now has a number of Center City exits, complete with overhead signs directing motorists to the best routes. The main east-west highway through the city, the **Schuylkill Expressway** (Interstate 76), has been completely reconstructed, though the shoulders still seem narrow in places. Also, some entrance ramps converge suddenly with speeding traffic. Be careful! The **Vine Street Expressway (**Interstate 676) connects the Schuylkill Expressway with Interstate 95, and provides a fast way to cut through Center City. Except during rush hour, traffic on these highways generally moves smoothly.

A neat little grid system developed in 1682 by **Thomas Holme,** surveyor for **William Penn,** makes it easy to figure out Center City. The grid's boundaries comprise the two square miles between the Delaware and Schuylkill rivers, and Vine and South streets.

Numbered streets run north-south, while those with names run east-west. The **Benjamin Franklin Parkway,** Philadelphia's version of the Champs-Elysées, cuts diagonally across the grid from City Hall to the Philadelphia Museum of Art and Fairmount Park.

Ferries

Before suspension bridges existed, commuters used to ferry across the Delaware River every day; now it's mostly tourists who do so. When weary of pounding the city pavement, put your feet up aboard the **Riverbus Ferry** to Camden for breathtaking views of Philadelphia and the sleek **New Jersey State Aquarium**. Departing every 30 minutes from Penn's Landing (Delaware Avenue and Walnut Street), the 400-passenger ferry takes 10 minutes to cross and docks one hundred yards from the aquarium. Grab a snack from a hot-dog vendor before you go (there's no food or drink served aboard). For further information, contact the Riverbus Ferry at 800/634.4027.

Parking

Half the automobiles in the city at any one time seem to be cruising for parking. Meter parking in Center City is hard to find, plus, for the most part, it's restricted to two hours. (Warning: Parking regulations are strictly enforced!) Your best bet is to leave the car at your hotel or in one of the many garages in Center City, then walk or take public transportation from there. The **Philadelphia Parking Authority (PPA)** operates several downtown garages with slightly lower rates than at the commercial garages. PPA's "Early Bird" rates (in by 9AM or 10AM and out by 6PM) are as cheap as you'll find. (Call PPA at 563.7670 for locations.) If you insist on trying your luck with meters, come with a bankroll of quarters: downtown meters cost 25 cents per 15 minutes. (Meter parking around the museums on the Parkway is less expensive and more practical since most spots offer 12-hour parking.) Unless you have a permit, neighborhoods generally restrict parking to two hours.

Subways

The **Broad Street** subway runs north-south through the city, while the **Market-Frankford** line runs east-west. While the Market East Station in Center City fairly gleams, most others are pretty grim. Avoid the subway at night unless you're going to a game at the sports complex (when you're sure to be part of a crowd).

Base fare on most routes is $1.50 and 40 cents for a transfer. Senior citizens ride free during off-peak hours and holidays; children under 12 pay 50 cents (have exact change; paper money is accepted). Discounted tokens and passes can be purchased at the SEPTA sales offices in the three Center City stations and in most Rite Aid drugstores. One of the best bargains going is SEPTA's **Day Pass,** which is good for a day's unlimited riding on all city transit vehicles, plus a one-way trip on the **Airport High Speed Line;** purchase the five dollar pass at the **Philadelphia Convention and Visitors Bureau** (16th Street and John F. Kennedy Boulevard).

Taxis

Cabs in Philly tend to be more expensive than in other Northeast cities. With a fleet of 1,400 taxis, however, they are plentiful, lining up to wait for business at hotels and designated taxi stops. Otherwise, step into the street and hail one with a whistle or a "Yo!" Taxi companies include **Quaker City Cab** (728.8000), **United Cab** (238.9500), and **Yellow Cab Company** (922.8400).

Trains

SEPTA's regional rail lines splay in every direction, hitting outlying areas of the city and the suburbs. Trains use three Center City locations: 30th Street Station (at Market Street), where you can make connections with **Amtrak** trains, Suburban Station (16th Street and John F. Kennedy Boulevard), and Market East Station (11th and Market streets).

For some wonderful day trips, take a train ride to **Doylestown, Merion** (site of the **Barnes Foundation** art museum), and other towns on the famous **Main Line.** See **Chestnut Hill** via the R8 Chestnut Hill West, which connects with the **Chestnut Hill Trolley,** a refurbished historic trolley that runs up and down Germantown Avenue. Fares on SEPTA's regional rail lines range from two to six dollars for a one-way ticket. For route information throughout the system, call SEPTA at 580.7800

The **Port Authority Transit Corporation (PATCO)** operates the Hi-Speedline that runs between four stops in Center City (Eighth and Market streets, 10th and Locust streets, 12th and Locust streets, and 16th and Locust streets), then crosses the Benjamin Franklin Bridge to points in southern New Jersey. To reach the **Camden Aquarium** take the Hi-Speedline to Broadway, then catch NJ Transit's Aqualink Shuttle. For information on PATCO, call 922.4600.

Walking

To get a feel for both old and new Philadelphia, you're best off hitting the pavement, where one minute you'll find yourself dwarfed by the recent crop of skyscrapers and the next winding your way through narrow streets lined with brick row houses dating back to the Revolution. **Center City's** hotels, historic sites, and museums are all conveniently close to one another, and parks and gardens offer a resting place when legs tire. You can easily stroll from the Delaware to the Schuylkill rivers in an hour; the most scenic route is along **Pine Street,** which starts in the residential neighborhood of **Society Hill,** turns into **Antique Row,** and ends near **Fitler Square** at the Schuylkill River.

The **Foundation for Architecture** leads some illuminating walking tours of the city's finer buildings, focusing on specific neighborhoods, architectural styles, or architects such as the influential **Frank Furness,** famous for his elaborate Victorian Gothic structures. Call 569.8687 for information. Warning: Beware motorists at intersections who have a habit of not yielding the right-of-way to pedestrians! Cars turning right on red pose great hazards to walkers.

FYI

Climate

Although prolonged spells of extreme weather are rare in any season, the prime time to visit Philadelphia is during the warmer months, April through October. September and October are the driest months, and also some of the prettiest since they coincide with the peak foliage season. In April and May the area runs rife with delicate new greenery and blossoms. On average, August brings the most sunny days, but that translates into hot and humid. Average daily highs in late April approach the 70s and hover in the 80s during the summer; temperatures cool back to the 70s in September.

Drinking

Pennsylvania's legal drinking age is 21. State-run stores throughout the city sell liquor and wine, but the selection of fine vintages in these stores is generally poor. Also, beer can't be purchased in supermarkets, as it can in more "enlightened" states, but you can buy a six-pack in a bar or at special distribution centers.

Publications

The *Philadelphia Inquirer,* the city's top all-around newspaper, has won 17 Pulitzers over the past 20 years, largely for investigative series on topics as wide-ranging as police brutality, the energy crisis, and America's blood supply. The Friday edition includes a "Weekend" section that has comprehensive listings of events and entertainment. The *Philadelphia Daily News,* a tabloid with no Sunday edition, emphasizes local news and sports. The *Philadelphia Tribune* serves the city's African-American population with editions on Tuesday, Thursday, and Friday. The *City Paper,* a freebie distributed at newspaper boxes throughout Center City and the suburbs, has especially thorough cultural and entertainment write-ups, as well as insightful political commentary on regional doings.

For a view of Center City from the people who live there, as well as entertainment and restaurant listings, pick up a copy of the *Welcomat,* a free paper published on Wednesday. *Philadelphia Magazine,* a full-color glossy sold at newsstands, offers slick, in-depth reporting of the region, plus film, theater, and cultural listings. Featuring an extensive dining directory, the magazine gives the "Best of Philly" awards you'll see hanging in area restaurants. *Business Philadelphia* caters to the city's business community. *PGN (Philadelphia Gay News)* serves the gays and lesbians. Refer to *Metrokids* and *Parents Express* for their monthly listings of children's events and other ideas about where to take the kids. Free newspapers can be found at bookstores, record stores, and some restaurants.

Radio and Television Stations
Radio

WHYY	Public Radio	91 FM
WRTI	Jazz/Blues	90 FM
WEAZ	Contemporary	101 FM
WFLN	Classical	95.7 FM
WMMR	Rock	93.3 FM
WYSP	Classic Rock	94 FM
WWDB	Talk Radio	96.5 FM
WXPN	Eclectic	88.5 FM
WXTU	Country	92 FM
KYW	News Radio	1060 AM
WDAS	Rhythm and Blues	1480 AM
WPHE	Spanish	690 AM

Television

KYW	Channel 3 (NBC)
WPVI	Channel 6 (ABC)
WCAU	Channel 10 (CBS)
WHYY	Channel 12 (PBS)
WPHL	Channel 17
WTXF	Channel 29 (FOX)
WGBS	Channel 57

Restrooms
In New York, everyone uses The Plaza Hotel; in Philadelphia, you'll have to settle for the Four Seasons, Ritz-Carlton, Sheraton, or Omni for a luxurious pit stop. Otherwise, fast-food restaurants and department stores won't turn you away in an emergency.

Sightseeing Operators
American Trolley Tours/Choo Choo
Trolley Company ....333.032●
Audio Walk and Tour ....925.123●
Centipede Tours, Inc. ....735.312●
Foundation for Architecture.......................569.318●
Liberty Belle Charters ....629.113●
Penn's Landing Trolley.............................627.080●
'76 Carriage Company ....923.851●
Spirit of Philadelphia ....923.141●

Smoking
Pennsylvania state law requires restaurants seating 75 or more people to have a nonsmoking section. Smaller restaurants must have a nonsmoking section or post a sign up front stating otherwise.

Street Smarts
The same rules apply here as they do to every other city—avoid down-and-out neighborhoods (especially **West Philadelphia** and **North Philadelphia**), guard pocketbooks and wallets, and, at night, stay in well-lit areas that have a lot of foot traffic. It's not a savvy idea at any time of day to venture into unfamiliar neighborhoods beyond the walking tours of this book. Keep your car doors locked no matter where you're driving, and whenever you park on the street.

Taxes
The 7 percent sales tax includes almost everything but clothing. The hotel tax is a whopping 12 percent, one of the highest in the country.

Telephone
All Philadelphia and suburban phone numbers have either the 215 or the 610 area code; numbers in South Jersey begin with a 609 area code.

Phone Book

Emergencies (Ambulance/Fire/Police) **911**
Dental Emergency **925.6050**
Medical Emergency **563.5343**
AAA Keystone Automobile Club.................569.4321
Children's Hospital 590.1000
Graduate Hospital.....................................893.2350
Hahnemann Hospital 448.7963
Hospital of the University of Pennsylvania ..662.3920
Thomas Jefferson Hospital.......................955.6840
Pennsylvania Hospital 829.3358
Poison Control Center 386.2100
Rape Hotline...985.3333
Rite Aid Pharmacies 464.3171

Visitor Information
Central City Ticket Office 735.1350
Foreign Language Translation 893.8900
Independence National Historical Park 627.1776
Philadelphia Convention and
Visitors Bureau................636.1666, 800/537.7676
Traveler's Aid 546.0571
Upstages (tickets) 567.0670
Visitors Information at the Bourse.............923.6317
Wanamaker's Ticket Office 568.7100

Other Important Numbers
Amtrak 824.1600
Bank Street Hostel...................................922.0222
Better Business Bureau 448.6100

Chamounix Mansion (youth hostel)............878.367●
Greyhound/Trailways Bus Lines ....931.400●
Handicapped Information...........................686.279●
SEPTA..574.780●
Time...846.121●
Weather ....936.121●
Western Union ....800/325.600●

Philadelphia has collected a large number of "firsts" in American history. In addition to the first paper mill, sugar refinery, and life insurance company, the city boasts the country's earliest private mental institution and its first hospital-performed amputation. Then there's the first American-made sulfuric acid, first steam-powered automobile, first federal housing project, first union strike, and first computer. But wait! There's even more: the revolving door, streetlight, ice cream soda, and merry-go-round were all introduced to the U.S. here as well.

"If you would not be forgotten as soon as you are dead and rotten, either write things worth reading or do things worth writing."

Benjamin Franklin

low to Read this Guide

HILADELPHIA ACCESS® is arranged so you can see
t a glance where you are and what is around you.
he numbers next to the entries in the following
hapters correspond to the numbers on the maps.
he text is color-coded according to the kind of place
escribed:

estaurants/Clubs: Red   **Hotels:** Blue

hops/ Outdoors: Green   **Sights/Culture:** Black

ating the Restaurants and Hotels

he restaurant star ratings take into account the
uality, service, atmosphere, and uniqueness of
e restaurant. An expensive restaurant doesn't
ecessarily ensure an enjoyable evening; however,
small, relatively unknown spot could have good
ood, professional service, and a lovely atmosphere.
herefore, on a purely subjective basis, stars are used
o judge the overall dining value (see the star ratings
bove at right). Keep in mind that chefs and owners
ften change, which sometimes drastically affects the
uality of a restaurant. The ratings in this guidebook
re based on information available at press time.

he price ratings, as categorized above at right, apply
o restaurants and hotels. These figures describe
eneral price-range relationships among other res-
aurants and hotels in the area. The restaurant price
atings are based on the average cost of an entrée for
ne person, excluding tax and tip. Hotel price ratings
eflect the base price of a standard room for two
eople for one night during the peak season.

Restaurants

★★★★	An Extraordinary Experience	
★★★	Excellent	
★★	Very Good	
★	Good	
$$$$	Big Bucks	($35 and up)
$$$	Expensive	($20-$35)
$$	Reasonable	($12-$20)
$	The Price Is Right	(less than $12)

Hotels

$$$$	Big Bucks	($175 and up)
$$$	Expensive	($125-$175)
$$	Reasonable	($75-$125)
$	The Price Is Right	(less than $75)

Map Key

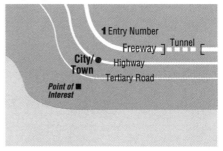

ear-Round Philadelphia

anuary
Mummers Parade, U.S. Pro Indoor Tennis
hampionships, Philadelphia International
uto Show

ebruary
Black History Month, Philadelphia Boat Show,
Philadelphia Home Show, Spectacor Presidential
azz Weekend

March
t. Patrick's Day Parade, Philadelphia Flower Show,
he Book and the Cook, Easter Promenade

April
enn Relays, Philadelphia Antiques Show

May
Philadelphia International Theater Festival for
hildren, Philadelphia Open House, Rittenhouse
quare Flower Market, Jambalaya Jam, Devon Horse
how, Mount Airy Day

une
Rittenhouse Square Fine Arts Annual, Elfreth's Alley
ays, CoreStates Pro Cycling Championship, Mellon
azz Festival

uly
uly Fourth Freedom Festival, Riverblues

August
Philadelphia Folk Festival

September
International In-Water Boat Show, Puerto Rican Day
Parade, Von Steuben Day Parade

October
Pulaski Day Parade, Super Sunday, Columbus Day
Parade

November
Philadelphia Craft Show, Thanksgiving Day Parade,
Fairmount Park Marathon

December
Army-Navy Football Game, Fairmount Park
Historical Christmas Tours, John Wanamaker's
Light Show, Pennsylvania Ballet's production of
The Nutcracker

The hoagie, a sandwich commonly referred to as
a "submarine" in other parts of the country, got its
name from Philadelphia's Hog Island Shipyard.
Workers there used to eat the sandwiches for
lunch; they became known as "hoggies" and then
"hoagies."

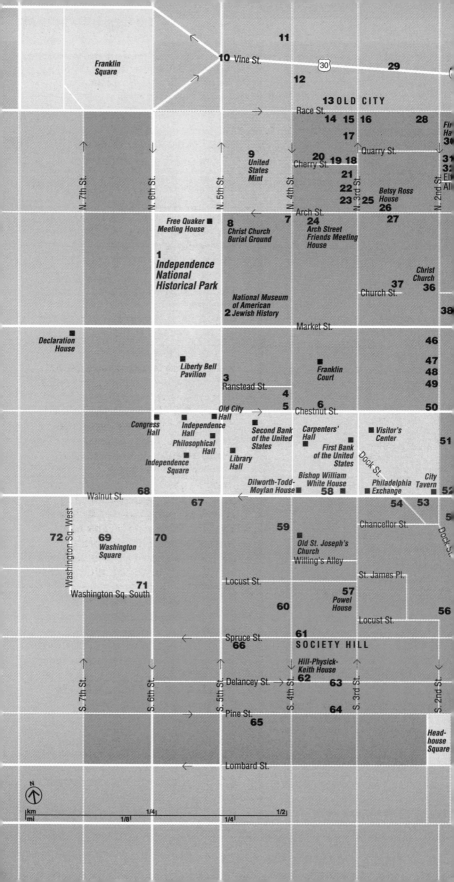

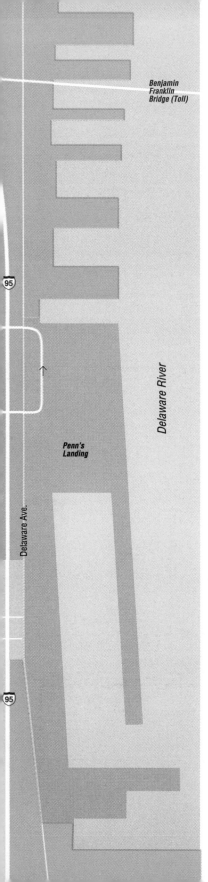

Benjamin
Franklin
Bridge (Toll)

95

Delaware River

Penn's
Landing

Delaware Ave.

95

Old
Philadelphia

Colonial America rose to its feet in a rectangular stretch of land along the Delaware River. Here, within the red-brick walls of **Independence Hall,** a group of determined colonists, risking execution by order of King George III, signed the **Declaration of Independence.** And after the Revolutionary War, the **U.S. Constitution** was written and made into law. At first glance Independence Hall appears too modest for the momentous role it played in U.S. history. But linger a while and you'll begin to see how its very simplicity is the perfect backdrop for the major events that took place.

You could easily spend a day or two touring **Independence National Historical Park,** the urban district that encompasses Independence Hall; the famous **Liberty Bell,** which called citizens to **Independence Square** for the first public reading of the Declaration of Independence in 1776; **Old St. Joseph's,** one of the oldest Catholic churches in the country; **Christ Church,** where brass plaques mark the pews once occupied by **George Washington** and **Benjamin Franklin;** the **Second Bank of the United States,** housing portraits of the government's founders; and more than 15 other historic buildings crucial to the country's early history. On the periphery of the park are the **National Museum of American Jewish History,** with exhibits on early Jewish settlements; the **United States Mint,** the largest money factory in the world; and the **Arch Street Friends Meeting House,** a lovely Quaker building circa 1804.

Two neighborhoods intertwine with Independence Park—**Society Hill,** a charming residential area that dates to colonial times, and trendy **Old City,** a warehouse district reborn as a mecca for art galleries and luxury condos. In Society Hill, located south of Independence Park, 18th-century

11

churches and modern town houses share the quirky brick and cobblestone pathways. You can see how the wealthy lived two centuries ago in the **Powel House** and the **Hill-Physick-Keith House,** then get a glimpse of how they live today on **Delancey** and **Spruce streets.** Happily, there's little evidence of the squalor that characterized Society Hill only 40 years ago, when the **Philadelphia Redevelopment Authority** took over the area, sold off historic properties one by one, and brought about the remarkable renewal.

Philadelphia's Old City, to the north and east of Society Hill, was the center of manufacturing and commerce and a crucial part of its bustling colonial seaport in the mid-1800s. Industry eventually moved west and the area declined. But like Society Hill, Old City has also been rejuvenated, and now contains the largest concentration of contemporary art galleries in the city, along with popular restaurants and historic sites, including the diminutive **Elfreth's Alley.** Every month from October to June, the neighborhood's galleries host a **First Friday** celebration, staying open until 9PM and serving free hors d'oeuvres.

1 Independence National Historical Park
Consider this L-shaped swath of land one large American history museum, with more than 20 buildings and monuments central to the early founding of the country. The 46-acre park is home to **Independence Hall, Old City Hall, Congress Hall, Philosophical Hall,** and the **Liberty Bell,** and covers 17 city blocks, blending into the neighborhoods of **Old City** and **Society Hill.** Operated by the **National Park Service,** it was created by an act of Congress in 1948. Rangers at the **Visitor's Center** can answer general questions about the park. Pick up a map at Independence Hall, the best starting place for your tour. Some sites can only be seen as part of a tour—including Independence Hall, the **Todd House,** and the **Bishop William White House.** Parking is available in the garage on Second Street between Chestnut and Walnut streets. ♦ Free. Daily 9AM-5PM. Bounded roughly by Walnut and Arch Sts, and Second and Sixth Sts. 597.8974

Within Independence National Historical Park:

Independence Hall So often has this brick building (shown here) been called the birthplace of American government that doing so seems a cliché. But the events that took place here were indeed momentous, and anyone with the slightest interest in American history will find beautifully preserved Independence Hall filled with all the integrity the history books suggest. Best of all, Independence Hall is allowed to speak for itself, with no hype or extraneous exhibits.

The Hall actually originated as headquarters of the Pennsylvania colony at a time when this plot of land stood on the outskirts of Philadelphia. In 1729 Pennsylvania leaders saw the need for a central government building, and **Andrew Hamilton,** a prominent lawyer and amateur architect who was Speaker of the Assembly, began planning the **State House** (as Independence Hall was then known) with master carpenter **Edmund Wooley.** They completed

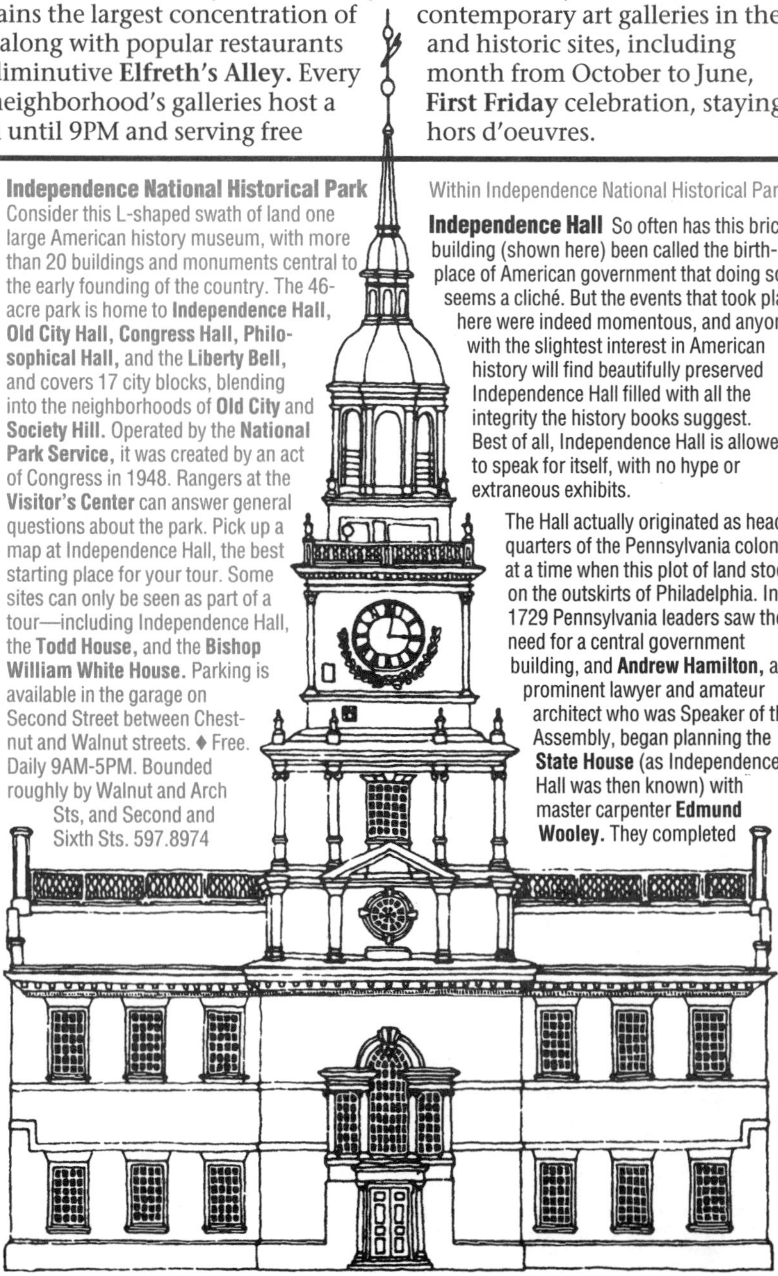

CHRISTINE LOZNER

construction in 1748, at a time when no one foresaw just how useful such a building might be as a meeting place for a fledgling federal government. Less than 30 years later, delegates from 13 colonies, including **Benjamin Franklin, Thomas Jefferson,** and **John Hancock,** congregated here and hotly debated the Declaration of Independence, which they finally approved on 4 July 1776 and signed a month later. (Hancock's bold and defiant signature is part of American lore—and American advertising.) The State House then went on to further fame: the **Second Continental Congress,** which drafted the Articles of Confederation, met here, and the first-floor **Assembly Room** served as the venue for the **Constitutional Convention,** which in 1787 produced the document that became the U.S. Constitution. Much later, on 22 April 1865, 85,000 people filed into Independence Hall to view the body of slain **President Abraham Lincoln.**

Independence Hall is one of the country's most outstanding examples of Georgian architecture, noted for its symmetry and for reflecting the city's early taste for Quaker plainness. It is restrained and unpretentious, with a white bell tower that seems a quaint souvenir in contrast to the monumental temples of government in Washington, DC. The brick and wood tower, also believed to be the work of Edmund Wooley, was added in 1750 to mark the 50th anniversary of **William Penn's** Charter of Liberties, which listed the founding principles of the Pennsylvania colony. The centerpiece is the great clock with its ornate dial plate, a replica of the original clock, installed in 1752. **William Strickland** designed the steeple, which was added in 1828.

The first floor's two rooms and large central hallway—all with handsome carved moldings—are decorated in mostly period furnishings that are not authentic to the rooms. (British troops used the building's earliest furniture as firewood when they occupied the city in 1777 and 1778.) The **Supreme Court Chamber,** on the right when you enter, is where Pennsylvania's highest court met. Note the large rendition of the Pennsylvania coat of arms, dating to 1785, over the judge's chair. **King George III's** coat of arms originally occupied the wall but was burned in Independence Square after the first public reading of the Declaration of Independence.

Across the hall is the Assembly Room, where the most significant events took place. The room's original fixtures include an inkstand made by silversmith **Philip Syng** in 1752 and used for the signing of both the Declaration of Independence and the U.S. Constitution, along with the chair used by **George Washington** during the Constitutional Convention. The back of the chair has a carving of the top half of the sun. After the Constitution was adopted,

Franklin reportedly said, ". . . now at length I have the happiness to know that it is a rising and not a setting sun." Two fireplaces and tables covered with green baize cloth, pewter inkstands, and brass candlesticks dominate the room. The beautiful cut-glass chandelier, added in 1976, resembles one that hung here in 1776.

On the second floor are the **Governor's Council Chamber;** the **Long Gallery,** used by British troops as a prison for American patriots during the Revolution; and the **Committee of the Assembly's Chamber,** which has a collection of weapons used during the war.

Every 15 minutes, the **National Park Service** offers brisk tours of this **National Historic Site** (you must be part of a tour to see the building), which vary in length from 15 to 30 minutes. Unless you're satisfied with a quick zip through the building, it's best not to come for a tour between 10AM and 2PM during the busiest times—May through June, the last two weeks of September, and October—when the rangers have less time to talk. ♦ Free. Daily 9AM-5PM. Chestnut St (between S. Fifth and S. Sixth Sts). 597.8974

Congress Hall Completed in 1789 as a county seat, the Federal-style west wing of Independence Hall housed the **U.S. Congress** from 1790 to 1800, when Philadelphia was the nation's capital. During that period Congress officially added the first 10 amendments, the **Bill of Rights,** to the Constitution; established the **United States Mint;** and admitted Vermont, Kentucky, and Tennessee to the union. Now a **National Historic Site,** the building has been authentically restored to its 1793 condition with a mixture of original and period furnishings. **George Washington** took the oath of office for his second term in the Senate chamber, an elegant room decorated with red silk curtains, an ornate plaster ceiling, and a huge carpet (a reproduction) bearing floral patterns, the seal of the U.S., and 13 state shields. Four years later, in 1797, **John Adams** was inaugurated in the room where the House of Representatives met, an event that gave the country's new Constitution an air of permanence. Off the second-floor chamber are various conference rooms. Note the immense portrait of **Louis XVI,** a gift from France, one of the colonial government's chief allies. ♦ Free. Daily 9AM-5PM. S. Sixth and Chestnut Sts. 597.8974

Independence Square The inviting plot of green behind the Independence Hall complex is filled with benches, arching trees, and rustic peace. It's a lovely place to sit or stroll, particularly when the trees take on the first delicate leaves of spring or the foliage turns lush and generous with shade in summer. At the rear of the colonial buildings, pathways radiate south to Walnut Street, west to Sixth Street, and east to Fifth Street. It was in this park that the **Declaration of Independence** had its first public reading. ♦ S. Fifth and Chestnut Sts

Philosophical Hall Directly behind Old City Hall stands the Federal-style headquarters of the **American Philosophical Society,** the nation's oldest learned society. Founded in 1743 by **Benjamin Franklin**—who else?—the organization's members have included **Thomas Jefferson, John Audubon, Marie Curie, Thomas Edison, Charles Darwin,** and **Albert Einstein.** In the 18th century, Philosophical Hall promoted astronomical research, silk cultivation, and canal development. Today it continues to encourage research in diverse fields, including quantum physics, neurobiology, computers, literary studies, and medical science. The building, a **National Historic Landmark,** was designed by **Samuel Vaughan** and completed in 1789. ♦ By appointment only. S. Fifth and Chestnut Sts. 440.3400

Old City Hall The "newest" part of the original State House complex is the east wing of City Hall, a Federal-style twin of Congress Hall designed by master carpenter **David Evans** and completed in 1791. Plans for the building, now a **National Historic Site,** were first discussed in the 1730s, but actual work didn't begin until after the Revolutionary War. Though built to house city government, the **U.S. Supreme Court** convened here from 1791 to 1800, when Philadelphia was the nation's capital. (**John Jay** was the first Chief Justice.) When the capital moved to Washington, DC, it served as City Hall; then, in 1901, local government relocated to Center Square. ♦ Free. Daily 9AM-5PM. S. Fifth and Chestnut Sts

Old City Hall

Liberty Bell Pavilion Here it is, the world-famous crack and the city's most popular tourist attraction. Every year, some 1.5 million people visit the glass and brick pavilion that houses the Liberty Bell. Commissioned to commemorate the 50th anniversary of the **Charter of Liberties,** which was enacted in 1701 by **William Penn** as Pennsylvania's constitution, the famous bronze bell was made by **Whitechapel Foundry** in London. The prophetic inscription on its surface from Leviticus 25:10 reads: "Proclaim liberty thro' all the land, to all the inhabitants thereof." In 1753 it was placed in the belfry of the **State House** (later known as Independence Hall) and tolled on important occasions, including 8 July 1776, when it rang out to call citizens to the first public reading of the **Declaration of Independence** in Independence Square. The bell cracked several times during the 1800s, and was silenced for good when it rang out for **George Washington's** birthday in 1846.

But the 2,000-pound bell—which could not be repaired—didn't gain widespread fame until the Civil War, when abolitionists adopted it and its Biblical inscription as a symbol of liberty. As more visitors began making a pilgrimage to Philadelphia to pay tribute to the cracked symbol of freedom, officials deemed Independence Hall too small to accommodate them and lobbied for construction of the bell's current home, a contemporary structure designed by **Mitchell/Giurgola Associates** and completed in time for the country's bicentennial. (The year 1976 didn't mark the first time the bell had left Independence Hall, however; in 1777, when the British occupied Philadelphia, patriots moved it to Allentown for safekeeping.) The bell, illuminated after dark, is now visible from Independence Hall. At night you can push a button outside the pavilion and hear a five-minute audio account of its history. During the day park rangers do the talking alongside the bell. ♦ Daily 9AM-5PM. Market St (between S. Fifth and S. Sixth Sts)

Declaration House "Neither aiming at originality of principle or sentiment, not yet copied from any particular document and previous writing, it was intended to be an expression of the American mind." So **Thomas Jefferson** said of the **Declaration of Independence,** which he drafted in

CHRISTINE LOZNER

rented rooms on this site. The 18th-century brick row house where he labored was demolished in 1883 and was then reconstructed the year before the U.S. bicentennial celebration. An eight-minute film featuring a rather unconvincing Jefferson plays regularly, and memorabilia from his life is displayed in large glass cases. The two upstairs rooms Jefferson rented from **Jacob Graff** have also been reproduced. ◆ Free. Daily 9AM-5PM. S. Seventh and Market Sts. 597.8974

Library Hall The **Library Company of Philadelphia,** the first subscription library in the colonies and a forerunner of the **Library of Congress,** established headquarters on this site in 1789 and stayed until the building was demolished some 99 years later. Built in its place in 1954 (with a reproduction of the original facade designed by **William Thornton,** architect of the Capitol building in Washington, DC), this structure by **Martin, Stewart & Noble** houses the library and offices of the **American Philosophical Society.** (The Library Company is now at 13th and Locust streets.) The 200,000-plus volumes and manuscripts in the library include historical treasures, such as first editions of **Newton's** *Principia* and **Darwin's** *Origin of Species,* **Lewis and Clark's** field notes, and a copy of the **Declaration of Independence** handwritten by **Thomas Jefferson.** The Philosophical Society rotates small exhibits from its collection in the lobby. ◆ Free. M-F 9AM-5PM. 105 S. Fifth St (between Chestnut and Walnut Sts). 440.3400

Second Bank of the United States Architecture students often come to admire **William Strickland's** 1824 marble-faced edifice, a **National Historic Site,** which established the trend in Greek Revival public buildings in the country. (Strickland, who modeled the bank after the **Parthenon,** also designed the Independence Hall steeple and other noteworthy buildings of the period.) At the time it was constructed, classical architecture was gaining in popularity as the country sought a more sophisticated image and a link between its democratic principles and those of ancient Greece.

The Second Bank held its own as the world's most powerful financial institution until **President Andrew Jackson** dissolved its charter in 1832 after disagreeing with the bank's conservative policies. From 1844 to 1935 the building served as home to the **U.S. Customs House,** then was restored in 1974. The main banking room is beautiful, with a barrel-vaulted ceiling in salmon and green tones, black-and-white marble floors, arched windows, and Doric columns. ◆ Free. Daily 9AM-5PM. 420 Chestnut St (between S. Fourth and S. Fifth Sts)

Within the Second Bank of the United States:

National Portrait Gallery Charles Willson Peale, the nation's most prominent early portraitist, opened the forerunner to this gallery on the second floor of **Independence Hall.** His museum, an idiosyncratic collection of portraits and mounted animal specimens (natural history fascinated him), closed in 1828.

Today the National Portrait Gallery houses many of Peale's paintings of the nation's founders, including Declaration of Independence signers **Alexander Hamilton, Thomas Mifflin,** and **Robert Morris.** Also on display are a **Henry Inman** portrait of **William Penn; William Rush's** lifesize likeness of **George Washington,** carved in pine; a copy of the first edition of the **Declaration of Independence** (the original document is in Washington, DC); a draft of the first official edition of the preamble of the **Constitution;** and early prints of Philadelphia, showing the city as it appeared when it was the nation's capital. ◆ Free. Daily 9AM-5PM. 597.8974

Carpenters' Hall Patterned after England's trade guilds, the **Carpenters' Company** has been active since it was founded in 1724, making it the oldest trade organization in the country. The group greatly influenced the creation of the city, spreading information about building techniques and setting prices. Its master carpenters, most notably **Robert Smith** (who also designed St. Peter's Church in Society Hill), often served as architects as well. Smith designed this handsome Georgian building (pictured above) as a meeting place for members of the Carpenters' Company, but it served as the site of the **First Continental Congress** in 1774, the year it was completed. Exhibits include Windsor chairs used by the delegates, a scale model of the building under construction, and early carpentry tools. ♦ Free. Tu-Su 10AM-4PM. Closed Tuesday in January and February. 320 Chestnut St (between S. Third and S. Fourth Sts). 925.0167

First Bank of the United States This is one of the oldest bank buildings in the country, designed and completed with a classical facade by architect **Samuel Blodgett, Jr.,** in 1797. The structure still conveys a sense of indomitable power, with its marble facing and two-story Corinthian portico. Note the carved American eagle in the mahogany pediment over the entranceway. (The eagle was gaining in stature as a national symbol at the time the bank formed.) The First Bank of the United States lost its federal charter in 1811, but the building, a **National Historic Site,** served as a working bank until 1926. ♦ Closed to the public. S. Third St (between Chestnut and Walnut Sts)

Philadelphia Exchange

Visitor's Center The glass roof and stark bell tower (so out of character with the rest of the neighborhood) make this modern brick building easy to spot. Designed by **Cambridge Seven Associates,** it was completed in 1975 to handle crowds for the bicentennial celebration the following year (the bell tower holds a bell donated by **Queen Elizabeth II** of Britain) and continues to serve a useful purpose, providing maps, restrooms, and park rangers to help you plan your day. *Independence,* a 28-minute film directed by **John Huston** and starring **Eli Wallach** as Benjamin Franklin, plays here 12 times a day. Rotating interactive exhibits will entertain those who like to press video screens and hear sound bites about American history.

The counter to the right of the entrance has literature on other Philadelphia attractions, along with information about services for non-English-speaking visitors and the disabled. Hour-long tours of the **Bishop William White House** and the **Dilworth-Todd-Moylan House** leave from here, and the bookstore and souvenir shop are just to the east. ♦ Free. Daily 9AM-5PM. S. Third St (between Chestnut and Walnut Sts). 597.8974

City Tavern **Paul Revere** arrived here on horseback in 1774 with news that Boston Harbor had been closed by the English Parliament, and **George Washington** enjoyed a lavish dinner here on his way to New York City for his inauguration in 1789. The present tavern building is a reconstruction of the 1773 structure that was a famous watering hole for delegates to both Continental Congresses and the city's elite. It is currently closed. ♦ S. Second and Walnut Sts

Philadelphia Exchange This masterpiece of Greek Revival architecture, with a sweeping semicircular Corinthian portico and a lantern tower, is a dramatic departure from the Federal and Georgian brick buildings in the area. Designed in the early 1830 by **William Strickland,** architect of the near by **Second Bank of the United States,** it is also notable for its adaptation to a very irre ular site. The **Philadelphia Exchange Company,** the oldest stock exchange in the country, opened here in 1834. Business transactions took place in the luxurious exchange room with marble columns and a mosaic floor until the Civil War. A **National Historic Site,** it's now used by the **Nationa Park Service** as an office. ♦ Closed to the public. S. Third and Walnut Sts

Bishop William White House Originall built in 1787 as the home of the first bisho of the Episcopal Diocese of Pennsylvania, this upper-class residence has been restored and is open to the public. The **Rig Reverend William White** was an esteemed civic leader, chaplain to the Continental Congress, and rector of **Christ Church** and **St. Peter's Church.** Furnished with 18th-century period pieces, the house has eight levels, including a root cellar, a wine cellar, and an ice pit, plus a feature that was a nov elty at the time: a clothes closet. You can only see the house on one of the daily park service tours, which depart from the **Visitor's Center.** (It's best to reserve a spo on these tours in the morning; sign up at th Visitor's Center.) ♦ Free. Tours daily (hour vary), except in winter. 309 Walnut St (between S. Third and S. Fourth Sts). 597.8974

Old St. Joseph's Church Hidden from view by an alley and courtyard, the church was built in 1733 as the first Roman Catholic church in the city, then rebuilt in 1838. Though state founder **William Penn** tolerated all religious practices, England forbade Catholic services, so this parish sought to be discreet (its pastor is said to have gone about town in Quaker dress). The original parishioners, less aristocratic than those at nearby St. Mary's, were mostly Irish and German craftsmen and domestics. Stop at the rectory to tour the church when services aren't taking place. ♦ Services M-F 12:05PM; Sa 12:05PM, 5:30PM; Su 7:30AM, 9:30AM, 11:30AM. 321 Willing's Alley (between S. Third and S. Fourth Sts). 923.1733

Dilworth-Todd-Moylan House Lawyer **John Todd** lived here until 1793, when he died of yellow fever (an epidemic that claimed the lives of many Philadelphians). His widow, **Dolley Payne Todd,** later married **James Madison,** the nation's fourth president. The Georgian brick house, a typical late-18th century middle-class dwelling constructed by carpenter **Jonathan Dilworth,** is only open as part of the daily tours led by park rangers from the **Visitor's Center.** (Sign up for a tour at the Visitor's Center in the morning.) ♦ Free. Tours daily (hours vary), except in winter. S. Fourth and Walnut Sts. 597.8974

Franklin Court The ghost of **Benjamin Franklin** appears everywhere in Philadelphia, but perhaps most vividly in Franklin Court, an area that holds special claim to his legacy. It was in the brick courtyard here that he built his 10-room, three-story house and printshop, nestled behind a row of tenements he rented out on **Market Street.** Now gone, the structures have been replaced by the underground **Franklin Museum,** with a towering postmodernist sculpture marking the spot once occupied by his house.

Before entering the courtyard, visit the restored rentals on Market Street, which contain exhibits about Franklin's life. At **322 Market Street** (a replica of the office of the *Aurora and General Advertiser*), you can see the newspaper published by **Benjamin Franklin Bache,** Franklin's grandson. Next door, at **320 Market Street,** are demonstrations of 18th-century printing and bookbinding equipment. The exposed foundation and original brick walls of **318 Market Street** explain how Franklin, influenced by the Great Fire of London, designed a fire-proof structure. At **316 Market Street** is the **B. Free Franklin Post Office,** a working post office where both the furnishings and the clothing of the postal workers are colonial. (Sorry, the postage prices are strictly contemporary.) Alongside is the **United States Postal Service Museum,** which offers narrative displays of U.S. postal history. Exhibits include pony express pouches and originals of Franklin's *Pennsylvania Gazette.* (Franklin was also the nation's first postmaster.)

To see the courtyard where the Franklin house once stood, pass through the archway in the center of the Market Street houses, where a sign reads: "Benjamin Franklin went to and from his house through this original passage." The painted steel sculptural outline of the buildings—known as **Ghost Structures**—was completed in 1976 according to designs by the noted Philadelphia architectural firm **Venturi & Rauch** with **John Milner Associates,** and rises 54 feet high. In the pavement beneath the metal frames are inscriptions by and about Franklin and concrete portals offering views into the foundation of his demolished home.

Next, visit the **Franklin Museum,** which celebrates the extent of Franklin's ingenuity. Displays showcase his many inventions: in

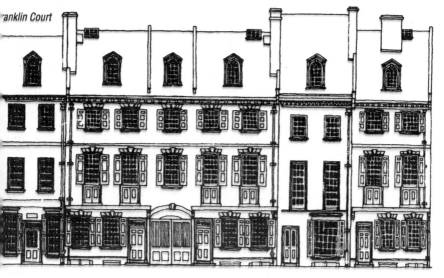

Franklin Court

addition to the Franklin stove, he invented the swim flipper; at age 80, he invented the wooden book clasp, a precursor of the shelf clasps now used in grocery stores; and he also developed an armchair with a seat that could be converted to steps for reaching books. The main room has a phone bank where you can dial numbers to hear comments made about Franklin by everybody from **George Washington** to **D.H. Lawrence;** and on a stage in the center of the room, a cast of moving dolls in period costumes acts out scenes of Franklin's life. There's also the obligatory 20-minute biographical film. ◆ Free. Daily 9AM-5PM. Market St (between S. Third and S. Fourth Sts). 597.8974

2 National Museum of American Jewish History This museum devoted to the history of Jews in America is also home to one of the oldest continuously meeting congregations, **Kahal Kadosh Mikveh Israel,** which traces its roots to 1740. In the earliest days of immigration, Jews came to the colonies in very small numbers and apparently did not encounter discrimination. In 1800, when the colonial population was about 5.3 million, the Jewish population was a mere 2,000, most of it concentrated in seaport towns. Jews received a high degree of acceptance: after a procession celebrating the adoption of the Constitution, for instance, kosher food was served, and **George Washington** sent a letter to Jewish supporters publicly thanking them for their congratulations on his appointment as President. Museum exhibits explain these events and examine Jewish involvement in the Civil War and in westward expansion. The museum, designed by **H2L2,** opened its doors and held its first service on 4 July 1976. Books and crafts are sold in the gift shop. ◆ Admission. M-Th 10AM-5PM; F 10AM-3PM; Su noon-5PM. 55 N. Fifth St (between Market and Arch Sts). 923.3811

3 The Bourse In striking contrast to the colonial structures nearby is this massive, columned brownstone, a 19th-century office building reincarnated as a multilevel retail and office complex in 1982 according to designs by **H2L2.** The block-long structure, designed by **George** and **William Hewitt,** architects of the Bellevue Stratford Hotel, features a red sandstone and Pompeian-brick exterior with flourishes of terracotta decoration. It opened in 1895 as home to the city's maritime, stock, and grain exchanges. After the financial center moved to the commercial core, the building fell into decline, until it was extensively renovated in the 1980s. The building's most dramatic space is its enormous great hall, illuminated by a huge skylight. Staircases with lacy railings ascend from the first floor, which is reserved for shops and food stalls. The ground-floor food court has plenty of places to sit, and offers hamburgers, salads, pizza, and sandwiches. Public restrooms can be found in the basement. ◆ M-Sa 10AM-6PM. 21 S. Fifth St (between Ranstead and Market Sts). 625.0300

Within The Bourse:

Bain's Deli $ Standard-issue corned beef brisket, tuna salad, and ham sandwiches are sold here. ◆ Deli ◆ Lunch. 925.6646. Also at The Gallery. 928.9323; The Gallery II. 592.1610; One Liberty Place. 567.1685

Liberty Chicken $ Rotisserie chicken, chicken kebab, spicy noodle chicken salad, and plain old chicken salad are some of the options. ◆ Chicken ◆ Lunch. 629.0815

4 Ritz at The Bourse This five-screen cinema shows foreign films and offbeat movies rarely played in more commercial theaters. Reduced parking rates are available. ◆ S. Fourth and Ranstead Sts (next to The Bourse). 925.7900

OMNI ✦ HOTELS

5 The Omni at Independence Park $$$ Combining the efficiency of a large chain operation with the comforts of an elegant small hotel, the Omni is the most luxurious place to stay east of Broad Street. When it opened in 1990, it filled a void in the historic area, which lacked deluxe accommodations. Most of the 143 rooms overlook Independence Park and are furnished with king-size beds and marbled bathrooms. Drinks and light fare, usually accompanied jazz on weekend nights, are served in the intimate lobby. A lap pool and fitness center, voice mail, and a gourmet restaurant round out the amenities. Weekend rates are especially reasonable. ◆ 401 Chestnut St (at S. Fourth St). 925.0000, 800/843.6664; fax 925.1263

Within The Omni at Independence Park:

Azalea ★★$$$ Plush and formal, the Omni's dining room is dressed in champagne tones with oversize cream-colored chandeliers, mirrored posts, banquettes, and white linen. The kitchen prides itself on using local produce, meats, and seafood (though the quality of the dishes fluctuates). Dinner might include roasted pheasant with applejack brandy and almond reduction or medallions of monkfish in a honey barbecue sauce. ◆ Eclectic ◆ Breakfast, lunch, and dinner; Sunday brunch. Reservations recommended. 931.4260

Using a camera fashioned out of a cigar box, Philadelphia clockmaker Joseph Saxton is thought to have taken the country's first photograph from a window at the United States Mint on Chestnut Street in Philadelphia. The date: 16 October 1839.

6 Philadelphia Maritime Museum Although life in Philadelphia no longer revolves around its port, water had everything to do with the city's initial development. The Delaware and Schuylkill rivers, with their links to the Atlantic Ocean, provided the prime means of transportation and trade in colonial times. Eighteenth-century Philadelphia was also the country's key entry point for immigrants (**Benjamin Franklin,** who arrived in 1723, was among those who came to the city by water). This fascinating museum (which will be moving to new quarters at **Penn's Landing** on the Delaware River in 1995) preserves that tradition by showcasing more than 10,000 maritime artifacts, including uniforms, flags, navigational instruments, and models of small crafts and ships. An interactive exhibit recounts Franklin's first day here and gives some idea of the role the waterways played in the daily life of the city. The **Workshop on the Water,** housed in a barge near Spruce Street at Penn's Landing, is the museum's floating education and exhibition area. Museum visitors who park in the garage at Fourth Street between Market and Chestnut streets receive a discount on parking. ◆ Admission. Tu-Sa 10AM-5PM; Su 1-5PM. Workshop on the Water: W-Su 10AM-5PM. 321 Chestnut St (between S. Third and S. Fourth Sts). 925.5439.

7 Holiday Inn Independence Mall $$ A short walk from Independence Park, this 364-room hotel has a pleasant lobby and comfortable rooms (those overlooking Arch Street don't have much of a view). You can relax in the shady courtyard of the **Arch Street Friends Meeting House** across the street, or take a dip in the hotel's small outdoor pool. ◆ 400 Arch St (at N. Fourth St). 923.8660, 800/843.2355; fax 923.4633

Within the Holiday Inn Independence Mall:

Benjamin's ★$$ Decorated with old prints of Philadelphia, brass chandeliers, and American colonial reproductions, this low-lit dining room has a Continental menu with a bit more flair than the average Holiday Inn restaurant. Among the offerings are prime rib, shrimp scampi, and chicken in a Chardonnay sauce. ◆ Continental ◆ Lunch and dinner. Closed Sunday. 923.8660

Plain & Fancy Cafe $ This pleasant dining room with floral prints, Windsor chairs, and large windows overlooking Arch Street serves three meals a day. Seafood salad, Buffalo wings, and fettuccine Alfredo are good bets for lunch. ◆ American ◆ Breakfast, lunch, and dinner. 923.8660

8 Christ Church Burial Ground Some of the country's first leading citizens are buried in this cemetery three blocks from Christ Church, including **Benjamin Franklin;** numerous Revolutionary War heroes and patriots; and the **Right Reverend William White,** chaplain of the Continental Congress and first Episcopal Bishop of Pennsylvania. Franklin's grave is visible through the iron gate on the Arch Street side. ◆ By appointment only. Closed in winter. N. Fifth and Arch Sts

9 United States Mint Every day, 32 million coins come out of the manufacturing rooms of this money factory—the largest mint in the world—and each year, more than 100,000 working dies used in coin presses are produced here. Blanks are stamped out of strips of metal, and, eventually, the finished coins drop into large canvas bags, which are sewn shut and loaded onto pallets. Visitors can watch the action through a plate-glass window on the second floor.

The monolithic, virtually windowless building, designed by **Vincent G. Kling and Associates** in 1969, is a descendant of the oldest mint in the country, which opened a few blocks away in 1792. **David Rittenhouse,** the famous mathematician and inventor, served as director of the first Philadelphia Mint, and the balance he invented in the 1700s is on display. All of the designs for commemorative coins made since 1892 are also here, plus numerous other samples of medallic art, including all the **Congressional Gold Medals,** and war medals such as the **Purple Heart** and the **Bronze Star.** A "hot off the press" display shows the latest mint medals authorized by Congress. In the lobby, two Tiffany glass mosaics dating to 1901 depict the history of coin making. **Peter the Eagle,** a real bird who adopted the mint as his home and was a mascot to mint workers in the early 19th century, has been stuffed and put on display (he may have been the model for the American eagle that appeared on silver dollars). Coins and medals can be purchased in the lobby store. ◆ Free. M-F 9AM-4:30PM. N. Fifth and Arch Sts. 597.7350

10 Bolt of Lightning . . . A Memorial to Benjamin Franklin Isamu Noguchi designed this 60-ton stainless-steel sculpture, which rises 101 feet to mark the axis of **Independence Mall** and the **Benjamin Franklin Bridge.** It was a gift to the city's public art collection by the **Fairmount Park Art Association,** which has been embellishing the city since 1872. ◆ N. Fifth and Vine Sts

11 Cafe Sorella ★$ On the northern edge of Center City, this restaurant located in two tiny storefront rooms features an innovative menu. Among the offerings are chicken with asparagus and black-bean sauce; pasta with backfin crab in a tomato-basil sauce; and pizza with shrimp, scallops, roasted peppers, scallions, mozzarella, and Romano. ◆ Eclectic ◆ Lunch and dinner; dinner only on Saturday. 314 N. Fourth St (between Vine and Callowhill Sts). 592.7075

Restaurants/Clubs: Red
Shops/ ♥ Outdoors: Green
Hotels: Blue
Sights/Culture: Black

12 St. George's Church St. George's is the oldest Methodist church in the U.S., and **Richard Allen,** founder of the African Methodist Episcopal Church, was licensed here as the first African-American to preach in the country. A historical center and museum adjoin the church. ♦ 235 N. Fourth St (between Race and Vine Sts). 925.7788

13 Old City In colonial days, Old City and nearby **Society Hill** constituted the city proper. But in the 1800s, as the city burgeoned into a major port and industrial power, Old City benefited from its position alongside the Delaware River (now separated from the neighborhood by Interstate 95) and became a thriving mix of factories, banks, warehouses, and retail stores. This hectic district included a world-renowned sugar refinery, textile manufacturers, and a hoop-skirt factory (probably responsible for the long-forgotten slogan, "Philadelphia Dresses the World"). Many commercial buildings of that period—in brick, cast iron, and granite—survive alongside early colonial buildings, such as the magnificent **Christ Church,** the **Betsy Ross House,** and the **Arch Street Friends Meeting House,** all giving Old City its character.

Eventually the city's manufacturing center moved west and Old City deteriorated. Then the construction of the highway along the river and the **Benjamin Franklin Bridge** cut the neighborhood off from the rest of the city. But with the gentrification of Society Hill in the late 1970s, many of Old City's former warehouses were converted into luxury apartments or condominiums and a number of small businesses opened their doors. The relatively cheap rent and spacious 19th-century buildings offered the perfect combination for contemporary art galleries. Today more than 30 galleries, many among the best in the city, call this unquestionably hip neighborhood home.

From October to June on the first Friday of each month, the galleries stay open late to host a big block party, attracting a generally young and fashionably bohemian crowd (dressed mostly in black). People tour the galleries for a few hours, sampling the free hors d'oeuvres, and then eat dinner in one of the neighborhood's restaurants. Some say Old City has found itself once again. ♦ Bounded by Market and Vine Sts, and N. Front and N. Fifth Sts

Contrary to popular opinion, the Declaration of Independence was signed on the 2nd of August—not on the 4th of July. The signers approved the resolution adopting the measure on 4 July 1776 in Independence Hall.

14 DiNardo's Famous Seafood ★$$ The casual atmosphere at this popular Philadelphia branch of the notable Wilmington, Delaware, seafood house is ideal for families. Dark strip paneling, nautical doodads, large tables, and roomy booths set the scene for cracking into the blue-clawed hard-shell crabs, which come steamed and seasoned (Baltimore style) or in a bowl of garlic sauce. The fish is always fresh, and the salty, slightly spicy french fries taste great with beer. You may be in for a wait on weekends. ♦ Seafood ♦ Lunch and dinner; dinner only on Sunday. 312 Race St (between N. Third and N. Fourth Sts). 238.9595

15 Philadelphia Furniture League A consortium of local artisans creates the handcrafted wood furniture and upholstered sofas and chairs here at prices well below what you'd pay in New York. Hand-painted desks and chests and stained wood pieces have been on display, including a baby cradle made of black walnut with ash spindles. ♦ Tu-Sa noon-5PM. 160 N. Third St (between Cherry and Race Sts). 440.7136

16 Mode Moderne Designer furniture and decorative objects from the 1920s to the 1960s are displayed in this offbeat showroom. ♦ Tu-Sa noon-6PM. 159 N. Third St (between Cherry and Race Sts). 627.0299

17 OLC Crystal chandeliers are too staid for this lighting and furniture showroom, which specializes in artsy, contemporary light fixtures with European labels. There's also furniture from **B & B Italia, Driade, Atelier International,** and others. Approximately 90 percent of sales are to designers and architects, but walk-in traffic is welcome. ♦ Tu-Sa 10AM-5PM. 152-154 N. Third St (between Cherry and Race Sts). 923.6085

18 Keiser-Newman Aggressively stylish contemporary furniture made of wood, glass, marble, aluminum, and porcelain fills this showroom. ♦ Tu-Sa 9AM-5PM; Su noon-5PM. 134 N. Third St (at Cherry St). 923.743

19 Jessica Berwind Gallery The side door of this handsome mid-19th century building with arched windows and cream-colored cast-iron columns leads to a stairway and a narrow loft gallery that displays high-quality contemporary art. ♦ Tu-F 10AM-6PM; Sa 10AM-5PM. 301 Cherry St (between N. Third and N. Fourth Sts). 574.645

Below the Jessica Berwind Gallery:

Snyderman Gallery Richard and Ruth Snyderman, a husband-and-wife team that also owns **Works Gallery** on South Street, opened this spacious gallery in 1992. Exhibits focus on contemporary art, furniture, and sculpture, such as artist **Randy Shull's** whimsical wooden wall fixtures, clocks, and cabinets. Shull's painted wood pieces feature small doors that open onto a surprise—in one, six tiny photographs of a human eye. Works of well-known furniture designer **Wharton Esherick** have also been displayed here. ♦ Tu-Sa 10AM-6PM. 303 Cherry St (between N. Third and N. Fourth Sts). 238.9576

20 F.A.N. Gallery The gallery's narrow room showcases contemporary art, such as **Lynne Clibanoff's** eerie drawings, photographs, and constructions of abandoned city buildings, desolate courtyards, and empty passageways. ♦ Tu-Su 11AM-6PM. 311 Cherry St (between N. Third and N. Fourth Sts). 922.5155

21 La Trattoria dell'Artista ★★$$ Devotees of Old City's art galleries and food lovers in search of Italian comfort food pack the tiny but festive dining room in this brick-walled trattoria. Diners sit elbow-to-elbow at tables with bright vinyl tablecloths. Try sausage with olives, fresh tomatoes, rosemary, and mozzarella. Be prepared to wait on weekend evenings. ♦ Italian ♦ Lunch and dinner. Closed Sunday. 130 N. Third St (between Cherry and Arch Sts). No phone

22 Rodger LaPelle Gallery Established in 1980, this highly regarded gallery exhibits contemporary paintings, sculpture, and graphics by local and national artists. ♦ W-Su noon-6PM; first Friday of every month noon-10PM. 122 N. Third St (between Cherry and Arch Sts). 592.0232

23 L'Osteria dell'Artista ★★$ This popular trattoria has bohemian charm much like its sister restaurant, **La Trattoria dell'Artista**. Checkered tablecloths, flea-market art, a contemporary mural of swirling human figures, and large mirrors decorate the colorful—and cramped—dining room. Best bets are the tuna steak with peppers and broccoli, the stuffed flounder, and the pasta with sausage, sun-dried tomatoes, and peppers. ♦ Italian ♦ Lunch and dinner; dinner only on Saturday and Sunday. 114 N. Third St (between Cherry and Arch Sts) 922.5595

24 Arch Street Friends Meeting House **Owen Biddle's** simple brick structure, the largest Quaker meeting house in the country, was built in 1804 on land donated by **William Penn**. It still hosts twice weekly meetings, though today's congregants usually fill only a small portion of the pews in the main meeting room. The austere style is common to all meeting houses, with white wooden shutters and none of the customary accoutrements of religious worship (statues, pulpits, stained-glass windows, and the like). Believing that God resides in each person, the Quakers don't look to sermons or ministers for direction. Feel free to ask questions of the person at the front desk. ♦ M-Sa 10AM-4PM. 320 Arch St (between N. Third and N. Fourth Sts). 627.2667

25 Moderne Expensive European and American Art Deco furniture and decorative pieces, including paintings and sculpture, are on display. The showroom has featured the ironwork of **Edgar Brandt** and furniture by **Dominique, Leleu,** and **Adnet.** ♦ M-Sa 11AM-6PM. 111 N. Third St (between Race and Arch Sts). 923.8536

26 Betsy Ross House Upholsterer and seamstress Betsy Ross lived either in this house or in the one that stood in the courtyard next door. Though she was long believed to have designed the American flag, this claim has now been disproved (meager—not firm—evidence does indicate that she sewed a flag for the early federal government). Ross, who lived from 1752 to 1836 and was widowed twice and married three times, is buried in the courtyard. The 1740 house is typical of the period and contains the accoutrements of her trade. ♦ Donation requested. Tu-Su 10AM-5PM. 239 Arch St (between N. Second and N. Third Sts). 627.5343

27 Solo Mio ★$ Stop here for lunch if you're sightseeing in Independence Park. The daily specials—rigatoni and garlic bread, if you're lucky—are inexpensive, and the shoe box of a dining room is loaded with charm. Abstract artworks by local artists are tacked to the walls, and Sinatra croons in the background. ♦ Italian ♦ Lunch and dinner. 232 Arch St (between N. Second and N. Third Sts). 625.9820

28 Café Einstein ★$$ A doodled sketch of **Albert Einstein** decorates the front door of this casual yet sophisticated dining room, with wood ceilings, brick walls, works by local artists, and a wood-burning stove. Too bad the menu is so unreliable. Linguine Einstein with sun-dried tomatoes and spinach, crab cakes, Cajun catfish, and chicken with yogurt and thyme are among the selections. ♦ Eclectic ♦ Dinner; Sunday brunch. 208 Race St (between N. Second and N. Third Sts). 625.0904

29 Painted Bride Art Center Located in a former elevator factory just under the Benjamin Franklin Bridge, this multicultural art center hosts dance performances, poetry readings, plays, art exhibits, and concerts

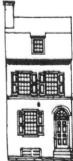

(mostly jazz, folk, and world music). Painted Bride was the brainchild of a small group of artists, who originally set up shop in 1970 in a former bridal store on South Street. The center has since grown into a full-fledged nonprofit center promoting multiculturalism in the arts, with funding from the **National Endowment for the Arts.** ♦ Daily 9AM-5PM. 230 Vine St (between N. Second and N. Third Sts). 925.9914. Box office 567.0670

30 Fireman's Hall A turn-of-the-century firehouse has been restored to showcase fire-related memorabilia spanning two centuries. Exhibits tell the story of firefighting, from its primitive beginnings in the American colonies to 20th-century sprinkler systems. (In the 1700s colonists typically kept a bucket just inside their front doors in case of disaster; by 1803 water from the Schuylkill River was stored in steel trunks.) The museum's high-ceilinged main room contains examples of 19th- and 20th-century firewagons, powered by hand, horse, or steam. Other highlights are a hand pump reputedly used by **Benjamin Franklin,** who founded the country's first fire company, and a radio dispatch system. Antique axes, helmets, badges, old posters, and ladders adorn the walls and fill the display cases. Don't miss the firemen's living quarters on the second floor. Children especially love this museum. ♦ Donation. Tu-Sa 9AM-5PM. 147 N. Second St (at Quarry St). 923.1438

31 The Clay Studio Part gallery, part art school, and part group salon, this cooperative of more than 30 ceramic artists produces an eclectic array of pieces, from the wildly avant-garde to vases you could give your parents for Christmas. Two first-floor rooms feature juried exhibitions by local and national ceramic artists, and a small shop sells distinctive, reasonably priced designs. ♦ Tu-F noon-6PM; Sa-Su noon-5PM. 139 N. Second St (between Race St and Elfreth's Alley). 925.3453

32 Nexus Foundation for Today's Art This nonprofit organization displays the works of its 15 or so members, and also hosts community art shows with a political message—perhaps the work of Cuban artists or an exhibit of Eastern European ceramics. ♦ Tu-F noon-6PM; Sa-Su noon-5PM. 137 N. Second St (between Race and Arch Sts). 629.1103

33 Elfreth's Alley Turn off Second Street into this postcard-perfect alley of 18th-century brick row houses (like the one pictured at right), said to be the oldest continuously inhabited street in the U.S. The fact that most of the houses are still private homes makes the alley all the more enchanting. Named after **Jeremiah Elfreth,** a blacksmith and speculator who built and rented out some of the homes, the alley was right next to the Delaware River during the 18th century. Artisans, sea captains, a school teacher, and a rabbi lived here, and most of them ran their businesses directly out of their homes.

Though at first glance the buildings look alike, take a closer look and you'll see signs of different periods. The oldest, **Nos. 120-122,** were built in the 1720s, and the newest in the early 1800s. Small panes of glass (shipped all the way from England in early colonial days), pent eaves, and modest doorways distinguish the earlier homes. Later dwellings have stairs leading up to elaborate entrances and larger windows. Note the mirror contraptions that jut from the second floors of some of the houses. Known as busybodies, they were used by residents as early as the 18th century to see who was knocking at their front doors below.

The **Elfreth's Alley Museum** occupies the house in the middle of the south side of the block. Built in 1750, it's a classic Philadelphia "trinity"—a miniature three-story structure with one room on each floor and narrow, winding staircases (the bane of furniture deliverers today). Halfway down the block is **Bladen's Court,** a tiny brick and cobblestone alley-within-an-alley that takes you to a small circular courtyard. ♦ Admission for museum only. Daily 10AM-4PM. Off N. Second St (between Race and Arch Sts). 574.0560

34 Rosenfeld Gallery Located in a former paint warehouse, this spacious first-floor gallery exhibits works by new artists from around the country. Popular shows have included clay monoprints by **Mitch Lyons** and handmade paper by **Doug Zucco.** ♦ W-Sa 10AM-5PM; Su noon-5PM. 113 Arch St (between N. Front and N. Second Sts). 922.1376

35 Smythe Stores This 1857 Northern Italian Renaissance-style warehouse turned office building is one of the neighborhood's few remaining grand cast-iron structures. With its rows of arched windows and fluted columns, it represents a significant departure from the area's original brick warehouses, which had small windows and little adornment. In 1900 plans to demolish the building so trolleys could turn around in the corner were averted with the ingenious idea of removing only the middle section, allowing trolleys to pass right through the center. The demolished portion was re-created with fiberglass in the 1970s, long after the trolley route had died. Can you tell where the old and new begin and end? ♦ N. Front and Arch Sts

36 Christ Church If you sailed into Philadelphia during the 1700s, the white steeple of Christ Church would have welcomed you, just as the Statue of Liberty held out her hand to travelers from afar in New York. Completed in 1744, the design owes much to **Sir Christopher Wren's** churches in London.

Dr. John Kearsley, a physician, is believed to have laid out the plans for the elegant Georgian structure (shown below), and **James Porteus,** of the Carpenters' Company, was the builder. Master carpenter **Robert Smith** added the tower and 200-foot steeple in 1754. The exterior, dominated by a Palladian window on the east front, is in Flemish bond brick, common to residential structures of the period, and urns bearing flames crown the balustrade that runs along the roof.

Inside, the church, a **National Historic Landmark,** rings with the history of 18th-century Philadelphia. **George Washington** and **Benjamin Franklin** were among the key historical figures who belonged to the Anglican congregation; the baptismal font in the rear of the church, sent

to Philadelphia in 1697 from **All Hallow's Church Barking-by-the-Tower** in London, is where **William Penn** was baptized; **Bishop William White** preached from the wine-glass-shaped pulpit for almost 60 years; members of the **Continental Congress** attended services here while meeting in Philadelphia; and the signers of the **Declaration of Independence** came here on 5 July 1776 to pray. Not long after the colonies achieved independence, the church separated from the mother country as well, and the Protestant Episcopal Church in the United States was established in conventions here in 1785 and 1789. The **American Book of Common Prayer** was also approved here in 1789. Christ Church was designated a national shrine in 1950. It remains an active parish. ♦ Donation. M-Sa 9AM-5PM; Su 1-5PM. Services Su 9AM, 11AM; W noon. S. Second St (at Church St). 922.1695

37 Old City Coffee ★$ Fresh-roasted coffee beans, brewed coffees, cookies, and oversize muffins are sold in this fragrant storefront. Pass through the little hallway to the cozy dining room with marble-topped tables, and relax over cappuccino, a cold lemonade, or a light lunch of Thai shrimp salad. ♦ Cafe ♦ Light breakfast and lunch. 221 Church St (between N. Second and N. Third Sts). 629.9292

38 Larry Becker Located on the first floor of a narrow brick building, this gallery has built a solid reputation representing a select roster of about a dozen contemporary painters and sculptors. Some of the better-known local names have included **Italo Scanga, Bill Walton, Darwin Nix,** and **Rebecca Johnson.** ♦ Tu-Sa 11AM-5PM; July-Sept by appointment only. 43 N. Second St (between Market and Church Sts). 925.5389

39 Penn's View Inn $$ This small inn, not far from the center of Independence National Historical Park, holds its own on a block of old warehouses that will probably someday be restored. The standard accommodations have windows with partial views of the Delaware River, while premium rooms feature Jacuzzis and full views of the river (and Interstate 95). All 28 rooms are furnished with colonial reproductions and come with a complimentary glass of wine and a Continental breakfast. ♦ 14 N. Front St (at Market St). 922.7600, 800/331.7634

Within Penn's View Inn:

Ristorante Panorama ★★★$$ A large wall mural of an Italian hill scene dominates the dining room of this less expensive cousin of the fastidious **La Famiglia.** To start, try *fantasie di mare,* a plate of crab, scallops, shrimp, shiitake mushrooms, and mozzarella, and choose from more than 120 wines by the glass. ♦ Italian ♦ Lunch and dinner. 922.7800

40 **Shane Candies** Open since 1876, this charming storefront bills itself as the oldest candy store in the country. Whether or not this is true, it has some of the best chocolates in Philadelphia (try the milk chocolate almond bark if you can't decide). At Eastertime, the store is packed full of chocolate crosses and coconut cream eggs. ♦ M-Sa 9AM-5:30PM. 110 Market St (between S. Front and S. Second Sts). 922.1048

41 **Montana** ★$ If price is the only standard, Montana is a decent place for a one-and-a-half-pound lobster or a 24-ounce rib-eye steak. Dark wood walls feature old photographs of Philadelphia, and the bar—buzzing with sports talk and games on TV—is decorated with photos of local college teams. Faded jeans are the appropriate attire. Barbecued ribs, grilled chicken, and hamburgers are also served. ♦ American ♦ Dinner. 6 S. Front St (between Market and Chestnut Sts). 922.5676

42 **La Famiglia** ★★★$$$$ First-class Italian cuisine is served in this formal and elegant drawing room with fine moldings and sconces, ornate mirrors, and plush chairs. The service is stiff, the menu high-priced, the wine list long and wonderful, and the food consistently excellent. Start off with wild mushrooms in a fresh tomato sauce or shrimp in butter, garlic, and parsley, and then dig into the homemade pasta, including small ravioli in a cream sauce. ♦ Italian ♦ Lunch and dinner; dinner only on Saturday and Sunday. Closed Monday. 8 S. Front St (between Market and Chestnut Sts). 922.2803

43 **La Truffe** ★★★$$$$ Set in an elegant dining room with the feel of a French country inn, La Truffe serves classic haute cuisine with contemporary touches. Co-owners **Jeannine Mermet** and **Leslie Smith** and chef **W. Todd Davies** have impeccable standards—and charge accordingly. All courses are à la carte. Begin with salmon gravlax with three caviars, chilled mussel and asparagus tart, or snails with mushrooms, Pernod, fennel, and radish, then move on to grilled quail stuffed with hazelnuts and currants or rack of lamb seasoned with thyme (the texture is so buttery that the waiters have been known to show off by carving it with a spoon). Beaded lamps, brocade chairs, silk wall coverings, and fresh flowers adorn the white brick dining room, carrying through the cozy but sophisticated atmosphere. ♦ French ♦ Lunch and dinner; dinner only on Monday and Saturday. Closed Sunday. Reservations recommended. 10 S. Front St (between Market and Chestnut Sts). 925.5062

Above La Truffe:

Jeannine's Bistro ★★★$$$ Escargots, classic French onion soup with Gruyere, and traditional cassoulet might all appear on the blackboard menu at this tony upstairs bistro. The owners, who also run the elegant—and twice as expensive—La Truffe downstairs, have created an intimate setting with stained-glass dividers, floral tablecloths, and Toulouse-Lautrec reproductions on the walls. Good bets are the spinach salad with warm brandy dressing, duck in sour cherry sauce, or a ragout of rabbit. For dessert, white chocolate mousse is a must. Cabaret-style music is featured on Friday and Saturday nights, and French-born co-owner **Jeannine Mermet** sometimes sings. ♦ French ♦ Lunch and dinner; dinner only on Monday and Saturday. Closed Sunday. Reservations recommended. 925.2928

44 **Kawabata Olde City** ★★$$$ Some of the freshest sushi in Philadelphia is prepared with artistry in this Japanese restaurant, and served in a dark series of dining rooms separated by Japanese screens. Those turned off by raw fish will like the offbeat selection of vegetarian sushi, including one with shiitake mushrooms and asparagus. ♦ Japanese ♦ Dinner; lunch on Thursday and Friday. 110 Chestnut St (between S. Front and S. Second Sts). 928.9564

45 **The Middle East** ★$$$ Brash, loud, low-lit and nearly windowless, this large Middle Eastern restaurant is owned by **City Councilman Jimmy Tayoun,** and plays up its name with an enormous plastic camel over the entranceway, Persian tapestries on the walls, belly dancers, and live Middle Eastern music. The beef and lamb kebabs are the best selections on the menu, which also features such standard dishes as moussaka, braised lamb shank, *hummus, baba ghanouj,* and stuffed grape leaves. ♦ Middle Eastern ♦ Dinner. Closed Monday. 126 Chestnut St (between S. Front and S. Second Sts). 922.1003

46 **Serrano** ★★$$ Exotic puppets dangle from the ceilings and gargoyles decorate the walls of this small international cafe. The menu has everything from Vietnamese meatballs to Hungarian chicken and Malaysian pork chops plus Indonesian satay, Texas chili, Asian-style fish, and Thai salads. On Monday nights Serrano puts on a reasonably priced multi-course ethnic meal, perhaps an Indonesian *rijsttafel* or a Brazilian feast. ♦ Eclectic ♦ Lunch and dinner; dinner only on Saturday. Closed Sunday. 20 S. Second St (between Chestnut and Market Sts). 928.0770

Sassafras Cafe &
ART GALLERY

47 Sassafras Cafe & Art Gallery ★$$ A carved wood bar, mosaic tiles, and a marble fireplace add charm to this small bistro, but the menu is less than inventive. Filet mignon, chicken teriyaki, and fettuccine in a peppered vodka cream sauce are among the choices. Order a hamburger instead. ♦ International ♦ Lunch and dinner. Closed Sunday. 48 S. Second St (between Chestnut and Market Sts). 925.2317

48 Los Amigos ★$ Mainstream Mexican food—tostadas, tacos, and enchiladas—is served in this restaurant with white stucco walls. Every plate comes with the standard rice and refried beans. ♦ Mexican ♦ Lunch, dinner, and late-night snacks. 50 S. Second St (between Chestnut and Market Sts). 922.7061

49 Rib-It ★$$ Pork, beef, and lamb ribs are the chief attractions in this chain operation. If you've cleared it with your cardiologist, try the Funion Loaf, which looks like bread but is actually onion rings. ♦ American ♦ Lunch and dinner. 52 S. Second St (between Chestnut and Market Sts). 923.5511

50 Philadelphia Fish & Co. ★$$ Walk through the extremely popular and noisy bar to reach this casual dining room that serves a wide selection of fresh seafood. The restaurant imports about a hundred pounds of mesquite from Texas every day to feed its grill and give the seafood a nice nutty flavor. In addition to grilled swordfish and tuna are rainbow trout in shallot butter, bluefish with mustard and grilled onions, and shark in a citrus sauce. Entrées are served with your choice of steamed red potatoes, rice pilaf, cole slaw, or vegetables. ♦ Seafood ♦ Lunch and dinner; dinner only on Sunday. 207 Chestnut St (at S. Second St). 625.8605

Philadelphia was a primitive town during the 1600s. Not only were the very first dwellings made of logs, but pigs and goats trotted about freely and raw sewage stagnated on Front Street.

estaurants/Clubs: Red   Hotels: Blue
ops/ ♣ Outdoors: Green   Sights/Culture: Black

51 Thomas Bond House $$ This bed-and-breakfast offers a country inn atmosphere in the middle of the city. Built in 1769 by **Thomas Bond,** an eminent colonial physician who helped found **Pennsylvania Hospital,** the elegant Georgian brick structure was a residence until 1810, then was used as a commercial building until it was restored as an inn in 1988. A marble fireplace warms the parlor, where wine and cheese are served nightly. Guests enjoy Continental breakfast during the week and a full breakfast on week-ends. The inn also has some 20th-century amenities: color TVs and hair dryers. Rates for the 12 rooms vary widely. ♦ 129 S. Second St (between Chestnut and Walnut Sts). 923.8523, 800/845.2663

52 Old Original Bookbinder's ★★$$$$ A Philadelphia fixture since the first restaurant opened on this site in 1865, Bookbinder's has kept its name in the news by flaunting its famous customers—Presidents, baseball players, Hollywood celebrities—whose photos line the walls. A thousand people can be seated in the dining room, which is decorated with old bell-shaped lamps, Philadelphia paraphernalia, and a collection of model fire trucks and guns. The food is pricey, conservative, and dependable, with enormous servings of fresh broiled fish and lobsters, taken from a live tank, that literally fall over the sides of the plates. ♦ Seafood ♦ Lunch and dinner; dinner only on Sunday. 125 Walnut St (at S. Second St). Reservations required. 925.7027

53 Pasta Blitz by Lamberti ★$$ Indulge a craving for garlic, tomatoes, and olive oil in this second-story glass-enclosed restaurant across the cobblestone street from the **Ritz Five** movie theater. As the name suggests, the menu is heavy on pasta, as well as Italian preparations of chicken, veal, and seafood. Try the fettuccine with baby shrimp, garlic, and white wine or the chicken with asparagus, sun-dried tomatoes, mushrooms, and melted mozzarella. A breezy outdoor terrace is open in warm weather. ♦ Italian ♦ Lunch and dinner. 212 Walnut St (between S. Second and S. Third Sts). 238.0499

54 Ritz Five This five-screen movie theater is popular with locals in search of something besides the latest Hollywood blockbuster. You can count on finding at least one good movie here, and it's clean and comfortable—with cushy chairs that lean back. Arrive early for weekend shows. ♦ 214 Walnut St (between S. Second and S. Third Sts). 925.7900

55 Society Hill Sheraton $$$ A block from Penn's Landing and steps from Old City, Society Hill, and Independence Park, this Sheraton is a convenient semiluxury hotel with 365 rooms, an indoor pool, and an atrium lobby. The brick exterior fits in nicely with the neighborhood. ♦ One Dock St (at S. Second St). 238.6000, 800/325.3535; fax 238.6652

Within the Society Hill Sheraton:

Hadley's ★$$$ Dressed up in the colonial colors of salmon and green, the Sheraton's formal dining room tries to depart from standard hotel fare with a menu that includes shad cooked on cedar with spring onions and crushed mustard seed sauce, duck with thyme and roasted apples, and homemade gravlax. ♦ Eclectic ♦ Lunch and dinner; Sunday brunch. 238.6000

The Courtyard ★$ Sink into a comfortable chair by the fountain in the Sheraton's sunny lobby for a drink, a cup of coffee, or a lunch of chicken salad or seafood chowder. ♦ American ♦ Lunch, light snacks, desserts, and cocktails. 238.6000

56 Society Hill Towers The only high rises in Society Hill are the result of a design competition in the late 1950s held to select a new building for the site of the demolished food distribution center. Architect **I.M. Pei** won with these concrete towers, completed in 1964. The apartments inside are spectacular, with floor-to-ceiling windows and views of the river. At the base of the West Tower is *Old Man, Young Man, The Future,* by **Leonard Baskin,** a work commissioned (as required) by Philadelphia's One Percent for Art program and completed in 1966. In the center of the adjacent square of town houses, also by Pei, is a second casting of **Gaston Lachaise's** *Floating Figure,* originally completed in 1927. ♦ S. Second and Locust Sts

57 Powel House **Samuel Powel** and his wife, **Elizabeth Willing Powel,** were legendary hosts who entertained **George Washington, General Lafayette,** and other prominent figures at this elegant Georgian town house. Powel was a wealthy patron of the Revolution, though evidently able to accommodate both sides of the dispute: he was the first mayor of Philadelphia after the war and the last mayor under the Crown.

Built in 1765, the house contains its original fixtures and furnishings, including a staircase made of Santo Domingo mahogany. Powel hired furniture carvers to create the intricate doorways, moldings, and paneling. (The woodwork from two of the original rooms is displayed in the **Metropolitan Museum of A** and the **Philadelphia Museum of Art.**) One amenity in short supply, however, is closet space. It was local custom at the time to lev taxes on all rooms that could be walked into including closets. One solution was to use a massive wooden wardrobe like the one on t second floor. Don't miss the elegant ballroo or the formal garden adjacent to the house, which contains trees and shrubs common t 18th-century gardens.

The Powel House is one of seven collective known as **Mansion Row,** which starts at 23 S. Third Street. Some of the city's leading ci zens had homes here in the 18th and 19th centuries, including **John Penn,** grandson c William and the last colonial governor of Pennsylvania, who lived in the house that stood at **No. 242** from 1776 to 1771. **No. 23** was built in 1824 by master bricklayer **Amo Atkinson.** Only the Powel House is open to public. ♦ Admission. Tu-Sa 10AM-4PM; Su 1-4PM. 244 S. Third St (between Locust an Spruce Sts). 627.0364

58 The Pennsylvania Horticultural Socie The Society is responsible for one of the cit most popular events of the year: the **Philadelphia Flower Show**—the largest indoor show of its kind. Held every March at the Philadelphia Civic Center (but scheduled to move to the Pennsylvania Convention Center in 1996), the flower show is synonymous with spring in Philadelphia. The headquarters and ground merit a visit even if you have just a mild inte est in horticulture, which the Society calls " slowest of the performing arts." The first-fl exhibit area features watercolors and pencil sketches of flowers, and the backyard is ho to a vegetable plot and an 18th-century forn garden with neat pathways, geometric flowe beds, and a delightful gazebo. ♦ Free. M-F 9AM-5PM. 325 Walnut St (between S. Thirc and S. Fourth Sts). 625.8250

59 The Philadelphia Contributionship for Insuring Houses from Loss by Fire One of the city's earliest insurance firms, formed by **Benjamin Franklin** in 1752, the Contributionship actually kept its own brigades to help in fighting fires. The Greek Revival-style headquarters was designed by **Thomas Ustick Walter** and completed in 1836. ◆ Closed to the public. 212 S. Fourth St (between Locust and Walnut Sts)

60 Old St. Mary's Church Built in 1763 by carpenter **Charles Johnson,** St. Mary's was Philadelphia's central Roman Catholic church during the Revolution and became the city's first cathedral in 1810 following the creation of the Philadelphia diocese. The **Continental Congress** attended services here four times; **George Washington** and **John Adams** both visited; and on 4 July 1779 the first public religious commemoration of the **Declaration of Independence** was held here. The earliest version of the building was plain brick, and the Gothic facade was added during the late 1800s when the church was expanded. The cemetery to the west has been a Catholic burial ground since 1759. ◆ Free. M-Sa 9AM-5PM; Su 8AM-noon. Services Su 9AM, 10:30AM. 252 S. Fourth St (between Locust and Spruce Sts). 923.7930

61 Society Hill One of the most pleasant city neighborhoods in the country, Society Hill boasts a delightful mix of 18th- to 20th-century residences, charming walkways with benches and greenery, and handsome colonial churches. The absence of tall buildings puts the area on an intimate scale, reminiscent of the city that stood here more than 200 years ago. Named after the **Free Society of Traders,** a stock company that invested in **William Penn's** new colony, Society Hill was one of the principal residential areas of colonial Philadelphia. When the city served as the capital of the nation from 1790 to 1800, many of the federal government's leaders lived here. But the neighborhood was not always so posh: in the 1940s Society Hill ranked as one of the worst slums in Philadelphia. Its rebirth is a story of ingenious urban renewal. Today the area contains more 18th-century architecture than anywhere else in America.

Fifty short years ago Society Hill was dominated by a food distribution center on Dock Street, commercial buildings, and run-down boardinghouses. Spurred in part by the renewal of **Independence Park,** the city relocated the food center to South Philadelphia in the 1950s, tore down the dilapidated commercial buildings, and surveyed the neighborhood's historical treasures. The **Philadelphia Redevelopment Authority** acquired many of these deteriorated colonial structures and sold them to private individuals for what would be considered a pittance today, but with a binding agreement

that required restoration of the buildings. During the next two decades more than 600 of the area's historic houses were renovated. And, fortunately, the architecture of the contemporary town houses constructed on empty lots doesn't attempt to replicate colonial structures, à la Williamsburg, Virginia, but complements the older buildings instead. Though a few historic houses are open to the public, notably the **Hill-Physick-Keith House** and **Powel House,** the vast majority are private residences. ◆ Bounded by Walnut and Lombard Sts, and S. Second and S. Fifth Sts

62 Hill-Physick-Keith House The only free-standing Federal mansion left in Society Hill is an excellent place to get a sense of how the wealthy lived in the early part of the 19th century. The 32-room house was built in 1786 by **Henry Hill,** an importer of Madeira wine, and later occupied by **Dr. Philip Syng Physick,** known as the father of American surgery. Physick lived here from 1815 to 1837, courageously remaining during the yellow fever epidemic. After his death, the house was remodeled by family members and then neglected until the 1960s, when the property was donated to the **Philadelphia Society for the Preservation of Landmarks** and restored, along with its original furnishings. Next to the house is a Federal-style garden with a serpentine path and antique cannons. ◆ Tu-Sa 10AM-4PM; Su 1-4PM. 321 S. Fourth St. 925.7866

63 Delancey Street This charming side street has an eclectic array of colonial structures and contemporary houses. It's one of a number of intimate narrow streets in Society Hill—others include **American, Cypress,** and **Philip**—that are ideal for a stroll. Most of the houses were built individually or in pairs instead of in speculative rows. In the 200 block of Delancey Street on the south side is a typical colonial courtyard with tiny houses that were once tenements rented out by the merchant who owned the main house in front. **St. Peter's Way,** between Fourth and Third streets, is a brick walkway that wends from Old St. Joseph's Church below Walnut Street to St. Peter's on Pine Street. **Lawrence Court,** off the 400 block of Spruce Street, is a similar walkway. Both have been enlivened with sculptures, and St. Peter's Way also has a small playground. ◆ Bounded by S. Fourth and S. Front Sts, and Pine and Spruce Sts

In 1793, in a prison yard at Sixth and Walnut streets (a part of what is now Society Hill), Jean Pierre Blanchard became the first person to ascend in a balloon. Lifting off before a crowd of spectators that included George Washington, the hydrogen balloon landed 46 minutes later in southern New Jersey.

64 St. Peter's Church Perhaps more than any other place in the city, this lovely 18th-century church and its serene, otherworldly graveyard will transport you to colonial times. Miraculously, the building has changed very little in its more than two centuries. The **William Penn** family donated the land for an Anglican church when the pews at Christ Church to the north filled to overflowing. Designed by master carpenter **Robert Smith,** the church opened for worship in 1761. In the first sermon, **Reverend Dr. William Smith** noted that St. Peter's was "decently neat and elegantly plain." Aside from the large Palladian window on the chancel wall and arched windows on the side walls, the earliest version of the church was spared of exterior ornament, in keeping with the Georgian style of the time. The intimate interior is unusual because the pulpit and altar are at opposite ends of the main aisles. The high-backed box pews, once occupied by **George Washington** and other leading citizens, were raised off the floor to keep out drafts. Two wooden angels flanking the organ case, brought here from **Old St. Paul's Church** in 1831, were made by well-known local sculptor **William Rush.** The tower and spire, designed by Philadelphia architect **William Strickland,** were added in 1842 and contain eight bells made at the **Whitechapel Foundry** in London, birthplace of the Liberty Bell.

Several Revolutionary War figures are buried in the churchyard, including **Dr. John Morgan,** chief physician of the Continental Army and founder of the University of Pennsylvania Medical School, and **John Nixon,** a Lieutenant Colonel who read the Declaration of Independence for the first time in public on 8 July 1776. Portrait painter **Charles Willson Peale** is also buried here, along with the chiefs of seven Indian tribes who died during the yellow fever epidemic of the 1790s. The churchyard, surrounded by a brick wall built in 1784, is shaded by beautiful trees, including robust hollies that spill over to the street side and Osage oranges, said to have been grown from seeds brought from the West by **Lewis and Clark.** St. Peter's still houses an active Episcopal congregation noted for its three choirs. ♦ Tu-Sa 9AM-noon (knock on the rectory next door if the church is locked). Services Su 9AM, 11AM. 313 Pine St (between S. Third and S. Fourth Sts). 925.5968

65 Old Pine Street Church Established in 1768 as the third Presbyterian church in the city, and the only colonial one still in existence, Old Pine dominates the block with its wrought-iron fence, yellow exterior, and classic columns. It was originally constructed as a simple Georgian church from plans by builder **Robert Smith.** In 1837, as the Greek Revival style came into fashion, Corinthian columns were added, giving it the appearance of a classic temple. During the British occupation of Philadelphia, royal troops used Old Pine as a hospital and stable. Later, several of the church's 19th-century pastors were in the forefront of the region's antislavery movement. As with St. Peter's down the street, Old Pine has a peaceful courtyard with tombstones standing in crooked rows. Mathematician, astronomer, and inventor **David Rittenhouse** is buried here, along with a number of Revolutionary War heroes, including **General John Steele,** field officer on the day the British surrendered at Yorktown in 1781. **Eugene Ormandy,** the famed conductor of the Philadelphia Orchestra, was also laid to rest here. ♦ Services Su 10AM. 412 Pine St (between S. Fourth and S. Fifth Sts). 925.8051

66 Society Hill Synagogue Designed by **Thomas Ustick Walter,** architect of the Capitol dome in Washington, DC, this Greek Revival building was erected in 1829 as a Baptist church. It was purchased by a Rumanian Jewish congregation in the early 1900s, and the attics and cupolas that originally stood atop the squat corner towers were removed. ♦ 426 Spruce St (between S. Fourth and S. Fifth Sts)

67 Penn Mutual Life Insurance Completed in 1970 and designed by **Mitchell/Giurgola Associates,** this 18-story office building overlooking Independence Square is actually an addition to the buildings next door, designed by **Edgar Seeler** in 1913 and **Ernest Matthewson** in 1931. Note how the dark glass and concrete facade of the old **Pennsylvania Fire Insurance Company** blends in with Penn Mutual's ground-level entrance. ♦ 510 Walnut St (between S. Fifth and S. Sixth Sts)

68 Curtis Center For more than half a century the **Curtis Publishing Company** was the country's leading publisher of popular magazines, its stable including the phenomenally successful *Ladies Home Journal,* begun in 1883. Curtis also bought the *Saturday Evening Post* in 1897, and increased circulation to 500,000 by 1903. Today the large brick and white marble building houses offices. A 15-foot-high **Maxfield Parrish** glass mosaic mural made by **Louis C. Tiffany Studios** in 1916 dominates the lobby of this building, designed by **Edgar Seeler,** which is open to the public. ♦ Independence Square West (S. Sixth and Walnut Sts). 238.6450

The Great Fire of London in 1666 had a profound influence on the development of early Philadelphia. City planners not only encouraged the use of brick for more fireproof buildings, they also created a grid pattern of streets to make it easier for firefighters to get around in an emergency.

59 Washington Square This square, one of the original five parks laid out by **William Penn**, is one of the most inviting and underused outdoor spaces in Philadelphia. Washington Square has had a checkered past: During the city's first decades, it was a ragged plot of green used as a cemetery for transients and paupers, and later, victims of the yellow fever epidemic. The **Tomb of the Unknown Soldier** in the center of the square commemorates the American patriots who were buried here during the British occupation of the city in 1778. When the neighborhood finally improved during the 19th century, the square became a gracious common, as the Federal town houses still standing on the southwest end attest. **Christopher Morley,** the famous Philadelphia writer, lived as a young man in the third house from the corner of Seventh Street. In the 1800s offices were built around the square, and it became the headquarters of the city's robust publishing industry. Today Washington Square has a balanced mix of residences, office buildings, and small businesses. On its streets, you can find the oldest publishing house in the country, a prestigious gallery for contemporary art, one of the city's oldest and most unusual private clubs, and a wonderful old Italian restaurant. Dominated by shade trees and furnished with benches, it's a good place to take a break and feed the pigeons. ◆ Bounded by S. Sixth and S. Seventh Sts at Walnut St

70 The Athenaeum of Philadelphia Two gaslit lampposts stand outside the front door of this private club, which opened as a sub-scription library for well-to-do bibliophiles in 1814. The elegant Italian Renaissance Revival building was one of the first brown-stones in the city, designed by **John Notman,** the Scottish-born architect who brought Gothic and Renaissance designs to 19th-century America. Inside, the elegant rooms seem made for sipping sherry and poring over texts by Aristotle or Virgil. In recent years the club has become a major reposito-ry of architectural drawings, including early sketches of the U.S. Capitol and Independence Hall, as well as decorative arts from the Victorian period. The building also serves as headquarters of the **Victorian Society of America** and houses a wide range of Victorian interior design samples that are often used by people restoring their homes. Exhibits on the first floor are open to the public. ◆ Free. M-F 9AM-5PM. Tours by appointment only. 219 S. Sixth St (between Walnut St and Washington Sq South). 925.2688

71 Locks Gallery The former headquarters of the **Lea and Febiger** publishing firm has been converted into this prestigious commercial gallery for contemporary art.

Behind the wrought-iron door and columned facade are three floors of exhibition space. Artists displayed here include **Elizabeth Murray,** known for her colorful, sculptural paintings and cartoonlike figures; sculptor **Nancy Graves,** who creates abstract bronze pieces out of everyday objects, such as farm tools or plants; and **Phoebe Adams,** whose sculptures in bronze, hair, and wax resemble parts of the body. ◆ Tu-F 10AM-6PM; Sa 10AM-5PM. 600 Washington Sq South (between Walnut and Spruce Sts). 629.1000

72 Thomas Moser Cabinetmakers The solid cherry Shaker- and Mission-influenced furniture sold in this fine Art Deco building designed by **Ralph B. Bencker** comes from a workshop in Auburn, Maine. ◆ M-F 10AM-6PM; Sa 10AM-5PM. 210 Washington Sq West (between Locust and Walnut Sts). 922.6440

A Stitch in Time: The Fabrication of the Betsy Ross Legend

When **John Ross** was killed in an explosion of gun-powder in 1776, his wife, **Betsy,** took over their upholstery business, running it out of a small house at Second and Arch streets. Despite what your kindergarten teacher may have told you, the story of Betsy Ross sewing the first flag of the American colonies—the ring of 13 stars bordered by stripes—is about as likely as that of **George Washington** chopping down the cherry tree. Most historians agree that the Betsy Ross legend is another of those enduring myths of American history, a legend that lives on despite meager evidence.

Like most cities, Philadelphia has been associated with its share of historical inaccuracies or embel-lishments. For instance, it didn't snow much during that infamous winter when Washington and his troops camped at Valley Forge. And the **Liberty Bell** did not crack on the Fourth of July—that myth was the invention of a popular 19th-century writer, **George Lippard.** Likewise, the Betsy Ross story was apparently created by her grandson.

Though a Quaker by birth, Ross broke with the religion's pacifist stance and supported the revolutionary cause. Evidence shows that she sewed small packets used to hold gunpowder for the rebel government. And though there is a gov-ernment receipt for a flag she made, there is no indication that it was the nation's first flag. Some Philadelphians find it annoying that the city contin-ues to propagate the myth by operating the Ross home as a public shrine. However, park officials argue that the house is a classic example of 18th-century Philadelphia architecture. Regardless of her part in the flag's creation, Betsy Ross can be considered a heroine of her time. After all, how many women in the 1700s ran their own business?

Aliza Green
Owner, Aliza Green Food Consulting Company

Seeing yet another unexpected angle of the most striking and boldest building on Rittenhouse Square: **The Rittenhouse.** Every side makes a different statement.

Visit the private **Rosenbach Collection** on Delancey Street. This magnificent Philadelphia town house (on *the* best block in Center City) houses some of **Maurice Sendak's** original paintings for his children's books, as well as theater sets. And the setting will make you feel part of the city's aristocracy.

Einstein Toys at the Mellon Independence Center (which used to be Lit Brothers Department Store—look for the sign at the corner that still says: "Lit Bros. Hats Trimmed Free"). Einstein's toys are the best, and the salespeople, who really care about kids, can help you choose something really special. It's not just another discount toy store.

A private dinner arranged by the famous **Toto** (the best maître d' in the city, a man born to his job) in the wine cellar at **Caffe Di Lullo,** at their original location in the Fox Chase section on the outskirts of Philadelphia.

Buying one terrific outfit a season from **Toby Lerner's** very personal boutique on South 17th Street. Her sophisticated taste married with a sense of humor always hits the spot. I only wish it could be more often. My long-term favorites—the clothes that always make me feel good—all seem to come from here.

Window shopping at **Nan Duskin.** Their series of full-size *vitrines* showcase the best in top designerwear. It's a great place for fantasizing, or for buying that very special dress or suit and really living it up.

My once-a-week trip to **Indian Rock Produce** at the **Jenkintown Farmer's Market,** where Al sells the kind of produce, fruits, and salad greens usually served in four-star restaurants. It's great to be able to cook with stuff this good, and there's always something new to try.

A picnic alfresco at the **Azalea Garden** behind the Philadelphia Museum of Art. There's sure to be a wedding party in all their finery being photographed at this site, a favorite of locals.

The Monday morning **Flea Market** at **Perkiomenville** (on Route 29), especially if you can get there early enough for the auction. I've been "hunting" there for 25 years and my house is full of treasures, especially jewelry and furniture. My best find was a bronze lamp covered by a stained-glass shade full of brilliant parrots.

Wander around at **Fante's** on Ninth Street in the Italian Market. The only problem is that there's too much temptation for a cookware junkie like me, because "Fante's has everything," especially baking supplies and European pans and molds. Their salespeople are extraordinarily helpful; it's a family-run business and it shows.

The **Italian Market** on any day but Sunday (too crowded) or Monday (closed), with all its grunginess is *the* place to see the real Philadelphia. Pick and choose at the stalls: some have top quality, others are best for bargains. In winter, the stall owners keep warm with fires built in 50-gallon drums.

The **Taste the Harvest Festival** held every fall at the Armory on 23rd Street, a farmer's market extravaganza showcasing fresh squeezed apple cider, chef demos, homegrown fruits, vegetables, herbs, and edible flowers, and wine tastings. There's even a country-music band, and live farm animals for the kids.

The Warthog, a bronze sculpture by local artist **Eric Berg** at the **Philadelphia Zoo,** is a favorite landmark.

Kalamata olive bread at **Breadsmith** in Chestnut Hill. This city has always had wonderful crusty Italian bread (try the loaves from **Caccia's** or **Lanci,** both in South Philly), but we've never had a serious bakery before. Witness the line out the door, even on weekdays.

A visit to **Assouline & Ting,** where the owner always has something new to try. It's great for high-quality baking ingredients that are usually only available to restaurants and bakeries. Try his store-brand chocolate—a great buy!

Patti LaBelle
Singer/Actress

Everyone's always surprised when they hear I still live in Philadelphia. The lights are certainly brighter in Los Angeles and New York, but in Philly they seem a whole lot warmer. Carry a smile when you come here and you'll be right at home.

Take a walk along the **Delaware River,** where you'll find trendy cafes filled with pretty young things—great scenery of both kinds!

Head to **Friday Saturday Sunday** on 21st Street for the best margaritas this side of Mexico.

Mezzanotte has the juiciest hamburgers.

When I'm really hungry for a big steak (and I mean *big*) I head for **The Palm** at The Bellevue.

Bookbinder's is a real Old City tradition; some Philadelphians consider it the only restaurant in town.

I wish my kids weren't all grown so I'd always have an excuse to go to the **Please Touch Museum,** where you get to play with everything!

The **Afro American Museum,** a great repository of arts and artifacts, is a must-see for anyone of African descent.

Jim's Steaks is the answer I always give when people ask where to get the best cheesesteak sandwich. Let that grease just drip down and you'll know why Philly is famous for this.

Cruise **South Street**—it's more fun and friendlier than Greenwich Village.

on't miss **Reading Terminal Market** for fish, fruit, nd vegetables. You might see me there squeezing e tomatoes.

llure is the best place to shop for my husband. rom Giorgio Armani to Donna Karan it has the neat- st menswear. My favorite store for *me* is **Knitwit**. rop by, you'll see why.

e love to get out of the city and often head to **eading** for all the discount marts. I love clothes, nd I love a bargain even more.

ry taking Route 30 into **Lancaster County** toward mish country. During the summer you can get the eshest vegetables here. In the fall go pick apples— 's unbelievably beautiful.

ly perfect evening out: drinks at the **Four Seasons otel**, dinner at **Le Bec-Fin**, jazz at **Zanzibar Blue**, en home to watch late movies (real late!).

ane Robelot
ews Anchor, WCAU-TV

o to the **Dilworthtown Inn** in West Chester for a ste of fine cuisine and an atmosphere that reflects hiladelphia's incredible history. It's a lovely, warm 50-year-old inn with the most diverse and delicious ontinental menu available.

o sample the city's menu go to **Jack's Firehouse** t's really an old firehouse, with a beautiful wooden eiling, walls, and floors). The owner, **Jack McDavid**, ill prepare a mouth-watering gourmet meal, Southern Style," that's also very healthy . . . every- ing served here is organically grown.

lurray's Delicatessen on Montgomery Avenue in ala Cynwyd (just outside of Philadelphia) has unfor- ettable chicken and turkey breast sandwiches, hitefish salad, and the freshest bagels (in fact, it's e best deli).

runch at the **Four Seasons Hotel**. Don't eat for three ays before you go because everything is delicious.

hiladelphia's heart is her history. And, though it ounds corny, you truly capture the spirit of this city nd our country with a park-service tour of **dependence Hall** and the **Liberty Bell**, followed by tour in a horse-drawn carriage (catch one outside dependence Hall).

t night, take **West River Drive** along the Schuylkill iver and look across the river to **Boathouse Row**. liniature white lights outline the delightful architec- re, a year-round holiday treat.

he **Philadelphia Museum of Art**, beautiful inside nd out, is certainly touted as one of the finest in the orld. It also has a wonderful cafeteria! And the kids houldn't miss the **Philadelphia Zoo**, with the rare ammals house and the new carnivore exhibit. . . . 's clean, beautiful, and educational.

nally, the greatest horticultural exhibit in the orld—**Longwood Gardens**—is just minutes from hiladelphia on Route 1. It's breathtaking any time f year.

ou'll love Philadelphia. Come see our City of rotherly Love.

David R. Boldt
Editor of the Editorial Page, *The Philadelphia Inquirer*

Best Place to Stroll, Jog, or Bike—along **East River Drive** on a summer evening when the rowing crews leave ripples in the water, which looks like molten pewter (runner-up: **Valley Forge National Park**).

Best Historical Attraction—**Independence Hall**, where it all began.

Historic Attractions Most Likely to be Missed That are Well Worth Seeing—**Franklin Court**, the **Graff House**, and the John Huston movie at the **National Park Visitors Center**.

Best Place for Breakfast—**au bon pain** at Penn Center (sit at one of the outdoor tables).

Best Place for Lunch—**The Rose Tattoo**.

Best Place for Cocktails—lobby of the **Ritz Carlton**.

Best Place for Dinner—**The Garden**. Have a "sum- mer (or winter) garden" as an aperitif, oysters, sole amandine, and a "Bonaparte" for dessert. (Or, for a completely different experience, have the buffalo at **Jack's Firehouse** and end the meal with fine bour- bon in a brandy snifter).

Places to Skip—**The Main Line** (if you've seen one affluent suburb, you've seen them all). If you want to visit a nice Philadelphia neighborhood, stroll along Germantown Avenue in **Chestnut Hill** on a Saturday, but don't tell anyone else about it.

Nicest Place to Go Christmas Shopping—**The Shops at Liberty Place** (**Shops at The Bellevue** is nice, but the selection isn't as broad nor the enter- tainment as good).

Best Vista—**Swann Memorial Fountain** (in Logan Circle) at night. Wednesday night is best, when the museums are open. (Best place from which to admire it: the **Fountain Room** at the Four Seasons Hotel.)

The World's Most Beautiful Ugly Building— **City Hall**.

Edmund N. Bacon
City Planner

Visiting the wonderful period rooms in the **Masonic Temple**.

Taking the **water taxi** between restaurants and nightclubs on the Delaware River.

Wandering along the greenway garden paths that lace through **Society Hill**.

Watching the ducks and having lunch at **Valley Green Inn** on Wissahickon Creek.

Riding the ferryboat from **Penn's Landing** to the **New Jersey State Aquarium**.

Sitting quietly in George Washington's pew at **St. Peters Church** on Pine Street.

Lunch under the trees in the **Fountain Court** of Commerce Square.

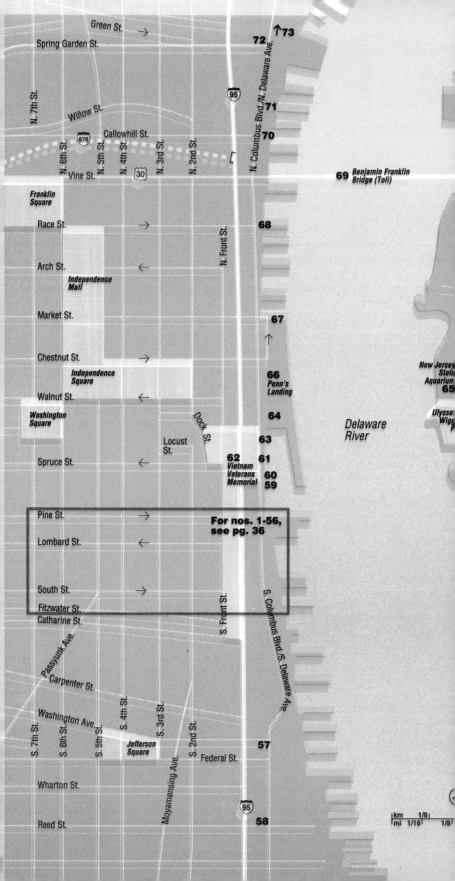

Green St. →

Spring Garden St.

72

↑73

I-95

71

70

N. 7th St.

Willow St.

676

Callowhill St.

N. 6th St.

N. 5th St.

N. 4th St.

N. 3rd St.

N. 2nd St.

Vine St.

30

69 **Benjamin Franklin Bridge (Toll)**

Franklin Square

Race St. →

68

N. Front St.

Arch St. ←

Independence Mall

Market St.

67

↑

Chestnut St. →

Independence Square

66
Penn's Landing

Walnut St. ←

Washington Square

64

63

Dock St.

Locust St.

62
Vietnam Veterans Memorial

61

60

59

Spruce St. ←

New Jersey State Aquarium
65

Ulysses Wigg

Delaware River

Pine St. →

For nos. 1-56, see pg. 36

Lombard St. ←

S. Front St.

S. Columbus Blvd./S. Delaware Ave.

South St. →

Fitzwater St.

Catharine St.

Passyunk Ave.

Carpenter St.

Washington Ave.

S. 7th St.

S. 6th St.

S. 5th St.

S. 4th St.

S. 3rd St.

S. 2nd St.

Jefferson Square

Moyamensing Ave.

Federal St.

57

Wharton St.

58

Reed St.

| km | 1/8 |
| mi | 1/16 | 1/8

N. Columbus Blvd./N. Delaware Ave.

South Street/Waterfront

South Street is trend central, the closest thing Philadelphia has to Greenwich Village. Its hip reputation was immortalized in the '60s, when a popular song intoned, "Where do all the hippies meet? South Street. South Street," and again in the '80s, when a song by the Dead Milkmen mentioned the **Philadelphia Pizza Company** and **Zipperhead**, two South Street hangouts. Though national chain stores started taking up residence in the '80s, South Street has managed to maintain its counterculture character with an eclectic mix of boutiques, restaurants, pubs, music clubs, and people (keep an eye out for the "Kazoo Lady" and other wacky street performers). If you have just one night in Philly, try to make it here to bask in the vibrant atmosphere.

As in other trendy urban neighborhoods, many of South Street's establishments come and go with the seasons. The water-ice shop that attracted hordes last summer may well vanish in the fall. Vacant storefronts suddenly become costume shops for Halloween, then hastily transform into last-minute gift centers in time for the winter holidays. Even the secondhand stores, which keep all the slackers looking frowsy-chic, change frequently. On weekends during warm-weather months, South Street closes to vehicular traffic from Eighth to Front streets, creating a wide walkway that grows more Dionysian by the hour. During any season, first-time visitors should start either at the river and work west or around 10th Street and walk toward the water.

While the bohemian pleasures of South Street are easy to explore on foot, restaurants and nightclubs on the piers along the nearby Waterfront are spread too far afield for walking. Despite water-taxi services and trolleys, it's difficult to bounce between nightclubs on the different piers, as some are miles apart. But waterfront establishments have taken care of the proximity problem with one-stop restaurant/nightclubs, dinner cruises on the Delaware, and theme "entertainment complexes," where you can dine, dance, and even swim the night away under one roof.

1 **Society Hill Playhouse** Over the last few years, this neighborhood theater has become one of the most consistent venues for drama in Philadelphia. Its two stages are small and rather ordinary, but the productions—most notably the long-running *Nunsense*—have received critical acclaim. The season runs from September through May, and there's cabaret-style late-night comedy on weekends. ♦ Call for schedules and ticket prices. 507 S. Eighth St (between South and Lombard Sts). 923.0210

2 **Montserrat** ★★$$ Locals and tourists while away the hours together in Montserrat's comfortable wood-and-beveled-glass bar, and the staff always has the latest news on Philadelphia's hippest neighborhood. Though the menu seems partial to salads and meatless dishes, Montserrat's Sunday brunch and charbroiled burgers are favorites. A deck offers streetside dining in friendly weather. ♦ American/Eclectic ♦ Lunch and dinner. 623 South St (between Sixth and Seventh Sts). 627.4224

3 **Comics And More** Both newsstand and collector comics are available in this small, invariably busy store. Comic-book fans will delight in perusing cards, models, buttons, T-shirts, and other superhero-related merchandise. On Sunday, an artist takes up residence to show patrons how to paint models of their favorite characters (the store provides paints when models are purchased). ♦ M-Th noon-10PM; F-Sa noon-midnight; Su noon-8PM. 620 South St (between Sixth and Seventh Sts). 625.9613

4 **Tower Records** Built on the site of Ripley's, a famed Philadelphia nightclub, the area's premier music store requires three floors (plus a separate location for classical across the street) to house all of its compact discs and cassettes. How does this Tower differ from others in the chain? Its extraordinarily deep jazz section caters to the area's discriminating listeners, and its rap bins contain a full line of local and

international hiphop. As in other Tower stores, the staff is knowledgeable and friendly. This location also has a **Ticketmaster** outlet for concerts and sporting events. ◆ Daily 9AM-midnight. 610 South St (Classical Annex: 595 South St). 574.9888

5 Mother Bethel African Methodist Church Considered the birthplace of the African-American church, the massive stone Mother Bethel is the most important historic building in the South Street area. **Richard Allen** and **Absalom Jones,** two prominent freedmen of colonial Philadelphia, founded this sanctum in 1787. It later served as a stop on the Underground Railroad. Four churches have been built on the site; the current one opened in 1890 and was restored in 1987, after some of its members tried unsuccessfully to move the church to West Philadelphia, where many in the congregation reside. Mother Bethel is known for its gospel choir and fiery preaching. The church museum can be visited by appointment. ◆ Services Su 10:45AM Sept-June; Su 10AM July-Aug. Sixth and Lombard Sts. 925.0616

6 South Street Antiques Market Many of the old houses a few blocks from the commercial area have been passed from generation to generation in the same family, proving a goldmine for the 28 dealers in this market. Vintage castoffs include clothing, postcards, jewelry, Depression-era glassware, and Art Deco furniture. The dealers are ready with information about their merchandise, but they're also aware that most people who wander in are just browsing. The lower level can be counted on for a few black velvet Elvis paintings, too. ◆ W-Th, Su noon-7PM; F-Sa noon-8PM. 615 S. Sixth St (between South and Bainbridge Sts). 592.0256

7 Garland of Letters When your inner child calls, this New Age bookstore with a welcoming, low-key environment offers music, crystals, and objets d'art, along with the expected instructional guidebooks. Come here to hook into Philadelphia's growing healing-arts scene. Sign up for yoga or meditation classes, and learn about lectures and community events. ◆ Daily 10AM-10PM. 527 South St (between Fifth and Sixth Sts). 923.5946

8 South Street Souvlaki ★★$ The city's preeminent Greek taverna has an open-flame grill and kitchen facing the street, so you can see—and smell—the options before ordering. Just about everything that comes off the grill is delectable. Best bets include such staples as gyro sandwiches and souvlaki, grilled fresh fish specialties, and roasted chicken. The swordfish kebabs—prime chunks of fish and veggies served on the stick over yellow rice, with a lemon cream sauce—are excellent. The cozy dining rooms, enlivened by murals, are crowded on Sunday nights, when zealous

musicians perform Greek songs during dinner. ◆ Greek ◆ Lunch and dinner. 509 South St (between Fifth and Sixth Sts). 925.3026

9 Original South Philly Water Ice ★★$ Lunch-counter foods (burgers, hot dogs, sandwiches) dominate the menu, but the ch attraction at this stylized 1950s diner is the sweet, cooling water ice, a local tradition in the summertime. Some entrepreneurs corru it into a popsicle and add too much sugar, b here the finely chopped ice is blended with fresh fruits for an ideal hot-weather treat. Lemon is the standard, but there are differen flavors daily. Genuine boardwalk-style soft i cream is another option for the dog days. ◆ American ◆ Daily 9AM-midnight. 506 Sou St (between Fifth and Sixth Sts). 629.1555

10 Philadelphia Record Exchange Well before chain stores brought the yuppies to South Street, young slackers swarmed the neighborhood, their only ambition to find the latest punk records on the cheap. This store still a haven for alternative-rock culture, and while it does a brisk used-CD business, the Exchange hasn't lost faith in vinyl, which ensures the business of the downwardly mobile. The store—packed to capacity, hot, and always loud—also carries local and national fanzines. ◆ Daily noon-9PM. 608 S. Fifth St (between South and Bainbridge Sts). 925.7892

11 The Book Trader A daunting, floor-to-ceiling repository of used books, The Book Trader may very well have those long out-of-print volumes you've been stalking. The fiction titles are crammed downstairs, while the more spacious second level has enough room for a miniature art gallery. An adjacent center for used records, while not as comprehensive, has been known to contain few gems. ◆ Daily 10AM-midnight. 501 Sou St (at Fifth St). 925.0219

Between 1955 and 1975, three out of every four industrial jobs in Philadelphia were eliminated.

Restaurants/Clubs: Red   **Hotels:** Blue

Shops/ 🌳 Outdoors: Green   **Sights/Culture:** Bla

12 Tiramisu ★★$$$ The closest thing South Street has to a cozy white-tablecloth trattoria, Tiramisu plays fast and loose with Southern Italian cuisine. Chef/owner **Alberto Del Bello** is from Rome's Jewish neighborhood, and he mixes elements of both traditions to create his imaginative if heavy dishes. The wood oven produces exceptional bread, but be sure to save room for the filling main courses. ♦ Italian ♦ Lunch and dinner; dinner only on Saturday and Sunday. 528 S. Fifth St (between South and Lombard Sts). Reservations recommended. 925.3335

13 Digital Underground Dealing exclusively in new and used CDs, this shop strives to offer titles the larger stores miss. That means lots of jangle bands on American independent labels, plenty of grunge, and the rare secondhand find. The sales clerks know what they're talking about. ♦ M-Th, Su 11AM-10PM; F-Sa 11AM-11PM. 526 S. Fifth St (between South and Lombard Sts). 925.5324

14 IPSO The coffeehouse society spreading through Philadelphia arrived late at South Street, but this dimly lit conversation spot makes up for its tardiness with literary pretension—an atmosphere that invites you to pull out a notebook and jot down grand thoughts. The espresso and flavored Italian-style drinks may well enhance creativity, but they're expensive, especially considering the clutter of books and newspapers that calls itself ambience. Homemade *biscotti* is a must with coffee. ♦ M-Th 4PM-midnight; F 4PM-1AM; Sa noon-1AM; Su noon-midnight. 517 S. Fifth St (between South and Lombard Sts). 922.6784

15 Tower Books The popular music store chain's attempt at book retailing is a hit on South Street. You'll find the most complete magazine (and scholarly journal) selection in the city, along with business books and computer manuals. Children's literature is also well represented. ♦ Daily 9AM-midnight. 425 South St (between Fourth and Fifth Sts). 925.9909

16 Cheers To You ★$ A few years ago this well-liked corner pub got a face-lift. Television sets, tuned to different channels, now radiate from various angles, and the bar area has been trimmed to accommodate additional tables. It's still a great place to drink, and especially busy on weekends. But come to socialize, not to eat—the food is unremarkable. ♦ Italian ♦ Lunch and dinner. 430 South St (at Passyunk Ave). 923.8780

All of the more than 35 beer-making facilities in Philadelphia from the 1930s—many affiliated with national brands or distributed across the country themselves—have closed. You can see the vacant shell of Ortlieb's brewery at Third and Popular streets, and the old Schmidt's plant at 127 Edward Street, between Front and Second streets.

16 Games Workshop Some epic game like Dungeons and Dragons is usually in progress at the huge game table in this store. Players talk strategy and mull over options with enough candor to help an alert beginner learn the basics. Fanatics and dabblers can select from science fiction and fantasy games for all ages and skill levels, as well as a large selection of individual playing pieces. ♦ M, W-Sa noon-8PM; Su noon-6PM. 424 South St (between Fourth and Fifth Sts). 829.0554

17 Philadelphia Pizza Company ★★$ Shun the mediocre by-the-slice pizza available elsewhere on South Street in favor of a delicious pie at Philadelphia Pizza Company. Friendly and comfortable, with spacious wooden booths, the restaurant starts with a fairly thick crust, baked until it begins to get crispy. Customers select from an exhaustive array of toppings, ranging from familiar pepperoni and mushrooms to more gourmet items. While the pizza is tops, the pasta dishes can be inconsistent. Sit at the bar upstairs or on the outdoor deck, which has a pool table. ♦ Italian ♦ Lunch and dinner. 418 South St (between Fourth and Fifth Sts). 627.3339

17 PhilaDeli ★$ Waitresses call everyone "hon" in this informal diner filled with local color. Breakfast, available all day, is a highlight; start with fresh-squeezed orange or grapefruit juice, and sample one of the various bagel treatments. The creamy cheesecakes and other gooey desserts are "to die for," just as the waitresses claim. If you're on the move, PhilaDeli also sells cold drinks and snacks, and will package sandwiches to go. ♦ Deli ♦ Breakfast, lunch, and dinner. 410 South St (between Fourth and Fifth Sts). 923.1986

18 Zipperhead On the leading edge when it comes to the latest fashion fads gripping American youth, Zipperhead has seen trends swing from safety-pin punk to biker leather and back again. Even if you're the khakis type, it's fun to examine the odd accessories, pre-ripped flannel shirts, and all types of gear in basic black. A skateboard shop upstairs caters to the skate-punk community. Both floors offer rock and rap T-shirts and other music-related items. ♦ M-W, Su noon-10PM; Th noon-11PM; F-Sa noon-midnight. 407 South St (between Fourth and Fifth Sts). 928.1123

19 Lickety Split ★$$ With its colorful jungle facade and second-floor waterfall, Lickety Split was a trend-setter on Philadelphia's restaurant scene when it opened some 20 years ago. Though the bar still serves innovative specialty drinks, and the menu always contains a few surprises, this tourist magnet is better for chatting and grazing than serious dining. ♦ Italian/Eclectic ♦ Lunch, dinner, late-night snacks, and Sunday brunch. 401 South St (at Fourth St). 922.1173

20 Eyes Gallery One of the first gift shops to locate on South Street in the 1970s, Eyes Gallery helped spark the South Street renaissance and spawned a number of neighboring imitators. The boutique features high-quality exotic jewelry and handicrafts from various undeveloped and Latin American countries, all artfully displayed. ♦ M-Th 11AM-7PM; F-Sa 11AM-8PM; Su noon-6PM. 402 South St (between Fourth and Fifth Sts). 925.0193

20 Jim's Steaks ★★$ The scent of fried onions wafting through the intersection of Fourth and South streets is the only advertising Jim's needs. At this black-and-white-tiled joint, a brawny bruiser behind the counter slaps together a classic Philadelphia cheesesteak: thin strips of steak cooked on an open grill, cheese, and usually onions, served in a hoagie roll. While some locals maintain that Pat's and Geno's in South Philly have a superior steak, Jim's has earned devoted followers with its special sauces, fresh toppings, and excellent fries. Pick up your meal at the ground-level cafeteria, then sit upstairs for an excellent view of the street action. ♦ American ♦ Lunch, dinner, and late-night snacks. 400 South St (at Fourth St). 928.1911

21 The Pink Rose Pastry Shop ★★★$ The pastry chefs at this bakery pour the finest ingredients and lots of TLC into the batter of their cookies, muffins, and cakes. Soothing music and an unhurried atmosphere make a weekday morning snack feel as relaxing as a Sunday brunch. Carrot cake is a must, and the coffee is great, too. ♦ Bakery ♦ Tu-Th 10:30AM-10:30PM; F 10:30AM-11:30PM; Sa 9AM-11:30PM; Su 9AM-8:30PM. 630 S. Fourth St (at Bainbridge St). 592.0565

22 Shippen Way Inn $ The area's only bed-and-breakfast inn has nine rooms, each with a private bath and reproductions of furnishings from the colonial era. Most have double beds.

Common areas include a living room, breakfast room, and courtyard. The family that owns the place lives next door and delights in preparing a full breakfast every day. Locals coping with spillover house guests favor the Shippen Way Inn, which has discount rates for stays exceeding three nights. ♦ 418 Bainbridge St (between Fourth and Fifth Sts). 627.7266, 800/245.4873

23 Famous 4th Street Deli ★$ Family owned and operated for three generations, the Famous Deli is one of the few remaining signs that South Street was once a Jewish enclave. The oversize sandwiches are legendary—try the pastrami or the Reuben—as are the bagels and homemade cookies, considered by many to be the best in the city. Don't judge this place by the decor or the paper plates. It's cluttered and feels a little chaotic when the line gets long, but the food is splendid, and the dining room is kept extraordinarily clean. ♦ Deli ♦ Breakfast and lunch. 700 S. Fourth St (at Bainbridge St). 922.3274

ESSENE

24 Essene ★$ With all the high-cholesterol food on South Street, it's comforting to know about this shrine to the fresh and wholesome just a few blocks away. In addition to an abundance of organically grown produce, this spotless health-food emporium has a restaurant in back that turns out vegetable juices, spicy sesame noodles, tofu hot dogs, and more. ♦ Health food ♦ Lunch and dinner. 719 S. Fourth St (at Monroe St). 922.1146

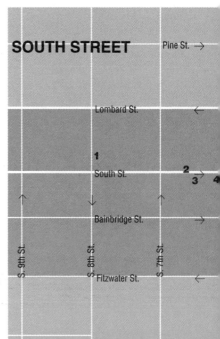

25 Alouette ★★$$$ Chef **Kamel Phutlok's** adventuresome spirit is reflected in the entrées of this Thai-influenced French restaurant. His exotic sauces, Thai curries, and unpredictable flavor combinations give such standard French dishes as veal medaillons (prepared with apple brandy and ginger sauce) a new kick. In warm weather, ask for a table in the pleasant and surprisingly quiet brick courtyard. ♦ French ♦ Lunch, dinner, and Sunday brunch. 334 Bainbridge St (at Fourth St). 629.1126

26 Alyan's ★$ Though short on decor, this Middle Eastern restaurant comes out a winner with tasty food and low prices. Such standbys as *hummus* and falafel are skillfully rendered, and the homemade fries—seasoned with onions and peppers—are a meal in themselves. ♦ Middle Eastern ♦ Lunch and dinner. 603 S. Fourth St (between South and Bainbridge Sts). 922.3553

27 Ishkabbible's Eatery ★$ A short-order lunch counter without the counter, Ishkabbible's tiny kitchen whips up an impressive array of foods. The business is mostly take-out, though there are a few tables inside and a picnic table on the sidewalk during summer months. Try the sizzling chicken cheesesteak, baked potato with choice of stuffing, and famous Fourth Street cookies (baked on the premises). ♦ American ♦ Breakfast, lunch, and dinner. 337 South St (between Third and Fourth Sts). 923.4337

28 Theater of Living Arts Once a cinema, then a venue for counterculture drama, followed by a repertory film theater, and then a theater dedicated to live music, the TLA is now a rock 'n' roll hall with no permanent seats, though folding chairs are brought in for the quieter shows. The generous stage, unobstructed sight lines, and good acoustics make this a terrific place for live music, and somebody interesting plays at least twice a week. **Lindsey Buckingham** (of **Fleetwood Mac**) stopped here on his first-ever solo tour, and the **Goats,** a local rap group, have rocked the house. A signboard beneath the marquee lists upcoming shows. A box office is on the premises. ♦ 334 South St (between Third and Fourth Sts). 922.1011

29 American Pie Kitschy cow-shaped wall clocks and other goofy, lowbrow items share the shelves with decorative contemporary crafts and an interesting selection of postmodern scrap-metal jewelry. Prices are fair, and the golden retrievers wagging their tails behind the counter are delightful. ♦ M-Th 11AM-9PM; F-Sa 11AM-10PM; Su noon-7PM. 327 South St (between Third and Fourth Sts). 922.2226

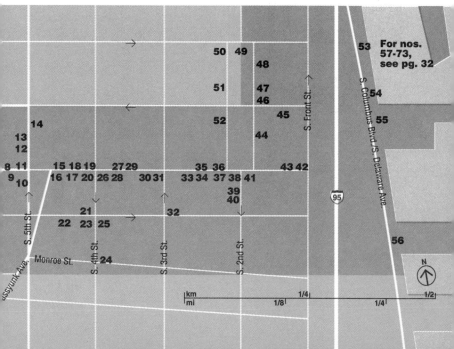

For nos. 57-73, see pg. 32

Philly on a Roll

Take a handful of sliced red meat, fry it in vegetable oil, slap some processed cheese on top, and you have a combination that will never win the endorsement of the American Heart Association. But put it on an Italian roll, throw in some fried onions, and you have the likewise unhealthy but ever so delicious cheesesteak, one of Philadelphia's better-known culinary feats.

The simple—and cheesy—cheesesteak may well encourage the impression that food in this city is less than sophisticated. Not so. Philadelphia kitchens have kept up with the ever-increasing demand for fine cuisine since the 1970s, when locals began to patronize restaurants more often. Nevertheless, the cheesesteak persists, and, in all fairness, has earned the right to do so.

Connoisseurs debate its origins, but the **Olivieri** family contends it all began at Ninth Street and Passyunk Avenue, where **Pat Olivieri** opened a hot-dog stand in 1930. After consuming a few too many franks, Olivieri asked his brother to pick up some thinly sliced steak at the butcher shop for him, and then proceeded to fry it on the grill. A taxi driver who happened by saw—and no doubt smelled—his creation, and said, "I'll take one of those." The rest is history.

In 1932 Olivieri opened **Pat's King of Steaks** directly across from its present location in South Philadelphia (his grand-nephew operates it today and a grandson runs **Olivieri's Prince of Steaks** at the Reading Terminal Market). On any given night, crowds line up outside Pat's King of Steaks, or at Pat's arch-rival, **Geno's**, across the street. At Pat's, you might hear a customer order a "cheesesteak wid', inside out." That's "Patspeak" for a cheesesteak with fried onions and a roll with the dough stripped from the inside.

Virtually every sandwich joint in the city, along with countless street vendors, pushes its version of the cheesesteak; plus the sandwiches pop up on menus all over town. An important tip: ask for provolone cheese instead of Cheez Whiz (aagh!). And, legend aside, Pat's in South Philadelphia does not make the cheesiest (read best) cheesesteak. Worthy contenders include **Jim's Steaks** and **Dalessandro's Steaks.** One might ask, however, how much variation is possible around so basic a theme. A very good question. Here are a few of the many cheesesteak venues you'll come across in Philadelphia:

Dalessandro's Steaks ★$ Enormous sandwiches are served in this Roxborough joint with booths and counter seating. Try a cheesesteak hoagie—steak with lettuce, tomato, cheese, onions, and Italian seasonings. ◆ Daily 11AM-1AM. Henry Avenue at Wendover Street, Roxborough. 482.5407

Geno's $ Picnic tables on the sidewalk allow for luxury dining of sorts. Both Geno's and Pat's (just across the street) are hopping when the bars close on weekends. Each has its loyal following, but Geno's sandwiches are a slight cut above Pat's. ◆ Open daily 24 hours. Ninth Street and Passyunk Avenue. 389.1455

Jim's Steaks ★★$ Your sandwich is made as you peek over a glass divider while standing in line. The steaks here are decent but somewhat overrated; contrary to legend, Jim's falls just short of ranking among the city's top culinary experiences. ◆ M-Sa 10AM-1AM; Su noon-1AM. Fourth and South streets. 928.1911

Olivieri's Prince of Steaks ★$ This offshoot of Pat's prides itself on a thicker, finer grade of beef. Sit down at the counter or get your sandwich to go. ◆ M-Sa 10AM-4PM. Closed Sunday. Reading Terminal Market. 625.9369

Pat's King of Steaks $ Stand at the counter or eat your steak in the car. Those with normal appetites can easily consume two of these slim sandwiches. ◆ Open daily 24 hours. Ninth Street and Passyunk Avenue. 468.1564

30 J.C. Dobbs Up-and-coming national hotshots vie with local talent for time on Dobbs' crowded stage—and for a place on the wall of publicity stills. Regulars throng the chatty bar area, though the crowd generally reflects the booking—from good old rock 'n' rollers to thrash-metal bands. The club's only fixture is Tuesday's **Last Minute Jam,** which features some of Philadelphia's most accomplished musicians along with rank amateurs trying desperately to convince their buddies that they have the blues. Take refuge in the upstairs bar if the sound system becomes overwhelming. ◆ Cover. Daily 4PM-closing. 304 South St (between Third and Fourth Sts). 928.1943

31 Jon's Bar & Grille ★★$ Large umbrella-covered tables, comfy chairs, and trees with Christmas lights create the most pleasant outdoor-dining experience on South Street. The menu is typically eclectic, ranging from nachos to grilled chicken sandwiches. A plaque in the bar area marks this site as the birthplace of **Larry Fine,** one of the **Three Stooges.** ◆ American ◆ Lunch, dinner, late-night snacks, and weekend brunch. 606 S. Third St (at South St). 592.1390

32 Judy's ★★$$ Stuffed meat loaf, superlative buttery mashed potatoes, and other wholesome unpretentious eats have kept Judy's going for some 15 years. The menu changes with the seasons, and the daily specials are truly special. Ask about the catch of the day—the baked or broiled fresh fish is always good. ◆ Eclectic ◆ Dinner. Third and Bainbridge Sts. 928.1968

Restaurants/Clubs: Red	**Hotels:** Blue
Shops/ 🍴 Outdoors: Green	**Sights/Culture:** Black

33 The Blue Marble Shops that promote eco-conscious consumerism are popping up faster than fast-food outlets, and this nook—which carries skin- and hair-care products as well as games, books, and office supplies made from recycled paper—celebrates the earth without too much sermonizing. Essential urban-tourist items include canvas bags (rather than paper or plastic) and an ozone-friendly spray that will clear the air on a smelly subway platform or in a stuffy hotel room. ♦ M-Th 11AM-8PM; F-Sa 11AM-10PM; Su 11AM-6PM. 234 South St (between Second and Third Sts). 829.9289

34 Knave of Hearts ★★$$$ This romantic candlelit hideaway filled with sentimental curios serves imaginative cuisine with Asian, Tex-Mex, Italian, and French touches. The mesquite-grilled tuna topped with sesame sauce is a good choice. ♦ Eclectic ♦ Lunch, dinner, and Sunday brunch. 230 South St (between Second and Third Sts). Reservations recommended. 922.3956

35 Chef's Market Put together a picnic or last-minute brunch at this upscale market. In addition to the fresh fish and meat counters, it stocks innumerable cheeses and gourmet sauces, and has the best selection of bread on South Street—crispy French baguettes, sourdough rolls, round Italian loaves. When you order one of the specialty coffees (by the cup or pound), it's hard to resist the cookies and other enticing home-baked goods, placed to encourage impulse purchases. ♦ M-Th 8:30AM-9PM; F 8:30AM-11PM; Sa 8AM-11PM; Su 8AM-9PM. 231 South St (between Second and Third Sts). 925.8360

36 Funny Bone Semiknown and aspiring local comedians perform in cushy surroundings for a well-heeled clientele at this popular comedy club. ♦ Cover. Show times: Tu-Th 8:15PM; F-Sa 8:30PM, 11PM. 221 South St (between Second and Third Sts). 440.9670

37 Ristorante San Carlo ★★$$$ Small, elegant, and unpretentious San Carlo has earned the devotion of many discerning pasta lovers, who rave over the sauces. Fresh tomatoes and garlic are the primary ingredients in the full-bodied but never heavy tomato sauce. ♦ Italian ♦ Dinner. 214 South St (between Second and Third Sts). 592.9777

38 Bridget Foy's South Street Grill ★$$ The most recent menu change sent this restaurant upscale. Burgers and chili, former star attractions, are played down in favor of more elaborate (and expensive) grilled chicken and seafood, plus light salads and stir-fry dishes prepared in a display kitchen. The warmer months bring sidewalk dining to this busy corner, and patrons can quench their thirst with German EKU lager or a hearty house microbrew. ♦ American ♦ Lunch and dinner. 200 South St (at Second St). 922.1813

39 Russia House ★★★$$ Residents of Philadelphia's Russian and Ukrainian communities frequent this tiny family-run restaurant, which strives for authenticity above all. The waitstaff tries to help the uninitiated navigate a menu full of Russian, Georgian, and Ukrainian dishes, including *zharkoye* (boiled potatoes with boiled beef and vegetables, covered with Stroganoff sauce). The management buys its caviar directly from Russia, eliminating costly brokers and resulting in fair prices for the consumer. ♦ Russian ♦ Lunch and dinner. 614 S. Second St (between South and Bainbridge Sts). Reservations recommended. 629.4888

40 Cedars ★★$ The Lebanese fare in this family-owned storefront is impressive—from the grape-leaves appetizer and the tabbouleh salad to the *kafta* combination platter. ♦ Lebanese ♦ Lunch and dinner. 616 S. Second St (between South and Bainbridge Sts). 925.4950

41 Monte Carlo Living Room ★★★$$$$ Ambitious Northern Italian creations, an understated yet elegant atmosphere, and attentive service make Monte Carlo the most outstanding restaurant in this part of town. The pasta is homemade, and gourmet taste buds rate the beef and veal dishes among the best available anywhere. Dessert options include an incredibly smooth gelato. The dance floor in the upstairs lounge is especially cozy. ♦ Italian ♦ Dinner. Upstairs club open until 2AM. 150 South St (at Second St). Jacket, tie, and reservations required. 925.2220

42 Downey's ★$$ Happy hour brings a happy crush to this Irish bar with turn-of-the-century decor, and many stay on for dinner. The bartenders are skillful and generous, and the waiters cheerfully steer indecisive diners toward the best items on the enormous menu of steaks and seafood. A second-floor balcony, open in nice weather, overlooks the Delaware River, and there's a rooftop deck, too. ♦ American ♦ Lunch, dinner, and late-night snacks. 526 S. Front St (at South St). 625.9500

43 Ritz Club Decked out in neon, this club is the place to dance to disco, rhythm and blues, funk, or (from time to time) rap. An adjacent restaurant, the **Back Porch** (★$$), serves Southern specialties, such as blackened fish and red beans and rice, as well as late-night munchies. Those who dine at the restaurant don't pay a cover—usually $10—to get into the club. ♦ Cover. W-Su 5PM-2AM. 121 South St (between Front and Second Sts). 925.3042

44 Pizzeria Uno ★$ The chain's trademark thick-crust deep-dish pie and faux-antique decor are served with a view of one of Philadelphia's oldest commercial areas from the second-floor windows. On weekend nights there's live musical entertainment upstairs. ♦ Lunch and dinner. 511 S. Second St (between South and Lombard Sts). 592.0400. Also at: 1721 Locust St (between 17th and 18th Sts). 790.9669

45 Le Champignon of Tokio ★★$$$ This cozy bistro with live jazz on the weekends has a globe-trotting menu of inventive Japanese food (including artfully prepared sushi), Thai standbys, and French cooking. Just reading the regular menu can take an evening, and the house specialties—lobster hara, bouillabaisse—are augmented by a weekend lunch menu that features Japanese-style dim sum. ♦ Japanese/French/Thai ♦ Lunch and dinner; dinner only Wednesday through Friday. Closed Monday and Tuesday. 122-124 Lombard St (between Front and Second Sts). 922.2515

46 Koffmeyer's Philadelphians revere the chocolate-chip cookies made by this little bakery, but the must-have item is the Headhouse Square, a vanilla brownie with chocolate chips and nuts. If you become addicted, don't worry: Koffmeyer's ships anywhere. ♦ Bakery ♦ M-Th 11AM-11PM; F-Sa 11AM-1AM; Su 11AM-9PM. Second and Lombard Sts. 922.0717

Just after President Ronald Reagan was shot in 1981 outside the Washington Hilton, he echoed the comment of former Philadelphian W.C. Fields, saying, "All in all, I'd rather be in Philadelphia."

47 The Lay Up Hiphop culture thrives in Philadelphia, and this store is one of the force that fosters it. The salespeople know rap mus and will discuss developments in the rap com munity with anyone who drops by. Cassettes CDs, T-shirts, and caps are sold, and the stor acts as an informal clearinghouse for information on appearances by hiphop artists both local and national. ♦ Tu-W noon-7PM; Th-Sa noon-11PM. 417 S. Second St (betwee Pine and Lombard Sts). 625.9302

48 Dickens Inn ★★$$$ Founded in 1980 by t owners of the Dickens Inn in London, Philly's version attracts tourists and devoted regulars with its warm atmosphere, long list of libations, and generous portions of English fare. Located in a Federal-style town house, t restaurant and bar are decorated with sculptures and paintings of Charles Dickens' characters, while dark, woody adjoining room host dart players. The inn is sometimes cramped with college students, but if you're a brew connoisseur, push on in. The bar stock beers and ales from all over the world (ask about the changing specials), as well as 20 single-malt whiskeys. The restaurant does a surprisingly brisk business in English pub grub—meat pies, fish-and-chips—but also serves serious meals like Cornish game hen and roast duckling. Desserts are made in-house, and taste that way. ♦ English ♦ Lunch and dinner. 421 S. Second St (between Pine and Lombard Sts). 928.9307

49 Headhouse Square In 1745 sheds were erected on this square between Pine and Sout streets to facilitate commerce; then fire-engin houses, called "headhouses," were built at either end of the square in the early 1800s. Bo headhouses had cupolas and alarm bells, and on the second floor of each was a firemen's social club. The fire station at Second and South was torn down before 1860, but its market shed remained until 1950, when it was razed to make room for a parking lot. The she between Lombard and Pine, called the **Shambles,** was restored in the early '60s, and continues to serve as an open-air market for crafts in the summertime. The remaining Georgian-style headhouse, at Second and Pin was built in 1805. Its single-room interior is under restoration. ♦ Second St (between Pine and South Sts)

50 Artful Dodger ★★$ While Dickens Inn represents the high end of British dining, the Artful Dodger is a classic pub—with above-average pub food. One room is a bar, the oth has large wooden booths and a fireplace. In addition to the expected sandwiches, the kitchen makes excellent stews and chili that's spicy enough to warm you up in the middle of winter. The specials are worth considering as are the preparations of fried fish. ♦ British/American ♦ Lunch and dinner. 400-402 S. Second St (at Pine St). 922.7880

51 The Morning Cup A Seattle native runs the efficient counter at this coffeehouse, putting his roots in that Northwest mecca of quality java to good use. The excellent espresso is appropriately strong, the cappuccino is robust, and the *biscotti* is superior. ♦ Coffeehouse ♦ M-F 6:30AM-6PM; Sa 8AM-6PM; Su 8AM-3PM. 422 S. Second St (between Pine and Lombard Sts). 629.1795

52 TGIFriday's ★$ Across the street from Pizzeria Uno is another recognizable name: TGIFriday's. Inside, picture windows overlook Headhouse Square. The food is standard Friday's fare. ♦ American ♦ Lunch and dinner. 500 S. Second St (between Lombard and South Sts). 625.8389

53 Liberty Belle II ★$$$ Where there's a waterfront there's a dinner cruise operation. The small *Liberty Belle II* covers the basics, with at least two entrée options at lunch and dinner, and an all-you-can-eat buffet during the moonlight cruise. A cash bar is available. Ask about theme cruises. ♦ Continental ♦ Lunch and dinner. Leaves from S. Columbus Blvd (at Pine St). Reservations required. 629.1131

54 Chart House ★$$$$ A salad bar loaded with fresh veggies and seasonal fruits, excellent treatments of surf and turf, and spectacular views of the Delaware make the Chart House the waterfront's most notable expense-account restaurant. Tops among the seafood choices are steak-size cuts of grilled swordfish and tuna, served with various sauces, some of them light enough to satisfy those who tally their fat grams. ♦ Continental ♦ Lunch and dinner. 555 S. Columbus Blvd (at Lombard St). Reservations recommended. 625.8383

55 Penn's Landing Trolley Another alternative mode of waterfront transportation, these restored turn-of-the-century streetcars travel along Columbus Boulevard from the Ben Franklin Bridge to Fitzwater Street. The round trip takes 25 minutes (these are antiques, after all). Boarding stops include Race, Market, Walnut, Dock, Spruce, and Lombard streets. A day pass costs $1.50. ♦ Sa-Su 11AM-dusk Easter-Labor Day; Th-Su 11AM-dusk July-Aug. 627.0807

56 Eli's Pier 34 ★$$ Enjoy great views of the river and passing ships while dining on the open-air deck or in the glass-enclosed dining room at Eli's. In mild weather a pleasant breeze rustles the interior's many hanging plants. This is one of the few new waterfront establishments that remains open year-round. The menu, printed on a paper bag, includes seafood and barbecue. ♦ American ♦ Lunch and dinner. 735 S. Columbus Blvd (between Bainbridge and Fitzwater Sts). 923.2500

57 Chef Theodore ★★★$$ Don't be put off by the nondescript strip shopping center location. Chef Theodore creates delicious traditional Greek cuisine. House specialties—shrimp casserole and various combination plates—are famous for their generous size. Be sure to order appetizers and side dishes as well: try the roasted potatoes, one of the exceptional salads, or Saganaki Opa! (a lightly fried cheese that's flamed tableside). ♦ Greek ♦ Dinner. 1100 S. Columbus Blvd (at Washington Ave, in the Riverview Plaza shopping center). Reservations recommended. 271.6800

58 Philly Rock Bar & Grill $ A knockoff of the Hard Rock Cafe, this restaurant has an extensive memorabilia collection. But you can't eat a poster, and the bargain-priced food—everything on the menu is less than $5—is lackluster. ♦ American ♦ Lunch and dinner. 1400 S. Columbus Blvd (at Reed St). 463.5771

59 Philadelphia Water Taxi This dispatch-operated water taxi services all the waterfront attractions (including stops at Piers 3, 19, and 25; the New Jersey State Aquarium; and Wiggins Park Marina), allowing you to park and cruise from one club to another. Charters are available. ♦ Call for rates and hours. Columbus Blvd and Spruce St. 351.4170

60 USS Olympia One of America's first steel ships, the USS *Olympia* was **Admiral Dewey's** flagship at the battle of Manila Bay in 1898, and one of the few survivors of the Spanish-American War. Its final assignment came in 1921, when it brought the body of the Unknown Soldier from France to Arlington National Cemetery. The ship has been transformed into a museum, where you can climb around and view the restored cabins, top deck, and boiler room. ♦ Admission. Daily 10AM-4:30PM Oct-May; daily 10AM-6PM Memorial Day-late Sept. S. Columbus Blvd and Spruce St. 922.1898

60 USS Becuna Berthed a few feet from the *Olympia*, the submarine USS *Becuna* is a 1,526-ton vessel commissioned in 1944. The *Becuna* saw action in the South Pacific during World War II and served in the Atlantic during the Korean and Vietnam wars before being decommissioned in 1969. Veterans of World War II volunteer time to answer questions on board. Warning: A submarine is no place for the claustrophobic. ♦ Admission. Daily 10AM-4:30PM Oct-May; daily 10AM-6PM Memorial Day-late Sept. S. Columbus Blvd and Spruce St. 922.1898

61 Maritime Museum's Workshop on the Water A floating exhibition and education center is housed on the barge *Maple,* where shipwrights demonstrate boat-building techniques. Visitors can watch the construction of a small craft, or participate in a workshop. ♦ Admission. W-Su 10AM-5PM. S. Columbus Blvd and Spruce St. 925.7589

62 Vietnam Veterans Memorial This outdoor plaza, dedicated in 1987, was built with volunteer contributions to honor the 80,000 Vietnam veterans from the Philadelphia area. A semicircle of wide brick steps faces a high black-granite wall painted with a mural depicting military scenes—aircraft carriers, fighter jets, and the like. Another wall is inscribed with the names of Philadelphians killed in the conflict. Both the American flag and black MIA flag fly over-head. ♦ Open daily 24 hours. Spruce and S. Front Sts

63 World Sculpture Garden This grassy two-acre sculpture garden is a welcome respite in the midst of Philadelphia's frenzied waterfront development. Attractions at this favorite picnic spot stretching along the waterfront include a bronze statue of **William Penn** at the age of 38 in 1682, an obelisk erected in 1992 commemorating **Christopher Columbus,** and a 20-foot totem pole from Canada. ♦ S. Columbus Blvd (between Spruce and Walnut Sts)

64 Port of History Museum This museum is currently being renovated and will reopen in 1995 as the new home of the **Philadelphia Maritime Museum.** ♦ S. Columbus Blvd and Walnut St. 925.3804

64 Riverbus Known locally as the "Delawhale," this hundred-foot-long vessel offers quick passage between Philadelphia and Camden's **New Jersey State Aquarium** on the hour and half-hour. The ship takes 400 passengers on a 10-minute trip that retraces the route of 19th-century ferries that **Walt Whitman** rode, providing a scenic view of both waterfronts: Camden, once the biggest naval shipyard in the country, and Philadelphia, the largest freshwater port in the world. The Riverbus allows you to avoid traffic, bridge crossings, and parking fees. ♦ Admission. M-F 7AM-6:45PM, Sa 9AM-8:45PM, Su 9AM-5:45PM 16 Sept-14 May; M-F 7AM-9:45PM, Sa 9AM-11:45PM, Su 9AM-7:45PM 15 May-15 Sept. S. Columbus Blvd and Walnut St. 800/634.4027

65 New Jersey State Aquarium Opened in 1992, the area's largest aquarium concentrates on native mid-Atlantic sea life. Exhibits and sea environments change often and are explained in the accompanying easy-to-understand literature. An auditorium with sweeping views of a huge aquarium offers an up-close look at large fish, and children love to pick up the starfish and sea anemones in the touch tank. ♦ Admission. Daily 9:30AM-5:30PM. One Riverside Dr, Camden, New Jersey. 609/365.3300

66 Penn's Landing The area known as Penn' Landing, a tract of waterfront land extending from South Street to Vine Street, has been developed into one of the city's most important recreational sites. Once the city's primary commercial area, this is where **William Penn's** surveyor, **Thomas Holmes,** started parceling out land grants. Early settlers dug caves into the steep slope rising from the water until housing could be built, and by 1700, most Philadelphians lived with three or four blocks of the river on tiny congested lots—a far cry from Penn's dream of a green country town.

Philadelphia's port area has always been busy. Through the 18th and 19th centuries and well into the 20th century, the docks we central to city commerce. Sailors, pilots, riggers, and shipwrights worked and lived nearby. In 1967, with most of the shipping concentrated in the south end of Philadelphi the rotting piers were replaced with the current system of walkways and the tiered river-view amphitheater known as the **Great Plaza.** In the summer the Plaza is the site of outdoor concerts—including a Memorial weekend New Orleans festival and a July blu festival—as well as themed neighborhood celebrations. The plaza also contains a large map and historical account of Philadelphia's waterfront. Pedestrian walkways at Market, Chestnut, and Walnut streets cross Interstat 95 to connect the city with the waterfront. ♦ From I-95, take Exit 16 (Columbus Blvd/Delaware Ave); from I-76, follow 676 to I-95 South; from Ben Franklin Bridge, follow 95 South. For parking information, call 923.8181. SEPTA bus routes 21 and 42 stop nearby. For information on events at the Gre Plaza, call 923.4992.

67 Spirit of Philadelphia ★$$$ Another large dinner-cruise operation, the *Spirit of Philadelphia,* which has both open and enclosed decks, takes to the water from March through December and offers lunch, dinner, and moonlight cruises up and down the Delaware. Live dance music follows the dinner show. Inquire about the theme cruise which have included a '50s sock hop and Jamaican and Caribbean meals. There's a cash bar. ◆ Continental ◆ Lunch and dinner. Columbus Blvd and Market St. Reservations required. 923.1419

57 Gazela The **Philadelphia Ship Preservation Guild** maintains and operates this 177-foot-long square-rigged sailing ship built in 1883. The *Gazela* was the oldest of the tall ships to participate in the 1976 **OpSail** tall ship celebration in New York and was on hand for the Statue of Liberty Centennial in 1986. The ship, which functions as a training vessel and is a permanent working exhibit, has a busy sailing schedule during the summer. ◆ Admission. Sa-Su noon-5PM Labor Day-Memorial Day; daily 10AM-6PM Memorial Day-Labor Day. Columbus Blvd and Market St. 923.9030

58 Rock Lobster ★$$$ One of the first in the deck 'n' tent brigade that disappears when the winter winds blow, Rock Lobster has an upscale Cape Cod-style beach house atmosphere, and prices to match. The seafood—particularly the lobster and shrimp salads—is worth the investment, but the rest of the menu is just so-so. ◆ Seafood ◆ Cover after 8:30PM. Lunch and dinner. 221 N. Columbus Blvd (at Race St). 627.7625

59 Benjamin Franklin Bridge After City Hall, Philadelphia's defining piece of public architecture is the Ben Franklin Bridge, designed by **Paul Philippe Cret** and completed in 1926, when it was the largest suspension bridge in the world. Rising from the buildings of Old City and towering over the waterfront piers, the bridge's massive blue hulk is visible for miles, a symbol of the city's solid traditionalism. It has served as the backdrop for movie sets and album-cover photographs, and is much more than just a conduit for cars, bikes, and commuter trains. To fully appreciate the bridge, you must see it at night, when it becomes a veritable light sculpture. A computer-driven lighting system, designed by Philadelphia architect **Stephen Izenour** of **Venturi, Scott Brown and Associates,** was added during the U.S. Bicentennial. Each cable is illuminated, and as the trains pass, the lights blink in a sweeping, dominolike succession that reminds one of the bridge's beauty. ◆ To South Jersey

70 Meiji-En ★★$$$ All things Japanese are served with style in this 600-seat restaurant (and jazz club on weekends). The massive dining rooms are divided by food type—tempura in one, sushi in another, and so on—and the understated decor of each room makes the most of the river view. But the real star is the artfully presented cuisine. The sushi, while pricey, is fresh and consistently excellent. ◆ Japanese ◆ Dinner; Sunday brunch. 19 N. Columbus Blvd (at Callowhill St). Reservations recommended. 592.7100

71 Katmandu ★$$ The ambitious menu runs the gamut from New Orleans-style red beans and rice to grilled fish and oversize sandwiches at this busy restaurant with a lineup of reggae and world music. ◆ Eclectic ◆ Lunch, dinner, and late-night snacks. Pier 25, N. Columbus Blvd (between Callowhill and Spring Garden Sts). 629.7400

72 Egypt A split-level dance floor, impressive sound and light systems, pyramids, and other thematic decorations make Egypt one of Philadelphia's top places to dance the night away. The club recently opened a glass-enclosed restaurant called the **Oasis** (★$$$; Continental; dinner only), signaling its intention to be more than just a late-night dancing destination. ◆ Cover varies. Closed Monday. 520 N. Columbus Blvd (at Spring Garden St). 922.6500, 800/622.3497

73 The Beach Club ★$$ As the name suggests, the beach is the theme of this waterfront club, where you can swim in a heated pool, play volleyball on regulation sand courts (with beach sand imported from the Jersey Shore), and have dinner. Come here to have fun, but don't expect an excellent meal. ◆ Continental ◆ Cover varies. Dinner. Pier 42, Columbus Blvd (2 blocks north of Spring Garden St). 829.1900

73 Maui Billing itself as the largest entertainment complex on the river, Maui has an array of indoor and outdoor options—from dining and games to live music and dancing. The **Kaanapali Beach Grill** (★$$) serves surprisingly tasty burgers, meats, and grilled fish in a beach-bungalow atmosphere, and there's a stage and sound system outside where island-style music reigns. A more traditional dance club and a comedy cabaret are located inside. ◆ Continental ◆ Cover varies. Dinner. Pier 53, Columbus Blvd (1/2 mile north of Spring Garden St). 423.8116

73 The Barbary If all the glitz (and long entrance lines) of the waterfront clubs gets you down, take your blues to the Barbary. Talk about counterprogramming: While the river clubs try to cater to every yuppie whim, this dive celebrates skid row. It's a dark and dirty roadhouse bar with a small stage and a mean sound system, not to mention a more enlightened blues-oriented music policy than any of the neighborhood's more corporate ventures. ◆ Cover varies. Music starts 9PM. Frankford and Columbus Aves. 739.3330

"American Bandstand," the TV series that introduced rock 'n' roll to millions of viewers, was taped in Philadelphia, using local high-school students as dancers at a simulated sock hop, with Dick Clark as host. The show debuted in the summer of 1957 as a daily afternoon program, later went weekly, and then moved from Philly to Los Angeles in the early 1970s.

staurants/Clubs: Red   **Hotels:** Blue

ops/ 🌳 Outdoors: Green   **Sights/Culture:** Black

Bests

James Nelson Kise
Architect/Planner, Kise Franks & Straw

Walking through **Rittenhouse Square** almost any day of the year, but especially in spring.

The fountain in **Logan Circle.**

Crucifixion with the Virgin and St. John by Roger van der Weyden in the **Philadelphia Museum of Art.**

The selection at **Joseph Fox,** bookseller.

The great bell that sounds the hours from the top of the **PNB Building.**

Shopping for hardware at **Killian's** in Chestnut Hill.

Walking **Forbidden Drive** in Wissahickon Park.

The Great Court of **John Wanamaker** when the organ is playing.

The view of the city from the East Terrace of the Philadelphia Museum of Art.

River Road between Lumberville, New Hope, and Yardley.

Tea at the **Bellevue** or the **Four Seasons.**

Reading Terminal Market.

The spectacle of **Rowing on the Schuylkill,** especially the regattas.

The unmitigated opulence of the **Academy of Music's** interior.

The **Philadelphia Flower Show.**

Walking anywhere in **Center City.**

Exploring the "little streets": Camac, Panama, Elfreth's Alley, Rodman, Quince, and Cypress.

The **Benjamin Franklin Bridge.**

Signe Wilkinson
Editorial Cartoonist, *Philadelphia Daily News*

You can never visit the **Liberty Bell** and **Independence Hall** too many times. For one, the park guides' official story line (especially on the bell) keeps changing. For another, even tough talkers cry when ushered into the room where the Declaration of Independence and the Constitution were signed. It's as close as America gets to a sacred shrine.

Also visit the four-acre **Fairhill Burial Grounds** at Germantown and Indiana avenues in the heart of what's cheerfully called "the badlands." You can get your nonprescription drugs and a glimpse at the graves of **Robert Purvis,** a wealthy black abolitionist, and the great Quaker abolitionist and early feminist **Lucretia Mott.** Watch out for used syringes, stray bullets, and the sudden realization of how unexpectedly the world goes on without us.

Nestled among housing projects and oil refineries, the newly renovated **Bartram's Gardens,** once home of America's first botanist, Quaker **John Bartram,** echoes etchings of what the banks of the Schuylkill River must have looked like to **William Penn** and early settlers. Peace.

Anne d'Harnoncourt
The George D. Widener Director of the Philadelphia Museum of Art

Philadelphia City Hall—the view from Conversation Hall, the buffalo heads over the arched entrance doors, the way it frames two great urban vistas.

Albert Laessle's bronze billy goat in **Rittenhouse Square**—one of the smallest and most beloved public sculptures in a city with a wealth of them.

Eating Japanese food at the **Meiji-En** and watching the eerie and magical pattern of light on **Ben Franklin Bridge** designed by Venturi, Scott Brown and Associates.

That amazing walk from river to river (Delaware to Schuylkill) on **Pine Street,** watching the city grow from the early 18th-century to the Edwardian era in an almost uninterrupted flow of domestic architecture.

Reading Terminal Market and **Bassett's** ice cream.

George Washington as seen by Charles Willson Peale and by Gilbert Stuart facing himself in the **Pennsylvania Academy of the Fine Arts.**

The beautiful marble-walled banking floor of the **PSFS Building.**

Horse chestnut trees in bloom along the **Museum of Art Drive.**

Penny Balkin Bach
Executive Director, Fairmount Park Art Association

Ten favorite public works in Philadelphia:

All Wars Memorial to Colored Soldiers and Sailors (circa 1934; J. Otto Schweitzer), Lansdowne Drive near Memorial Hall

Clothespin (1976; Claes Oldenburg), Centre Square Plaza, 15th and Market streets

Cowboy (1908; Frederic Remington), Kelly Drive north of Girard Avenue Bridge

Fingerspan (1987; Jody Pinto), Wissahickon Creek trail near Livezey Dam

Gates and Lighting Fixtures (1923; Samuel Yellin), Packard Building, 15th and Chestnut streets

Lion Crushing a Serpent (1832; Antoine Louis Barye), Rittenhouse Square

Swann Memorial Fountain (circa 1924; Alexander Stirling Calder), Logan Circle, Benjamin Franklin Parkway at 19th Street

Three-Way Piece Number 1: Points (1964; Henry Moore), Benjamin Franklin Parkway between 16th and 17th streets

Washington Monument (1897; Rudolf Siemering), Benjamin Franklin Parkway at Eakins' Oval

White Cascade (1976; Alexander Calder), Federal Reserve Bank (interior), 100 North Sixth Street

...rtha B. Aikens
...perintendent, Independence National
...torical Park

...ry visit to the city should begin with
...ependence National Historical Park. We don't
...ve only historic structures; although what we do
...ve is pretty impressive (**Independence Hall,**
...ngress Hall,** plus over 30 more). Then, there's the
...erty Bell,** which is in a class by itself, and the
...autiful **18th-Century Garden, Magnolia Garden,**
...se Garden, Tea Garden,** and countless numbers of
...aller landscaped areas. If you don't believe me,
...t stop by during the months of May and June when
...'ll see wedding parties and photographers
...rywhere.

...ce I live and work in **Center City,** my discoveries
...ve generally been in that area. If I'm in a pensive
...od, I turn left at the corner of my block and slowly
...oll down **Pine Street,** taking in all of the antique
...ps.

...uth Street,** which is a right turn from my block, is
...ticularly fun on weekends. An outing to South
...eet is a package deal that includes an ice cream
...ne, trying on hats in **Hats at the Belfry,** and
...ecking out the vendors at **Headhouse Square,**
...ich is conveniently nestled in the middle of three
...taurants—**TGIFridays, Artful Dodger,** and
...kens Inn.** A bit more sugar may be warranted.
...n't fret, there's a cookie store just a stone's
...ow away.

...tening to anyone or anything on a summer night at
... **Mann Music Center.**

...rimp at **Philadelphia Fish & Co.**

... matter how many times I see it, I still can't get
...er the magnificence of the **Mother Bethel A.M.E.
...urch.** The stained glass and the sound of their
...an take my breath away.

...joying lunch in the **Azalea Restaurant** at the Omni
...ile overlooking the park's **Tea Garden.**

...moment for a prediction: The Philly steak-and-
...ese sub will soon be recognized as a world-class
...dwich. Exporting is risky business, however. I've
...d some *interesting* ones in other cities, but none
...mpare to its namesake. The **Plain and Fancy Cafe**
...the Holiday Inn) makes a real one. If it isn't juicy
...d messy, it's an imposter.

...z at **Zanzibar Blue** and the **Afro-American
...storical and Cultural Museum.**

... evening harbor cruise on the *Spirit of Philadelphia.*

...e **Back Porch** for serious down-home Southern
...sine.

...llowhill Restaurant,** where my favorite dish is pork
...derloin with gravy, mashed potatoes, and a
...getable.

...nch at **Hotel Atop the Bellevue.**

...s it's true, if I had more space I'd only list more
...taurants. I seem to have unconsciously narrowed
... scope of exploration. What can I tell you? I think
...ing is one of life's simple pleasures. It goes well
...h anything.

John L. Cotter
Curator Emeritus American Historical Archaeology,
University Museum of Archaeology and
Anthropology, University of Pennsylvania

I like to pack a copy of *The Buried Past, an
Archaeological History of Philadelphia* with me and
explore **Independence National Historical Park** and
Society Hill on foot. (I know this part of the book
has got to be okay—I wrote it myself.) When you're
ready to sit down and eat, try **City Tavern,** where
John Adams and his pals planned the Revolution.
Good food and drinks kept them going, and will you,
too. Then go see the site of **Ben Franklin's** house
and the other archaeological discoveries I spent 20
years planning and supervising for the National Park
Service.

Walk up **Walnut Street** from the Delaware River
toward Broad Street. Dewey's Spanish-American
War flagship, *Olympia,* is boardable, as are sailing
ships. Go on past **Washington Square** and the
2,000 unknown soldiers of the American Revolution,
and the **Walnut Street Theater,** the oldest English-
speaking theater in the world, to the **Academy of
Music** to hear the Philadelphia Orchestra (If there's
no concert, tour the Academy—the finest opera
house in the United States).

While you're on Broad Street, take a look at **City
Hall,** the biggest such boodle box in the nation,
started in the 1870s, finished in 1900. It's full of
Alexander Stirling Calder statuary, with one of
William Penn at the top of the building. Then see
the **Pennsylvania Academy of the Fine Arts, Frank
Furness'** masterpiece of 1876, restored and
glorious.

Now backtrack two blocks and visit the
Pennsylvania Convention Center and **Reading
Terminal Market** beneath the old Reading Railroad
trainshed. There's every kind of gourmet food in the
market, from Amish pretzels to Häagan Dazs ice
cream. Eat some on the spot.

Downtown Philly is small, and on a predictable grid.
Its best-kept secrets are its magnificent museums,
restaurants, and the largest city park in the world—
Fairmount Park—complete with the Schuylkill River
running through it for miles and miles clear up
beyond Wissahickon Creek. Jog it, bicycle it, walk it,
drive it.

Discover the **University Museum,** one of the great
archaeological museums of the world, and probably
the least known, in a glorious building on the
University of Pennsylvania campus (tell taxi drivers
it's opposite Franklin Field on Spruce Street—then
they'll find it).

As you enter Fairmount Park there's the
Philadelphia Museum of Art, the last great Classical
Revival building in the country—a real glory inside
and out. Picassos, Renaissance worthies, Oriental
splendors galore.

Still hungry? Go to the **Italian Market** on Ninth
Street—all outdoors on the sidewalk; best antidote
for junk food in the world.

Center City East

Old bricks are making way for the new in Center City East, a neighborhood of multiple personalities extending from Washington Square to Broad Street. Robbed of its commercial heart by a slump in retail business, the area is currently in the midst of urban renewal. Adding considerably to the area's revitalization was the 1993 construction of the massive brick **Pennsylvania Convention Center**, strategically positioned in the downtown core between **Independence National Historical Park** and the **Parkway's**

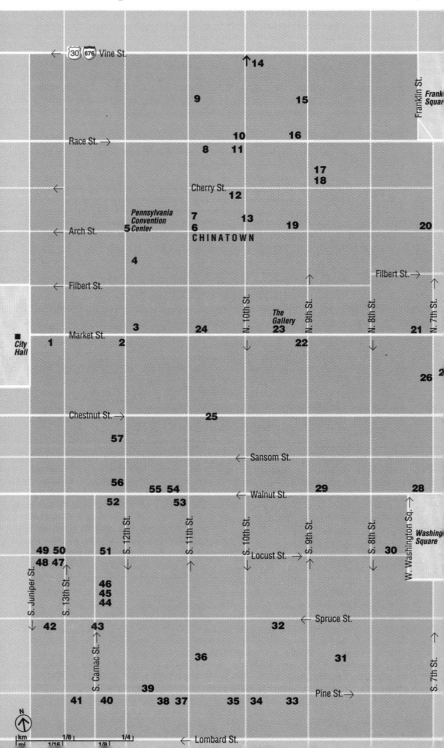

useums to encourage visitors to take advantage of the city's history and ommerce. Philadelphians are crossing their fingers that the convention omplex and other new construction, along with the restoration of old uildings, will help **Market Street** flourish as the important commercial oulevard it was in the days before suburban malls siphoned away ustomers.

eminders of Philadelphia's development from colonial seaport to onfident metropolis are visible in this varied neighborhood. Foxglove, ueen of the prairie, and saffron crocus growing in the brick walls of the 8th-century garden at **Pennsylvania Hospital** are reminiscent of a time hen the city's doctors relied on medicinal plants as remedies. A few blocks the north, gaslights flicker outside the **Walnut Street Theater,** as they id in the days when **Sarah Bernhardt** contracted a fatal cold while erforming here. And just west of the theater, one of the world's first modrnist skyscrapers, the **PSFS Building,** rises with clean, elegant lines above he busy street.

larket, Chestnut, Walnut, Spruce, and Pine streets—long, walkable horoughfares that traverse Center City from the Delaware to the Schuylkill ivers—characterize Philadelphia as much as red brick and cobblestones. trolling down these streets, you can find farmers selling produce at the eading Terminal Market, as they have since 1893; step into the brandew convention center; then join the crowd that gathers for the daily rgan concerts at the **John Wanamaker Store,** a local institution since 911. If you still have time, indulge in some "cheese fries" at **The Gallery,** a ontemporary shopping mall, and while away an afternoon browsing in hinatown for oyster sauce or bok choy, perhaps, or along Pine Street's ntique Row, with its eclectic stores, shade trees, coffee shops, econdhand bookstores, and small park dedicated to renowned hiladelphia architect **Louis I. Kahn.** Pine and Spruce streets, with larger, nore-stately row houses than those in **Society Hill,** have none of the hard dges found in the commercial districts just a short distance away.

1 John Wanamaker Store No one would think of installing a 30,000-pipe organ or crystal chandeliers in a department store these days. But the John Wanamaker Store is a magnificent survivor from a bygone era (a time when department stores often looked like palaces) designed in the Italian Renaissance style by famed Chicago architect **Daniel Burnham.**

John Wanamaker began his career as a clerk in a trading house on Market Street, and became a multimillionaire and politician, serving as Postmaster General under **President Benjamin Harrison.** He built this granite and limestone monolith in 1902-11, with construction proceeding even as he ran his original store on the site. At the time, the concept of selling everything from stationery to lingerie in a single building was still novel. The 1.9 million-square-foot Wanamaker store dazzled the public with a post office, children's playrooms, a books and periodicals department large enough to publish its own newsletter, and pneumatic tubes that carried money from every part of the building to the cashier's office on the second floor.

As with so many department stores, Wanamaker has suffered through some hard years. Retail business is now conducted only on the first five floors, with the rest of the building devoted to offices. But it's still a fun place to shop, carrying a good selection of moderately priced clothing and housewares. The interior and exterior were recently restored. Center-stage in the interior is the original five-story **Grand Court,** a lofty work of marble and arches. The bronze statue of an eagle in the court, purchased at the 1904 **Louisiana Purchase Exposition** in St. Louis, has become an important Philadelphia icon (and the phrase "meet me at the eagle" part of the local vernacular). You'll inevitably find at least one impatient-looking soul perched on the eagle's ledge. The famous pipe organ can be seen (and heard daily) just above the Grand Court. Generations of Philadelphians have flocked here to Wanamaker's annual Christmas light and music show, which remains unchanged year after year. ♦ M-Tu, Th-Sa 10AM-7PM; W 10AM-8PM; Su noon-5PM. Organ concerts daily 11:15AM-noon, 5:15-6PM. S. 13th and Market Sts. 422.2000

Within the John Wanamaker Store:

Terrace on The Court $ Renovations to Wanamaker have led to the closure of one of its greatest assets, **The Crystal Room,** an elegant paneled restaurant on the top floor. Talk of reopening it continues, but in the meantime this restaurant overlooking the Grand Court offers lunch fare, including sandwiches, salads, jambalaya, chicken potpie, quiche, and medaillons of pork. ♦ American ♦ Lunch; early dinner on Wednesday. Closed Sunday. 422.2000

2 Philadelphia Saving Fund Society Building (PSFS Building) Philadelphians often overlook this subtle masterpiece, though architecture lovers remain devoted to it. Designated the first modernist skyscraper in the world, the PSFS Building combines rich materials—marble, stainless steel, and polished granite—with sleek lines. When Philadelphia architect **George Howe,** also known for the Bird House at the zoo, and

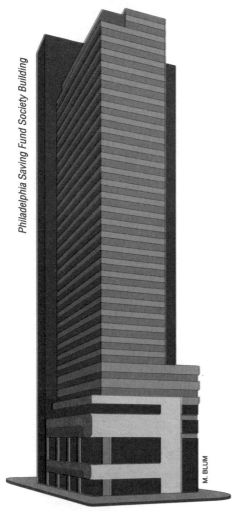

Philadelphia Saving Fund Society Building

M. BLUM

Walter Lescaze, a Swiss architect, finished their building in 1932, it embodied the very latest in European design, referred to as the International style. (It was also the second skyscraper in the world to be air-conditioned Notice the sculptural curve of the gray grani base. The original banking floor, a grand, op room of marble, glass, and stainless steel, i on the second level, where you see the limestone on the exterior (just below the boxlike tower and its vertical columns). To create a unified work of art, the architects likewise designed the interior hardware (clocks and doorknobs, among other things) and furnish ings, including chairs, wastebaskets, and water fountains. PSFS occupied the building until 1992, when it was purchased by a ban. that later became insolvent. The future of th internationally significant building remains i doubt, but for now, another bank, **Mellon PSFS,** has a branch on the banking floor. ♦ 12 S. 12th St (at Market St)

3 Reading Terminal Once a hurry-scurry commuter rail station built by the Philadelph and Reading Railroad in 1892, the Reading Terminal is about to embark on a new caree as a welcoming point for visitors. It's the sit of two of Philadelphia's most distinctive lan marks, the **Reading Head House** and the **Reading Train Shed,** designed by the **Wilsc Brothers** and completed in 1893. Both struc tures will eventually form the grand entranc to the new **Pennsylvania Convention Cente** Waiting rooms and offices once occupied th Head House, distinguished by its ornate Italian Renaissance exterior, wrought- and cast-iron columns, terracotta details, brick floors, and copper cornice. The nation's onl surviving single-span, arched train shed adjoins it. The region's transit system was reconfigured in the late 1970s, when **Marke East Station** became the major transportati hub. ♦ N. 12th and Market Sts

4 Reading Terminal Market When the Philadelphia and Reading Railroad decided build their terminal at 12th and Market stree in 1892, they faced the prospect of having t displace two 30-year-old farmers' markets. a compromise, the railroad company had a stroke of genius and built a market underneath its train shed. Today people trea sure this chaotic bazaar. Cooks depend on market for high-quality groceries, and local say it's the best lunch spot in the city.

In its early years the market was a marvel of turn-of-the-century technology, with sawdu covered floors, 78,000 square feet of aisles and stalls, a 400-line telephone system, anc 250,000 cubic feet of cold storage in the ba ment. It instantly flourished, appealing to al classes and tastes. Ordinary folks came for the New Jersey seafood and corn, Lancaste County poultry and vegetables, cranberries from the Pine Barrens, and huckleberries fr the Poconos. Chefs from the city's fanciest hotels, the **Bellevue Stratford** and the **Barclay**, stocked up on fresh produce and fancy herbs.

The market survived the Depression, when Philadelphians waited in line for rationed meat, but met its enemy with the advent of the modern supermarket and the exodus of the middle class to the suburbs. Thus began a serious decline. As the *Trenton Times* put it, "it became easier to find a secondhand paperback [there] than a fresh fish for dinner." In the 1970s there was talk of tearing the market down to make way for new development along Market Street, but sympathetic management took over in 1980. Farmers and purveyors signed new leases, and merchants who had been there for years decided to stay. Happily, the demand surged for local produce, quality meats, fresh fish, and superior lunch fare. Once again the market is jammed during lunch hours and on weekends, and recent renovations have created an even more cheerful atmosphere.

Pick up supplies for a picnic dinner, or shop for gourmet staples to take home. The northwestern corner of the market is still almost exclusively for Amish merchants from Lancaster County, known for their superior poultry and produce. Grab a bite to eat at one of the tempting food stalls (barbecued ribs at **Delilah's,** grilled chicken sandwiches at **Fireworks!,** and fried seafood at **Pearl's Oyster Bar** are among the choices). At lunchtime, long lines form at the Amish pretzel stall, origin of the very best soft pretzels on earth. (Note: Most of the food stalls close by 3PM, and the Amish businesses are open from Wednesday to Saturday only.) Dinner isn't served anywhere in the market. If you park in a lot, bring your ticket and merchants can stamp it for a parking discount. Maps of the market hang from the walls and are available at the office near the Arch Street entrances. ♦ M-Sa 8AM-6PM. N. 12th St (between Filbert and Arch Sts). 922.2317

Within Reading Terminal Market:

12th Street Cantina ★★$ Just a tiny stand until renovated in 1993, this is now a full-fledged eat-in and take-out Mexican restaurant. You can get the standard fast food—tacos, burritos, and enchiladas—as well as excellent homemade dishes: Oaxacan beef stew, turkey in classic red mole, Yucatán-style chicken tamales, or spicy vegetable casseroles. Salsas, tortillas, and fresh peppers can be purchased here, too. ♦ Mexican ♦ 625.0321

Spataro's ★$ Cold buttermilk and old-fashioned sandwiches have been standouts at Spataro's since 1947, where such choices as ham, liverwurst, turkey, tuna salad, and cream-cheese-and-olive spread are the same as when Truman was president. Just one of these substantial sandwiches can satisfy two restrained appetites. ♦ Deli ♦ 925.6833

Fisher's Soft Pretzels and Ice Cream ★★★$ If the only kind of soft pretzel you've ever tasted came from a street vendor, you're in for a treat. Here, Amish women roll out the dough just before it's placed in the oven, and waitresses brush the baked pretzels with butter. The result is as memorable as a warm slice of homemade bread. If you want a scoop, however, you're better off going to **Bassetts Ice Cream** around the corner. ♦ Snacks ♦ 592.8510

Bassetts Ice Cream ★★★★$ Even when the market was desolate in the 1960s and 1970s, you could always find people lining up at Bassetts. **Louis DuBois Bassett** started an ice cream business out of his backyard in Salem, New Jersey, in 1861, which makes Bassetts the oldest commercial ice cream operation in the country. The family moved their business from the Garden State to the Reading Terminal in the 1890s, where they've been ever since. It's no wonder the customers sitting at the counter have glazed looks of contentment. Heavy, smooth, and intensely flavored, this ice cream has a treacherously high butterfat content. Double chocolate chip, Irish coffee, French vanilla, butter almond, and rum raisin are the most highly recommended flavors. The Bassett family has also introduced its own frozen yogurt, and they expanded nationally in the 1980s. ♦ Ice cream ♦ 925.4315

Jill's Vorspeise ★★$ Health-conscious diners prize this take-out counter, named after the Yiddish word for hors d'oeuvres. Black-bean chili, Cajun bean salad, smoked mozzarella, and bulgur salad could be among the many choices. Pâtés, vegetable pizza with whole-wheat crust, fresh-brewed iced tea, and homemade cakes and cookies are available every day. ♦ Vegetarian ♦ 925.5415

Kamal's Middle Eastern Specialties ★★$ Falafels, made fresh daily, are stuffed into pita with the requisite salad greens and tahini sauce. There's also shish kebab, *hummus, baba ghanouj,* rice pilaf, and Greek pizza. ♦ Middle Eastern ♦ 925.1511

Famous 4th St. Cookie Co. ★★★$ Few of the usual shopping-mall cookie stands match the quality here. The selection typically includes oatmeal raisin, several varieties of chocolate chip, white chocolate, and peanut. ♦ Snacks ♦ 629.5990

Dienner's Bar-B-Q Chicken ★★$ If you see someone at a market table bent over a piece of aluminum foil and a rising pile of bones, you know they've been to Dienner's, where hot roasted chicken is sold whole or in part. (Contrary to the name, Dienner's makes simple roasted chicken with salt and mild seasonings, not barbecued chicken in a spicy sauce.) Crack it open here or take it out. ♦ 925.8755

Le Bus Bakery ★★$ The breads, almond croissants, muffins, breads, cakes, and cookies are oven-fresh. ♦ Bakery ♦ 592.0422

5 Pennsylvania Convention Center
Philadelphia hopes to become a major player in the competitive "meet market" with this new 1.3 million-square-foot complex. With a final bill of more than $500 million, the center is the costliest construction project in Philadelphia history. Architects **Thompson, Ventulett, Stainback & Associates** of Atlanta, Georgia, designed the handsome brick and limestone mammoth, with a main hall that covers four square blocks. Eventually the old Reading Railroad's ornate terracotta **Head House** and spectacular **Train Shed,** unusual structures that distinguish the center from blander public buildings, will become the hall's grand entrance, connected to the convention complex by a glass walkway over Arch Street.

From the moment officials proposed it, the convention center was one of the city's hottest controversies. Many adamantly opposed building in this already extremely dense neighborhood with narrow streets. But conventioneers—once they get there—will probably find the location very convenient. It's within easy walking distance of **Chinatown, The Gallery, Liberty Place,** and the commercial core of **Center City; Independence National Historical Park** is a mere six blocks away; and the **Reading Terminal Market** has been renovated and made part of the convention complex.

Driving and parking in the area remain a problem, but the center can be reached by mass transit. Commuter rail lines, including the **Airport Express,** stop at the Market East Station; there are subway stops at 11th and Market streets and 13th and Market streets; and buses run along Market Street and will stop right outside the door of the 1,200-room **Marriott Hotel,** scheduled for completion in 1994. ♦ Bounded by N. 11th and N. 13th Sts, and Arch and Race Sts. 636.3300

6 Chinatown The area's Chinese roots date back to the mid-19th century, when the first Chinese came to Philadelphia from the Guangdong Province. In the 1860s **Lee Fong** opened a laundry at 913 Race Street, the first business in what is now known as Chinatown. Today the eight-block area is home to dozens of Chinese restaurants, groceries, shops, churches, a cultural center, a hotel, fortune-cookie bakeries, an Asian bank, and about 3,000 people, a fraction of Philadelphia's Asian community.

Chinatown is a dense little neighborhood that has had to fight for its survival. After vying for space with the city's red-light district, it was further threatened by the expansion of the **Vine Street Expressway** and then construction of the **Pennsylvania Convention Center** right next door in 1993. It remains to be seen how the thousands of tourists brought in by the convention center will affect the area.

Though Chinatown is much more than restaurants, most visitors come here to eat, whether it be Chinese, Vietnamese, Taiwanese, Burmese, or Thai. There are a number of good places, and prices are always reasonable. Street parking can be difficult, so resign yourself to paying for a space in a lot if you don't find anything after a couple of swings around the area. ♦ Bounded by N. Eighth and N. 11th Sts, and Vine and Arch Sts

7 Van's Garden ★★$ A veteran among the city's Vietnamese restaurants, Van's is located in a plain storefront with vinyl-covered chairs. It's a favorite with Vietnamese residents, and the menu is a survey course in their native cuisine: soups with slippery rice noodles and beef, skewers of grilled meatballs, lobster salad with herbs and shredded vegetables, shrimp fried rice, and grilled pork on rice vermicelli. Prices are unbelievably low. Bring your own wine or beer. ♦ Vietnamese ♦ Lunch and dinner. 121 N. 11th St (between Arch and Cherry Sts). 923.2438

The world's first Automat opened in Philadelphia at the Horn and Hardart restaurant on Chestnut Street in 1902. People considered the Automat (essentially a wall of glass cubicles) an ingenious, fast method of serving restaurant food: customers put their money in, turned a handle, and opened the door of their choice. By the 1960s, fast-food restaurants had replaced Automats.

8 Joy Tsin Lau ★$$ The gaudy red decor, featuring columns festooned with dragons, live fish tanks, and lots of mirrors, is quite a backdrop for a traditional Chinese restaurant. Moo shu pork, roast duck, *wu-nan*-style lamb, and lemon shrimp are among the dozens of listings. Whole lobster is also available, and dim sum, offered daily, includes stuffed crab claws and shrimp dumplings. ◆ Chinese ◆ Lunch and dinner. 1026 Race St (between N. 10th and N. 11th Sts). 592.7227

9 Lee How Fook ★★$$ Refreshing lemon chicken, steamed sea bass, and hacked fried chicken with seasoned salt are among the nice and light dishes served at this spartan Chinese restaurant. ◆ Chinese ◆ Lunch and dinner. Closed Monday. 219 N. 11th St (between Race and Vine Sts). 925.7266

10 Imperial Inn ★$$ If you've never had dim sum (Chinese finger foods in a variety of wrappings, sauces, and dumplings), the Imperial Inn is a good introduction. Choices on the dim sum carts rolled around by servers at lunchtime range from spareribs, steamed dumplings, and a chewy Chinese version of lasagna to the more exotic chicken feet in brown sauce. The massive restaurant has one of those booklike menus packed with all the Cantonese, Szechuan, and Mandarin standards. ◆ Chinese ◆ Lunch and dinner. 142 N. 10th St (at Race St). 627.2299

11 Chinatown Quality Inn $$ The only place to stay in the heart of Chinatown is this 97-room hotel. Every room has a full kitchen with a small refrigerator and stove. ◆ 1010 Race St (between N. 10th and N. 11th Sts). 922.1730

11 Sang Kee Seafood Restaurant ★$$ Steamed sea bass; shrimp with mushrooms, vegetables, and cashews; and a filling seafood noodle soup are served in a no-frills dining room. ◆ Chinese ◆ Lunch and dinner. 1004 Race St (at N. 10th St). 625.9898

12 Cherry Street Chinese ★$$ It doesn't look Jewish—and, indeed, it's thoroughly Chinese—but this pleasant pastel room is deemed kosher (except on Saturday) by the city's rabbis. You'll see pork, beef, and poultry on the menu, but it's all made from wheat gluten. A special low-fat Pritikin menu is offered. ◆ Chinese ◆ Lunch and dinner. 1010 Cherry St (between N. 10th and N. 11th Sts). 923.3663

13 Friendship Gate This decorative arch is hard to miss as you stroll down 10th Street. It's one of the most attractive landmarks in Chinatown, a neighborhood with lots of commercial signs but almost no outdoor artwork. The arch was a joint project between Philadelphia and its Chinese sister city, Tianjin. Chinese artisans completed it in 1984 with materials brought from Tianjin. ◆ N. 10th St (between Arch and Cherry Sts)

14 Spaghetti Warehouse ★$ This massive, barnlike family restaurant has a train dining car in the middle of it and walls decorated with nostalgia signs. The approach is simple and successful: meals consist of a fresh-baked loaf of bread, huge drinks, a garden-variety salad, and a good-size plate of pasta with a choice of sauces. The 15-layer lasagna is popular. ◆ Italian ◆ Lunch and dinner. 1026 Spring Garden St (between N. 10th and N. 11th Sts). 787.0784

14 Siam Lotus ★★$$ North of Chinatown's main action in a dingy industrial neighborhood, this Thai restaurant holds forth in an unprepossessing building that was formerly a taproom. The easy parking, reasonable prices, and exotic food attract a young crowd. Try the beef or pork satay, red snapper with curry paste, fried noodles, squid salad, or curried duck. ◆ Thai ◆ Lunch and dinner; dinner only on Saturday and Sunday. 931 Spring Garden St (between N. Ninth and N. 10th Sts). 235.6887

15 Sang Kee Peking Duck House ★$ The dishes here are a cut above those served at neighboring restaurants, though the dining room can get noisy and crowded. Try the shrimp with black pepper sauce, spicy beef and eggplant, or chicken in black-bean sauce. Regulars recommend the noodles with ginger and scallions, and the huge servings of wonton noodle or wonton vegetable soup are almost a meal in their own right. ◆ Chinese ◆ Lunch and dinner. 238 N. Ninth St (between Race and Vine Sts). 925.7532

15 Riverside ★$$ The large dining room with Formica tables and booths may remind you of the last time you attended a very modest but happy wedding reception. Order beef *chow-fun* with gravy and broccoli and you'll get a solid rendition of the thick rice-noodle dish. ◆ Chinese ◆ Lunch and dinner. 234 N. Ninth St (between Race and Vine Sts). 923.4410

16 Joe's Peking Duck House ★★$ A select Chinese menu is available in this proverbial hole-in-the-wall. Best bets are the crispy duck in its natural juices; the mussels, in a variety of Asian sauces; and the dumplings. ◆ Chinese ◆ Lunch and dinner. 925 Race St (between N. Ninth and N. 10th Sts). 922.3277

Restaurants/Clubs: Red
Shops/ 🌿 Outdoors: Green

Hotels: Blue
Sights/Culture: Black

Getting Jazzed

Trumpeter **Miles Davis** looked to Philadelphia when recruiting for his legendary jazz quintet and came away with some extraordinary musicians: **John Coltrane, Philly Joe Jones,** and **Red Garland.** Not surprising, considering the deep roots jazz has in this city, that a partial list of musicians with a Philadelphia connection constitutes a jazz honor roll. **Dizzy Gillespie, McCoy Tyner, Bessie Smith, Shirlie Scott, Grover Washington, Jr.,** and the **Heath Brothers** (**Jimmy, Percy,** and **Tootie**) all hailed from Philadelphia's large and influential African-American community, which has kept this town prominent on the national jazz scene. From the 1940s to the 1960s, this was a world-class club town, with the likes of the **Showboat,** where John Coltrane, **Thelonius Monk,** Miles Davis, and **Stan Getz** performed, and the **Earl,** where Dizzy Gillespie played.

Today's jazz scene—though not as renowned as New York City's—remains lively. Although the number of full-time clubs has dwindled since the heyday, most nights you can still find a joint that's jumping—whether it's a bar, restaurant, church, or even the **Academy of Music.** And the **Mellon Jazz Festival** draws jazz superstars to the city each August. To find out more about the local scene, call **204-JASS,** the hot line operated by **WRTI-FM Radio (90.1),** a 24-hour jazz station affiliated with **Temple University.** Here are a few clubs that regularly offer live jazz:

J.J.'s Grotto Located in the basement of a turn-of-the-century mansion, this casual spot on the western edge of Center City schedules jazz standards. Regulars include guitarist **Jimmy Bruno** and **Jimmy King and Band.** ♦ Cover charge on Friday and Saturday only. Th-Sa 8:30PM-closing. 27 South 21st Street. 988.9255

L.G.'s Blue Note When you're in the mood for the blues, this neighborhood tavern and restaurant in East Germantown is the place for musical melancholy. They play straight-ahead jazz, too. ♦ No cover charge. M 6-10PM; F 9PM-1AM. 7400 Limekiln Pike. 924.7324

Ortlieb's Jazzhaus There's lots of 1940s charm in this club located north of Old Philadelphia. First-rate national and local musicians hold court six nights a week, with a jam session on Tuesdays. ♦ No cover charge. Tu-Th 8:30PM-closing; F-Sa 9:30PM-closing; Su 7PM-closing. Reservations recommended. 847 North Third Street. 922.1035

Mill Creek Jazz and Cultural Society A house band and well-regarded soloists are the attractions at this popular West Philadelphia jazz loft located inside a community center. Jazz workshops for children are held prior to each concert. ♦ No cover charge. F 8PM, 10PM; workshops: F 4-5:30PM. 4624 Lancaster Avenue. 473.4273

Painted Bride Art Center The legendary avant-garde art center is also daring in the jazz arena, hosting internationally known musicians who play everything from be-bop to cutting edge. ♦ Admission. Schedule varies. 230 Vine Street. 925.9914

Zanzibar Blue Sometimes as many as three bands a night get a chance to strut their stuff at this popular restaurant. A cafe and a bar offer plenty of space for serious riffing seven nights a week by many of the top local musicians. Its concert series attracts national names, too. ♦ No cover charge. Two drink minimum per set. W-F 5PM-1:30AM; Sa-Tu 9PM-1:30AM. Reservations are not required but seating is on a first-come, first-serve basis. 305 South 11th Street. 829.0300

M. BLUM

17 Ray's Cafe ★★$ Never have you seen coffee  served with more finesse than in this compact, contemporary cafe, which serves specialty coffees and Taiwanese cuisine. The coffee beans are roasted daily, and water is heated in an elaborate glass siphon over a tiny flame—all very mysterious and elegant. Your small, expensive cup of coffee comes in a china cup or exotic mug on a delicate wooden tray with a gold spoon and a butter cookie topped with sugar sprinkles. Daily coffee specials range from Jamaican blue mountain to Brazilian bourbon santos, Sumatra mandheling, Yemen mocha, and plain Columbian. The "amazing iced coffee" takes 12 hours to prepare, as spring water must drip drop by drop through a vertical crystal ball. No hot water is used in the brewing process, so the result lacks bitterness.

The Taiwanese menu features excellent dumplings stuffed with vegetables or pork and cabbage; and the house noodle soup is a meal in itself, thick with shrimp, pork, chicken, egg, and vegetables. Taiwanese rice noodles come with stir-fried pork, mushrooms, and vegetables. Ray's is bright and clean compared to many of the restaurants in this neighborhood. ♦ Coffeehouse/Taiwanese ♦ Lunch and dinner. 141 N. Ninth St (between Arch and Race Sts). 922.5122

18 Harmony Chinese Vegetarian ★★$$ All the "meat" and "seafood" dishes here are imitations fashioned from wheat gluten and soy protein, using no real meat or fish. The "shrimp" may not taste like it was just pulled from the Atlantic, but it's a dish that stands on its own. Small dining rooms add to the cozy atmosphere. ♦ Chinese vegetarian ♦ Lunch and dinner; dinner only on Saturday and Sunday. 135 N. Ninth St (between Arch and Race Sts). 627.4520

19 Siam Cuisine ★★$$$ Cold grilled beef salad, jumbo shrimp and porcelain noodles, Thai herbal cake, and grilled chicken marinated in sweet lemon oil have kept Siam Cuisine busy for 10 years. Linen tablecloths—still a rarity in Chinatown—and pastel walls distinguish the large dining room. ♦ Thai ♦ Lunch and dinner. 925 Arch St (between N. Ninth and N. 10th Sts). 922.7135

Every summer since 1975, the Philadelphia Green Program has converted dozens of abandoned lots into urban gardens, replacing litter and broken glass with sunflowers and patches of tomatoes and corn.

20 Afro-American Historical and Cultural Museum Built in 1976 on land that was once part of a historic black community, this contemporary building with concrete ramps and parquet floors exhibits African-American art and historical photographs and artifacts in four galleries. Displays might illustrate the migration of blacks from the southern states, the civil rights movement, or the rise of the black church. Other popular shows have included the abstract collages of the late **Romare Bearden** and narrative silk screens by **Jacob Lawrence.** Don't miss the museum's gift shop, which has an excellent collection of books on black history and culture, as well as notecards, prints, jewelry, and T-shirts. ♦ Admission. Tu-Sa 10AM-5PM; Su noon-6PM. N. Seventh and Arch Sts. 574.0380

21 Market Place East Without this delightful block of five Victorian buildings, miraculously spared from demolition in the 1970s and later restored, the city would be diminished. Their gay and ornate facades designed and built between 1859 and 1907 by **Collins and Autenreith** create a creamy white wedding cake that profoundly enhances the character of Market Street east of Broad Street. One of the structures is cast iron and the others are brick with marble or granite sheathings and galvanized iron trim, but their arched windows and common color give the appearance of a single exterior with octagonal towers at either end. Notice the sign, evocative of another era, that reads: "Hats Trimmed Free of Charge."

Lit Brothers Department Store occupied the Victorians from 1893 until it went out of business in 1977. In 1987 the buildings were converted into an office and shopping complex, a triumph for preservationists who had championed their survival. The first-floor and basement retail sections are situated around a bright and attractive six-story atrium. Be sure to see the splendid paneling by **John Haviland,** designed originally for Independence Hall, installed near the elevator lobby. ♦ M-Sa 10AM-6PM; some stores Su 11AM-5PM. 701 Market St (between N. Seventh and N. Eighth Sts). 592.8905

Within Market Place East:

Pagano's Gourmet $ Hurried lunchtime crowds descend on this mall outlet for a better-than-average selection of sandwiches, salads, and hot entrées, such as carved turkey, hot corned beef, Italian hoagies, seafood salad, crab cakes, and chicken potpie. Breakfast includes muffins, cinnamon buns, and scones. ♦ American ♦ Breakfast, lunch, and take-out dinner. Closed Sunday. 922.7771. Also at: 601 Walnut St. 627.5656

au bon pain ★$ Tarragon chicken salad, smoked turkey, and ham are stuffed into croissants—assembly-line style—at this popular chain operation. ♦ French cafe ♦ Breakfast and lunch. 625.0677. Also at: Liberty Place, 1650 Market St. 567.9005; S. 15th and Ranstead Sts. 567.8539; 841 Chestnut St. 922.8105

22 **National Archives** A total of 42,000 cubic feet of paper records are housed here, including the papers of the **Continental Congress,** passenger lists for the ports of Philadelphia and Baltimore from 1800 to 1950, and the federal census records for the entire country from 1790 to 1910. The Archives hosts two major exhibits from its collections each year. ♦ Admission. M-F 8AM-5PM; second Saturday of every month 8AM-4PM. S. Ninth and Market Sts (in the Post Office Building, room 1350). 597.3000

23 **The Gallery** If you like the variety and convenience of a suburban shopping mall but want to do your buying in the city, get thee to The Gallery. When the initial phase of this complex was completed in 1977, it was the first major retail building in Philadelphia in more than 40 years. At the time, the idea of putting a retail center in the middle of the city was new and exciting. Now you can find shopping malls like this (with skylit atriums, escalators, glass-enclosed elevator, and fountains) in other urban centers across the country.

Designed by **Bower and Fradley/Bower Lewis Thrower** and **Cope Linder Associates, Gallery I** and **Gallery II** cover a six-block area, with the main entrance at Ninth and Market streets. **Strawbridge & Clothier** and **JCPenney** are the two anchor department stores. A third, **Gimbels,** went out of business, and its building on 12th and Market streets awaits a tenant. The other stores (175 on four levels) are mostly chain outlets, such as **Radio Shack, The Gap,** and **Kaybee Toys.** There are three busy food courts, with the main one at mall level in Gallery I (between Ninth and 10th streets). ♦ M-Tu, Th, Sa 10AM-7PM; W, F 10AM-8PM; Su noon-5PM. Market St (between N. Eighth and N. 11th Sts). 625.4962

Within The Gallery:

Hardshell Cafe ★★$$ With crab logos and lobster bibs, this place should be somewhere along the waterfront. But here it is in a shopping mall on Market Street, with large windows overlooking city buses instead of boats and docks. Come in the early evening to get the biggest crabs; the colossals just about

fall off the plate. Ask for the Baltimore-style seasoning (with a distinct but not peppery edge), and request the house honey-mustard sauce if you order french fries. ♦ Seafood ♦ Lunch and dinner. 592.9110

Strawbridge & Clothier If you see lots of people on Market Street clutching bright green shopping bags, you'll know it's "Clover Day," one of the big sales events at this local retail giant. In 1861 **Justus Strawbridge** opened a dry-goods store on what was then known as High Street. He later formed a partnership with **Isaac Clothier** and launched one of the most successful businesses in Philadelphia. Strawbridge's eight-story building dates from 1896 and has been expanded several times, with the last addition in the 1930s. The local chain is now in the hands of fifth-generation Strawbridges, a family that has fended off merger offers and a takeover attempt by a New York investor. First-rate service and good sales are hallmarks of the store. ♦ M-Tu, Th, Sa 10AM-7PM; W, F 10AM-8PM; Su 11AM-6PM. 629.6000

Within Strawbridge & Clothier:

The Food Hall Chocolate-chip cookies, smoked-turkey sandwiches, pasta salad, fresh-roasted coffee, chocolates, and excellent breads are all sold in a marketlike setting on the first floor. ♦ 629.6000

24 **Market East Station** You can access the commuter rail lines and subway through **The Gallery** shopping complex. The station entrance is right across from **JCPenney** on the mall level. Notice the colorful tile wall mural designed by **David Beck.** ♦ N. 11th and Market Sts. 580.7800

25 **Chestnut Street** In the early 1970s, city officials closed Chestnut Street (then one of Philadelphia's premier shopping streets) to car traffic between Eighth and 18th streets, widened and bricked the sidewalks, and added modern light fixtures and benches. The street was reincarnated as a "transitway" for the exclusive use of buses and pedestrians, which unfortunately coincided with downtown losing business to suburban shopping malls and their ample free parking. So Chestnut Street never regained its former stature; it's now a haven for cut-rate drugstores and low-end retail shops. However, west of Broad Street,

the street's appearance improves noticeably. Two of the outstanding buildings found there are **Liberty Place** and the old **Jacob Reed's Store**, now a **Barnes and Noble** bookstore with a cafe. Longtime independent retailers include **Boyd's for Men.** ♦ Open to car traffic daily 7PM-6AM

26 The Balch Institute for Ethnic Studies

Well-conceived exhibits of photographs and artifacts in the small museum here celebrate the city's ethnic diversity. Learn about the successive waves of immigration to the Philadelphia area, including that of German Jews who arrived in the 18th century and Italians who worked as stonemasons and laborers on the first skyscrapers in the 1920s. Photographs capture the **Head House Square** marketplace around 1916 and stooped laborers in early sweatshops. A research library open to the public houses 60,000 volumes and 12,000 photographs. Don't forget to punch in your heritage on the computer in the lobby to find out which city organizations cater to your ethnic group. The institute also hosts workshops, film screenings, and lectures. ♦ Donation. Museum: M-Sa 10AM-4PM. Library: M-Sa 9AM-5PM. 18 S. Seventh St (between Market and Chestnut Sts). 925.8090

27 Atwater Kent Museum, The History Museum of Philadelphia

Objects of everyday life in Philadelphia over three centuries are showcased in this museum. The collection includes Native American stone tools; an 18th-century cockroach trap; a wooden pipe that carried water from the Schuylkill River; and photographs of some of the city's seedy types in an 1890 rogues' gallery from the **Philadelphia Police Department. John Haviland** designed the Greek Revival structure (the original home of the **Franklin Institute**), which was completed in 1827. ♦ Free. Tu-Sa 9:30AM-4:45PM. 15 S. Seventh St (between Market and Chestnut Sts). 922.3031

28 Pileggi Boutique

Good-looking womenswear with an emphasis on younger New York and European fashion designers is sold in this store adjoining a trendy beauty salon. The owners keep the selection unusual and fresh, favoring designers such as **Byron Lars, Nicole Miller, Robin Picone,** and **Kathryn Dianos.** There's also a large selection of costume jewelry. Prices range from moderate to expensive. ♦ M-Sa 9:30AM-6PM. 715 Walnut St (between S. Seventh and S. Eighth Sts). 922.3526

Restaurants/Clubs: Red   Hotels: Blue

Shops/ 🌳 Outdoors: Green   **Sights/Culture:** Black

29 Walnut Street Theater

The oldest theater in continuous operation in the country is located here in a restored Greek Revival building designed by **John Haviland** and built in 1809. The theater filled a void in a city slow to embrace the stage, and soon became a nationally recognized center for the dramatic arts. Many famous actors graced the Walnut Street's stages, including **Sarah Bernhardt,** the **Barrymores, Lunt and Fontaine,** the **Marx Brothers, Katharine Hepburn,** and **Helen Hayes.**

In 1983 the theater opened its own nonprofit production company, drawing actors from around the country. Its main theater seats more than a thousand and hosts a five-show season, usually with a big Christmastime production and a new musical at the end of the season. A mix of comedy and drama round out the rest of the year. Small, intimate productions are staged in an 80-seat studio theater from January to May. Walnut Street also manages the **Concerto Soloists Chamber Orchestra,** one of only two full-time professional chamber groups in the country, performing here and at the **Church of the Holy Trinity** at Rittenhouse Square. ♦ Box office M-Sa 10AM-6PM; Su noon-4PM. 829-833 Walnut St (at S. Ninth St). 574.3550

30 Ristorante La Buca ★★★$$$$

Descend an indoor staircase a few steps from Washington Square and you'll find yourself inside a grottolike basement with brick and stucco walls, wine racks, elegant brocades, pottery, and baskets. Ristorante La Buca draws businesspeople at lunch and a well-heeled older clientele in the evening. The somewhat staid Italian menu is executed with high-quality ingredients, and the kitchen's strengths are manifested in grilled foods: sweet, smoky-tasting langoustine; veal loin with radicchio; and chicken cooked on a stand of hot bricks are among the highlights. ♦ Italian ♦ Lunch and dinner; dinner only on Saturday. Closed Sunday. 711 Locust St (between S. Seventh and S. Eighth Sts). Reservations recommended. 928.0556

31 Pennsylvania Hospital

From its Spruce Street entrance, there's no hint of the central role this hospital played in colonial times. But approach the complex from Pine Street and you'll get a sense of its significance. The lovely brick building with a rotunda was the country's first full-fledged hospital, and its domestic scale, at once modest and majestic, proves a dramatic contrast to more modern hospitals. Designed by **Samuel Rhoads** (a friend of **Benjamin Franklin,** who helped raise funds for the building), the hospital was built in three parts: the East Wing was completed in 1756 (a time when the surrounding neighborhood was well on the outskirts of the city); the West Wing opened two years later; and the center building, an outstanding example of Federal architecture, was completed in 1804.

Thomas Bond, the eminent colonial physician, founded the hospital, initiating the first clinical studies of medicine in the country when he took his students on hospital rounds. Early modern surgical techniques were performed in the domed amphitheater at the top of the center building, which now houses the **History of Nursing Museum** and the **Historic Library of Pennsylvania Hospital,** said to be the country's oldest medical library. **Benjamin West's** painting *Christ Healing the Sick in the Temple* hangs in the gallery pavilion in the **Cathcart Building,** and there's a lovely 18th-century herb garden on the hospital's original grounds on Pine Street. For information on 30-minute self-guided tours, stop by the marketing office on the second floor of the **Pine Building** (enter on Spruce Street). Group tours available by special arrangement. ♦ Self-guided tours M-F 9AM-4:30PM. S. Eighth St (between Spruce and Pine Sts). 829.3971

32 Portico Row In the 1830s a speculator hired architect **Thomas Ustick Walter,** known for designing the Capitol dome in Washington, DC, to draw the plans for a block of elegant row houses here in what was then a very posh area. Compared to earlier homes built closer to the Delaware River, the residences were extremely large, with protruding porticos (each is actually an entrance to separate houses) and marble columns distinguishing their brick exteriors. The interiors of these private residences, which were restored in the 1980s, are richly detailed with walnut, mahogany, and marble. ♦ 900-930 Spruce St (between S. Ninth and S. 10th Sts)

33 Antique Row In the early 1800s cabinetmakers who set up shop on **Pine Street** crafted some of the finest furniture of the century. But when factories started churning out furniture, the street turned to antiques and earned a reputation for dusty, intriguing shops and idiosyncratic dealers. Some of the finest antiques in the country have been bought and sold on these blocks, along with a few rather ingenious fakes.

In recent years antique shopping at auction houses and traveling shows has increased, but Pine Street is still a prime haunt for veteran shoppers who thrive on ferreting out obscure treasures. You'll find more than a dozen stores stocked with furniture, lamps, and accessories, as well as boutiques offering an eclectic selection of '50s kitsch, estate jewelry, contemporary painted furniture, and South American crafts. ♦ Pine St (bounded by S. Ninth and S. 13th Sts)

34 M. Finkel and Daughter A striking quilt typically hangs in the window of this refined shop, which has turned to catalogs to market much of its stock of samplers, needlework, and, of course, antique quilts. The store also carries expensive, high-quality American antique furniture. ♦ By appointment only. 936 Pine St (between S. Ninth and S. 10th Sts). 627.7797

35 Jeffrey L. Biber Antiques Predominantly a dealer in decorative antiques, this shop offers an appealing selection of bronze statuettes, paintings on ivory, lamps, vases, and lots of silver (letter knives, vases, toilet pieces and tea sets). European antiques are also sold—perhaps a Louis XVI walnut settee, a Chippendale looking glass, or a 19th-century Scottish grandfather clock. ♦ M-Sa 11AM-5PM. 1030 Pine St (between S. 10th and S. 11th Sts). 574.3633

36 Zanzibar Blue ★★★$$$ Before brothers **Robert** and **Benjamin Bynum** went into business a few years ago, Philadelphians needed a place where they could dine well *and* hear good music, and this combination jazz club and restaurant successfully filled the void. Pink banquettes and a billowy blue-satin ceiling set the stage for such eclectic dishes as scallops and raspberries in a red wine sauce, seared tuna with *wasabi,* jambalaya, and grilled lamb with goat cheese. Recorded music—Betty Carter or Miles Davis would be typical choices—plays in the background. ♦ International ♦ Dinner; Sunday brunch. 305 S. 11th St (between Spruce and Pine Sts). Reservations recommended for dinner. 829.0300

Within Zanzibar Blue:

The Jazz Cafe The red vinyl seats, black ceiling, and contemporary paintings by local artists look like a movie set for a jazz club, replete with clouds of cigarette smoke. Some of the best musicians from the Philadelphia area—most with recorded albums—play here, including vocalist **Sheila Jordan,** pianist **Cedar Walton,** the **Harper Brothers** quartet, and trumpet player **Red Rodney.** Weekends are busy, so it's best to arrive by 8PM for a seat. The music begins at 9PM. ♦ Two-drink minimum for each jazz set. M-Tu 7PM-2AM; W-F 5:30PM-2AM; Sa 6PM-2AM; Su 9PM-2AM. 829.0300

Blue Bar One flight up from the cafe, this mellow room features live jazz and sometimes blues on weekends. There's a wonderful wall mural in brash pinks and turquoise, and blue satin drapes the stage. The Blue Bar is more intimate than The Jazz Cafe downstairs and the music is as good. Both draw an eclectic crowd, from college students to senior citizens. ◆ Two-drink minimum for each jazz set. F-Sa 7PM-2AM. 829.0300

37 Indigo The emphasis is on earthy Third World handicrafts, though 60 countries are represented in the jewelry and decorative items at this boutique. Pick through kilims from Afghanistan, Mexican clay sculpture, Haitian iron figures, and American-Indian jewelry made of coral, spiny oyster, turquoise, and the like. There are also hand-dyed batiks and contemporary Mexican prints. ◆ Tu-Sa 11:30AM-6:30PM; Su noon-6PM. 1102 Pine St (between S. 11th and S. 12th Sts). 440.0202

37 Maidie Franklin Designs Edwardian and Victorian wedding bands, earrings, and brooches are sold alongside lovely contemporary pieces made of sterling silver, beads, vermeil, cut glass, or gold. Prices vary widely, so don't be put off if you have less than $50 to spend. ◆ Tu-Su 11AM-6PM. 1106 Pine St (between S. 11th and S. 12th Sts). 923.3550

38 Studio Diaboliques Brothers **Stephen** and **Robert Carb** carry whimsical accessories and hand-painted furniture in vivid colors. ◆ Tu-Sa 11AM-6PM. 1114 Pine St. 238.0860

39 More than Just Ice Cream $ The apple pie in this neighborhood ice cream parlor and restaurant measures about four inches thick. ◆ American ◆ Breakfast, lunch, and dinner. 1141 Pine St (between S. 11th and S. 12th Sts). 574.0586

40 Jamison's ★$ Stop by this small coffee shop for morning coffee and a crisp almond croissant or cinnamon roll. But don't plan on whiling away the hours here: it's too small to linger in and work on your novel. Lunch and dinner feature quiches, salads, and earthy entrées, perhaps chicken crepes or turkey breast with mashed potatoes. The pancakes—especially the banana—make one of the best breakfasts in town. ◆ American ◆ Breakfast, lunch, and dinner. 1220 Pine St (between S. 12th and S. Camac Sts). 735.2240

41 Sabra ★$ Brick walls and cafe tables create a casual atmosphere for a quick bite to eat. Order chicken kebab, falafel, or *hummus* at the counter and they'll bring it to your table. Sodas come in cans. ◆ Middle Eastern ◆ Lunch and dinner. Closed Monday. 1240 Pine St (at S. 13th St). 735.4424

42 Chanterelles ★★★$$$$ Several of the city's noteworthy French restaurants have passed through this simple brick town house, including the famed **Le Bec Fin** and **Ciboulette,** both still in business elsewhere in the city. Chef **Phillipe Chin** oversees Chanterelles' 35-seat dining room, which has been simplified with white walls, fresh flowers, and colorful paintings of vegetables. Chin prepares classic French cuisine with a contemporary twist, making some concessions to light eaters. Appetizers include a crab bisque *en croute,* Asian *gravlax,* and lobster timbale. Seared aged beef tournedos, roasted rack of lamb with ratatouille quiche, and skillet-grilled salmon "chop" follow. The six-course degustation menu is worth the steep price. A vegetarian version includes wild mushroom soup, char-grilled vegetable ravioli, salad with champagne vinaigrette, and a phyllo dough "beggars purse" with niçoise vegetables and grilled tofu. ◆ French/Eclectic ◆ Dinner. Closed Sunday. 1312 Spruce St (between S. 13th and S. Juniper Sts). Reservations required. 735.7551

43 Camac Street Though **William Penn** hoped that each house in his "Greene Country Town" would be surrounded by open space, the lots he sold to various individuals were soon divided and subdivided. The city's well-to-do built large dwellings on the main streets, while workers erected modest row houses on the smaller streets and back alleys. (Panama, Iseminger, Jessup, and Quince streets, which lie just west of Washington Square, are only a few of the narrow, almost hidden, pockets of tiny houses and trees within steps of the city's skyscrapers.) Camac Street (pronounced cuh-MACK) offers a mix of early 19th-century row houses. Between Locust and Spruce streets, Camac becomes the "Street of Clubs," so nicknamed because it's a haven for the city's oldest artists' organizations. Some of the clubs remain, buoyed by the large numbers of artists drawn to the neighborhood since World War II. (The **Franklin Inn Club,** on the northeast corner of Camac and Locust streets, is a literary club founded in 1902—**Christopher Morley** and **Howard Pyle** were dues-paying members.) ◆ Between S. 12th and S. 13th Sts

44 Plastic Club A small sign on the door points out that this is the location of the country's oldest art club for women, opened in 1897. (At that time, the word "plastic" was commonly used to refer to an artist's molding of various materials and to the idea that a piece of art is never completely finished.) The club hosts one or two exhibits a year that are open to the public. ♦ 247 S. Camac St (between Spruce and Locust Sts). 545.9324

45 The Charlotte Cushman Club Started in 1907 (in another location) as a boardinghouse for actresses, this private theater club continues as a gathering place for people in the theater business and their avid followers. The club's collection of memorabilia includes **Sarah Bernhardt's** crown from *Medea,* antique theater bills, and a grand piano donated by **Fanny Brice.** "Speak with clarity, wit, and eloquence and you never know what might happen," advises the voice on the club's answering machine. Past recipients of the annual **Charlotte Cushman Award** (in honor of the famous 19th-century actress) include **Katharine Hepburn, Richard Burton, Helen Hayes,** and **Julie Harris.** Though there are no regular hours for the public, it's worth calling in advance to arrange a visit. ♦ Visitors by appointment. 239 S. Camac St (between Spruce and Locust Sts). 735.4676

46 Philadelphia Sketch Club Thomas Eakins, N.C. Wyeth, and **Thomas Anshutz** all belonged to this 133-year-old artist's club. Regular exhibits are open to the public. ♦ During exhibits: F-Su 2-5PM. 235 S. Camac St (between Spruce and Locust Sts). 545.9298

47 Historical Society of Pennsylvania Visitors to the city who don't stop in here to see "Finding Philadelphia's Past: Visions and Revisions" miss out on the lively narrative and artfully arranged displays, an excellent introduction to the area's history. After viewing such local artifacts as **William Penn's** baby cradle, **Benjamin Franklin's** music stand, and an intriguing portrait of **Benedict Arnold's** wife, you can step into a re-created streetcar and watch great old movie clips of Philadelphians in streetcars, factories, and their homes. Founded in 1824, the Historical Society owns a number of valuable documents, including the first two drafts of the **U.S. Constitution,** the original plan for **Independence Hall,** Benjamin Franklin's *Poor Richard's Almanack,* and the largest collection anywhere of William Penn's letters. Ten percent of the collection is on view each year. There's also a research library on the second floor. The building was designed by **Addison Hutton** and **Savery, Sheetz & Savery** and completed in 1910. ♦ Free. Tu, Th-Sa 10AM-5PM; W 1-9PM. 1300 Locust St (between S. 13th and S. 14th Sts). 732.6200

48 Library Company of Philadelphia This organization founded by **Benjamin Franklin** and his associates in 1731 maintains the largest collection of rare books in the area, including the libraries of **James Logan** and

Benjamin Rush. When the Continental Congress, Constitutional Convention, and U.S. Congress were meeting in Philadelphia from 1774 to 1800, the Library Company served as the Library of Congress. Stop in to see the changing exhibits on Philadelphia's history. ♦ M-F 9AM-4:45PM. 1314 Locust St (between S. 13th and S. 14th Sts). 546.318

49 Clarence Moore House Built as the home of businessman **Clarence Moore** in 1890, the delightfully complex mansion was designed by **Wilson Eyre,** an Italian-born architect known for his playful, imaginative residential structures. The exterior is an appealing mixture of rough-cut and smooth limestone, brick, and slate, and features a Venetian loggia, French tower, arched windows, sculptures, and gargoyles. The building now houses offices. ♦ 1321 Locust St (between 13th and S. Juniper Sts)

50 Girasole ★★★$$$
Named after the Italian word for "sunflower," this noisy trattoria with golden walls and summery lighting will seem especially appealing on a winter night when gray envelops the city. Chef **Andrea Covino** and his brother-in-law, **Franco Covino,** maintain consistently high standards. Pastas— *orecchiette* with broccoli *rabe* and sun-dried tomatoes, and *farfalle* with smoked salmon, name a few—are made by hand, not by food processor; carpaccio, prepared warm or cold is served with arugula and parmigiana or smoked mozzarella and endive; and chicken paillard, veal with mozzarella and arugula, and daily fish entrées are made at the grill. Most popular of all are the pizzas, baked in a wood-burning oven lined with volcanic lava. Choose from a variety of toppings, including arugula and prosciutto or four cheeses. ♦ Italian ♦ Lunch and dinner; dinner only on Saturday. Closed Sunday. 1305 Locust St. Reservations recommended. 985.4659

51 Deux Cheminées ★★★$$$$
Deux Cheminées now seems a bit of a misnomer for this first-class French restaurant, which was named for the original building and its two huge fireplaces. Fire destroyed the old location on Camac Street in the late 1980s, and today the restaurant occupies a former town house designed by **Frank Furness,** with five fireplaces and four elegant dining rooms furnished with silks, Oriental rugs, and fine old portraits. Chef **Fritz Blank's** changing fixed-price menu includes soup, salad, entrée, vegetable, dessert, and coffee. Crab velouté sauce laced with Scotch

whiskey, poached asparagus with orange-onion vinaigrette and curried whipped cream, and rack of lamb *à la périgourdine* or salmon sautéed with a crust of chopped seasoned peanuts were on the menu during a recent visit. ♦ French ♦ Dinner. Closed Monday and Sunday. 1221 Locust St (between S. 12th and S. 13th Sts). Reservations required. 790.0200

52 Ziggy's ★$$ Televisions blare Japanese videos and cartoons in a "Punk-Japanese" setting, with three levels of black decor and low lighting. For a wide sampling of the food, order the sushi/sashimi combination entrée, which includes 20 pieces of raw fish. There are also buckwheat noodle dishes, chicken teriyaki, beef tempura, and an exotic salad bar, with fried ice cream balls and fruit tempura for dessert. ♦ Japanese ♦ Lunch and dinner; dinner only on Saturday and Sunday. Closed Monday. 1210 Walnut St (between S. 12th and S. 13th Sts). 985.1838

53 Forrest Theater *Cats, Tommy Tune, Les Miserables,* and most of the other big hits eventually make their way to this stage, which has been hosting major Broadway shows for more than 60 years. The 1,800-seat theater opened in 1927 as an offshoot of the original Forrest at Broad and Sansom streets. ♦ Box office: daily 10AM-8:30PM when a show is playing; Tu-Sa 10AM-6PM during off-season. 1114 Walnut St (between S. 11th and S. 12th Sts). 923.1515

54 Lai Lai ★$$ A quick walk from the Academy of Music, the Forrest Theater, and the Walnut Street Theater, this pretty Chinese restaurant serves such dishes as chicken with garlic sauce, butterfly shrimp with bacon, crispy orange-flavored beef, pepper steak, and sautéed lamb with scallions. ♦ Chinese ♦ Lunch and dinner; dinner only on Sunday. 1119 Walnut St (between S. 11th and S. 12th Sts). 440.7866

55 Caribou ★$ This homey Parisian-style cafe with a large storefront window, marble tables, and an amiable French-speaking owner offers croissants and muffins for breakfast, and croque monsieur, salmon mousse, and croissant sandwiches for lunch. Try the satisfying version of the standard French onion soup, vegetarian lasagna, chicken cordon bleu, or baked escargots for dinner. ♦ French ♦ Breakfast, lunch, and dinner. 1121 Walnut St (between S. 11th and S. 12th Sts). 625.9535

56 Maccabeam ★★$ If you try to get an idea of Philadelphia's demographics from its ethnic restaurants, you would think the Chinese population was huge and the Jewish relatively small. In fact, the reverse is true, though Maccabeam is one of the few kosher restaurants in Center City. The tidy storefront with a galley kitchen, framed posters, and black lacquer chairs offers homey Israeli cooking, including turkey *kubba,* a mixture of turkey and cracked wheat formed into a ball and stuffed with pine nuts, and outstanding homemade falafels. ♦ Israeli/American ♦ Lunch and dinner; lunch only on Friday. 128 S. 12th St (between Sansom and Walnut Sts). 922.5922

57 Odeon ★★★$$$ Set in a former Victorian flower shop (look for the old lettering above the inside front doors), Odeon has the feel of a Parisian bistro. Among the restaurant's chief charms are the handsome wooden bar with its massive mirror and a staircase leading to a little upstairs balcony that hangs over the main room. Chef **Anders Divack's** specialties include crab cakes in lemon butter sauce, breast of moulard duck with yam puree and a ginger and star anise sauce, roasted chicken with rosemary, and panfried fish, all artistically presented on the plate. Indulge in a slice of fruit tart or chocolate torte with vanilla ice cream and caramel sauce for dessert. ♦ French ♦ Lunch and dinner; dinner only on Saturday. Closed Sunday. 114 S. 12th St (between Chestnut and Sansom Sts). Reservations recommended. 922.5875

Bests

Paul Levy
Executive Director, Center City District

Brunch on weekends at the **Famous Deli**—great food and lots of interesting Philadelphia personalities.

Walk to the top of the **Benjamin Franklin Bridge** for a breathtaking view of the waterfront and the skyline—it's free (most Philadelphians don't even know you can walk on the bridge).

A walk to **Valley Green Inn** and surrounding trails in **Fairmount Park,** the largest urban park in the world. You can wander for miles in the woods in the middle of the city.

Boathouse Row along the **Schuylkill River,** lit up at night.

A leisurely stroll along colonial **Delancey Street** in Society Hill.

Restaurants/Clubs: Red	Hotels: Blue
Shops/ 🌳 Outdoors: Green	Sights/Culture: Black

Broad Street/South Philadelphia

Philadelphia wears Broad Street like a fine old tuxedo. Twelve miles long and 69 feet wide, this grand avenue lined with some of the city's best architecture is ready-made for parades and presidential motorcades. Most of the buildings date from the late 19th and early 20th centuries, recalling a time when the area was the city's nerve center of banking, business, and local government. Though many businesses have moved to the modern glass and steel skyscrapers west of here, Broad Street remains a prestigious address and hub of activity.

A walk south along Broad still stirs memories of Philadelphia as it was before the 1940s, with all its self-confidence, hopes, and pretensions. Highlights include the **Pennsylvania Academy of the Fine Arts,** housed in a spectacular Victorian building designed by Philadelphia architect **Frank Furness; City Hall,** a Second Empire colossus and the largest municipal building in the world; the **Union League,** an elegant club for the city's conservative elite since the Civil War; the **Land Title Building,** an early skyscraper of classic proportions; and the famed **Academy of Music,** the oldest concert hall in the country and home to the Philadelphia Orchestra. Also on this stretch of Broad are the opulent exterior of the former **Bellevue Stratford Hotel,** now a hotel, shopping, and office complex, which dresses up its surroundings like a fancy bow tie; and the **Girard Trust Company** building, a classical temple in marble

South of Pine Street, Broad Street loses its grandeur. But this lackluster area has discovered new hope in plans for an **Avenue of the Arts,** where city officials are plotting to establish a major performing arts center in the next few years. Proposals call for several theaters, a concert hall, a recital hall, a graphic arts center, and wide sidewalks with outdoor cafes along Broad between Locust and South streets. Even if just a few of these plans come to fruition, the area will have more vitality.

Just below South Street, Broad enters South Philadelphia, a neighborhood with a distinct working-class personality. In the early years of the century many immigrant groups settled here, though Italians dominate today. South Philly is characterized by neat rows of brick houses with metal awnings, spaghetti and meatballs, **Mario Lanza, Mummers,** the **Italian Market,** and more than its share of funeral homes. The best walking routes are in the vicinity of the Italian Market at Ninth and Christian streets. Drive or take the subway even further into South Philadelphia to reach the city's sports centers **Veterans Stadium** and the **Spectrum,** home of the **Phillies, 76ers, Eagles,** and **Flyers.**

---

1 Pennsylvania Academy of the Fine Arts

Frank Furness designed this High-Victorian building for the oldest art school and museum in the country (founded in 1805 in another location). The compact foyer leads to a stair-hall bursting with color. Bronze ornamental railings, carved marble posts, ceramic tile mosaics, a star-studded cerulean blue ceiling, and a multitude of floral patterns (some cut in stone and gilded) combine for an exhilarating effect. The gilded walls were painted over and the floors covered with carpeting at one point (when some critics deemed the Academy excessively ornate), but, happily, opinions changed and the interior was restored according to designs by **Day and Zimmerman** for the 1976 Bicentennial.

This is the third home of the Academy (pictured on page 62), built just in time to celebrate the country's 1876 Centennial. Furness chose brick, sandstone, terracotta, and Conshohocken rough-cut stone for the exterior, and further embellished them with a mansard roof and an eclectic mix of decorative details.

Founded by portraitist **Charles Willson Peale** and artist **William Rush,** the Academy's distinguished art school has had a number of famous teachers: **Thomas Eakins, Gilbert Stuart, Cecilia Beaux,** and **Alexander Stirling Calder,** to name a few. (Eakins taught at the Academy from 1876 to 1886 and introduced the study of human anatomy to American artists. Though prized

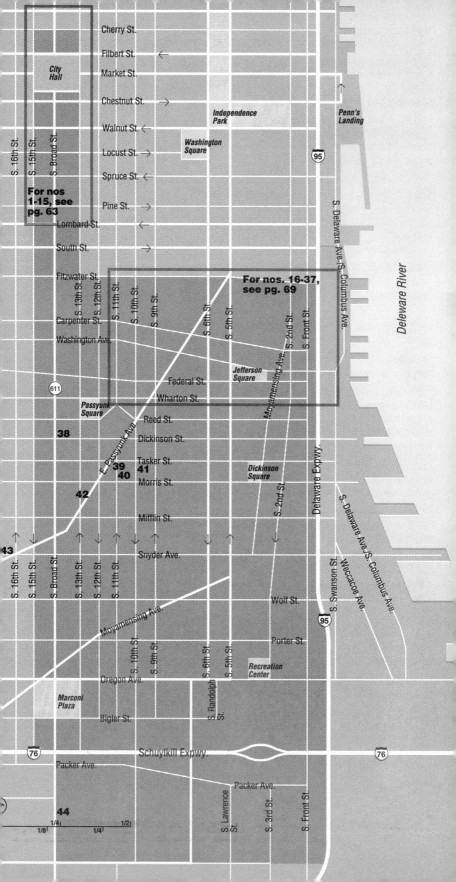

Pennsylvania Academy of the Fine Arts

by the school today, the Academy dismissed him from the staff after he allowed nude male models to pose in front of his female students.) The Academy likewise boasts a superb museum with a permanent collection of more than 1,700 paintings, 300 sculptures, and 14,000 works on paper, a portion of which is always on display. The inventory includes **Benjamin West's** *Death on a Pale Horse,* spared from destruction when a firefighter cut the canvas from its frame during a blaze; portraits of **George Washington;** *The Cello Player* by **Thomas Eakins;** and sculptures by **Red Grooms, Nancy Graves,** and **Louise Nevelson.** The first-floor **Morris Gallery** usually contains the work of contemporary Philadelphia artists.

Classes meet in a separate building (at 1301 Cherry Street), where the school gallery exhibits works primarily by students and faculty. The **Museum Shop** sells art books and gifts. Check the schedule for lectures, films, concerts, and workshops. ♦ Admission. Tu-Sa 10AM-5PM; Su 11AM-5PM. Guided tours Tu-Su 12:30PM, 2PM. 118 N. Broad St (at Cherry St). 972.7600

2 Masonic Temple The first American Freemasons (now the largest fraternity in the world) met in Philadelphia in 1732, and this 1873 building was their sixth temple in the city. **James Windrim,** a 27-year-old Freemason, designed the opulent structure, which resembles a medieval Norman church with its imposing carved doorway and stone facade. **George Herzog,** one of a number of distinguished German craftsmen who came

to this country in the second half of the 19th century, designed the halls. These main rooms vary dramatically in style, with the **Oriental Hall** modeled after the Palace of the Alhambra in Spain, and the **Egyptian Hall** after the temples of Luxor. **Renaissance Hall, Gothic Hall, Ionic Hall,** and **Norman Hall** are among the others. The **Masonic Museum** houses such memorabilia as **George Washington's** Masonic apron (a ceremonial garment designed after the working clothes of stonemasons). ♦ Tours M-F 10AM, 11AM, 1PM, 2PM, 3PM; Sa 10AM, 11AM. Closed Saturday in July and August. 1 N. Broad St (at Filbert St). 988.1917

3 City Hall Few buildings are as fascinating, controversial, grandiose, expensive, misunderstood, and, some would say, beautiful as Philadelphia's City Hall. With more than 600 rooms, 14 entrances, and 14½ acres of floor space, it is the largest municipal building in the world. It took $25 million and 30 years to build, and has been undergoing renovation and restoration virtually from the moment it was completed in 1901.

When **Thomas Holme,** the colonial surveyor-general, laid out his plans for five public squares in Philadelphia, he designated the 10 acres in the center of the city for civic buildings. Years later, the architect, **John McArthur, Jr.,** said of his own plan to put an enormous and spectacularly ornate City Hall at Center Square, "it cannot fail to make that portion of our city one of the choicest architectural spots in America." Still later, in 1953, City Councilman **Victor Moore** expressed a commonly held opinion at the time when he called McArthur's final product "an ugly monstrosity which sooner or later must come down."

A work of sculpture as well as architecture, the building exemplifies the Second Empire style briefly in fashion before the turn of the century. The granite and white marble exterior is adorned with an eclectic mix of columns, pilasters, pediments, dormers, and sculptures. Note how the tall marble columns at the entranceway and each corner make the building appear as if it has three stories instead of eight. Crowning it all is a 548-foot tower (believed to be the world's tallest masonry-bearing structure) and **Alexander Milne Calder's** famous bronze statue of **William Penn** (at 37 feet in length, it's the largest single piece of sculpture on any building in the world—the nose alone is 18 inches long). Calder also designed the other 250 sculptures on the building, most of them allegorical figures representing seasons, elements, virtues and vices, heroes, and trades. A sculptured face sits above each of the four archways leading to both sides of Broad and Market streets, representing Penn, Benjamin Franklin, Moses, and Sympathy.

Attempts to accommodate the workings of city government have led to the destruction or obscuring of many of the original interior details—the polished marble, coved ceilings, and carved woodwork, to name a few. But some rooms still point to what the building once was—and may someday be again. **Philadelphia Hospitality Style** offers tours of the impressive public spaces, including the **Mayor's Reception Room,** which features Honduran mahogany paneling, a three-ton chandelier, and portraits of the city's mayors. Be sure to see the marble balconies in the **City Council Room;** the rotunda ceiling and pedimented niches in the **Council Caucus Room;** and the marbled walls, hand-set mosaic floors, and ceiling ornamented with gold leaf in the beautifully restored **Conversation Hall.** Plans call for all of City Hall to be restored by the building's centennial in 2001. In 1991 **Mooreland Studios** of Stockton, New Jersey, completed a $24.5 million restoration of the Penn statue and the tower, replacing the latter's deteriorated cast-iron plates with new steel ones.

For a breathtaking view of Philadelphia, visit the **Observation Deck** at the base of the Penn statue (to reach it, take the elevator to the seventh floor, an escalator up two more flights, and then a five-passenger elevator to a platform 30 stories up). A Fairmount Park ranger is always standing by to answer questions about the view. In addition to the guided tours of the public rooms, the

Foundation for Architecture offers occasional tours of the exterior (call 568.3351 for tours of the interior, and 569.3187 for tours of the exterior). ♦ Guided tours of interior: M-F 12:30PM. Tours of exterior: schedule varies. Observation Deck: M-F noon-2:45PM Labor Day to mid-June; M-F 10AM-2:45PM mid-June to Labor Day. Broad and Market Sts. 686.9074

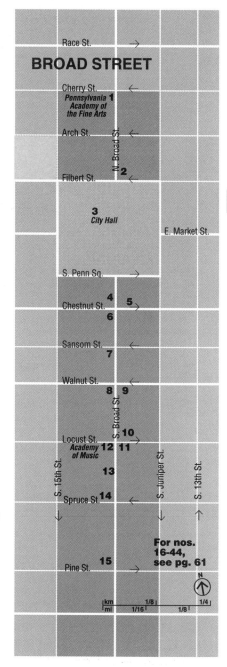

Girard Trust Company

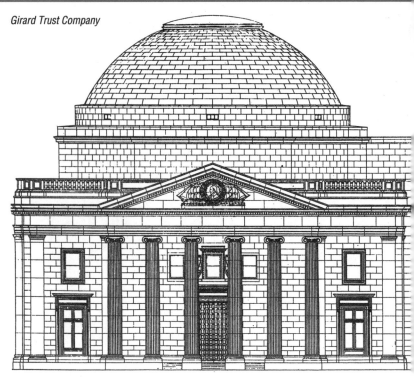

4 Girard Trust Company Tucked among high-rise offices, this classical bank building with a distinctive white marble facade, Ionic columns, and dome (illustrated above) is evocative of Rome's Pantheon. A joint effort by the architectural firms of **Frank Furness** and **Stanford White,** it was completed in 1908. **McKim, Mead & White** built the adjacent 30-story skyscraper at **1400 Penn Square** in 1923. Note the way the marble exterior and Italianate windows pay homage to the earlier bank building. ♦ 34-36 S. Broad St (at Chestnut St)

In 1956, the elegant marble stairway outside the famous ballroom of Philadelphia's Bellevue Stratford Hotel (now The Bellevue) was the scene of tragedy when, during a dinner dance, socialite Louise Schoettle plummeted to her death while trying to demonstrate how she had slid down banisters as a youngster.

In 1945, the writer Struthers Burt described Philadelphia's City Hall as "one of the most expensive, ugliest city halls ever conceived by the mind of man; a monstrosity of bad taste, inconvenience, and graft." Architectural historians would later describe it as the finest example of the Second Empire style in America.

5 J.E. Caldwell & Co. When local architect **Horace Trumbauer** designed this elegant Beaux Arts structure in 1916, he adorned this first-floor jewelry store with black and gold Belgian marble floors, terracotta tile ceilings, and Baccarat chandeliers. Philadelphia's premier jeweler—a family-owned business since it opened in 1839—Caldwell operated a fleet of Rolls Royces to dispense diamonds, engraved calling cards, and European china to the homes of the city's elite. But the seven-store chain fell on hard times in 1992 and is now in the hands of a corporation that plans to market less exclusive merchandise. ♦ M-Sa 10AM-5PM. 1339 Chestnut St (between S. Juniper and S. Broad Sts). 864.7800

6 Land Title Building Chicago architect **Daniel Burnham** designed this 16-story "skyscraper." The Ionic arcade running along the two-story base of the buff brick and granite facade seems to lift the distinguished building upward, and the arches, projecting and flat windows, and decorative cornice set apart from its neighbors. This was Burnham's first East Coast commission, completed in 1897. ♦ Southwest corner of S. Broad and Chestnut Sts

7 Union League Club Known widely for two things—its conservatism and its magnificent building—the Union League Club is a descendant of an organization that raised money for the Union cause during the Civil

Restaurants/Clubs: Red   **Hotels:** Blue
Shops/ 🌳 Outdoors: Green   **Sights/Culture:** Black

War. Today it offers the city's lawyers and businesspeople a place to meet and lunch. In the 1980s, after much fuss, the club allowed women to join for the first time. The dark brick and sandstone building—designed by **John Fraser** and built in 1865, despite the Civil War—is a fine example of the Second Empire style, with a mansard roof, dormer windows, and a sweeping semicircular staircase. **Horace Trumbauer's** 1909 Renaissance Revival addition to the west of the building is a sharp contrast to the earlier structure. ♦ 140 S. Broad St (at Sansom St)

8 **The Bellevue** Prussian immigrant **George Boldt** opened the **Bellevue Stratford Hotel** in 1904. (Boldt had previously owned the city's two top hotels, the Bellevue and the Stratford, but he demolished the latter and built the enormous French Renaissance-style Bellevue Stratford for $8 million.) His hotel became one of the fanciest in the world, with in-house orchestras, three ballrooms, a rooftop rose garden, and rooms ranging from Colonial to Greek in style. Designed by **G.W.** and **W.D. Hewitt** at the turn of the century, this elaborate behemoth features a slate-covered mansard roof with dormers and chimneys and an exterior of terracotta, slate, and rusticated stone.

The hotel began losing its luster in the 1950s, and then, in 1976, as Philadelphia celebrated the country's Bicentennial, tragedy struck at a convention of the American Legion at the Bellevue. **Legionnaires' Disease,** as the media dubbed it, killed 29 Legionnaires and forced the hotel to shut down. (A bacteria transmitted in the hotel's air ducts apparently caused the disease.) The Bellevue changed hands, reopened in 1979 as the **Fairmont Hotel,** and then closed again seven years later. In 1989, after a reported $100 million in renovations, the building gave it a third shot as The Bellevue hotel, office, and shopping complex. Many of the building's outstanding features were beautifully restored or spared from further deterioration, including the hotel's legendary 14,000-square-foot ballroom, which had been slated for destruction. Philadelphia's socialites continue to hold balls and lavish fund-raisers there, just as they have for more than 80 years. ♦ 200 S. Broad St (at Walnut St)

Within The Bellevue:

Shops at the Bellevue The former lobby of the Bellevue Stratford is now a grand entranceway to this elegant retail complex with some of the city's most exclusive chain boutiques. Among the 14 stores are **Gucci, Tiffany,** and **Neuchatel Chocolates.** On the first floor, **Suky Rosan,** a branch of the store on the Main Line, carries formal gowns and bridalwear. ♦ M-Sa 10AM-6PM; W 10AM-8PM. 875.8350

Broadway ★$$ From matzoh ball soup to hot corned-beef sandwiches, this wood-and-tile deli in the basement of The Bellevue offers a full New York-style menu, complete with a gratis plate of pickles. The waiters often come forth at the spur of the moment with show tunes—hence the name of the place. Sometimes they can even sing. ♦ Deli ♦ Breakfast, lunch, and dinner. 732.3737

The Palm ★★$$$$ Saddle-size steaks and chops, grilled fish, and fancy hash brown potatoes make this branch of the coast-to-coast chain as popular as it is in other cities. The Palm has an in-the-know atmosphere, with well-turned caricatures of local celebrities on the walls. The ceilings are painted to look like old-fashioned pressed tin. ♦ American ♦ Lunch and dinner; dinner only on Saturday and Sunday. Reservations required. 546.7256

Ciboulette ★★★★$$$$ Behind a series of large French doors at the top of The Bellevue's escalator, this incurably chic restaurant awaits its audience in high-ceilinged splendor. Owner-chef **Bruce Lim** preserved the ornate moldings, columns, mosaic tiles, and hardwood floors of the Bellevue Stratford's Pink and Gold Rooms, once the scene of formal receptions, and added white linens, fresh flowers, and bright modern paintings. Lim, a perfectionist, creates dishes that are at once earthy and elegant: a terrine of goat cheese, eggplant, and zucchini wrapped in pasta; saddle of lamb with sweet garlic sauce; venison loin with apple compote; and potato *gnocchi* with bay scallops and thyme. Excellent crème brûlée, opera cake, and tarts with seasonal fruit follow. Ask for a table overlooking Broad Street. ♦ French Provençal ♦ Lunch and dinner; dinner only on Saturday. Reservations required. 790.1210

Hotel Atop The Bellevue $$$ Today only the top seven floors of the old Bellevue Stratford are devoted to a luxury hotel. With its richly paneled library bar, hushed elegance, palatial Grand Ballroom, and intriguing nooks and crannies, it would make the perfect setting for a murder mystery. All 173 rooms come with two-line telephones, minibars, videotape players, stereo systems, and use of the adjacent **Sporting Club.** Some rooms overlook a wonderful skylit conservatory.

From the hallway known as **The Promenade,** you can look past the city's row houses east to the Delaware River. The dining rooms and lounges have been beautifully restored. ♦ 1415 Chancellor Court (at S. Broad St). 893.1776, 800/221.0833; fax 732.8518

Within Hotel Atop The Bellevue:

Founders ★★★$$$$ Decorated with prints of old Philadelphia, statues of Benjamin Franklin and David Rittenhouse, and handsome upholstered chairs, Founders is a luxurious institution with wonderful views of the city's skyline. Chef **Jean-Paul Lucy** prepares American classics with French touches: salmon smoked over oak and served with potatoes and caviar or a rack of lamb for two roasted simply with rosemary. The dessert flan is outstanding. ♦ American/French ♦ Lunch and dinner. Reservations required. 790.2814

The Ethel Barrymore Room ★$$ Enjoy afternoon tea, light snacks, and evening cocktails in what looks like an oversize boudoir. Floral murals and ornate plasterwork enhance the sky-blue domed ceiling. ♦ Tea ♦ Daily 5PM-midnight; tea W-Sa 3-5PM; dancing and live music F-Sa 10PM-1AM. 893.1776

Philadelphia Library Lounge ★★$$ Th type of aristocratic wood-paneled library you see in movies is re-created here, complete wi Oriental rugs, rows of old books on the shelv and a fire in the hearth. Stop in for drinks, ho d'oeuvres, or pastries. ♦ American ♦ M-Th 11:30AM-1AM; F-Sa 11:30AM-2AM; Su 11:30AM-midnight. 893.1776

9 Baci ★$$ A trendy Italian menu, eclectic interior with neon and kitschy statues, and glass-enclosed cafe area jutting onto the Broad Street sidewalk all bring in a steady crowd. Pizzas pulled from the wood-burning oven are topped with such fashionable ingredients as eggplant, goat cheese, arugul and prosciutto. Also on the menu are shrimp scampi made with rosemary, garlic, and bacon, and chicken cooked on a rotisserie. ♦ Italian ♦ Lunch and dinner. 211 S. Broad S (at Walnut St). 731.0700

10 Upstares at Varalli ★★$$ Diners in the upstairs windows here always seem to be having such a great time, perhaps because they're looking down on so many others still searching for parking spaces. They also have great views of the Academy of Music and the lighted trees on Broad Street. Pasta, pizza, a

Pennsylvania's Founding Father: William Penn

As the state's name suggests, **William Penn** was a towering figure in Pennsylvania history. He arrived in what was first known as **Penn's Woods** in 1682 to claim the land granted him by **King Charles II.** The land grant was made in repayment for a loan Penn's father, **Sir William Penn,** an admiral in the British Navy, made to the crown. But the colony was actually named for the elder Penn. The younger William Penn, who was raised in privileged circumstances, adopted a fiercely idealistic Quakerism by the time he was a young man. He later would land in jail in Ireland and in London's famous Tower for attending Quaker meetings and writing religious pamphlets. (Viewed as anti-Royalists, Quakers were strictly forbidden to practice their religion.)

On his first trip to the New World, Penn left England in May 1682 on the *Welcome* and arrived at the site that was to become Philadelphia in September with about 65 colonists, most Quakers like himself. If King Charles hadn't insisted that the colony be named for Admiral Penn, Philadelphia might be in a state with a different name. William Penn, son, considered the "Penn" prefix too vain, preferring instead "Sylvania" or "New Wales." However, the crown prevailed, and the largest territory ever owned outright by an individual British subject became known as "Pennsylvania."

In populating his colony, Penn was one of the original advocates of diversity, seeking both an ethnic and occupational mix. He recruited among the Germans, Swedes, and Dutch, and most of the land-purchasers in the colony were artisans and craftsmen.

In planning Philadelphia's layout, Penn chose a simple pattern: two broad central axes paralleled b narrower streets, the basic look of **Center City** today. Penn wanted to avoid the congestion of Europe's densely populated cities, which he felt b crime, disease, and slums. Aside from leaving a geographic imprint on the city, Penn contributed t the intellectual framework of both the city and the New World. His democratic idealism, inspired by h devout Quakerism, was generations ahead of its time and foreshadowed the principles embodied ir the **Declaration of Independence** and the **U.S. Constitution.** His original constitution for the colo for instance, called for religious liberty, free elections, and a guarantee of trial by a jury of peers Penn's legacy is honored by the 37-foot bronze statue by **Alexander Milne Calder** that sits atop City Hall.

For all he accomplished, Penn's stewardship of Pennsylvania was marred by political disputes and controversy. He had to divide his time between the colony and his affairs in England, and left his depu governors in charge during his absences. Frequen arguments took place between the provincial Assembly and these deputies. Ultimately, Penn turned over the management of the colony to **Jam Logan,** the provincial secretary, and a series of deputy governors. Penn died in 1718, 69 years before a delegation, meeting in Philadelphia, ratifi his ideals by incorporating them into the U.S. Constitution.

risotto are the kitchen's specialties. If you aren't famished, have a half order of risotto with duck and artichokes, pasta with sun-dried tomatoes and cheese, or *agnolotti* with sweet sausage, peas, cream, and parmigiana. The pizza with duck and fontina cheese and the arugula salad with roasted pine nuts, seasonal berries, red onion, Gorgonzola, and orange poppy seed dressing are superb.
♦ Northern Italian ♦ Lunch and dinner; dinner only on Sunday. 1345 Locust St (at S. Broad St). 546.4200

11 Philadelphia Hilton & Towers $$$ If you want to be in the center of Center City, this 26-story hotel with 430 rooms and tall windows is a good choice. Two floors of luxury accommodations come with minibars, Continental breakfast, and afternoon hors d'oeuvres. Regular rooms include access to the health club, a rooftop track, and an indoor pool. Ask for a room facing Broad Street.
♦ S. Broad and Locust Sts. 893.1600, 800/445.8667; fax 893.1663

Within the Philadelphia Hilton & Towers:

Cafe Academie $$ Overlooking the Hilton's atrium lobby and decorated with large Parisian cafe murals, Cafe Academie offers a pleasant place to sit, though typical hotel fare.
♦ American ♦ Breakfast, lunch, and dinner. 893.1600

12 Academy of Music The late Philadelphia writer **John Francis Marion** once described the sense of contentment and pride Phila-delphians feel when they sit in the plush red seats of this beautiful concert hall: "They are secure, enfolded, enveloped in one of their favorite monuments to a rich and colorful

past." For many, the Academy of Music is a more important cultural symbol than the Liberty Bell, particularly because it is home to the premier **Philadelphia Orchestra.**

Plans for the building, completed in 1857, initially called for a more elaborate exterior, but funds ran short and architects **Napoleon LeBrun** and **Gustave Runge** settled on a dark brick facade with Italian Renaissance arches (pictured below). No expense was spared on the baroque interior, however, a gilded setting for performances and social events modeled after La Scala in Milan. German artist **Karl Heinrich Schmolze,** who died in his thirties from lead poisoning, painted the fresco on the domed ceiling with allegorical figures representing Poetry, Music, Dance, Comedy, and Tragedy. Medallions, urns, and sculptured figures ornament the barrel-shaped interior, and Corinthian columns flank the proscenium.

Many famous musicians and speakers have appeared on the Academy's stage, ranging from **Tchaikovsky** to **Garrison Keillor.** The Philadelphia Orchestra, once described by the *New York Herald Tribune* as the city's "chief contribution to civilization," first performed here in 1900 and has been at the Academy since, with three legendary conductors: **Leopold Stokowski, Eugene Ormandy,** and **Riccardo Muti. (Wolfgang Sawallisch** took over after Muti's resignation in 1992.) The conductors have sometimes tangled with the city's conservative tastes. Stokowski, who led the orchestra from 1912 to 1936 and preferred modern composers to Bach and Beethoven, received a lukewarm response when he conducted Stravinsky's *Le Sacre du*

Academy of Music

Printemps and supposedly resigned in frustration.

Though once celebrated for its acoustics as an opera house (LeBrun and Runge placed a dry well under the floor near the orchestra pit to enhance the music), the Academy is considered inadequate for orchestral music according to today's standards. The Philadelphia architectural firm of **Venturi, Scott Brown and Associates** has been commissioned to design a new orchestra hall with better sound farther south on Broad Street, but half the money for the project has yet to be raised. The Academy of Music would continue to host groups and performers other than the orchestra. The **Luciano Pavarotti International Voice Competition** and the **Opera Company of Philadelphia** also call this building home. ◆ Box office M-Sa 10AM-9PM (5:30PM when there's no evening performance). S. Broad and Locust Sts. 893.1930. Tickets by phone: 893.1999; fax 545.4588

13 Merriam Theater When the old **Shubert Theater** opened here in 1918, dozens of big-name Broadway stars appeared on its stage, including **Laurence Olivier, Ethel Merman,** and **Gertrude Lawrence.** The **University of the Arts** purchased the 1,668-seat theater in 1971 and, in the 1980s, restored the inside, renovated the lobby, and refurbished some of the theater's original murals and bas-reliefs. Now managed by the **Philadelphia Theater League,** the Merriam presents Broadway hits, gospel shows, and some stand-up comedy, as well as performances by **The Pennsylvania Ballet** and **Pennsylvania Opera Theater.** ◆ Box office M-Sa 10AM-5:30PM. 250 S. Broad St (between Locust and Spruce Sts). 732.5997

14 Ruth's Chris Steak House ★★★$$$$ Marble and wood contribute to the clubby feel of this gregarious and comfortable link in the upscale steak-house chain on the ground floor of the **Atlantic Building.** Obscenely large crustaceans stock the lobster tanks, and the marbled steaks, seared in the broiler and served on burning-hot plates, are huge. Beware: the sizzle you hear under your porterhouse or filet mignon is the sound of butter (you can ask the waiter to omit it). For extras, order the simple broccoli or fried shoestring potatoes. ◆ American ◆ Lunch and dinner; dinner only on Saturday and Sunday. 260 S. Broad St (at Spruce St in the Atlantic Building). Reservations recommended. 790.1515

15 University of the Arts Two art schools, the **Philadelphia College of Art and Design** and the **Philadelphia College of Performing Arts,** joined in 1987 to create this university. Housed in a Greek Revival-style building originally designed by **John Haviland** in 1825 for the **Asylum for the Deaf and Dumb,** the university offers degree programs in fine arts, graphic arts, dance, theater, and music. (It also operates the **Merriam Theater,** where student dance and theater performances are held.) In 1875 **Frank Furness** designed the additions in the back. The university's first-floor gallery hosts rotating exhibits of acclaimed artists, such as conceptual sculptor **Donald Lipski** and figurative painter **Gregory Botts.** ◆ Free. Gallery M-F 10AM-5PM; W 10AM-9PM; Sa-Su noon-5PM. Closed in August. S. Broad and Pine Sts. 875.1117

16 Dante's and Luigi's ★$$ Stucco walls and white linoleum set the scene in this South Philly classic. Start with roasted peppers and proceed to one of the standbys: osso buco, sweetbreads sautéed in wine sauce and mushrooms, pork chops cacciatore, sautéed broccoli *rabe,* or good old spaghetti and meatballs. Order a side of spaghetti with any of the dishes for a taste of the neighborhood's typically rich tomato "gravy." (Only outsiders use the word "sauce" for pasta toppings in South Philly.) ◆ Italian ◆ Lunch and dinner; lunch only on Monday, Tuesday, and Sunday. 762 S. 10th St (at Catharine St). 922.9501

17 L. Sarcone & Son Bakers Three times a day, hot Italian bread—seeded, plain, round, or oblong—comes out of the brick oven in this no-frills storefront, which opened 71 years ago. There might be a line, but the bread (dense and spongy with a thick crust) is worth the wait. There are also rolls, rings, twists, bread sticks, and pepperoni breads. Count on empty shelves if you come right before closing. ◆ M-Sa 7:30AM-4PM; Su 7:30AM-1PM. 758 S. Ninth St (between Catharine and Fitzwater Sts). 922.0445

In the 1930s, before air-conditioning was common, Philadelphia's public pools were so popular that swimmers were allowed only a limited time in the water. City officials cleared the pools at regular intervals and then reopened them minutes later—anyone with a wet swimsuit was not allowed back in. To dupe the pool police, children would place their dripping suits on the hot pavement and let cars ride over them to squeeze the water out.

William Wagner, a wealthy merchant and amateur scientist, gave free science lectures at his home in the 1840s and eventually established the Wagner Free Institute of Science in North Philadelphia to educate the public. His collection of stuffed animals, fossils, minerals, dinosaur bones, and birds fills the museum at 17th Street and Montgomery Avenue. The institute's Greek Revival building was designed by John McArthur, Jr., architect of City Hall.

Restaurants/Clubs: Red   **Hotels:** Blue
Shops/ 🌳 Outdoors: Green   **Sights/Culture:** Black

18 Ralph's ★$$ The room downstairs at Ralph's (pictured above) is sedate and plain, so ask to be seated upstairs in the huge hall with old-fashioned Italian murals. Try the mussels in white wine sauce, breaded veal cutlet, or spaghetti with meatballs. ♦ Italian ♦ Lunch and dinner. 760 S. Ninth St (between Catharine and Fitzwater Sts). Reservations recommended. 627.6011

19 Palumbo's Nostalgia Room ★$$$ The late **Frank Palumbo** was famous in Philadelphia for his nightclub, a hot spot in the 1960s and 1970s, where such singers as **Al Martino** performed between stints on the Atlantic City stages. Hanging lamps with orange and red fringe illuminate the dark, narrow dining room, and stucco walls peek out from behind rows of celebrity photographs. The food pays tribute to Palumbo's Southern Italian roots, with everything from eggplant parmigiana to stuffed pasta shells. The batter-dipped, deep-fried squid may be the lightest in South Philadelphia, where calamari is an everyday event. Cioppino (an Italian version of paella) combines crab, mussels, clams, shrimp, lobster, and fish in a broth with herbs and spices. ♦ Italian ♦ Lunch and dinner; dinner only on Sunday. 807 S. Ninth St (between Catharine and Christian Sts). 574.9091

20 Italian Market Scruffy and unkempt but full of life, this five-block stretch of open-air market stalls and specialty stores is the focal point of South Philadelphia's Italian neighborhood, where local residents gather to shop, gossip, and people-watch. Plucked geese and whole pigs hang in the butcher windows; fish lie wide-eyed on packs of ice; and a huge variety of olive oils, vinegars, capers, pasta, and Italian cheeses line the store shelves. The atmosphere is particularly electric around Christmas and Easter. On Friday and Saturday, the sidewalks become nearly impassable as crowds try to squeeze past the outdoor vegetable, fish, and dry-goods vendors. In winter, merchants burn their packaging materials in metal barrels to keep warm, emitting a thick, unpleasant odor, and in the sweltering summer heat, the street again becomes very fragrant—sometimes too much so. But the low prices and selection of products found nowhere else in the city draw crowds from all over Philadelphia. Even though it's legal, don't attempt to drive up Ninth Street during market hours. Local parking lots don't charge much and you can often find spaces on the streets nearby. Hours vary for the different vendors. ♦ M-Sa 9AM-5PM. S. Ninth St (from Christian St to Washington St)

21 D'Angelo Brothers Forty kinds of sausage and eight types of pâté can be found in this 79-year-old family run shop. The sausages include *boudin*, seafood, Turkey Santa Fe (turkey, cilantro, and jalapeño), and pork with spinach, pine nuts, and ricotta cheese. Run by **Sonny D'Angelo,** the store also claims to be the country's largest retail distributor of game meats, selling alligator, llama, ostrich, and 57 other kinds of exotic animals. If you *must* take home some turtle stew or buffalo chili, D'Angelo's will happily pack it up in one of

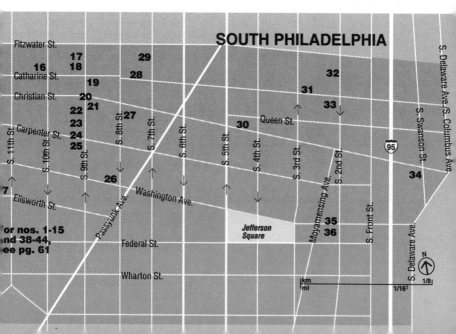

SOUTH PHILADELPHIA

Fitzwater St.
Catharine St.
Christian St.
Carpenter St.
Ellsworth St.
Washington Ave.
Federal St.
Wharton St.
Queen St.
Jefferson Square

S. 11th St
S. 10th St
S. 9th St
S. 8th St
S. 7th St
S. 6th St
S. 5th St
S. 4th St
S. 3rd St
S. 2nd St
S. Front St
S. Delaware Ave.
Passyunk Ave.
Moyamensing Ave.
S. Swanson St.
S. Delaware Ave./S. Columbus Ave

95

16 17 18 29 28 19 20 22 21 23 24 25 27 26 30 31 32 33 35 36 34

7

or nos. 1-15 and 38-44, see pg. 61

their coolers. ♦ Tu-Sa 10:30AM-6:30PM; Su 10:30AM-3:30PM. 909 S. Ninth St (between Carpenter and Christian Sts). 923.5637

22 Claudio King of Cheese Fat wheels of Parmigiano-Reggiano, oily jars of sun-dried tomatoes, slabs of prosciutto, and vats of olives fill this redolent shop. **Claudio Auriemma,** who likes to gab, doles out samples as he hacks away at his cheeses and meats. ♦ M-Sa 9AM-6PM; Su 9AM-2PM. 926 S. Ninth St (between Carpenter and Christian Sts). 627.1873

23 Villa DiRoma ★$ Everybody's "hon" to the waitresses dressed in the neighborhood's trademark black outfits in this traditional redbrick pasta joint with three plain-as-can-be dining rooms. Lasagna, cannelloni, and manicotti are mainstays, and the chicken and veal dishes come with tomato "gravies" (sauces), mozzarella, peppers, and sausages in a variety of familiar combinations. Mussels are served in a choice of an atypically thin red gravy or a white garlic sauce. The cannoli are made at a local bakery. ♦ Italian ♦ Lunch and dinner; dinner only on Monday and Sunday. 934 S. Ninth St (between Carpenter and Christian Sts). 592.1295

24 Talluto's Authentic Italian Food This all-around Italian deli sells olive oils, fresh and frozen pastas, olives, pizza, meats, and antipasti. The smoked mozzarella and the fresh cannoli—crisp shells filled with sweetened ricotta cheese and chocolate chips—are both excellent. ♦ Italian deli ♦ Tu-W, Sa 8:30AM-5PM; Th-F 8:30AM-6PM; Su 8:30AM-1PM. 944 S. Ninth St (at Carpenter St). 627.4967

25 Fante's Cookware Cooking enthusiasts may have to muster some willpower at Fante's. There's always one thing more you could use, whether it be a $250 copper pot or $3 worth of plastic cake decorations. The prices aren't discount, but the selection of kitchen gadgets, knives, pot racks, cookbooks, earthenware, and high-quality pots and pans is unbeatable. A small shop adjoining the main store peddles gourmet oils, chocolates, coffees, and spices. ♦ Tu-Sa 9AM-5:30PM; Su 9:30AM-12:30PM. 1006 S. Ninth St (between Washington Ave and Carpenter St). 922.5557

26 Tu Do ★$ The Vietnamese food, not the atmosphere, is what counts in this small, plain storefront. Good choices are the fragrant noodle soup with beef and rice, pressed shrimp with sugarcane and rice wrappers, and a main entrée of two quail stuffed with ground pork and mushrooms. The crispy *pho xao don*—panfried rice-stick noodles—is perfect. ♦ Vietnamese ♦ Lunch and dinner. Closed Tuesday. 1030 S. Eighth St (at Washington Ave). 829.9122

27 Vinh Hoa ★$ Vietnamese and Chinese cuisine are well prepared in the kitchen of this low-key restaurant, with a slight nod to the Vietnamese dishes. Asparagus and crabmeat soup, shrimp rolls, boneless duck with lemongrass and chile sauce, and whole fish fried and served with a spicy sauce are all worth a try. Hanging lamps, bamboo screens, and Vietnamese musical instruments decorate the pleasant dining room. ♦ Vietnamese/Chinese ♦ Lunch and dinner. Closed Tuesday. 746 Christian St (at S. Eighth St). 925.0307

28 Samuel S. Fleisher Art Memorial In 1898 **Samuel S. Fleisher,** a wealthy woolens manufacturer, founded a free art school called the **Graphic Sketch Club,** which he eventually moved to this unusual series of buildings (an Episcopal church, a church school, and four residential abodes). The former house of worship, designed by the architectural firm of **Frank Furness** and completed in 1886, far outshines its immediate neighbors. Modeled after a medieval Italian church, the narrow brick structure is profoundly beautiful. Fleisher purchased the church (along with the adjoining houses) in 1922, renamed it "the sanctuary," and filled it with treasures of medieval and Renaissance ecclesiastical art. The **Philadelphia Museum of Art,** which now administers the galleries and school, added to the sanctuary collection with 15th- and 16th-century European paintings and sculpture. Highlights of the collection include two large paintings by Spaniard **Pablo Vergos,** 13th- and 14th-century statues of saints, old Russian icons, a 15th-century French abbot's chair, stained-glass windows by **John LaFarge** and **Nicola D'Ascenzo,** wrought-iron gates by **Samuel Yellin,** and an altarpiece by **Violet Oakley.**

The school is still in operation, and students and faculty frequently exhibit their works here. **Louis I. Kahn** studied at Fleisher, and today a sparse lecture room by artist **Siah Armajiani** pays tribute to his ideas. Each year the museum hosts four art shows; more than 200 artists vie for the chance to exhibit their work at one of these prestigious, high-visibility events. ♦ Free. M-Th 11AM-5PM, 6:30-9:30PM; F 11AM-5PM; Sa 10AM-noon, 1-3PM. 709-721 Catharine St (between S. Eighth and S. Seventh Sts). 922.3456

29 Saloon ★★★$$$$ Dress in your finery if you want to mesh with the fur coats and finely tailored suits in this chic Italian restaurant. Super-cushy chairs, reddish walls, and oversize paintings set the mood for an innovative menu featuring veal cordon bleu stuffed with prosciutto and cheese; shrimp with wild rice in a cognac cream sauce; and clams filled with shrimp, crabmeat, and cheese. ◆ Italian ◆ Lunch and dinner; dinner only on Monday and Saturday. Closed Sunday. 750 S. Seventh St (between Catharine and Fitzwater Sts). Reservations required. 627.1811

30 Mario Lanza Museum Born **Freddie Cocozza** on Christian Street near Sixth Street, **Mario Lanza** is South Philadelphia's favorite expatriate. The singer, who died in 1959 at the age of 38, achieved fame in seven Hollywood movies, including his most famous film, *The Great Caruso,* in 1951. Lanza never gained widespread respect as a serious opera singer, but this small, homey museum in the **Settlement Music School** is a touching memorial to his aspirations. ◆ Free. M-Sa 10AM-3:30PM. 416 Queen St (between S. Fourth and S. Fifth Sts), third floor. 468.3623

31 Dmitri's ★★★$$ On any given night, a hundred or more people may descend on this tiny two-room restaurant, which seats only 25 (reservations aren't accepted). If you're up to the wait, pass the time on a bar stool at the marble counter with a view of the open kitchen. Owner-chef **Dmitri Chimes** prepares some of the best grilled fish in town, including whole baby salmon, swordfish steaks, and mackerel. The Greek *avgolemono* soup—chicken stock with lemon, egg, and rice—is excellent, as are the *baba ghanouj* and *hummus.* Bring your own wine. ◆ Seafood/Middle Eastern ◆ Dinner. 795 S. Third St (at Catharine St). 625.0556

32 La Grolla ★★$$$ Peach walls adorned with paintings of the Piedmont region set this lovely restaurant apart from the usual spaghetti joints. Chef **Giovanni Massaglia** often experiments with game, creating such dishes as venison fillet with peppercorn-mustard sauce or antelope braised with wild mushrooms. Homemade pasta, osso buco, cioppino, and a veal chop broiled with olive oil and rosemary are other possibilities. Those square crackers on the table are actually baked pasta. ◆ Italian ◆ Dinner. Closed Sunday. 782 S. Second St (between Fitzwater and Catharine Sts). Reservations recommended. 627.7701

33 Walt's ★$$ Crab comes deviled, steamed Baltimore-style, fried, or stuffed into two jumbo fried shrimp at this plain but bustling restaurant. The decor in the two dining rooms consists of standard-issue tables and simple wooden chairs. ◆ Seafood ◆ Lunch and dinner; lunch starting at 1PM on Sunday. 804 S. Second St (at Catharine St). 339.9124

34 Gloria Dei (Old Swedes' Church) Swedish Lutherans first settled what is now Philadelphia—not English Quakers, as is commonly assumed. The Swedes built a simple log church on this site in 1643, and replaced it with this brick structure (illustrated above) in 1700. With its white steeple, classical gables, and steep roof, it resembles colonial churches built by British settlers more than the earliest log architecture of the Swedes. Today the church and its quiet graveyard—where **Johan Printz,** governor of the New Sweden colony, is buried—seem out of place along this industrialized section of the Delaware River. Old Swedes' became an Episcopal church after the American Revolution, when Sweden cut off aid to its churches in the former colonies. ◆ M-F by appointment only; Sa-Su 9AM-5PM. 916 S. Swanson St (between Columbus Blvd and Christian St). 389.1513

35 Snockey's $$ You'll know the instant you walk in that this oyster bar—around, in various locations, since 1912—is no-frills South Philly. Maybe it's the linoleum brickwork on the walls and the little red lobster prints on the white curtains. Ask to be seated in the front room, where you can watch the shucking at the raw bar, rather than in the main dining room in back. Most of the seafood is breaded or fried, so lighten it up with an appetizer from the raw bar. A typical dinner is the seafood combo platter, with a deviled clam, fried scallops, fried oysters, a fried flounder fillet, cole slaw, and french fries. ◆ Seafood ◆ Lunch and dinner; dinner only on Sunday. 1020 S. Second St (at Washington Ave). 339.9578

Philadelphia's first major labor strike occurred in 1903 when 100,000 textile workers—including 10,000 children—refused to work until guaranteed a 55-hour week. The strike failed but successfully dramatized the plight of child laborers.

British rocker David Bowie, one of the many artists attracted to the Philadelphia scene, recorded portions of his 1975 "Young Americans" album at Sigma Studios on 12th Street.

36 Mummers Museum The annual **Mummers Parade,** which takes place New Year's Day, is Philadelphia's Mardi Gras, when thousands of working-class citizens draped in elaborate costumes made of feathers and sequins strut down Broad Street to the sound of tinny string music. Crowds stationed on the sidewalks shout and heckle—and drink a fair amount of beer. Discussing the pagan roots of Mummery, Temple University Professor **Morris J. Vogel** writes: "We can imagine the despair of primitive European peoples as autumn and winter brought ever less daylight, ever colder temperatures, fewer nuts and berries to gather, and fewer animals to hunt." At today's glitzy, televised Mummers Parade, however, thoughts of "nuts and berries" inevitably get lost in the revelry.

This museum, designed by **Veland and Junker** and completed in 1976, has two floors filled with items related to Mummers.

In one particularly eerie room, mannequins model prize-winning costumes made over the years. A large digital clock ticks away the time remaining until New Year's Day, and plaques and photographs memorialize some of South Philadelphia's champions, such as the late **Mayor Frank Rizzo.** Stringed band concerts entertain weekly in the parking lot from May to September. ♦ Admission. Tu-Sa 9:30AM-5PM; Su noon-5PM. S. Second St and Washington Ave. 336.3050

37 Felicia's ★★$$$ Pictures of the Old Country brighten the main dining room of this row-house Italian restaurant, where the versatile kitchen turns out calamari sautéed with olives, capers, and fresh tomato; strip steak with brandy, marsala, cream, and black peppercorn; grilled veal chop; and a fresh fish of the day. ♦ Italian ♦ Lunch and dinner; dinner only on Saturday and Sunday. Closed Monday. 1148 S. 11th St (at Ellsworth St). Reservations recommended. 755.9656

Mummer's the Word

Every New Year's Day, some 25,000 sequined, feathered, face-painted, banjo-playing men (plus a handful of women and children) dance and strut along a two-mile stretch of South Broad Street. These colorful characters (known as **Mummers**) make their way up the urban boulevard to the hoots and hollers of dense, boisterous crowds.

The **Mummers Parade,** an official city function since 1901, has been called the oldest continuous folk festival in the United States. "Mumme" is a German word for mask, thus a Mummer is one who disguises or masquerades. Whether the Mummers tradition originated from **English Mummery Plays** (an early form of burlesque featuring harlequins dressed in silk and satin) or from a Swedish and Finnish custom of roaming bands of merrymakers who observed "Second Christmas" remains unclear. In the 1700s, Philadelphia's first Mummers wandered the city on New Year's Eve, and at midnight shot pistols; they were nicknamed Shooters at the time. The bands became larger (and cut out the gunshot salute) in the 1850s, parading around the lower part of the city as far as Market Street by 1876. Eventually Broad Street from South Philadelphia to City Hall became the official site of the Mummers Parade.

Unless you've seen it firsthand, the Mummers' strut is hard to visualize (try to imagine a kind of high-stepping, arm-flapping walk). It probably evolved from the **Cakewalk,** a popular late 19th-century dance. The Mummers march to music produced by bands made up of (and limited to) accordions, saxophones, drums, violins, banjos, bass fiddles, glockenspiels, and clarinets—a tinny sound that some people find grating and others rousing.

The Mummers (who come from clubs representing different neighborhoods) devote a full 12 months to practicing the music, devising the routines, and, most importantly, designing and creating the costumes (elaborate productions of sequins, dyed feathers, lamé, and mirrors). One of the remarkable feats of the Mummers is that they manage to move at all in these getups, let alone march for hours. A typical costume worn by a string-band member weighs 150 pounds and consists of a steel-rod frame covered with cardboard, fabric, and gaudy ornaments. Each costume includes hundreds of ostrich feathers, which the Mummers buy for about $50 a dozen.

Four divisions of Mummers trek down Broad Street: **Comic, Fancy, String,** and **Fancy Brigade.** The Comic Division (a.k.a. the Clowns), which steps off first, specializes in first-class, unadorned strutting. They precede the more disciplined Fancies, who in turn are followed by the String Division, the true stars of the parade. Every year each string band picks a different theme for its five-minute routine. It could be a Broadway show, say *The Sound of Music;* a fairy tale; or a concept, maybe pirates or savages. Bands perform their routines at various intervals along Broad Street and again before the judging stand at City Hall, where they compete for modest prizes. Like the Fancy Brigade, a division with elaborate choreographed routines, the string bands have 55 members each.

The parade starts at 7AM and has been known to last well over 12 hours, a bit much unless you're a true Mummerphile. If you're averse to the cold (or to hard-drinking crowds), you can always watch the antics on television. Better yet, catch a live performance; the string bands stage concerts at the **Civic Center** every spring and in the **Mummers Museum** parking lot a few months later.

38 Victor Cafe ★★★$$$ Waiters break into song at regular intervals in this special restaurant, founded in 1925 by the late **John DiStefano** and named after the recording company. (A replica of the RCA Victor mascot, **Nipper,** stands guard above the door.) Starched linens cover the tables, pictures of opera greats hang from the walls, and a back room houses a collection of 20,000 records. This is how it works: recorded opera music plays until a waiter rings a little bell; then a record starts—perhaps an old show tune, more likely an aria—and the waiter begins to sing. The scene is repeated every 15 minutes or so. Most of the performing waiters are opera students or professionals between contracts. All the hoopla might seem hokey if the food wasn't worthy of applause. Now run by the third generation of DiStefanos, the kitchen prepares outstanding fettuccine with cream, smoked salmon, vodka, and red caviar; lamb chops with artichokes and capers; and spaghetti with prosciutto and mozzarella. ♦ Italian ♦ Dinner. 1303 Dickinson St (between S. 13th and Broad Sts). Reservations recommended. 468.3040

39 Frankie's Seafood Italiano ★$$$ Blue-lit coves in the walls, plastic fish hanging from the ceiling, and blond-wood tables with Italian money underneath the varnish carry out Frankie's Italian seafaring motif. Try the steamed seafood combination, a mix of shrimp, clams, and mussels in red gravy or white wine sauce (the better choice). Veal wrapped in prosciutto and cooked in red wine, rosemary, and garlic, and filet mignon stuffed with shrimp are other possibilities. ♦ Italian ♦ Lunch and dinner; dinner only on Saturday and Sunday. Closed Monday. 11th and Tasker Sts. 468.9989

In February 1968, only a few months after the Spectrum sports arena opened in South Philadelphia, the roof blew off in a fierce windstorm. Two weeks later, it blew off again.

In 1961, the Phillies baseball team boasted the longest losing streak on record—23 games.

Philadelphia used to be a very quiet town on Sundays. Before the 1930s, baseball, football, fishing, movies, plays, orchestral performances, and shopping were all illegal on Sunday. The Blue Law statute, passed by the Pennsylvania legislature in 1794, forbade "any wordly employment or business whatsoever on the Lord's Day." The penalty for violation was six days in jail. Most of the prohibitions gradually were repealed, though one Blue Law is still in force: all liquor stores close on Sunday.

Restaurants/Clubs: Red   Hotels: Blue
Shops/ ♠ Outdoors: Green   Sights/Culture: Black

40 Caruso ★$$ Indulge in homemade pasta while you relax in a cross between a comfy living room and a 1950s rec room. Regulars favor Caruso for its Northern Italian cream, wine, and tomato sauces. Try the pasta sampler, which may include penne in cheese sauce and spinach-stuffed shells. The mixed grill comes with lamb, veal, pork, and chicken. ♦ Italian ♦ Dinner. Closed Monday. 1533 S. 11th St (at Tasker St). Reservations recommended. 755.8886

41 East Tasker Cafe ★$$ Owned and operated by the same family since 1919, this trattoria has a chummy bar and all the South Philly mainstays: ravioli, spaghetti with meatballs, ziti with broccoli, mussels marinara, and shrimp scampi. Calamari rings, mozzarella sticks, and chicken fingers round out the menu. ♦ Italian ♦ Lunch and dinner. Closed Sunday. 1601 S. 10th St (at Tasker St). 339.8605

42 Marra's ★$ Philadelphia's first pizzeria now serves veal, chicken, and pasta in every Southern Italian variation, but stick with the pizza. Ease into one of the old red upholstered booths, ask for the Marra Special, and sit back and anticipate the classic, thin South Philly pie with mushrooms, pepperoni, and roasted peppers. Take a look at the oven in the foyer, made with bricks brought from Naples 70 years ago. South Philly lore has it that the bricks get hotter than their American counterparts. ♦ Italian ♦ Lunch and dinner; dinner only on Saturday and Sunday. Closed Monday. 1734 E. Passyunk Ave (between S. 12th and S. 13th Sts). 339.9042

43 Royal Villa Cafe ★★$$ The home cooking in this dark row-house taverna is well worth traveling just a few blocks south of the beaten path. Recommended dishes are the pastas with Southern Italian tomato gravy; veal Sorrento in a sharp medium-brown gravy with spinach and mushrooms; and an unusual boneless capon stuffed with mozzarella cheese and prosciutto. ♦ Italian ♦ Lunch and dinner. 1700 Jackson St (between Wolf St and Passyunk Ave). 462.4488

44 Sports Complex At the far end of South Philadelphia, the residential streets empty into sports fan heaven, site of both **Veterans Stadium** and the indoor **Spectrum.** The Sports Complex is easy to reach. It's right off Interstate 95 and the Schuylkill Expressway exits and within walking distance of the Pattison Avenue Subway Station. Both "the Vet" and the Spectrum are used year-round. ♦ S. Broad St and Pattison Ave

Within the Sports Complex:

Veterans Stadium On game nights, the Vet lights up the sky, and the raucous shouts and applause of the crowd thunder through the nearby neighborhood. Opened in 1971 and designed by **George Ewing Co., Stonorov and Haws,** and **Hugh Stubbins, Jr.,** Veterans Stadium is home to the **Phillies** baseball team and the **Eagles** of the National Football League, as well as the **Temple University** football team and the annual **Army-Navy** game. Though it lacks the charm of Franklin Field at the University of Pennsylvania or the old Connie Mack Stadium, the Vet does offer 60,000 colorful seats, flashy scoreboards, clear sight lines, artificial turf, and plenty of parking spaces. Still, Philadelphia baseball fans look enviously at Boston's venerable Fenway Park and Camden Yards, the new old-style stadium in Baltimore. The city and team ownership have discussed building another stadium, but funding is always a problem.

Philadelphia's sports teams are enormously popular: the Phillies can count on drawing more than two million fans a season, and the Eagles sell out almost every game. Since most Eagles seats are held by season-ticket holders, the best you can hope for on game days are seats near the end zones or in the upper reaches of the stadium. While the Phillies pull in a great crowd, they rarely sell out, so it's usually possible to buy tickets at the gate. Try either to eat before you get to the Vet or to bring something along—the food is stadium-bad and stadium-priced. The guards will confiscate alcoholic beverages brought from outside, however, so buy your beer from the concessions. A word about seating: the section numbers increase with the levels, which means the 100 and 200 sections put you close to the field. For the most part, avoid the 700 level unless you're not afraid of heights. The best seats for baseball games are near Gates A, B (at home plate), and C. For football, Gates E and A are at midfield. Gate ▮ near the left-field foul pole for baseball and t▮ end zone for football, does hold a special attraction: from the 700 level, you get a magnificent view of the Center City skyline. ♦ Phillies box office M-F 9AM-8PM; Eagles box office M-F 9AM-5PM. 3501 S. Broad St. Phillies box office 463.1000; Eagles box offi▮ 463.5500

Spectrum Built in 1967, Philadelphia's mo▮ versatile and oft-used arena is home to both the **Philadelphia 76ers** of the National Basketball Association and the **Philadelphia Flyers** of the National Hockey League. Some 300 other events are held here each year as well, including the **Ringling Brothers Barnu▮ & Bailey Circus, Disney on Ice,** and the **U.S. Pro Indoor Tennis Tournament.** The Spectrum, designed by **Skidmore Owings and Merrill,** is considerably smaller than the Vet, with seating broken down into far fewer sections. Lettered seats are near rink and court levels, sections 1 to 40 are in the next level, and 41 to 80 in the highest level. Whether you're watching the Sixers shoot hoops or the Flyers play hockey, Sections G and T put you at center court and center ice. Tickets can almost always be purchased on game days.

While the Spectrum is in far better shape tha▮ say, the Boston Garden, the Flyers and Sixer▮ plan to move into a brand-new arena at the nearby site of the demolished **JFK Stadium. Spectrum II,** as it is called, will be connected to the Spectrum by a tunnel and will seat mo▮ than 20,000, compared with about 18,000 a▮ the Spectrum. ♦ Box office M-F 9AM-6PM; Sa-Su 10AM-4:30PM. Pattison Pl (at S. Broa▮ St). General information 336.3600. 76ers 339.7676

Betsy Z. Cohen
Chairman/CEO, Jefferson Bank

Feast on focaccia bread at **La Verandah** while tankers and tugs float by on the Delaware River. And then, for a true maritime experience, catch the ferry to the **New Jersey State Aquarium.** At night, you can check the color of the aquarium dome for a weather forecast: blue means clear skies, red is for rain, purple warns of approaching thunderstorms. Another great sight: the **Benjamin Franklin Bridge** at night, when crossing trains trigger a dramatic display of lights in motion.

Jog or bike the **Schuylkill River Bike Path,** a leisurely 22-mile ride to **Valley Forge Historic National Park.** Serious bikers can challenge the famous uphill **Manayunk Wall** along the way, or coast downhill just for fun.

Pretend you're in Paris at Le Bec Fin's **Bar Lyonnais,** chef **Georges Perrier's** private oasis—classy and intimate.

Eating a **soft pretzel** on the steps of the **Philadelph▮ Museum of Art.** Sure, you can eat them all over the city, but a pretzel here is a masterpiece. Of course, don't miss the museum.

There must be a hundred Italian restaurants in Sou▮ Philadelphia, but for me, there's only **Felicia,** serving real Italian food, South Philadelphia-style. For the best Jewish-Italian cuisine outside of New York or Rome, try **Tiramisu.** And when other restaurateurs go out to eat, they go to **Dmitri's.** Opera buffs will love **Victor Cafe,** where the waiters sing for your supper.

For the classic Philadelphia-at-night postcard photograph, position yourself on **West River Drive** opposite the silhouetted houses of **Boathouse Row** Imagine Philadelphian **Jack Kelly,** world-class rower, taking daughter **Grace** out for a ride on the Schuylkill River.

Reading Terminal Market, for the freshest produc▮ and poultry in Philadelphia and an eclectic collectio▮ of take-out food. Don't miss the breads at **Le Bus.**

e's Peking Duck—lots of Chinese restaurants
ve ducks in the window, but Philadelphians know
at Joe's are the best. It's one of those secrets that
erybody shares.

r the best seats in the house, attend a Friday
ernoon rehearsal of the **Philadelphia
chestra**—music in the making.

end a country day in historic **Chester County.**
ter the **Brandywine Museum,** visit **Longwood
rdens** for the orchids and the acres of other
wers and landscaping. In summer, stay for
ening concerts and Longwood's spectacular
untain-light show. Bring a blanket and a basket.

even Izenour

nior Associate/Architect, Venturi, Scott Brown
d Associates, Inc.

nnsylvania Academy of the Fine Arts—Frank
rness' great museum, particularly the stairhall.

e **Furness Building** at Penn—restoration of one
the great 19th-century spaces in America.

FS Building—one of the first modern
yscrapers in America.

ading Terminal Market—the pluralistic,
stronomic, and social experience in Philadelphia.

e **Schuylkill River Bike Path** starts at the
iladelphia Museum of Art and goes to **Valley
rge Historic National Park,** passing through
irmount Park; Main Street, Manayunk; and
nshohocken. This 22-mile trail touches upon
e geological, industrial, and social history of
th- and 19th-century industrial Philadelphia.
great ride!

ain Street in **Manayunk**—the new South Street for
iddle-aged suburban Philadelphians.

dy Wicks

mmunity Activist/Owner, White Dog Cafe

eeing an art exhibit at **Taller Puertorriqueno,** the
erto Rican cultural center, then walking up **"El
oque de Oro"** (The Golden Block) to Fifth and
merset streets for a dinner of roast pork, beans
d rice, fried plantains, and coconut pudding at **El
hio.** Afterward, it's across the street to
aymond's Night Club for dancing to salsa and
erengue.

ding my bike along **East** and **West River Drive,**
pecially in the spring when the fruit trees along
e river and the azaleas behind the **Philadelphia
useum of Art** are in bloom, and the scullers from
athouse Row are out on the water. Be sure to
op by the sculpture of three horn-blowing angels,
th geese often gathered below.

nch on the porch of **Valley Green Inn,** watching
e parade of joggers, dog walkers, and bicyclists
ss along the Wissahickon Creek trail.

n Saturday nights, eating clams and drinking beer
hile listening to the love songs of the toothless
ad singer in the old men's band at the **Triangle
vern** in South Philly.

Enjoying a home-style dinner at **Daffodil's** in North
Philadelphia, then walking around the corner to see a
performance at **Freedom Theatre,** America's oldest
black theater.

Breakfast at the **Fountain Room** in the Four Seasons
Hotel with a window seat looking out at the **Swann
Memorial Fountain** in Logan Square. The branches
of the catalpa trees, adorned with purple flowers in
the spring, encircle the fountain, and immaculate
flower gardens, which change with the seasons,
skirt the base.

Watching the polar bears underwater in the
Philadelphia Zoo. You can see right into their
mouths, inches from their big teeth, when they dive
into the water from the rocks and swim up to the
glass.

The live oak charcoal grill set right on the table at
Kim's Korean, where you cook beef and vegetables
and wrap them in lettuce leaves with spicy
condiments. Next door there's a store of Korean
goods, including excellent music and books.

Shopping and eating and eating and shopping at
the **Reading Terminal Market** on Saturday. All of
the food here is at its best, including the big ripe
vegetables at the produce stands, homemade
pretzels at the Amish booth, fresh crab sandwiches
at **Coastal Cave Trading Company,** grilled chicken
at **Fireworks,** and rich ice cream at the **Bassetts**
counter.

A driving tour of Philadelphia's outstanding
community wall murals, including the *Tribute to
Diego Rivera* at 17th and Wallace streets; the
African-American family farmers at 22nd and
Dauphin streets, with community garden plots at
its base; the powerful story of Philadelphia's
immigrants at Second and Callowhill streets; and
the *Boy with Raised Arm* at 40th Street and Powelton
Avenue, with a Walt Whitman quote, "I am large, I
contain multitudes." While you're at this last stop,
get your wheels cleaned in front of the mural at
House of Clowns car wash, which supports area
youth projects.

Riding the **water taxi** up and down the Delaware
River, stopping for Japanese food at **Meiji-in,**
dancing to reggae at **Katmandu,** and sometimes
taking a trip across the river to the **New Jersey State
Aquarium.**

Getting dizzy from the nosedive aerial shots of the
city in *Philadelphia Anthem* at the **Omniverse
Theatre** in the Franklin Institute. The four-story
wraparound screen there is the biggest in the world,
and the sound quality is incredible, especially when
the gospel singers burst forth and the Mummers'
band goes by.

On George Washington's birthday in 1861,
President-elect Abraham Lincoln made a speech
from the balcony of the Continental Hotel in
Philadelphia. "There is no need of bloodshed or
war," he said. That same year, the Civil War
began.

Center City West

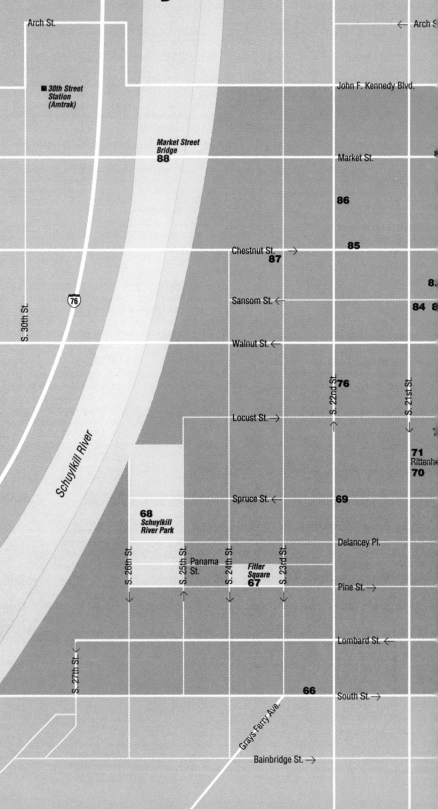

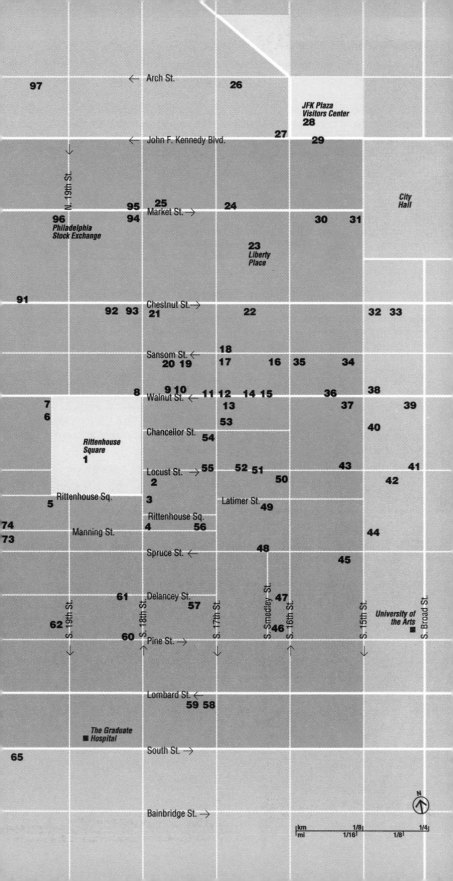

The engines of investment and commerce roar from on high in the sleek glass towers of Center City West, the city's principal downtown core and site of the **Philadelphia Stock Exchange.** A fashionable residential area in the 19th century and a stronghold of investment houses and banks in the early 20th century, Center City West's skyline was transformed with the 1987 construction of the $225 million, 60-story **Liberty Place** skyscraper (home to **The Shops at Liberty Place** and **The Ritz-Carlton** hotel).

On weekdays **Chestnut Street** and the main thoroughfares of **Market Street** and **John F. Kennedy Boulevard** teem with businesspeople scurrying to and from their high-rise offices. Retail outlets stand shoulder to shoulder with little boutiques, hobby shops, great restaurants, and smart cafes in the stylish area south of Chestnut Street. Farther down, on **South Street,** distinctive town houses (hardly changed since the 1890s) dominate the shady streets. Some of the city's finest shops are located along **Walnut Street** between **Rittenhouse Square** and **Broad Street,** drawing an older, well-heeled clientele, while chic urbanites frequent the specialty shops that appear on the numbered cross streets and on narrow **Sansom Street.** Rittenhouse Square, a well-landscaped island of civility, is the most inviting public space in Philadelphia and the site of art exhibitions and flower shows. World-renowned Philadelphia architects **Frank Furness** and **John Notman** built many of the neighborhood's fine homes. Even subdivided into apartments, these brownstone or brick structures retain their character and originality. Also on these tree-lined streets are art galleries and several of the city's most unusual museums: the **Rosenbach Museum and Library,** with its priceless collection of literary manuscripts and first editions; **The Mütter Museum,** a wealth of medical exotica; and **The Civil War Library and Museum,** which displays some lesser-known war memorabilia.

Except for restaurants, theaters, and a few outposts of commerce, Center City West above Walnut Street shuts down at night, essentially clearing the street of people. However, the Rittenhouse Square area and nearby Pine and Spruce streets remain lively and safe, particularly in the warmer months. The faded first-run movie theaters on Chestnut Street, which cater to rambunctious adolescents, show slick Hollywood fare (if you attend a late-night show, expect to be frisked at the door by security guards) while the neighborhood's sole remaining art house, **The Roxy Theatre,** screens more sophisticated films.

1 Rittenhouse Square The most beloved of the five city squares laid out by **William Penn** and **Surveyor-General Thomas Holme** originally served as a pasture for stray cows, pigs, and chickens. Then the neighborhood's mid-19th century gentrification bestowed it with great Victorian mansions. Now stately apartment buildings frame the square, which boasts a children's wading pool, wooden benches, overarching trees, and fine statuary. It's a perfect place to enjoy a sandwich and a cold drink, but refrain from bringing a beer: the park police strictly enforce the no-alcohol rule.

Much of the park's intimate ambience is due to **Paul Philippe Cret,** founder of the famous architecture school at the University of Pennsylvania, whose designs for the small wading pool, central plaza, and entrances, reminiscent of European parks with fountains and statuary, were completed in 1913. The square (originally called **Southwest Square**) is named after 18th-century Philadelphia astronomer and mathematician **David Rittenhouse.** (His orrery, a clocklike device that describes the positions of the planets as they orbit around the sun, is displayed at the **Van Pelt Library** on the University of Pennsylvania campus.) People are always milling about in Rittenhouse Square, whether it be office workers on a break, shoppers resting their feet, or the elderly ladies who live in nearby apartments, out with their nurse's aides for a breath of fresh air. Whatever the current ills of the city, you're reasonably safe walking through here any time of the day or night.

On the west side of the square by Locust Street, parents of young children have staked out the "nursing circle": infants nap under the trees and toddlers stretch their legs under the watchful gaze of *Billy* (1914), the goat statue by Philadelphia sculptor **Albert Laessle.** The classically sculpted *Duck Girl* (1911) presiding over the fun at the wading pool is by **Paul Manship,** a leading American sculptor of the first half of this century, who also created the *Aero Memorial* outside the Franklin Institute. In the center of the square is *Lion Crushing a Serpent* by French sculptor **Antoine Louis Barye,** who cast the statue in 1832 as a commentary on the triumph of monarchy over the rabble of democracy (it was installed in 1892). In a less symbolic pose crouches **Cornelia Van A. Chapin's** stone carving *Giant Frog* (1941). At the entrance, two nymphs hoist a sundial as a *Tribute to Evelyn Taylor Price* (1947), the community leader who helped beautify the square between 1916 and 1946. **Beatrice Fenton,** graduate of the Pennsylvania Academy of the Fine Arts and friend of famous painter **Thomas Eakins,** sculpted the classical bronze figures, which contrast nicely with the Art Deco-ish base beneath them. ♦ Bounded by S. 18th, S. 19th, Walnut, and Locust Sts

2 The Curtis Institute of Music What better place to study the world's great composers than under the frescoed and carved wood ceilings of these dignified buildings? **Mary Louise Curtis Bok,** daughter of *Saturday Evening Post* publisher **Cyrus Curtis,** founded the music school, which, since 1924, has counted **Leonard Bernstein, Samuel Barber, Anna Moffo,** and **Peter Serkin** among its alumni. On summer nights, students sometimes serenade Rittenhouse Square from the windows on the upper floors of the main building. Music lovers can listen to the students more regularly at free recitals held three nights a week during the school year in the institute's **Curtis Hall.** (The hall also is used for faculty recitals, chamber music concerts, and occasional rehearsals of the **Curtis Symphony Orchestra.**) The three buildings that make up the institute were once four private houses built at the turn of this century; the main building, for instance, was a mansion designed by **Peabody & Stearns** in 1893 for banker **George Childs Drexel.** The firm of **Cope and Stewardson** constructed the house at 1718 Locust Street in 1903, and **Horace Trumbauer** designed **Knapp Hall,** where you'll find the library, in 1908. ♦ Free. Recitals M, W, F 8PM. 1726 Locust St (at S. 18th St). 893.5261

3 The Barclay Hotel $$ Dark wood paneling, an enormous tripartite gilt mirror, marble tables with fresh flowers, and crystal chandeliers decorate the intimate lobby, harking back to a time when the Barclay was one of the fanciest places in town. Famous authors and celebrities used to stay here on their stops in town—**Eugene Ormandy,** the famous conductor, lived in one of the posh upper-floor apartments—and the ballroom saw many a lavish debutante party and wedding reception.

An ever-ready porter stands at attention outside the revolving door of the hotel (designed by prominent local architect **Frank Watson** and completed in 1929), and many of the 240 rooms have four-poster beds and genuine antiques. No hotel in Philadelphia can boast a better location, directly across from Rittenhouse Square, in a very walkable neighborhood filled with shops, restaurants, and museums. A number of the rooms feature views over the square. The Barclay also offers some unbelievable deals. On weekends, a double room with breakfast costs as little as $68. Complimentary breakfast is included in the rates. ♦ 237 S. 18th St (between Locust and Spruce Sts). 545.0300, 800/421.6662; fax 545.2896

Within The Barclay Hotel:

Le Beau Lieu ★$$$ Could this opulent dining room actually have cheesesteaks and turkey clubs on its menu? Ostrich plumes in white urns, velveteen drapes and banquettes, chandeliers, and a maître d' in jacket and tie suggest the restaurant is more exceptional than it really is. In addition to sandwiches, there's New York strip steak, grilled lamb chops with mustard sauce, and broiled salmon with lemon butter. ♦ American ♦ Breakfast, lunch, and dinner. 545.0300

Lobby Bar With Oriental wall hangings, tiny black tables, and extremely low lighting, the Lobby Bar is a romantic place for a drink. A pianist entertains here three nights a week. ♦ M-Th, Su noon-midnight; F-Sa noon-2AM. Piano music: W 8PM-midnight; F-Sa 8PM-2AM. 545.0300

Creative Artists Network (CAN) The co-op presents group shows of artists who have an established body of work but haven't been discovered by a gallery—yet. CAN's prices usually run significantly lower than the tags at conventional galleries. ♦ M-F 9AM-5PM. Suite 3-A. 546.7775

staurants/Clubs: Red   **Hotels:** Blue
ops/ ♣ **Outdoors:** Green   **Sights/Culture:** Black

4 Philadelphia Art Alliance Ornate granite columns flank the entranceway of the Rittenhouse Square mansion, built in 1906 for **Samuel Price Wetherill. Frank Miles Day,** an architect known for buildings at Princeton and Yale universities, designed the house, which the Art Alliance purchased in 1926 to serve as a place for all the muses (according to its 1915 charter), with art exhibitions, concerts, and readings. **R. Tait McKenzie's** terracotta bas-relief of the alliance's founder, **Christine Wetherill Stevenson,** enlivens the arch above the dining-room door. The outdoor garden is open in the summer. ♦ Free. M-F 11AM-5:30PM; Sa noon-5PM; Su noon-4PM. 251 S. 18th St (between Locust and Spruce Sts). 545.4305

Within the Philadelphia Art Alliance:

The Cafe $ Pop in for a light lunch—Greek salad, pasta primavera, and ham-and-cheese sandwiches—after viewing the exhibits in the building. ♦ American ♦ Lunch. Closed Saturday and Sunday. 545.4305

5 Philadelphia Ethical Society Sunday morning talks on a variety of topics are held in this center for humanism. Evening courses are offered as well. ♦ 1906 S. Rittenhouse Sq (between S. 19th and S. 20th Sts). 735.3456

6 The Rittenhouse Hotel $$$$ **Alexander Cassatt,** president of the Pennsylvania Railroad and brother of early 20th century impressionist painter **Mary Cassatt,** lived in the house that once occupied the site of this deluxe hotel and condominium tower, designed by **Alesker, Reiff and Dundon.** The Rittenhouse project was begun in the early 1970s, but the development stalled, leaving the white, horizontal ziggurat designed by local architect **Don Reiff** an empty shell for seven years. With time and good maintenance, The Rittenhouse has found its place among the square's other mammoth apartment towers, and ranks as the best place to stay in this part of the city. The hotel's 98 spacious guest rooms occupy the 33-story building's first nine floors. Each has two floor-to-ceiling windows overlooking either the square or the city's west side.

Out-of-town stars frequently stay here (**Denzel Washington** and **Tom Hanks** called The Rittenhouse home while shooting **Jonathan Demme's** film *Philadelphia*). **Topper's Spa,** with an indoor pool and fitness machines, is open to guests (fee on weekdays, no charge on weekends). Works by local artists are showcased throughout the building, and each floor has a Philadelphia scene by painter **Dan Cavaliere.** The hotel goes out of its way to welcome children, with kid-oriented events and family packages. ♦ 210 W. Rittenhouse Sq (between Walnut and Locust Sts). 546.9000, 800/635.1042; fax 546.9858

Within The Rittenhouse Hotel:

Restaurant 210 ★★★$$$$ A curved marble staircase with brass railings leads to the hotel's luxury dining room, where floor-to-ceiling windows almost make Rittenhouse Square a fixture of the plush, airy space. The pricey menu features such innovative dishes as free-range pheasant with a shiitake and mustard-seed waffle; medaillons of Texas antelope with a sweet corn and sage strudel; and veal chop with roasted elephant garlic. ♦ Contemporary Continental ♦ Lunch and dinner; dinner only on Saturday. Closed Sunday. Reservations recommended. 790.2534

TreeTops ★★★$$$ Most of the art on the walls—except the four antique temple carvings from the Lombok Islands of Indonesia—is by local artists, including a watercolor of the Italian Market in Philadelphia. The eclectic menu includes lamb chops grilled with ratatouille orzo; a mixed grill of marinated chicken breast, apple and chicken sausage, and smoked duck breast; and turkey steak with wild mushrooms. There's an additional seafood menu on Friday and Saturday nights. Try to get a seat on the bottom deck by the windows. ♦ American ♦ Breakfast, lunch, and dinner; dinner only on Saturday and Sunday. Reservations recommended. 790.2533

Cassatt Lounge ★★$$ Right off the lobby, this delightful tearoom looks onto a courtyard with outdoor furniture and pastel garden murals. The dramatic walls of the Holy Trinity Church next door add further interest to the scene. Afternoon tea includes tomato-and-arugula finger sandwiches, smoked salmon on Viennese bread, and citrus scones. ♦ Tea ♦ Afternoon tea, cocktails, and desserts. 546.9000

Boathouse Row Bar This upscale pub adorned with Schuylkill River rowing memorabilia, including a scull owned by Olympic star **Jack Kelly,** brother of the late **Princess Grace,** also serves light food. ♦ M-F, Su 11:30AM-11:30PM; Sa 11:30AM-2AM. 546.9000

Nan Duskin A tony, expensive, women's clothing store, Nan Duskin has been an arbiter of good taste on Rittenhouse Square for more than 65 years. When the shop moved here from 18th and Walnut streets several years ago, it became a more forbidding place, tucked into the corner of the glamorous Rittenhouse Hotel. But don't be intimidated: there's no law against looking. Boutiques of **Armani, Chanel, Yves St. Laurent,** and **Valentino,** along with racks of ready-to-wear clothing by high-end designers such as **Joan Vass, Byron Lars, Todd Oldham, Gemma Kahn**, and **Emmanuel** provide material for your imagination if not for your closet. Perfumes, jewelry, exquisite shoes, handbags, delicate housewares, men's shirts and ties, and stationery are also available. ◆ M-Tu, Th-Sa 10AM-6PM; W 10AM-8PM. 735.6400. Also at: 508 Lancaster Ave, Strafford. 688.6816

7 Holy Trinity Church Scottish-born architect **John Notman,** whose mark is on some of Philadelphia's prettiest churches, including **St. Mark's** on Locust Street and **St. Clement's** on Cherry Street, designed this Romanesque Revival brownstone, which opened as an Episcopal Church in 1859. Philadelphia architect **George W. Hewitt** completed the tower in 1868, the same year the church's rector, **Phillips Brooks,** composed "O Little Town of Bethlehem." ◆ Services Su 8:30AM, 11AM; Th 12:15PM. 1904 Walnut St (between S. 19th and S. 20th Sts). 567.1267

8 Urban Outfitters Now occupied by a street-smart clothing store, this former home of Drexel heiress **Sara Drexel Fell** and **Alexander Van Rensselaer** is a Beaux Arts standout, with columns, projecting bays, and a panelled dome at the top of the grand winding staircase. The best-preserved part of the **Peabody & Sterns** building, completed in 1898, is the **Doges Room** on the first floor, the mansion's former dining room. Mrs. Van Rensselaer, born a Quaker, converted to Catholicism and decorated accordingly: the ceiling portraits include four popes and several Venetian magistrates surrounded by festoons, anthemia, and cartouches. Men's clothing can be found on the second floor, and hip housewares in the basement. ◆ M-Sa 10AM-8PM; Su noon-6PM. 1801 Walnut St (at S. 18th St). 569.3131

9 Borders Can a single store change a city? It must be possible, because no one can recall what Philadelphia was like before this small chain of big bookstores opened its Walnut Street doors in 1990. Ground zero for ultracool literati types, Borders reinvigorated the entire Rittenhouse Square area, even inspiring other booksellers in the neighborhood. In addition to selling new publications on all subjects, this is a place to meet other readers, sip coffee (at the espresso bar upstairs), and fantasize about the novels you'd read if you only had the time.

The espresso bar offers a full range of coffees, teas, exotic soft drinks, scones, dipping biscuits, and other sophisticated desserts. In the basement, a comfy children's department invites young readers (and their parents) to sprawl in the aisles. Borders is a stop on the book-tour circuit, with author readings several times a week, and a children's hour every Saturday. Most author readings of adult books start at 7:30PM on the second floor; come early if you want a seat. ◆ M-F 7AM-10PM; Sa 9AM-9PM; Su 11AM-7PM. 1727 Walnut St (between S. 17th and S. 18th Sts). 568.7400. Also at: 1149 Lancaster Ave, Bryn Mawr. 527.1500; 515 Rte 73 South, Marlton. 609/985.5080; Springfield Square Shopping Center, Baltimore Pike, Springfield (Delaware County). 543.8588

10 Helen Drutt Gallery Owner **Helen Drutt** has helped elevate such crafts as ceramics, textiles, and jewelry to fine art. Her prestigious gallery features prominent artists such as goldsmith and painter **Breon O'Casey** and **Rudolf Staffel,** who specializes in translucent porcelain vessels. ◆ W-F 11AM-5PM; Sa 10AM-3PM, or by appointment. 1721 Walnut St (between S. 17th and S. 18th Sts). 735.1625

11 The Nature Company For those who see the great outdoors as an inspiration to shop, The Nature Company delivers, with science kits and instruments, science-related toys, a lovely gem collection, books, and a knowledgeable staff. Talks, demonstrations, and field trips for children and adults are sponsored by this store and other Nature Company outlets in the Philadelphia region. ◆ M-Tu, Th-Sa 10AM-7PM; W 10AM-8PM; Su noon-6PM. 1701 Walnut St (at S. 17th St). 977.8696

12 The Latham Hotel $$$ Located near Center City West shopping, this unpretentious first-class hotel has 139 sunny guest rooms. The staff is friendly and well-informed, particularly doorman **Joe Broderick,** who has worked at the Latham since the former apartment building, erected in 1906, became a hotel in 1970. Amenities include same-day valet and laundry service, business facilities, and free use of a health club a block away. Ask for a room on one of the five newly refurbished nonsmoking floors. ◆ 135 S. 17th St (at Walnut St). 563.7474, 800/528.4261; fax 563.4034

Within The Latham Hotel:

Bogart's ★$$$ A romantic room with contemporary artwork, banquettes, and slatted ceilings, Bogart's occupies the corner of the Latham lobby. Recent changes in the menu have resulted in lighter, more imaginative fare: asparagus Napoleon, scallop taco, and a breast of duck with ginger and currants, to name a few of the dishes. For lunch there are crab cakes, oyster and chicken salad, and hamburgers; dinner offers osso buco, steak, and salmon with spinach and garlic. ◆ Continental ◆ Breakfast, lunch, and dinner. 563.9444

More than 2,000 original drawings by children's author Maurice Sendak are part of the extensive literary collection at the Rosenbach Museum and Library at 2010 Delancey Place near Rittenhouse Square.

13 Schmidt/Dean Gallery You might see the work of stone sculptor **Bradford Graves,** who draws inspiration from primitive cultures; local artist **Stephen Estock** and his abstract paintings on linen; or photographer **Linda Adlestein,** who creates multilayered negatives of Rome and Venice. Everything shown here—prints, paintings, sculptures, photographs—is contemporary. ♦ Tu-Sa 10:30AM-6PM, or by appointment. 1636 Walnut St (between S. 16th and S. 17th Sts). 546.7212

14 Newman Galleries A Philadelphia institution, Newman Galleries has been in business since 1865—and its dated stock of landscapes and portraits clearly reflects it. Nevertheless, some noteworthy pieces can be found in its huge inventory, including items of historic interest. Newman wasn't always a place for the affluent (as it is now); in the 1870s the gallery exhibited art on the streets with a handsome horse-drawn "Art Cart." ♦ M-F 9AM-5:30PM; Sa 10AM-4:30PM. 1625 Walnut St (between S. 16th and S. 17th Sts). 563.1779

15 Temple University Center City Campus With its main campus in North Philadelphia, Temple's downtown outpost offers continuing education courses and occasional events, including live music performances. ♦ 1616 and 1619 Walnut St (between S. 16th and S. 17th Sts). 204.5528

On the Temple University Center City Campus:

Stage III Run by the Temple theater department, Stage III showcases graduate and undergraduate actors and actresses. Professional productions occasionally rent out the 160-seat space. ♦ 204.1122

Gallery Potluck art with talented and less-interesting contemporary artists is displayed. ♦ Free. Tu-Sa 10AM-5PM. 204.5041

The Writer's Voice Open readings for writers of poetry, prose, or essays take place here. ♦ Free. 8PM, the first Monday of every month. 787.1527

16 How-To-Do-It Book Shop Artisans, hobbyists, foreign language enthusiasts, and browsers will find reason to pause at this shop. Titles showcased in the store window have included *How to Talk to Your Cat, How to Lie with Maps,* and *Light Your House with Potatoes.* ♦ M-Tu, Th-F 9:30AM-5:30PM; W 9:30AM-7:30PM; Sa 9:30AM-5PM. 1608 Sansom St (between S. 16th and S. 17th Sts). 563.1516

17 First Baptist Church A brooding brownstone completed in 1899 and designed by **Edgar V. Seeler,** this church combines Byzantine and Romanesque features. The 12 panels in the dome are Byzantine stained glass. ♦ Daily 11:30AM-2PM. Concerts: Wednesday at noon followed by services at 12:15PM. S. 17th and Sansom Sts. 563.3853

18 American Institute of Architects Bookstore The tall store windows reveal a terrific variety of books on architecture, especially about Philadelphia and the region, as well as posters, mobiles, T-shirts, cards, bookmarkers, and other design-oriented gift items. Surely you know someone who would love a model airplane kit based on Leonardo da Vinci's drawings of flying machines, or adult building blocks that teach architecture principles. ♦ M-Sa 10AM-5:30PM. 117 S. 17th St (at Sansom St). 569.3188

19 Dandelion Come here for the city's best selection of casual jewelry in silver, brass, bronze, and gold. You might find an inlaid turquoise-and-lapis bracelet from the Zuni Indian reservation in New Mexico; a silver necklace from Italy; or a 14-karat gold ring by Circle Round the Moon, a company in Maine. The store sometimes focuses on one of the many countries represented, perhaps Kenya or Mexico. Notecards and small, expensive crafts are sold, too. ♦ M-F 10AM-6:30PM; Sa 10AM-6PM. 1718 Sansom St (between S. 17th and S. 18th Sts). 972.0999

20 Joseph Fox Book Shop Descend the steps to this homey, sensitively stocked bookstore (with a superb art section) that boasts a devoted clientele. The family-run business, which opened in 1951, is refreshingly personal compared to the newer mega-bookstores nearby. ♦ M-Sa 10AM-5:30PM. 1724 Sansom St (between S. 17th and S. 18th Sts). 563.4184

20 Urban Objects Nouvelle housewares—cotton throws, sculptural clocks, and high-tech teapots—are the mainstay here. The shop maintains an active bridal registry for the couple that scorns traditional china. ♦ M-F 10AM-6PM; Sa 10AM-5PM. 1724 Sansom St (between S. 17th and S. 18th Sts). 557.9474

21 Condom Nation One might be surprised at the variety of prophylactic sheaths cheerily sold here in card-store surroundings. ♦ M-Sa 9:30AM-6PM. 1734 Chestnut St (between S. 17th and S. 18th Sts). 563.7811

22 The Art Institute of Philadelphia (WCAU Building) Built in 1928 for the **WCAU** radio station, this child of the Jazz Age uses all kinds of glass to show off its Art Deco charms. It was designed by **Harry Sternfeld** (who specialized in Art Deco) with his student **Gabriel Roth,** and renovated in 1983 by the local firm of **Kopple Sheward and Day.** Glass and metal chevrons run alongside the frosted glass tower, which glowed blue at night when the station was broadcasting. The wall surface is composed of blue glass chips set in plastic. Inside, note the Deco brushed-metal elevator doors and mailbox. The institute, an independent art school, has occupied the premises since 1982. ♦ 1622 Chestnut St (between S. 16th and S. 17th Sts). 567.7080

23 Liberty Place Philadelphia possessed a relatively low skyline until 1987, when developer **Willard G. Rouse** and Chicago architect **Helmut Jahn** completed this 60-story mixed-use complex, the first structure to exceed the height of the hat worn by *William Penn* on City Hall. (A "gentlemen's agreement" had previously limited the height of buildings in Philadelphia to that of the statue's hat.) The postmodernist **One Liberty Place,** with its blue-glass, neon-trimmed facade reminiscent of Art Deco skyscrapers (especially New York's Chrysler Building), is easily the most important building erected in Philadelphia since World War II, and one of the great examples of the current architectural era. Jahn also designed the tower's 58-story twin, **Two Liberty Place,** a less distinguished structure despite its similarity in design and material. The complex, which is the home of **The Shops at Liberty Place** and the plush **Ritz-Carlton** hotel, has transformed commercial life in the neighborhood.

Unlike so many "signature" buildings of 1980s America, One Liberty Place is an integral part of its city environment: every downtown corner provides a different view of the tower, and every change in the weather or time of day is reflected on its surface. ♦ S. 17th and Market Sts. 851.9000

Within Liberty Place:

The Shops at Liberty Place Seventy shops, including a food court and stalls of craft merchandise, occupy the first and second floors of this upmarket urban mall with a breathtaking rotunda topped by a windowed dome. There's often piano music on the skylit rotunda floor; at Christmastime, troupes of Mummers march in with pageantry and song. ♦ M-Tu, Th-Sa 9:30AM-7PM; W 9:30AM-8PM; Su noon-6PM; extended hours during holiday season. 851.9055

Within The Shops at Liberty Place:

Handblock Shades of Laura Ashley run through Handblock's selection of linens and women's clothing. Look for beautiful—and relatively inexpensive—pillowcases, tablecloths, and linens in country florals and vivid French Provençal prints. Care for a very feminine white blouse? Handblock carries two dozen varieties in rayon, cotton, and linen, as well as those full white nightgowns worn by Victorian heroines. ♦ 981.0350

Celebrate America: The Philadelphia Store For the souvenir hunter, this store has T-shirts printed with hoagie recipes, Pennsylvania Dutch tiles, pillowcases, gift baskets, and Hershey's chocolate. ♦ 567.1976

The Artisans Store All those country doodads—quilts, wind chimes, and dried-flower wreaths—needed to decorate your suburban home are here. The prices, however, can't compete with what you'd find in a real country store. ♦ 567.1355

Liberty Place

M. BLUM

Time Works With Charlie Chaplin clocks and an extensive selection of fake gold watches, Time Works is a store utterly devoted to keeping track of time. ♦ 564.3752

Platypus A cross between Conran's and Williams-Sonoma, this urban country store has ample housewares for the young professional. Tapestrylike cotton throws, Calphalon cookware, British pine tables, and fresh coffee beans account for only part of the extensive selection. Search out the great silverware, especially the Twigware—stylish utensils with gnarled iron handles. ♦ 963.0755

Fire & Ice This fascinating store is almost a museum of rocks, gems, minerals, fish fossils, and corals. Glass cases display hand-carved soapstone from Kenya, malachite necklaces, earrings in sterling silver and onyx, and tigereye figurines. ♦ 564.2871

Goods For the little girl in your life, buy a tiered hat stand for her bonnets or a pastel *poudreuse* (powder desk) for her brush and comb. This source for expensive wedding and baby-shower gifts also carries Liberty of London sheets, down comforters, and bed trays. ♦ 567.2162

Candy Barrel Hard candies from all over the world are sold by the pound. ♦ 851.0764

Flags Unlimited Just what it says: flags from all the latest countries, plus hokey items for the extreme nationalist in everyone. Surely you need a placard that reads "Parking for Albanians Only!" ♦ 567.2445

Shops entered from South 17th Street:

Chiasso If there's unconquered territory on your office desk, consider purchasing some of Chiasso's super-fashionable paperweights and black matte and chrome accessories or knickknacks in crayon colors. ♦ 41 S. 17th St (between Market and Chestnut Sts). 563.0175

Rand McNally Map and Travel Store Whether you're looking for a map of a newly formed Eastern European nation or a topographical map of your own backyard, it's probably here. The prices aren't discount, but the selection is good. You'll also find globes, travel-related toys, and games. ♦ S. 17th and Market Sts. 563.1101

The Ritz-Carlton $$$$ The 290-room Ritz-Carlton is furnished in a European style, with 18th-century oil paintings, antiques, and hand-woven rugs. In the afternoon, a pianist plays classical music, and the evenings are given to jazz. Ask for an upper-floor room on the east side for great nighttime views of the Liberty Place rotunda and the extraordinary frosted-glass Art Deco facade of the Institute of Art. Guests enjoy a fitness center and sauna. Enter the hotel directly from the Liberty Place shopping area or from South 17th Street, and take an elevator up to the third-floor lobby. ♦ S. 17th and Chestnut Sts. 563.1600, 800/241.3333; fax 564.9559

Within The Ritz-Carlton:

The Dining Room ★★$$$$ Cloistered from the rest of the hotel, this formal, high-ceilinged room serves eclectic cuisine, ranging from steamed red snapper with polenta and sun-dried tomatoes to tenderloin of beef with *gnocchi* and Dover sole with a potato crust. ♦ Eclectic ♦ Lunch and dinner; lunch only on Monday. Closed Sunday. Reservations recommended. 563.1600

The Grill ★★$$$ Prices are lower midday in this masculine room. Lunch might feature tuna steak with fennel, peppered Gulf shrimp on fettuccine, or a chicken-breast club sandwich. Raspberry crème brûlée or Key lime pie are among the dessert choices. ♦ Continental ♦ Lunch and dinner. 563.1600

$FU᠎ZZ᠎I

Sfuzzi ★★$$$ Designed to look like a remnant of the Roman Empire, with faux frescoes on the walls and faux parchment menus, this chain of Italian bistros has found its niche: the young professional crowd. The food is Nouveau Italian: pizza with smoked chicken and caramelized onions, grilled shrimp with saffron orzo, linguine with rock shrimp, and roasted Portobello mushrooms. Some of the tables look out on Market Street. ♦ Italian ♦ Lunch and dinner. 1650 Market St. Reservations recommended. 851.8888

24 The Turf Club This wood-paneled and brass-railed betting parlor broadcasts live from **Philadelphia Park** and other local horsetracks. The Turf Club attracts a diverse mix of bettors: retirees, brokers from neighboring investment firms on their lunch hour, and regular players. There's also a restaurant and a bar. ♦ M-Tu, F-Su 11AM-11:15PM; W-Th 6-11PM. 7 Penn Center (at N. 17th and Market Sts). 246.1556

25 Mellon Bank Center The pyramid that covers the cooling system of the Mellon Bank Center has become a distinctive element of the city's new skyline, and its gray granite and white marble base dominates the block at street level. The building's tapering corners, which evoke an Egyptian obelisk, culminate in a latticework pyramid that's dramatically illuminated at night. Construction of the 54-story building was completed in 1990 to the designs of **Kohn Pederson & Fox,** though the terrazzo floors and other stylish furnishings suggest an edifice of much greater age. Be sure to see the silvery vaulted ceilings inside. The underground concourse connects to **Suburban Station.** ♦ 1735 Market St (between N. 17th and N. 18th Sts)

26 Firefighting Exhibit Sponsored by **CIGNA,** the descendant of the **Insurance Company of North America,** this exhibit showcases the history of insurance. But the main attraction is a lobby display of 19th-century firefighting equipment. Constructed when this equipment had a ceremonial as well as practical function, the **Spider Hose Reel** (circa 1855), **Philadelphia Hose Company No. 1 Steam Engine** (1858), and **Silsby Steam Fire Engine No. 1013** are charming pieces of American craftswork. Note the collection of firefighters' hats. ♦ Free. M-F 9AM-5PM. 1650 Arch St (between N. 16th and N. 17th Sts)

27 Suburban Station Downstairs in this recently refurbished 1930 Art Deco marble and brass building by **Graham, Anderson, Probst, and White** (the Chicago firm that also designed **30th Street Station**) are a shopping concourse and commuter rail station for trains to and from the Philadelphia suburbs. (You can also catch a fast train here to the airport.) Entrances to the concourse run from City Hall to 18th Street along John F. Kennedy Boulevard and Market Street. ♦ N. 16th St and John F. Kennedy Blvd. 580.7800

28 JFK Plaza Visitors Center Like a UFO that has just landed in the city, this circular building awaits tourists who want to stock up on information about Philadelphia. The staff is friendly and helpful, and there's a full selection of brochures and pamphlets. (Warning: Don't even *try* to park around here.) ♦ Daily 9AM-5PM Labor Day-Memorial Day; daily 9AM-6PM Memorial Day-Labor Day. N. 16th St and John F. Kennedy Blvd. 636.1666, 800/537.7676

29 John F. Kennedy Boulevard The elevated **Pennsylvania Railroad** tracks, which ran from 30th Street Station to City Hall, stymied development of Center City West for decades. Nicknamed the "Chinese Wall," the tracks were finally torn down in 1953, making room for this thoroughfare and for the 14-acre **Penn Center** office complex, which is connected by an underground concourse to **Suburban Station.** ♦ Between Market and Arch Sts

30 Milord la Chamarre Philadelphians predictably called it "the Mummer," though French artist **Jean Dubuffet** named his 1973 sculpture-and-drawing installation *My Lord in the Fancy Vest.* ♦ Market St (between S. 15th and S. 16th Sts)

31 The Clothespin This sculpture is exactly what it appears to be, a towering steel clothespin rising 54 feet above Center Square Plaza. It's the work of Swedish-born artist **Claes Oldenburg,** known for other famous pop art icons, such as *Bat Column,* a hundred-foot-high baseball bat in Chicago, and *Split Button* at the University of Pennsylvania (see page 119). ♦ S. 15th and Market Sts

31 Top of Center Square ★$$$ The commanding view of Center City is the main attraction of this dressy restaurant, situated on the 41st floor of an office tower across from City Hall. The kitchen turns out Continental fare: grilled salmon teriyaki steak; veal scaloppini; and shrimp with pasta, black olives, diced tomatoes, and Boursin cheese in a garlic-butter wine sauce. Live music entertains on Friday and Saturday nights. ♦ Continental ♦ Lunch and dinner; dinner only on Saturday and Sunday. S. 15th and Market Sts (in the First Pennsylvania Bank Tower), 41st floor. 563.9494

32 Packard Building Early 20th-century artist **Samuel Yellin,** whose wrought-iron fixtures adorn several Philadelphia landmarks, designed the gates and lighting fixtures on the Chestnut Street side of this structure. Note the detailing above the 15th Street entrance. (Trivia buffs: The Packard's gates weigh 10 tons apiece.) ♦ S. 15th and Chestnut Sts

33 Barnes & Noble Book Store The former **Jacob Reed's Sons** men's store, an eclectic building designed by **Price and McLanahan** and completed in 1904, was converted into a mega-bookstore in the 1980s. Note the terracotta tilework from **Mercer Tileworks** in Doylestown in the foyer arch at the store's entrance. The factory was commissioned by Jacob Reed's Sons to re-create scenes from the garment industry. Stained glass, more Mercer tiles, and frescoes by muralist **C.T. Monaghan** depicting the early 20th century leisure class line the store's walls. Barnes & Noble is a great place to pick up remaindered titles, especially historical works. It also has an all-inclusive magazine section and occasional author readings. ♦ M-F 9AM-8PM; Sa 10AM-7PM; Su 11AM-6PM. 1424-1426 Chestnut St (between S. Broad and S. 15th Sts). 972.8275

The highest recorded temperature in Philadelphia was 104˚ Fahrenheit in July 1966; the lowest temperature was 7˚ below zero in January 1984.

Eddie Sawyer, former manager of the Phillies baseball team, quit three games into the 1961 season, one of the team's worst. The reason? "I'm 49," he said at the time, "and I want to live to be 50."

staurants/Clubs: Red   Hotels: Blue
ops/ 🌳 Outdoors: Green   **Sights/Culture:** Black

34 Samuel Adams Brew House ★$ The first brew house to open in the city since the 1700s sits above the **Sansom Street Oyster House.** Huge stainless-steel casks hold the brewing beer, and there's a tavernlike room for quaffing the varieties on tap (the darks are especially interesting). New York strip steaks, barbecued brisket, pizza, and ample hamburgers and fries trigger your thirst. ♦ American ♦ Lunch and dinner. Closed Sunday. 1516 Sansom St (between S. 15th and S. 16th Sts), second floor. 563.2326

34 Sansom Street Oyster House ★★$$$ Owners **David** and **Judi Mink** run this veteran seafood restaurant adorned with old pictures of Philadelphia food purveyors, colorful oyster plates, and raw clams and oysters on ice. House specialties include crab Imperial, broiled or fried sea scallops, and slabs of fish grilled and served with pepper hash. ♦ Seafood ♦ Lunch and dinner. Closed Sunday. 1516 Sansom St (between S. 15th and S. 16th Sts). 567.7683

35 Gross McCleaf Gallery Most of the artists who exhibit landscapes and representational paintings here hail from the Philadelphia region. They include **Joe Sweeney,** whose paintings have portrayed traditional scenes of Boathouse Row along the Schuylkill River; **Bertha Leonard** and her fanciful interiors; and **Jacqueline Chesley,** a neo-impressionist who has used Longwood Gardens as a subject. ♦ M, F-Sa 10AM-5PM; Tu-Th 10AM-6PM. 127 S. 16th St (at Sansom St). 665.8138

36 Le Bec-Fin ★★★★$$$$ You don't just drop in on Le Bec-Fin, you plan a meal here for months. Owner-chef **Georges Perrier** oversees one of the most celebrated restaurants in the nation, a place of high formality, extravagant prices, and classic French cuisine. Philadelphians look at Le Bec-Fin as a setting for special occasions. The dining room features elegant fabrics, plush chairs, ornate mirrors, and classic moldings. Massive chandeliers dangle from the two-story ceiling and spectacular flowers line the fireplace. The fixed-price meals—appetizer, fish, main course, cheese, salad, and dessert—are elaborate, leisurely, and rich. Thin-sliced hearts of palm with caviar and quail eggs, salmon with morel mushrooms and goose liver, and squab with juniper berry sauce typify an evening here. The grand finale is the dessert cart—from which patrons happily choose as much as they wish, maybe raspberry Napoleon, caramel ice cream, melon sorbet, or Floating Island (a custard). Sample the same food for less money downstairs in the **Le Bar Lyonnais** (★★★$$$) ♦ French ♦ Lunch and dinner; dinner only on Saturday. Closed Sunday. Reservations required. 1523 Walnut St (between S. 15th and S. 16th Sts). 567.1000

37 Susanna Foo ★★★$$$ Chef-owner **Susanna Foo's** wide-ranging imagination is set free in this handsome restaurant. Though basically Oriental, the cuisine borrows heavily from other cultures: shrimp in a curry of pears, wonton ravioli stuffed with veal, grilled quail on a bed of watercress, grilled chicken with melon and honeyed walnuts, and a crispy duck from which all signs of fat have been meticulously removed are among the eclectic dishes. The fried bananas come with honey, almond slivers, and warm coconut sauce. ♦ Eclectic Chinese ♦ Lunch and dinner; dinner only on Saturday. Closed Sunday. 1512 Walnut St (between S. 15th and S. 16th Sts). Reservations recommended. 545.2666

38 Drexel and Company Building Originally the offices of the Drexel financial company, this Italian Renaissance palazzo, designed in 1927 by **Day and Klauder,** echoes the Strozzi Palace in Florence. Bas-relief panels above the ground-floor windows depict the signs of the zodiac. From the outside, the building seems impervious; its walls are solid granite, and the massive doors swing shut on hammered-steel hinges. The red canopy that the current owners have erected in front of the door compromises the effect, however. For now, at least, this office building stands empty. ♦ 135-43 S. 15th St (at Walnut St)

39 Tiffany & Co. The jewelry is real, but the granite-and-marble building is faux, closely modeled after Tiffany's flagship store in New York. It was built in 1990 by local developer **Richard Rubin.** The statue of *Atlas,* hoisting the clock, is a replica of the 1853 original in New York by **Henry Frederick Metzler.** ♦ M-S 10AM-5:30PM 1414 Walnut St (between S. Broad and S. 15th Sts). 735.1919

40 Bookbinders Seafood House ★★$$$ The Bookbinder family became famous locally after founding their original Society Hill restaurant, which they've since sold. They opened this second restaurant in the 1940s, and the family remains in charge. The cuisine that thrilled crowds years ago is still prepared with the freshest of ingredients, but it's a bit dull by today's nouvelle standards. Shipwheel lamps, dark red tablecloths, and full-length curtains decorate the main room, which seats 400 people. Plump banquettes and a more relaxed atmosphere characterize the rear dining rooms. The house trademarks are steamed lobster (the largest weigh in at four pounds), snapper soup, and broiled fish. Fruity cheesecakes tempt for dessert. ♦ Seafood ♦ Lunch and dinner; dinner only on Saturday and Sunday. 215 S. 15th St (between Walnut and Locust Sts). 545.1137

In 1959, the establishment of two "One Percent Programs" required that a percentage of all construction and redevelopment funds in Philadelphia go to public art.

41 Di Lullo Centro ★★★$$$$ Philadelphia's most urbane Italian restaurant is located in the lobby of the former **Locust Theater.** Contemporary murals in deep greens and purples, low lighting, and glass partitions dominate the sumptuous main dining area, and a glass elevator descends to lavish private banquet rooms. Chef **Donna Vahey** oversees a kitchen that turns out meticulous food in diminutive portions. Start with tender fried squid, prosciutto and figs, or roasted sweet peppers and mozzarella. Some of the legendary pastas include angel hair with fresh herbs, garlic, and cheese; spinach pasta with cream and shrimp; and tortellini with crabmeat in a tomato cream sauce. Manzo, a beef fillet, is served on a bed of spinach with balsamic vinegar and pearl onions. The best desserts are ricotta cheesecake, homemade gelato, and chocolate mousse. ♦ Italian ♦ Lunch and dinner; dinner only on Saturday. Closed Sunday. 1407 Locust St (between S. Broad and S. 15th Sts). Reservations required. 546.2000

42 Marabella's ★$$ The unremarkable but trendy Italian fare served here ranges from vegetarian lasagna with goat cheese and spinach to sausage and fennel calzone and shrimp pizza with red pepper. The children's menu earns brownie points among tired parents. ♦ Italian ♦ Lunch and dinner; dinner only on Sunday. 1420 Locust St (between S. Broad and S. 15th Sts). 545.1845. Also at: 1700 Benjamin Franklin Pkwy. 981.5555

43 Tequila's ★★$$$ Mexican food *can* be complex and serious. Owner **David Suro,** of Guadalajara, serves such traditional dishes as *mole poblano* (chicken in a sauce of peppers, chocolate, and peanuts). But branch out and try *molcajete* (named after the bowl-shaped mortar used to crush ingredients with a pestle), a mix of crunchy pork skin, shredded beef, chiles, toasted tomatoes, garlic, cilantro, and cheese. The Guadalajaran specialty, *huarache,* is shredded pork and beef in a spicy sauce with refried beans. ♦ Mexican ♦ Lunch and dinner; dinner only on Saturday. Closed Sunday. 1511 Locust St (between S. 15th and S. 16th Sts). 546.0181

44 Copa, Too! ★★$ If you're wondering about the name, it's a takeoff on its South Street sister restaurant called **Copa Banana Cabana.** Copa, Too! serves the juiciest hamburgers and crispiest french fries in town, plus lots of standard bar food: nachos and refried beans, potato skins with melted cheese, and even enchiladas. Tiny, lively, and casual, the restaurant plays up a nautical theme and has an interesting selection of fish (for watching, not eating) swimming about in a tank. The burgers come with some unusual toppings— Boursin cheese and alfalfa sprouts, among others. ♦ American/Mexican ♦ Lunch and dinner. 263 S. 15th St (between Locust and Spruce Sts). 735.0848. Also at: 344 South St. 923.6180

45 The Drake Tower Apartments Formerly **The Drake Hotel** and now an apartment house, **Ritter and Shay's** 36-story tower, completed in 1929, is a sterling example of Philadelphia's first skyscrapers—its graduating tiers were ordered by the city's then-new zoning codes. Terracotta ornamentation recalls the travels of **Sir Francis Drake,** with images of sailing ships, globes, and domes: Pompeian brick covers the building's steel frame. ♦ 1512-14 Spruce St (between S. 15th and S. 16th Sts)

46 The Three Threes ★$$$ During Prohibition, The Three Threes was a speakeasy. Long since a legitimate restaurant, it has a candlelit main dining area and some small rooms upstairs—much like the town house restaurants of Quebec City. The food is simple Continental with an Italian edge: Caesar salad, stuffed clams, chicken Marsala, Cornish game hen with wild rice, and filet mignon with mushrooms. ♦ Continental ♦ Lunch and dinner; dinner only on Sunday. 333 S. Smedley St (bounded by S. 16th and S. 17th Sts, and Spruce and Pine Sts). 735.0667

47 Warsaw Cafe ★★$$$ Only 30 people fit into the Warsaw Cafe's dining room, decorated with Art Deco posters, etched-glass windows, and crimson tabletops. All of the dishes turn out lighter than you might expect. Try fresh borscht; a Baltic Sea salad with fish, olives, and pasta shells; or cabbage leaves stuffed with ground veal, herbs, onions, rice, and mushrooms and baked in a subtle tomato sauce. ♦ Eastern European ♦ Lunch and dinner. Closed Sunday. 306 S. 16th St (between Spruce and Pine Sts). 546.0204

Philadelphia's turn-of-the-century political boss, Boies Penrose, a Republican state legislator for 12 years and a U.S. senator for almost 25 years, was a larger-than-life figure. He weighed about 300 pounds and supposedly polished off a dozen eggs and as many rolls with his morning cup of coffee.

48 The Garden ★★★$$$ In the 1970s owner-chef **Kathleen Mulhern** took over this cream-colored Center City town house—built in 1870 for the **Philadelphia Musical Academy**—and oversaw its beautiful reconstruction. The Garden has since become a Philadelphia institution, known for its classy rooms and unwavering standards. Beyond the dark-wood oyster bar is the main dining room, decorated with luxurious floral wallpaper and handsome mirrors. Several years ago Mulhern expanded the operation to an adjoining town house, filling one room with antique decoys and another with horse prints. The secluded garden area out back opens in the summertime.

The menu, which has changed imperceptibly over the years, elevates the term "Continental cuisine." Crab salad in avocado, beef carpaccio with herbs and capers, and spinach *gnocchi* with Gorgonzola sauce stand out among the appetizers. Dover sole, filet mignon in red wine sauce with *pommes frites,* and a veal chop with linguine and wild mushrooms are stellar entrées. Desserts include profiteroles (pastry puffs with ice cream and chocolate sauce) and the Bonaparte (a thin pastry with ice cream and strawberries). ♦ Continental ♦ Lunch and dinner; dinner only on Saturday. Closed Sunday. 1617 Spruce St (between S. 16th and S. 17th Sts). Reservations recommended. 546.4455

49 The Print Club Since 1915, the Print Club has promoted fine art prints, photographs, and art books through temporary exhibitions in its two large galleries. Purchase prints and books in the **Gallery Shop.** ♦ Free. Tu-Sa 11AM-5:30PM. 1614 Latimer St (between S. 16th and S. 17th Sts). 735.6090

50 Magnolia Cafe ★★$$ Once the home of a top French restaurant, this handsome town house with high ceilings, carved woodwork, and a crystal chandelier is now the setting for casual Cajun cuisine. The daily fish entrées—usually four or more—come blackened or broiled with mustard hollandaise. Other choices include spicy barbecued shrimp and shrimp rolled in coconut and beer, then deep-fried and served with orange marmalade sauce. Live jazz fills the two dining rooms on Tuesday night. ♦ Cajun ♦ Lunch and dinner; dinner only on Saturday and Sunday. 1602 Locust St (between S. 16th and S. 17th Sts). 546.4180

51 Locust Street From 1848 to 1908, a number of wealthy Philadelphians hired prominent architects to design some of the city's finest town houses along a portion of this lovely street. Scottish-born **John Notman,** whose early Gothic Revival **St. Marks Church** dominates the middle of the block, is also thought to be responsible for building Nos. 1604, 1620, and 1622. Italian-born Philadelphia architect **Wilson Eyre** renovated No. 1618 (note the first-floor window and the human face hidden in the floral motif), and **Cope and Stewardson,** renowned for buildings on the University of Pennsylvania campus, designed the Georgian Revival houses at Nos. 1631 and 1633. **Horace Trumbauer's** white limestone house at No. 1629 represents the Beaux Arts school (Trumbauer also designed the Free Library on the Parkway and famous mansions in the Philadelphia suburbs, New York City, Washington, DC, and Newport, Rhode Island. ♦ Between S. 16th and S. 17th Sts

52 St. Marks Church John Notman's striking 1851 church was self-consciously constructed in the medieval Gothic style revived by the Anglican reform movement. The interior is richly carved and decorated; note the silver altar in the **Lady Chapel.** ♦ 1625 Locust St (between S. 16th and S. 17th Sts)

53 Janet Fleisher Gallery Local artists whose works tend to have a visceral feel are displayed here. The gallery also offers the works of the legendary, anonymous **"Philadelphia Wireman"** found years ago in the trash of a gentrifying neighborhood. Constructed from wire and assorted debris, these small pieces are believed to have been used in African-American religious rites. ♦ M-F 10:30AM-5:30PM; Sa 11AM-5:30PM. 211 S. 17th St (between Walnut and Chancellor Sts). 545.7562

54 Belgian Chocolate House Fine chocolates are flown to this shop from Brussels to preserve their freshness. Owner **Willy Rajter,** a former diamond merchant, displays his confections in glass cases. The prices are astronomical (how about $28 a pound?) and the intense little chocolates taste so rich they will make you light-headed. Rajter recommends the pieces filled with crème fraîche. Rumor has it that the shop might move to another location in the neighborhood, so call before visiting. ♦ M-F 10AM-6PM; Sa 10AM-5PM. 220 S. 17th St (between Chancellor and Locust Sts). 735.3975

In 1993 Mayor Edward Rendell asked the Streets Department to replace many traffic lights in the city with stop signs in order to save money. The results so far have been denounced by many city residents, who contend traffic lights are safer.

55 Warwick Apartments and Hotel $$$ The Warwick opened for business in 1926, the night of the **Dempsey-Tunney**

fight in Philadelphia, and ongoing renovations recall its Jazz Age glory. Designed in the English Renaissance style by local architect **Frank Hahn,** the 22-story building now has 210 guest rooms and 150 apartments for longer stays. Among its principal competitors—the **Barclay** and the **Latham**—the Warwick's lobby is more dazzling and spacious. The hotel has made its third-floor rooms especially accessible for disabled guests, and has set aside six nonsmoking floors. Guests enjoy free use of a nearby fitness club and pool, as well as complimentary cable television service. ♦ 1701 Locust St (at S. 17th St). 735.6000

Within the Warwick Apartments and Hotel:

Capriccio ★$ Fancy coffees and an eclectic selection of desserts characterize this stylish cafe, a popular Center City hangout despite its slow and chaotic service. ♦ Coffee shop ♦ Daily 6:30AM-1AM. 735.6000

1701 Café ★$$ Enjoy a simple hamburger or a fancier entrée (maybe grilled tuna with wasabi butter or pizza with Black Forest ham and goat cheese) in this woody dining room with recessed lighting, mirrored posts, and candlelit tables. ♦ Eclectic ♦ Lunch and dinner. 735.6000

Newport Bar and Grill $$ Stuffed trophy fish and old photos of the upper crust hobnobbing at Newport line the walls of this boisterous singles hangout. It's very spacious and noisy, with a separate room for billiard tables and a huge octagonal bar with an overhanging brass rack for glasses. The 18-ounce strip steak, grilled scallops, and fettuccine primavera are all reasonably priced. But don't choose Newport for the food, come for the scene. ♦ American ♦ Dinner. Live music most Friday and Saturday nights. 735.6000

When it opened in 1929 at 20th and Market streets in Center City, the famous Mastbaum Theater was the third-largest movie theater in the world. The opulent movie palace, decorated with crystal and gold leaf, seated 5,000 people. It was destroyed in 1958.

56 Mangel Gallery The well-regarded Mangel Gallery presents a range of prestigious contemporary artists, from realist **Alex Katz's** images of high-society figures to **Robert Motherwell's** abstractions and **Red Groom's** funky portrayals of everyday life. ♦ Tu-Sa 11AM-6PM. 1714 Rittenhouse Sq (between S. 17th and S. 18th Sts). 545.4343

57 The Plays and Players Theatre Founded in 1911, the oldest amateur theater group in the country performs here in its original building. Under the leadership of its first president, **Maud Skinner,** wife of actor **Otis Skinner,** the theater became a fixture of Philadelphia high society. It continues to produce about four shows a year—usually contemporary American plays such as *Miss Firecracker*—renting its space to other companies the rest of the time. Murals by local artist **Edith Emerson** enliven the walls of the auditorium, which seats 324 people. Children's productions often run concurrently. ♦ 1714 Delancey St (between S. 17th and S. 18th Sts). 735.0630

58 Shahrzad ★★$$ Glass-topped tables with vinyl tablecloths, house plants, and framed posters decorate this miniature storefront Iranian restaurant, located in one of Center City's nicest residential neighborhoods. Start with *mast-o-khiar* (yogurt with cucumber and dried mint) or *dolmeh moe* (stuffed grape leaves with spring onion, leek, and mint). Grilled kebabs of beef, shrimp, swordfish, and chicken flavored with lemon and saffron come with long-grained basmati rice. ♦ Iranian ♦ Lunch and dinner. Closed Monday. 1700 Lombard St (at S. 17th St). 546.2300

59 Astral Plane ★★$$$ The small dining rooms in this funky town house evoke the '70s, which is when the restaurant opened. The decor is an artsy jumble, with discordant florals on the tables, mismatched dinnerware, and chandeliers that hang from parachute-silk ceilings. Choices from the eclectic menu include a simple filet mignon with shallot and tarragon, grilled mako shark with grapefruit tequila salsa, and three-cheese lasagna. ♦ Eclectic ♦ Lunch and dinner; dinner only on Saturday. 1708 Lombard St (between S. 17th and S. 18th Sts). 546.6230

60 The Civil War Library and Museum This little-known, historically rigorous museum devoted to Civil War memorabilia holds ample evidence of Philadelphia's close ties to the conflict. During the war **General Ulysses S. Grant** made his home at 20th and Chestnut streets, while **General George Gordon Meade,** the commanding Union officer at Gettysburg, lived at 19th and Delancey streets. Both generals have rooms devoted to their artifacts (check out the stuffed head of Meade's horse). The museum's collection includes several life masks of **Abraham Lincoln,** as well as a lock of his hair and the dress in which his nemesis, **Jefferson Davis,** attempted to escape capture. For non-buffs, the room dedicated to the belongings of ordinary soldiers may prove more interesting (note the soldiers' sewing kit, called a "housewife"). Scholars have access to the manuscript collection and 16,000-volume library. ◆ Admission. M-Sa 10AM-4PM. 1805 Pine St (between S. 18th and S. 19th Sts). 735.8196

61 Delancey Street Like many Philadelphia streets, Delancey runs through one neighborhood for several blocks, then disappears into a T-junction with another street, rematerializing a few blocks away as if there had been no break. This preternaturally persistent street, on most blocks shady and well kept, is a pleasant place for a contemplative walk among fine houses. One recommended stretch runs between 18th and 20th streets, where most of the houses hail from the mid-19th century. Late 19th-century architect **Frank Furness** designed the **Horace Jayne Mansion** (1900 Delancey Street), with its balcony, carved stone at the entrance, and cherubim and seraphim on pediments.
◆ Between Spruce and Pine Sts

62 Bag & Baggage Bed & Breakfast $ There's no shingle outside this eclectically furnished B&B inn (a row house with three rooms, two with shared bath), but once you find it you'll feel right at home. Its convenience and warmth make it one of the best bargains in Philadelphia. ◆ 338 S. 19th St (between Delancey and Pine Sts). 546.3807

63 Rosenbach Museum and Library The nation's preeminent museum for rare books and manuscripts continues to expand its collection, providing an important resource to literary scholars. Rare books dealer **Dr. A.S.W. Rosenbach** and his brother **Philip H. Rosenbach,** a local art dealer, lived on Delancey Street from 1926 until the early 1950s. Their Victorian mansion—with its Georgian interior—is furnished with early English, French, and American pieces.

The Rosenbachs' most important holding is **James Joyce's** manuscript of *Ulysses,* which played a key role in the recent controversy over the novel's "corrected" edition (try to follow the novelist's crabbed handwriting). Three-quarters of all **Joseph Conrad's** manuscripts also have found their way here, as have the first four pages of **Bram Stoker's** *Dracula,* which he began while staying at the long-gone **Stratford Hotel** on Broad Street. "Rosy," as his friends called A.S.W., also got his hands on the 1519 editions of **Erasmus'** *New Testament*

(with prints by **Holbein**); **Cervantes'** *Don Quixote de la Mancha* (1605); and the first tit■ published in North America, *The Bay Psalm Book* (1640). All are on display, along with temporary exhibitions and a permanent instal■ lation re-creating the poet **Marianne Moore's** Greenwich Village apartment. Guides escort visitors through the museum on hour-long tours; they will tailor the itinerary to your interests. ◆ Admission. Tu-Su 11AM-4PM; last tour begins at 2:45PM. Open to scholars by appointment. Closed during August. 2010 Delancey Pl (between S. 20th and S. 21st Sts■ 732.1600

64 Waldorf Cafe ★★$$$ A friendly bar, candlelit tables, and sprigs of fresh flowers enhance the bottom floor of this corner town house. The Waldorf Cafe has a long track record in the neighborhood and the food wins steady approval, if not raves. Some of the trademark dishes: wild mushrooms sautéed ■ cream and cognac; spicy grilled shrimp with black beans, sour cream, and a citrus dressing; sweetbreads with Dijon mustard; and a half duck cooked in soy and molasses. For dessert, try the bitter chocolate and white mousse. ◆ American ◆ Dinner. 20th and Lombard Sts. Reservations recommended. 985.1836

65 Pastabilities Fresh pasta and tasty sauces are prepared in this shop by **Michael Divirgilio.** Pasta flavors include ginger, cayenne pepper, and squid. ◆ M-Sa noon-8PM; Su noon-6PM. 1942 South St (between S. 19th and S. 20th Sts). 545.1959

66 South Street Stained Glass Curious illuminations in transoms, skylights, and doorways enliven many house interiors in Philadelphia. Some of these date to the 19th century; others were custom made last week at local stained-glass workshops such as this one owned by **Forrest Smith.** South Street Stained Glass also sells fetching glass curios ◆ M-F 10AM-6PM; Sa 10AM-4PM. 2209 South St (between S. 22nd and S. 23rd Sts). 735.2415

Plans are under way for a recreation path and park along the Schuylkill River from the Fairmount Waterworks to Spruce Street. The asphalt path, intended for use by joggers, strollers, and cyclists, should be completed by 1994.

67 Fitler Square An idyllic, shaded park treasured by city residents, Fitler Square's small size is one of its chief charms, along with the fountain, brick walkways, and bronze statues. In the summer it tops the list of places in the city to read or eat lunch. First established in 1896, the park has been refurbished several times, most recently in 1980. It was named after **Edwin W. Fitler,** a wealthy cordage manufacturer who became Philadelphia's first mayor under its 1885 city charter (which was supposed to end corruption but in fact only refined it). ♦ Pine St (between S. 23rd and S. 24th Sts)

68 Schuylkill River Park Overlooking the (admittedly fetid) waters of the lower Schuylkill River, this is a real recreational park, with a children's playground, tennis courts, basketball courts, and leased lots for local gardeners. ♦ Between Locust and Pine Sts

69 Spruce Street Two fine blocks of brownstones were erected here during the second half of the 19th century, the mansard roofs and round-headed windows showing their Second Empire influence. Brownstone has never been as common in Philadelphia as it is in New York City, but during the 1800s, it appealed to builders because it was relatively cheap yet handsome. The earthen tones of these elegant blocks offer a pleasing contrast to the brick and stucco facades of nearby houses. No. 2111-13 and No. 2132-34 are attributed to **Frank Furness.** Local architect **Wilson Eyre,** known for his picturesque residences, designed the Colonial Revival house at No. 2123-25. The Victorian on the corner at No. 2100, designed by Philadelphia architect **George Hewitt,** is complemented by the red and white brick building opposite at No. 2044. ♦ Between S. 20th and S. 22nd Sts

In the early 1980s, a bronze statue of prizefighter Rocky Balboa, the lead character from the *Rocky* movies, was erected outside the Philadelphia Museum of Art. The museum had provided a backdrop for a classic scene from the first film of the blockbuster series, when Rocky (played by Sylvester Stallone) triumphantly ran up its steps. However, some—not all—Philadelphians considered the statue innappropriate for a world-class museum, and Rocky was eventually moved to the front of the Spectrum sports arena.

The Schuylkill, Delaware, Susquehanna, Lehigh, Monangahela, and Allegheny rivers course through Pennsylvania, representing more miles of running water—45,000 in all—than in any other state in the country. Also the most flood-prone state, Pennsylvania experienced $3 billion in flood damage between 1970 and 1993.

70 Friday, Saturday, Sunday ★★$$$ For two decades, this intimate town-house restaurant has endured while others fell by the wayside. The menu is written on a Day-Glo board between the two little downstairs dining rooms. Fabrics hang across the walls and form a ceiling of cloth to make the place seem bigger than it really is. A little bar, lined with a large fish tank, and an additional dining room are located upstairs. The meal-size salads, grilled swordfish, rack of lamb, poached salmon in sorrel sauce, and Cornish hen haven't changed much since the '70s. ♦ American Eclectic ♦ Lunch and dinner; dinner only on Saturday and Sunday. 261 S. 21st St (between Locust and Spruce Sts). 546.4232

71 Thomas Hockley House Local architect **Frank Furness,** known for his eccentric buildings, designed (and 21 years later enlarged) this home for **Thomas Hockley,** a lawyer who was his friend and early supporter. It was completed in its earliest version in 1875. As in Furness' other buildings, the variations in the cut and lay of the brickwork create a pattern of texture and silhouette, an effect strived for by later Philadelphia craftspeople. ♦ 235 S. 21st St (between Locust and Spruce Sts)

72 Book Mark A pleasant, unhurried second-hand bookstore tucked away on a quiet street, Book Mark offers a solid architectural selection and a strong mail-order business. ♦ M-F 10AM-5PM; Sa noon-5PM; and by appointment. 2049 W. Rittenhouse Sq (between S. 20th and S. 21st Sts). 735.5546

73 asta de blue The unpredictable selection of trendy women's clothes in this tiny boutique may include a short-sleeved, fly-away jacket with wide-legged trousers; a long, feminine, floral sundress; or a denim sarong with a sleeveless vest, cowboy boots, and a baseball cap. Cutting-edge hats and shoes, expensive but hard to lay your hands on elsewhere, can be found here, along with pricey jeans that fit like a glove. ♦ M-Tu 11AM-7PM; W 11AM-9PM; Th-F 11AM-8PM; Sa 11AM-6:30PM; Su noon-5PM. 265 S. 20th St (between Manning and Spruce Sts). Also at: Suburban Square, Ardmore. 732.0550

Restaurants/Clubs: Red	**Hotels:** Blue
Shops/ ♣ Outdoors: Green	**Sights/Culture:** Black

74 Carolina's ★★$$$ "In" from the moment it opened in the mid-1980s, and still a hit with a thirtyish crowd in suits, Carolina's attractions include American comfort food and a prime location near Rittenhouse Square. Calf's liver in raspberry sauce, steamed pork dumplings, and roast chicken with sausage corn-bread stuffing stand out on the dinner menu. The veal loaf, with a dense gravy and mashed potatoes, is especially popular. For lunch try the Cobb salad with chicken, olives, bleu cheese, tomatoes, and avocado in a taco shell. The interior features an old tin ceiling that looks down on a room with large storefront windows and tightly positioned tables. ♦ American ♦ Lunch and dinner; dinner only on Saturday; Sunday brunch. 261 S. 20th St (between Locust and Spruce Sts). 545.1000

75 Sande Webster Gallery The 20-year-old Sande Webster Gallery works hard to assemble innovative, varied shows featuring local artists. Contemporary abstract painters **Moe Brooker, James Brantley,** and **Charles Searles** are among the best-known exhibitors. ♦ M-F 10AM-6PM; Sa 11AM-4PM. 2018 Locust St (between S. 20th and S. 21st Sts). 732.8850

76 English Village Built in 1923, **Spencer Roberts'** English Village was a successful experiment in urban design, with attached houses arranged around a well-tended flagstone court (no cars or other vehicles allowed). The tall mansard roofs contribute to the Elizabethan flavor. Why aren't there places like this in more American cities? ♦ S. 22nd St (between Walnut and Locust Sts)

77 William H. Allen Bookseller Countless used and antiquarian books have changed hands in these musty surroundings. The selection on classical history and literature is particularly flush. ♦ M-F 8AM-5PM; Sa 8:30AM-1PM. 2031 Walnut St (between S. 20th and S. 21st Sts). 563.3398

When Thomas Jefferson wrote the Declaration of Independence, he said his objectives were ". . . to place before mankind the common sense of the subject in terms so plain and firm as to command their assent and to justify ourselves in the independent stand we are compelled to take . . ."

78 The Compleat Strategist Dragon slayers can find kindred spirits to duel with by looking at the listings on the bulletin board here. The Compleat Strategist carries a full line of adventure, fantasy, and war games, including board games. ♦ M-Th, Sa 11AM-6PM; F 11AM-7PM. 2011 Walnut St (between S. 20th and S. 21st Sts). 562.2960

79 Irish Pub ★$$ Nothing here elevates the reputation of Irish food, but people come for the drink and the live-it-up atmosphere. Portraits of Irish-American celebrities grace the walls of both Center City locations. Stained glass, high ceilings, and bars of carved cherry wood recall older pubs in Ireland. The Dublin Irish stew is the best thing on the menu, which also includes chili, salmon, and steak. On many nights, a DJ spins records from 9PM on, and a high-decibel crowd takes over. ♦ Irish American ♦ Lunch and dinner. 2007 Walnut St (between S. 20th and S. 21st Sts). 568.5603. Also at: 1123 Walnut St. 925.3311

80 Fat Jack's Comicrypt A full line of superheroes, from *Adam Strange* to *Zot,* plus an extensive collection of back issues, is available in this shrine to the comic book. Anyone interested in a few copies of *Love and Rockets,* a magazine of graphic short stories for adults? ♦ M-Th, Sa 10AM-6PM; F 10AM-7:30PM. 2006 Sansom St (between S. 20th and S. 21st Sts). 963.0788

81 Home Sweet Homebrew What exactly is a zymurgist? Well, you could easily become one in **George H. Hummel's** hobby shop, which has everything you need to make your own wine and beer ("except the time," Hummel advises): starter kits, labels, bottles, bottle caps, T-shirts, you name it. ♦ Tu, Th-F 11:30AM-6PM; W 11:30AM-8PM; Sa 11AM-6PM. 2008 Sansom St (between S. 20th and S. 21st Sts). 569.9469

82 The Roxy Theatre The neighborhood's only remaining art film house screens first-run and recent art films, offbeat films, cult films, and would-be cult films, along with lots of Japanese science fiction, and more conventional fare. The two screens each seat about a hundred people. ♦ 2021 Sansom St (between S. 20th and S. 21st Sts). 563.9088

The Green Boys, a guerrilla group that staged raids on the British occupying Philadelphia, depended on a little-known Revolutionary War heroine known as Mom Rinker for word of enemy movements. Legend has it that she sat knitting on the cliffs above Wissahickon Creek. Whenever British troops passed, she would write a warning message on a scrap of paper, roll it up in a ball of yarn, and toss it to the Green Boys 250 feet below her.

83 The Wilma Theater Jiri and Blanka Zizka emigrated from Czechoslovakia in the 1970s and within a decade opened their innovative theater, albeit in cramped, no-frills surroundings. They've leaned toward political or philosophical drama, earning a reputation for originality and courage. Well-received comedies, including the contemporary political satire *Halcyon Days,* have played here, as well as dramas such as *Lady Day at Emerson's Bar and Grill,* **Vaclav Havel's** *Temptation,* and *Oedipus the King.* One measure of their success: plans for a new 300-seat theater on Broad Street, across from the **Merriam Theater.** The Wilma seats 106 people. ◆ 2030 Sansom St (between S. 20th and S. 21st Sts). 963.0345

84 The Classical Guitar Store All kinds of guitars, many of them secondhand, are sold here. The mellow, nylon-stringed classical guitar is the house specialty. ◆ M-F noon-6PM; Sa 10AM-5PM. 2038 Sansom St (between S. 20th and S. 21st Sts). 567.2972

85 First Unitarian Church In 1886 architect **Frank Furness** designed this two-story structure for his father, the **Reverend William Henry Furness.** While the church's exterior has undergone much alteration, the sanctuary remains intact, with a ceiling the architect stenciled with gold-leaf daffodils. ◆ 2125 Chestnut St (between S. 21st and S. 22nd Sts)

86 College of Physicians and Surgeons Founded in 1787 by **John Redman, Benjamin Rush,** and other prominent physicians, the college is the oldest existing honorary medical society in the U.S. It is also the home of the **F.C. Wood Institute for the History of Medicine** and an important library of medical literature, which has rare editions of **Aristotle** and paintings by **Thomas Eakins, Charles Willson Peale, John Singer Sargent,** and **Gilbert Stuart.** The building was completed in 1908 according to designs by **Cope and Stewardson.** ◆ Free. M-F 10AM-4PM. 19 S. 22nd St (between Market and Chestnut Sts). 563.3737

Within the College of Physicians and Surgeons:

The Mütter Museum For those with strong stomachs, the Mütter is a repository of frightful medical curiosities, including the tumor extracted from **President Grover Cleveland's** cancerous jawbone, the liver shared by famous 19th-century Siamese twins **Chang** and **Eng Bunker,** and a skeleton of a 7'6" giant alongside that of a 3'6" dwarf. The Mütter also houses **The Chevalier Jackson Collection of Foreign Bodies**—that is, drawer upon drawer of objects that the "Father of Laryngology" extracted from people who had accidentally swallowed them.

Despite the squeamish delight that generations of Philadelphians have taken in Mütter's wonders, these exhibits were not collected for their shock value. When the distinguished **Dr. Thomas Dent Mütter** retired in 1856, medical science was growing out of its metaphysical stage, when doctors attributed diseases to various "ill humours." In the mid-19th century medical education was based on gross anatomy and pathology, and diseases were observed by watching their clinical course in the patient, followed by autopsy. These exhibits were a boon to students of the era. Cleveland's jawbone, by the way, was replaced by a rubber prosthesis in a secret ship-board operation in 1893, leaving his constituents none the wiser. ◆ Donation requested. Tu-F 10AM-4PM 19 S. 22nd St (between Market and Chestnut Sts). 563.3737

87 2300 Chestnut Street Mural The 1983 painted trompe l'oeil mural by **Richard Haas** draws in a series of Philadelphia landmarks, seemingly placed in the building's interior: statues of *William Penn* and *Benjamin Franklin,* and behind them the ghost of architect **Frank Furness'** long-demolished **Baltimore & Ohio Railroad Station.** At ground level, the parking lot seems to abut the Schuylkill River. ◆ At S. 23rd St

88 Market Street Bridge The great granite eagles at each end of the bridge may look familiar to New Yorkers. Designed by **Adolph Alexander Weinman,** the 5,500-pound birds were installed on the roof of New York's Pennsylvania Station in 1903. After they lost their perch in the '60s, with the demolition of the station, the eagles were moved to diverse places, including this otherwise undistinctive bridge. None of the Schuylkill bridges are recommended for a casual walk; the traffic and wind can make them unpleasant for pedestrians. ◆ Market St (between S. 23rd and S. 30th Sts)

89 Commerce Square I.M. Pei, architect of prominent buildings throughout the country, and **Henry Cobb,** who designed the John Hancock Tower in Boston, teamed up to create these 40-story twin corporate towers of textured gray granite (completed in 1987 and 1992). The diamond-shaped cutouts that adorn the top floors make the buildings easy to spot from blocks away. A wonderful mid-block park designed by landscape architect **Hannah Olin** separates the towers. ◆ Market St (between N. 20th and N. 21st Sts)

90 Cutters Grand Cafe ★★$$$ Grand in style with high ceilings, marble, chandeliers, and a dramatic staircase, Cutters rates high among singles and young professionals. The bartenders add to the theatricality by climbing a tall ladder to pull items from the two-story bar. Popular beers and malt whiskeys include 60 single malt scotches and **Orval,** a triple-hopped ale from Belgium. The cuisine emphasizes Cajun spices, with mesquite-grilled fish, chicken, and steak. Salads and pastas, such as shellfish fettuccine, are also available. ♦ American ♦ Lunch and dinner; dinner only on Saturday and Sunday. 2005 Market St (at N. 20th St). 851.6262

91 Whodunit Creaky floors and dim lighting set the stage for mystery lover **Art Borgeau's** bookshop, which offers thousands of new and used crime books, including some long-out-of-print items. You might call it a bookstore *noir.* ♦ M-Sa 11AM-6:30PM. 1931 Chestnut St (between S. 19th and S. 20th Sts). 567.1478

92 Boyd's for Men Holding forth in a 1907 Beaux Arts building that once housed the art school for the **Pennsylvania Academy of the Fine Arts,** this top-of-the-line men's store offers ready-to-wear labels and custom-made items. Boyd's may have the finest selection of men's clothes in the city, but it's not really a store for browsers; the platoon of eager, obsequious salesmen chills the atmosphere. White balustrades, marble columns, and prints enhance an already-elegant interior. **BLT's** (★$), a cafe in the store, serves gourmet sandwiches and light entrées such as grilled filet mignon on foccacia with sweet onion relish. ♦ M-Tu, Th-Sa 9:30AM-6PM; W 9:30AM-9PM. 1818 Chestnut St (between S. 18th and S. 19th Sts). 564.9000

93 Freeman Fine Arts Not everything for sale at this auction house is a fine antique, and that makes the two-figure bidding all the more fun. The furniture on the floor of the cavernous salesroom can range from Mission buffets to Naugahyde recliners, and some of the paintings are valuable only for their frames. Look for the quality stuff on the days before the auctions, which take place every Wednesday beginning at 10AM (glassware and paintings go first). Written bids are accepted. Catalogued auctions of antiques and paintings are held several times a year in the handsome third-floor gallery. ♦ M-F 9AM-5PM. 1808 Chestnut St (between S. 18th and S. 19th Sts). 563.9275

94 Holiday Inn Center City $$ Ongoing renovations should enliven this hotel, which offers 445 standard Holiday Inn rooms. The convenient location is close to the stock exchange and a short bus trip to the convention center. ♦ S. 18th and Market Sts. 561.7500, 800/464.4329; fax 561.4484

95 The Family This outdoor sculpture of a man, woman, and child was completed by **Timothy Duffield** in 1981. ♦ N. 18th and Market Sts

96 Philadelphia Stock Exchange Dating to 1790, the Philadelphia stock exchange was once a key institution in the early American economy, though now it is overshadowed by the Big Board in the Big Apple. In 1981 the exchange moved into its current comfortable quarters, designed in 1981 by **Cope/Linder and Associates** with an eight-story atrium under a greenhouse skylight as its centerpiece. Student guides lead tours around lunchtime, when the action is somewhat less frenzied. Three selling floors, littered with call slips, offer stock equity, stock options, and foreign currency options (the latter activity occurs all night to take advantage of overseas trading hours). The traders stare at computer monitors like NASA flight controllers, furiously auctioning stocks and currency, signaling their bids across the floor, and then shouting the puts and calls at each other, all making for good theater. After a sale, they relax over computer games and lollipops. The traders are friendly, yet always on the lookout to turn a profit: charmed recently by a seventh-grade class of visitors, they *sold* the children their lollipops, at 25 cents apiece. ♦ Free tours by appointment. 1900 Market St (at S. 19th St). 496.5200

97 Apollo Hotel $ It may be a few blocks away from the main action, but this small hotel is not at all inaccessible. Its 84 rooms are scheduled for remodeling in a style that the management assures will not drastically change the inexpensive rates. ♦ 1918 Arch St (between N. 19th and N. 20th Sts). 567.8925

When the Connie Mack Stadium (a.k.a. Shibe Park) opened in 1908, it was the first concrete-and-steel ballpark ever built. People in neighboring row houses erected bleachers on their roofs to watch the Philadelphia Athletics play baseball until John Shibe, the owner, installed a 38-foot addition, blocking the view. The stadium closed in 1970, a victim of the neighborhood's lack of parking spaces.

Between 1820 and 1860, Philadelphia's population grew from 110,000 to 560,000 as its factories multiplied.

In February 1991, fire broke out in One Meridian Plaza, a 39-story office building directly across from Philadelphia's City Hall. Three firefighters were killed in the blaze, accidentally started by rags soaked with linseed oil (used as a cleaning solvent), and the heavily damaged skyscraper still remains closed.

Bests

Patrick T. Murphy
Director, Institute of Contemporary Art

Walking Around—Philadelphia is an exciting and rewarding city to stroll. See a lexicon of American architecture from the early 18th century to today. Areas suggested: **Old City, Society Hill,** and **Rittenhouse Square.**

The **Italian Market,** where you can see what the Lower East Side of Manhattan must have been like at the beginning of this century. Try **Sarconi's** for bread, **Isgro's** for cannoli, **D'Angelo Brothers** for meat, and **Claudio King of Cheese** for cheese and salami.

Reading Terminal Market is a wonderful covered market with lots of fresh produce. Try **Le Bus** for the archetypal muffin.

Make a pilgrimage to the **Marcel Duchamp** collection at the **Philadelphia Museum of Art** and see *Etant Donnes.*

The **Mütter Museum at the College of Physicians** is one of the most eccentric museums in the country. Check out the collection of "things that people have swallowed."

Fabric Workshop features high-quality work by internationally known artists.

White Dog Cafe, for a unique combination of imaginative food and social conscience (with sister restaurants as far away as Hanoi and Havana).

Zanzibar Blue continues the tradition of sophisticated jazz in Philadelphia.

Frank's Bar, which has a beautiful interior and offers lively conversation after work, reminds me of a Dublin bar.

Allen's Bookshop is a truly great antiquarian bookstore. Browse for hours.

Philadelphians tend to be self-effacing about the **Mummers Parade,** but if you're in town on 1 January, don't miss this northeastern-style Carnival.

Tequila's—a great Mexican restaurant.

Victor's Cafe, for the Italian food and the professionally trained singers (waiting on tables as they anticipate their big break) who entertain with excerpts from the great operas.

Little Pete's—a perfect diner, with good food and waitresses who've seen it all.

Robert Bynum
Owner, Zanzibar Blue

First Fridays, when art aficionados gather to stroll and gawk among the many galleries and studios that fill Old City, a unique part of Philadelphia.

West River Drive, for a late-night cruise and the best view of the lights along **Boathouse Row.**

The **Fountain Room** in the Four Seasons Hotel and **Restaurant 210** at the Rittenhouse Hotel.

The **Rodin Museum,** home of *The Thinker,* when you need inspiration.

Philadanco, a dance troupe with soul.

The Astral Plane for atmosphere, and **Mama Rosa's** for soul food.

Di Lullo Centro and **Susanna Foo** for expensive Italian and Chinese dining (respectively) in lavish surroundings.

Ralph's and **Joe's Peking Duck House** for inexpensive, yet very good, Italian and Chinese food (respectively).

The **Philadelphia Zoo** in winter, when you feel closer to nature and the animals.

Wawa for hot dogs at 4AM.

Browsing through **Boyd's** (the men's clothier) and buying at **Ira Lish.**

Drinks at the bar at **Odeon.**

More than anything, the feeling that Philadelphia is the biggest small town in the United States.

Margaret E. Kuhn
National Convener, Gray Panthers

Go to **Independence Square** and visit the **Liberty Bell** and the great colonial buildings where the Continental Congress met and the Declaration of Independence was signed in 1776.

The **Philadelphia Museum of Art,** one of the city's artistic and architectural treasures.

Great conductors and world-renowned musicians have made the **Philadelphia Orchestra** revered and loved around the world. The chandeliers and columns of the **Academy of Music** are most appropriate settings for the music.

The William Penn statue atop City Hall overlooks the **John Wanamaker Store,** which has a Grand Hall that's a wonderful meeting place ("meet me at the eagle"), especially at noon when the great organ plays, holding shoppers and visitors spellbound.

Walk through the **Chinese Arch** and enjoy Chinese shops and delectable food in **Chinatown.**

Fairmount Park/Schuylkill River—One of the longest parkways in America. The trees, shrubs, grassy knolls, and stone bridges make driving, walking, and hiking a memorable journey.

Lunch or tea at **Valley Green Inn** on Wissahickon Creek was a favorite rest stop for colonial stagecoaches. The ducks, geese, and swans swimming in the creek are a delight for children and family groups.

Many scientific exhibits can be explored at the **Franklin Institute,** plus there's the **Fels Planetarium,** where you learn about the stars and planets, and the magnitude of the universe.

Restaurants/Clubs: Red   **Hotels:** Blue

Shops/ 🌳 **Outdoors:** Green   **Sights/Culture:** Black

Parkway/Fairmount Park

Extending in a single diagonal from City Hall, the **Benjamin Franklin Parkway** is a wide, tree-lined thoroughfare studded with palacelike neoclassical structures, flags, statues, and ornamental fountains. Look familiar? You might say it's a boulevard of brilliant imitations—a direct take on the **Avenue des Champs-Elysées** in Paris. The **Free Library** and **Family Court** are reminiscent of the **Place de la Concorde**. And the striking gateway to the **Rodin Museum** is even a replica of a replica, a copy of the one at

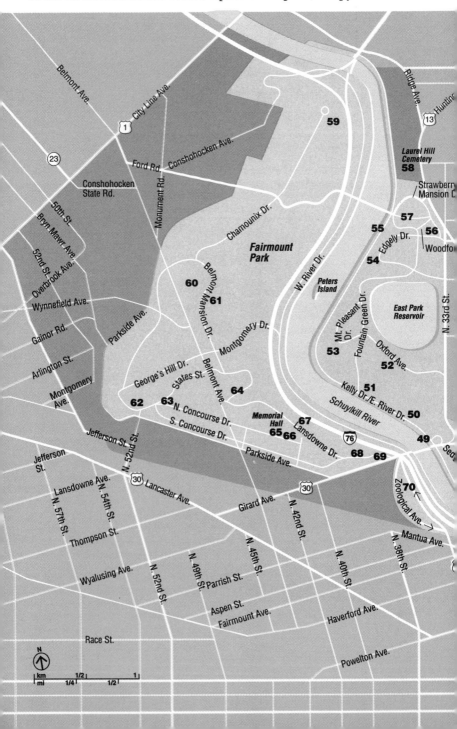

ulptor **Auguste Rodin's** home in Meudon, France, which was based on the trance to the **Chateau d'Issy.**

group of society figures spearheaded this massive public works project in 17 as a way of connecting Fairmount Park to the center of the city at City ll. French landscape designer **Jacques Greber** proposed a design that would t through existing neighborhoods, focus on City Hall, and be lined with pressive cultural institutions. The Parkway accomplished many of these als: its open expanses are a welcome release from the city's boxed-in precincts, and the **Museum of Art** and the **Franklin Institute** have earned world-class reputations. Nevertheless, few French visitors mistake the Benjamin Franklin Parkway for the Champs-Elysées, an urban boulevard of cafes and shops. In true American style, the Parkway caters to automobiles, and serves as a quick exit from Center City.

William Penn once praised the rocky bluff where the Museum of Art stands as the "Faire Mount." Thus **Fairmount** was the logical name for what later became a vast, landscaped park on both banks of the Schuylkill. Both Penn and **Benjamin Franklin** saw the river as an important water resource, but it was not until 1843 that the city began purchasing property upstream of the **Fairmount Waterworks** to protect the supply. In 1867 the area was designated a public park. After rejecting a plan by **Frederick Law Olmsted,** who designed New York's Central Park, the city turned to its own Prussian-born junior engineer, **Hermann Schwartzmann,** to lay out the winding drives on either side of the river and landscape the grounds. The park's moment of celebrity came in 1876, when 10 million people crowded its west side to visit the **Centennial International Exposition.** Fairmount Park continued to gain territory, as well as a good deal of fine statuary, into the 20th century, but the greatest change came with the development of the **Schuylkill Expressway** and the increase in commuter traffic along **East River Drive** (now called **Kelly Drive**).

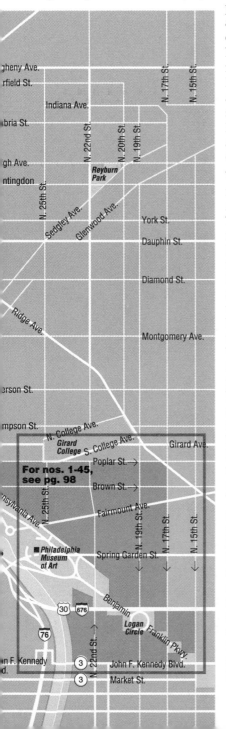

For nos. 1-45, see pg. 98

Parkway/Fairmount Park

The two highways separate the riverfronts from the park and leave much of it out of reach to anyone without a car. Visitors to the park's nether regions usually drive from sight to sight, through woods, and past fields, some of them unkempt. The well-maintained promenade along Kelly Drive, however, a lovely stretch of trees, rivers, and greenery, is the heart of the park, where most visitors go to stroll, jog, or bicycle. Along the walkway are places to picnic and rent rowboats, and the **Ellen Phillips Samuel Memorial** sculpture garden is a serene spot to watch the sculling crews race their shells. Riding the **Fairmount Park Trolley** bus is a relaxing way to see the area; it takes visitors on a 17-mile loop, stopping at the early American mansions in the park. Just north of the Parkway, the gentrified neighborhood of Fairmount, with pretty shaded streets of restored row houses, offers the best restaurants to visit while touring the vicinity.

1 LOVE Sculpture Robert Indiana's steel sculpture, located on the axis of the Parkway in Kennedy Plaza, is commonly referred to as "Philadelphia LOVE." It was erected in 1976. ◆ John F. Kennedy Blvd and N. 15th St

2 Three-Way Piece Number 1: Points Henry Moore's 1964 bronze sculpture weighs in at one ton and has been said to resemble a hefty animal (with three points for paws), a gnawed bone, and a hunched bird. ◆ The Pkwy (between N. 16th and N. 17th Sts)

3 Bell Atlantic Tower Philadelphia's favorite new office tower, by the hometown firm of **The Kling Linquist,** houses the corporate headquarters of the Bell Atlantic Company. Its faceted sides and ziggurat top, illuminated at night, are wrapped in red granite accentuated by polished brass trim at its base. Construction was completed in 1990. ◆ N. 18th and Arch Sts

4 Dock Street Brewing Company ★★$$ Boisterous crowds of professionals frequent this stylish contemporary alehouse, named for the brand of beer. Young lawyers loosen their ties and play billiards in the room behind the 40-foot cherry bar, while vats in the front produce five to seven brands of beer and ale each day. Sample the fresh brews in the appealing high-ceilinged dining room, furnished with cherry tables. The hit-or-miss menu includes real British pub fare: game pies, roast beef sandwiches with mustard dipping sauce, and (indigestible) fish-and-chips. Panfried crab cakes, Muscovy duck chili simmered in dark lager, rabbit cassoulet, and excellent homemade breads stylishly round out the offerings. ◆ Eclectic ◆ Lunch and dinner. 2 Logan Sq (N. 18th and Cherry Sts). 496.0413

5 Embassy Suites Hotel $$$ Recently opened after a remodeling of a 1963 apartment house designed by **Stonorov & Haws,** the cylindrical 28-story hotel offers 281 two-room suites. Each suite has two balconies that overlook either the Parkway or Center City. Catering to families, the hotel has a children's playroom on the premises, as well as a health club and sauna. ◆ 1776 Benjamin Franklin Pkwy (at N. 18th St). 561.1776, 800/EMBASSY; 963.0122

Within the Embassy Suites Hotel:

T.G.I. Friday's $ This popular chain restaurant, known for its hamburgers and salad bars, serves guests a complimentary cooked-to-order breakfast. ◆ American ◆ Breakfast, lunch, and dinner. 665.8443

6 United Fund Headquarters Designed by **Mitchell/Guirgola Associates** in 1969, this building is perhaps the finest example of this firm's work in the city. Each of the three main facades addresses its urban context, as well as its compass orientation: a monumental vertical scale in concrete facing the angled Parkway, horizontal concrete sunscreens facing Logan Circle, and a gray glass curtain wall facing north on Arch Street. It's a remarkable response to the design and development controls of the Parkway, including a trapezoidal site. ◆ The Pkwy (between N. 17th and N. 18th Sts)

6 Statue of Kopernik In the early 16th century, Polish astronomer **Nicholas Copernicus** came up with the theory that the earth moves around the sun. Commissioned by local Polish Americans to mark the 500th anniversary of his birth in 1473, the abstract sculpture recalls the astronomer's accomplishments and his original Polish name: **Mikolaj Kopernik.** The monument, by **Dudley Talcott,** features a 16-foot stainless-steel circle that symbolizes the earth's orbit, with soil from Copernicus' birthplace, Torun, Poland, placed beneath it. ◆ N. 18th St and the Pkwy

7 Wyndham Franklin Plaza Hotel $$$ A city unto itself, the 758-room hotel offers comfortable rooms, a pool, a sauna, a fitness club, squash courts, outdoor tennis courts, and a jogging track (for some of these facilities, however, guests must pay extra). **Geddes Brecher Qualls Cunningham** designed the hotel, which was completed in 1982. The massive atrium lobby, with its metal truss skylight, is far from cozy, the one intimate touch an 1869 tower clock imported from Manchester, England. A 15-minute walk brings you to either the convention center or the shopping areas of Walnut and Chestnut streets. Valet parking and a shuttle service from Philadelphia Airport are available. ◆ N. 17th and Race Sts. 448.2000

Within the Wyndham Franklin Plaza Hotel:

Between Friends ★$$$ Chippendale chairs, banquettes, and silk flowers adorn the hotel's most elegant restaurant. The menu surpasses the conventional meals offered elsewhere in the hotel with grilled swordfish daubed with peach salsa, panfried duck breast paired with onion confit, and Cajun-blackened sirloin steak. ◆ American ◆ Lunch and dinner; lunch only on Monday and Tuesday; Sunday brunch. Lobby level. 448.2000

The Terrace ★$$ An open dining area overlooking the massive lobby caters primarily to out-of-towners who don't feel like venturing outside. The menu—grilled chicken sandwiches, fried shrimp, and pasta primavera—isn't too adventurous either. ◆ American ◆ Breakfast, lunch, and dinner. 448.2000

The Lobby Bar This bar stays open late—a good thing, too, because there's little nightlife in the immediate area. ◆ Daily 3:30PM-1AM. Lobby level. 448.2000

8 Cathedral of Ss. Peter and Paul The seat of Philadelphia's Roman Catholic archdiocese was designed by **John Notman** and **Napoleon LeBrun** from plans drawn by **Reverends Mariano Maller** and **John B. Tornatore** and inspired by the Church of San Carlo al Corso in Rome. Notman is responsible for the Palladian Revival exterior, with the great copper dome and Corinthian portico (shown above). The inside of the dome was painted by **Constantino Brumidi,** who also frescoed the Capitol dome in Washington, D.C. Construction of the cathedral was completed in 1864; restoration and other new construction took place in the 1950s. The side chapels were recently turned into seven shrines, including one to Philadelphia's own **Blessed Katherine Drexel** (1858-1955), a Catholic convert whose many charitable works have made her a candidate for sainthood. ♦ N. 18th St and the Pkwy. 561.1313

In front of the Cathedral of Ss. Peter and Paul:

Statue of Thomas FitzSimons The Irish-born signer of the Declaration of Independence served in the Continental Congress and the first three U.S. Congresses.

9 Four Seasons Hotel $$$$ If you can afford it, this is indisputably the best hotel in the city. The lobby opens onto a series of sitting rooms, with comfortable niches from which to watch the well-dressed and well-heeled go by. Designed by **Kohn Pederson Fox Associates,** the 371-room hotel and the neighboring 30-story **One Logan Square** office tower feature a pool and health club facilities, as well as a dry cleaner and a beauty salon. Rooms are furnished with mahogany secretaries, marb baths, and minibars stocked with Belgian chocolates and Perrier. Free car service is available within the city limits. ♦ 1 Logan Sc (N. 18th St and the Pkwy). 963.1500, 800/332.3442; fax 963.9562

Within the Four Seasons Hotel:

The Fountain ★★★★$$$$ This is one o' those rare hotel restaurants that deserves t' acclaim it garners. The tastefully conservati dining rooms, with antique china place settings, shaded chandeliers, and an extravagant display of fresh flowers, look o Logan Square and Swann Fountain. Executi chef **Jean-Marie Lacroix** and chef **Martin Hamann** prepare imaginative dishes, culina artistry of the sort featured in gourmet magazines. Order à la carte, if you like, but fixed-price menu is the better value. You might start with roasted shad roe with cape or sweet corn and ginger soup, then move c to a consommé with quail eggs, grilled calf liver with sweet onion ravioli, or Muscovy duck breast with sweet potatoes and a gree peppercorn sauce. Or choose from their lighter menu: perhaps roasted rabbit tenderloins with asparagus tips and wild mushrooms, marinated artichoke heart with grilled quail and shavings of Locatelli chees or an impeccably grilled Hawaiian tuna fillet with a basil sauce. The wine list is extensive and the service is refined without being snooty. ♦ American/Continental ♦ Breakfast lunch, and dinner. Reservations recommended. 963.1500

Swann Lounge and Cafe ★★$$ A light menu is offered in an airy, elegant room overlooking the Parkway. The comfortable sofas and chairs make this a pleasant choic for afternoon tea or lunch. Choose from croissant sandwiches, pasta (perhaps with venison and eggplant), or a daily meat speci

On Friday and Saturday nights, the lounge s up an elaborate dessert table with tortes, cakes, mousses, tarts, and fruit. A set price lets you visit the **Viennese Buffet** as often as you wish. A jazz trio provides the entertainment. Return on Sunday for brunch—slightly pricey, but a cut above the all-you-can-stand hotel spreads. ♦ America ♦ Breakfast, lunch, afternoon tea; Sunday brunch. Viennese buffet: F-Sa 9PM-1AM. Reservations recommended for afternoon te 963.1500

10 Morton's of Chicago ★★★$$$$ Lawyer and businesspeople in well-cut suits descen from neighboring office towers to dine at th local entry of the national steakhouse chain. The place resembles an old-fashioned gentleman's club with dark woods, brass, a etched glass. Despite the fact that many of t appetizers are fish or seafood (such as broil sea scallops wrapped in bacon), and that the kitchen even serves lobster and a daily fish entrée, don't let it fool you. If you're not into red meat, you really don't belong here. The main attraction is beef, though the rib lamb chops are also good. Be prepared: Before you order, the waiter displays naked cuts of meat for your approval. ♦ American ♦ Lunch and dinner. 1 Logan Sq (entrance on N. 19th St, between Cherry and Race Sts). 557.0724

11 Logan Circle The recent restoration of the **Swann Memorial Fountain,** built in 1924, may prove a milestone in Philadelphia's current revival. **Alexander Stirling Calder's** spouting bronze figures represent the city's three main waterways: the male American Indian stands for the **Delaware River,** and the two women for the **Schuylkill River** and **Wissahickon Creek.** The bronze swans play on the name of **Dr. Wilson Cary Swann,** president of the Philadelphia Fountain Society, in whose honor the fountain was constructed. Calder collaborated with **Wilson Eyre, Jr.,** on the fountain and pool. At night the geysers and sprays glamorously reflect the city lights. During the day, the circle (one of the five original city squares) attracts lovers, readers, small children, and the homeless. **James Logan** (1674-1751) was **William Penn's** agent and mayor of Philadelphia. Mind the traffic signals as you approach the fountain on foot; one of the finest outdoor sculptures in America is, unfortunately, in the middle of a busy traffic circle. ♦ N. 19th St and the Pkwy

12 The Academy of Natural Sciences This is *the* place for dinosaurs. The oldest natural history museum in the country, the Academy often plays second fiddle to the more ostentatious **Franklin Institute.** But the Academy's collection of re-created dinosaurs and mounted animals is one of the finest in the country. Founded in 1812 by druggist **John Speakman** and his friends, the Academy began as a discussion group that met in a Market Street coffeehouse. It moved to its present site in 1876, bringing with it the beginning of its spectacular dinosaur collection, including the first bones ever attributed to dinosaurs. The bones of the Hadrosaurus were discovered in nearby Haddonfield, New Jersey, in the 1830s; in 1868 Academy curator **Joseph Leidy** used them to assemble the world's first mounted dinosaur skeleton. Now, many of the creatures stand in the dinosaur hall, a hit among young children. On the second floor,

another exhibit, "Dinosaurs—A Global View," demonstrates their evolution and extinction. Among the other exhibits is one on the ancient Egyptian process of mummification—with a real mummy, named Petiese, out of his wraps. Lifelike dioramas of mounted animals—lions, gorillas, wild yaks, buffalo, and polar bears—are shown in their natural settings. Mounted zebras drink from a stream in a re-creation of a **Serengeti Waterhole.** In the highly recommended third-floor children's museum, **Outside In,** kids can pet living animals, perhaps a tarantula or bunny, and play on a sandy beach. On the weekends, the museum has special events and sponsors field trips for adults as well as children. On display in the museum's library, which includes more than 150,000 volumes, is a folio copy of **John James Audubon's** *Birds of America.* There's a gift shop and, on the ground floor, vending machines and tables for eating. ♦ Admission. M-F 10AM-4:30PM; Sa-Su 10AM-5PM. N. 19th and Race Sts. 299.1000

13 Moore College of Art and Design Founded in 1848, the college is the only four-year art college for women in the U.S. Worth visiting are two galleries located on the ground floor: the **Goldie Paley Gallery** showcases emerging American and European artists, and the **Levy Gallery** focuses exclusively on Philadelphia artists, especially African-American and other minorities. ♦ M-Tu, Th-F 10AM-5PM; W 10AM-8PM; Sa-Su noon-4PM. N. 20th and Race Sts. 568.4515

14 St. Clement's Episcopal Church Looking as if it belongs amid serene graveyards and rolling English countryside instead of nondescript office buildings and row houses, this 1859 church is yet another **John Notman** project. When 20th Street was widened in 1929, this gracious Romanesque brownstone was moved 40 feet without sustaining any damage. The wrought-iron gates of the 1870 **Lady Chapel** are the work of **Samuel Yellin,** who, in the early part of the century, fashioned exquisite ironwork for the homes of the Rockefellers and Vanderbilts. ♦ M-F 10AM-3PM. 2013 Appletree St (between N. 20th and N. 21st Sts). 563.1876

15 Please Touch Museum One of the better examples of a genre that has spread across the country, parents depend on this fun house for pre-schoolers, especially on dreary days. The emphasis here is on play; education comes second. Park the stroller and head up a winding ramp. You're greeted by an obstacle course of balance beams, wooden slides, and climbing ropes. Next is "Move It," the museum's new transportation display. It features a real city bus with a working horn and steering wheel. Kids immediately climb into the driver's seat and demand spare change. A monorail that used to run through the Grand Court of the **John Wanamaker Store** is here, along with miniature trains and a 30-foot replica of the Delaware River, complete with water, toy ferries, and cranes to load cargo onto little freighters. Elsewhere in the museum, you'll find a mock television station with a working camera, a large wooden train set, and a life-size trolley. Computers scattered throughout the main floor are a big hit, as is the miniature supermarket, with cash registers, stocked shelves, and shopping carts. After filling their carts, children unpack and cook in the designer kitchen next door. (The same rubber chicken has been roasted thousands of times.) The museum gets crowded on weekends, so arrive early or try a weekday. Bring your own lunch unless hot dogs from the cart out front will do. The gift shop has a fairly expensive selection of books, educational games, and toys. ♦ Admission; pay as you wish on Wednesday from 3-4PM and Sunday from 9-10AM. Daily 9AM-4:30PM. 210 N. 21st St (at Race St). 963.0667

16 The Franklin Institute Science Museum Inspired as much by P.T. Barnum as by **Benjamin Franklin,** the Institute is a great theatrical enterprise that will entertain, amuse, and exhaust you, while it teaches you about science. The **Franklin Institute for the Promotion of Mechanical Arts** was founded in 1824 and became a major center for scientific study in the 19th century. The Science Museum, designed by **John T. Windrim,** opened in 1934 and has been significantly enlarged with designs by **Geddes Brecher Qualls Cunningham.** As you enter, you'll see a rotunda that is the national memorial to Franklin. Anchoring it is an imposing 122-ton marble monument of America's most famous scientist by **James Earle Fraser** (who also designed the buffalo nickel). The museum is made up of several entities, and the admission fee depends on which you visit. Decide how much time you have, and talk over the choices with the patient ticket sellers in the central atrium. The admission fees are higher than those of other

museums in the city, so expect a fairly expensive outing, especially if you come with a herd of children. Three gift shops and two restaurants are located in the Franklin Institute to ensure that you are completely broke before you leave. ♦ Admission. Daily 9:30AM-5PM. N. 20th St and the Pkwy. 448.1200

Within The Franklin Institute Science Museum:

The Science Center The exhibits in this section—the original part of the museum—are fascinating and instructive. One of the real crowd-pleasers is a two-story human heart: you walk through the arteries and ventricles, while the heartbeat echoes in your ears. The **Mechanics Hall** contains levers, pulleys, and other mechanical devices that demonstrate the laws of Newtonian physics (as you operate them, docents are on hand to explain the principles). Optical effects and electromagnetism all get good displays, and you can take a train ride (for about 10 feet) aboard a Baldwin locomotive. An entire room is devoted to trains and provides some of the best fun in the museum for kids.

Mandell Futures Center This section focuses less on science and more on technology: space travel, computers, and telecommunications, as well as their attendant problems. A sizable exhibit explores environment and waste disposal, and a giant globe plots the spread of the human population from the 18th century into the 21st. While the center goes out of its way to be interactive, small children are more likely to enjoy the many ramps leading to the exhibits rather than the underwhelming exhibits themselves. If you have a limited amount of time, skip this center and go on to the **Omniverse Theater.** ♦ M-W 9:30AM-5PM; Th-Su 9:30AM-9PM

Tuttleman Omniverse Theater The four-story dome contains a 79-foot-wide screen that wraps 180 degrees around the audience, and is operated using an eight-track sound system and 56 speakers. The result is your complete immersion in a thrilling science film. The feature presentation is preceded by a superb short, *Philadelphia Anthem,* a hyperkinetic look at the city, complete with stirring music and eye-opening shots. The features themselves—explorations that have ranged from Antarctica to the South American rain forest to outer space—are spectacular. Occasionally, the theater offers late-night showings of films with marginal scientific interest, like the Rolling Stones in concert. ♦ Hourly shows M-F 10AM-4PM; Sa-Su 10AM-5PM

Fels Planetarium Once planetariums used Zeiss projectors, those marvelous, multilensed, insectlike devices, to accurately re-create the night sky on their domes. Employing the projector, a narrator would conduct a sky tour of the universe, demonstrating the movement of the stars from season to season, and over the millennia. But now the Zeisses have been purged and the live sky tours replaced by canned space documentaries. The Fels Planetarium is no exception, though it still presents a sky show with live commentary on Saturday afternoons, as well as occasional evening jazz concerts. ◆ Showtimes vary

17 Aero Memorial The bronze sphere, designed by **Paul Manship** and unveiled in 1948, memorializes the Allied aviators who died during World War I. ◆ N. 20th St and the Pkwy

18 Shakespeare Memorial The 1926 monument by **Alexander Stirling Calder** was erected by the **Shakespere Society,** which honored the Bard's original spelling of his name. The grouping depicts Hamlet and Touchstone, the court jester, and commemorates several of the actors who brought Shakespeare to the Philadelphia stage, including **Thomas Wignell, John Drew,** and **Edwin Forrest.** ◆ Logan Circle (at N. 20th and Vine Sts)

19 The Free Library Boasting a collection of 10 million items, the Philadelphia public library system is an important resource for students of all ages. In 1894 University of Pennsylvania provost **Dr. William Pepper,** with a $250,000 bequest from his uncle **George Pepper** and private subscriptions, began The Free Library in **City Hall.** The main branch was designed by **Horace Trumbauer** in 1917 as part of the Parkway project. Trumbauer's chief designer was **Julian Abele** (1881-1950), the first African-American graduate of the University of Pennsylvania School of Architecture. (Trumbauer and Abele also designed the **Museum of Art.**) The library's stacks are closed for browsing, but a computerized card catalog and helpful librarians make finding books relatively easy. Tours of the Rare Book Department can be arranged. At closing time, the chimes of a replica of London's Big Ben resound throughout the building. The cafeteria on the fourth floor has lunch fare at bargain prices, and an outdoor terrace offers a lovely view of Center City. ◆ M-W 9AM-9PM; Th-F 9AM-6PM; Sa 9AM-5PM; Su 1-5PM. Closed Sunday in summer. Logan Circle (at N. 19th and Vine Sts). 686.5407

20 Bistro Callowhill Street ★★$$ This tasteful contemporary bistro with gray decor and lots of faux marble has gained a faithful following. Try the fresh rainbow trout and julienned vegetables broiled in parchment, the boneless chicken breast with a wild mushroom mousse and red wine sauce, or the ravioli stuffed with broccoli and ricotta cheese. The restaurant smokes its salmon right in the kitchen, and accompanies it with sour cream, red onion, capers, and fresh fruit—delicious. ◆ American ◆ Lunch and dinner; dinner only on Saturday and Sunday. Closed Monday. 1836 Callowhill St (between N. 18th and N. 19th Sts). 557.6922

21 Rose Tattoo Cafe ★★$$ A jungle of green plants hangs from the ceiling in this longstanding tenant of a dingy corner several blocks north of the **Free Library.** Head for the rear room with skylights if you can, and order the cold salad of grilled chicken and angel hair pasta. The casual menu also features classic jambalaya and veal tenderloins with cognac and apricot-cherry chutney. ◆ American/Continental ◆ Lunch and dinner; dinner only on Saturday. Closed Sunday. 1847 Callowhill St (at N. 19th St). 569.8939

22 Down Home Grill ★$ The owner of **Jack's Firehouse** bought a failed gyro-burger-pizza joint, adorned it with murals, and installed a menu of down-home cooking that draws the business crowd, students in jeans, and families (there's a good children's menu). Country home cooking and urbane diner food are the attractions here, though sometimes the quality fluctuates. The choices, at least, are interesting. Sandwiches include a smoked turkey club, a fried oyster po' boy, and foccacia bread with roast pork, peppers, and provolone. The myriad possibilities also include chili, hearty meat loaf, barbecued pork ribs, and pizza (regular or topped with duck, scallions, and Chinese plum sauce). ◆ American ◆ Breakfast, lunch, and dinner. 1800 Spring Garden St (at N. 18th St). 557.7510

In 1872, the Fairmount Park Art Association was formed "to protest against the universal standardization of machinery that is stamping out the artistic soul of the individual." The association first limited its scope to providing the park with outdoor sculpture but soon took on the whole city's appearance—one of the main reasons for the wealth of public art in Philadelphia today.

Popular recording artists who live in the Philadelphia area: Patti LaBelle; saxophonist Grover Washington, Jr.; singer Teddy Pendergrass; rappers DJ Jazz Jeff and the Fresh Prince, as well as the Goats; and pop-rockers The Hooters. (Fans of Eugene Ormandy, director and conductor of the Philadelphia Orchestra from 1936 to 1980, might remember "The Sound of Philadelphia" in a more classical version.)

23 Mezzanotte ★★★$$ Colorful plates of antipasti—roasted peppers, marinated mushrooms, frittata—are strategically placed near the entrance of this contemporary trattoria. Decorated with chrome, glass block, and muted lighting, Mezzanotte has several dining rooms, including a balcony for quiet conversation. The designer pizzas are a hit. Try the sweet-tasting pizza with sliced apples, Italian sausage, and Gorgonzola, or a more traditional pie with prosciutto, black olives, mozzarella, and red onion. If you prefer, dine more lavishly by ordering a regional specialty: black pasta with squid, white beans, tomato, and basil from Calabria or Sicilian duck marinated in sherry and grilled with currants and Marsala wine. One of Mezzanotte's moderately priced wines is a must on any table. ♦ Italian ♦ Lunch and dinner. 1701 Green St. 765.2777

24 Korman Suites at Buttonwood Square $$$ With 210 suites out of a total of 280 rooms, free parking, and a free shuttle service around Center City, this new hotel is a great deal, even if it is slightly out of reach of Philadelphia's principal attractions. A cobblestone courtyard with modern sculpture, enormous brass doors, and a pleasant lobby help give the hotel a modicum of elegance. Stay on one of the upper floors for an extraordinary view of the Philadelphia skyline. The fitness facilities and outdoor pool are available to all guests, and Continental breakfast is free. ♦ 2001 Hamilton St (at N. 20th St). 569.7000

Within Korman Suites at Buttonwood Square:

Catalina ★$$ A sunny California-inspired restaurant looks onto a garden courtyard that almost has you believing you're on the West Coast. The emphasis is on light, imaginative entrées that are low in cholesterol and fat. Grilled fish or steak comes with a choice of sauces that are a cut above: sun-dried tomato with olive relish, for example. Or try the baked oysters, barbecued shrimp, stir-fried beef, or one of Catalina's large inventive salads. ♦ American ♦ Lunch and dinner; dinner only on Sunday. Reservations recommended. 569.7500

25 Long's Gourmet Chinese Cooking ★$$ In a renovated strip of raised storefronts that was a former loading dock, a pastel dining room with well-spaced tables offers Chinese food and prices a notch above those in Chinatown. Daily specials usually feature fresh fish, such as salmon in an orange sauce. Try the crispy, boneless duck with Chinese vegetables, the hot curried lamb, or the baby shrimp with vegetables and peanuts. ♦ Chinese ♦ Lunch and dinner; dinner only on Saturday and Sunday. Closed Monday. 2018 Hamilton St (at N. 21st St). 496.9928

26 Civil War Soldiers and Sailors Memorial The two marble pylons at the entrance to the tree-lined section of the Parkway were designed by **Hermon Atkins MacNeil** and installed in 1927. On the sides facing the Philadelphia Museum of Art, important battles and naval engagements are listed. Two sidewalks lead from here to the museum; take the one on the right; it has a crosswalk at the end. ♦ N. 20th St and the Pkwy

27 The Rodin Museum The largest collection of **Auguste Rodin's** sculptures outside of France, the Rodin Museum opened in 1929. Two Frenchmen who already had much to do with designing Philadelphia, **Paul Philippe Cret** and **Jacques Greber,** were the architects of the French Renaissance-style museum. The collection of statuary belonged to **Jules Mastbaum,** an early motion picture exhibitor who died before the museum could be built. The sculptures he donated to the people of Philadelphia include *The Thinker* (which sits brooding at the front gate), *The Burghers of Calais, The Age of Bronze,* and *The Kiss.* Also, more than 100 drawings, paintings, and plaster studies are part of the collection. Though they don't seem revolutionary today, in Rodin's time, the intensely expressive human figures represented a dramatic departure from the stiff, idealizing statues of civic and cultural heroes that were the norm.

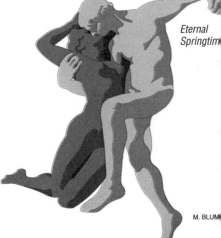

Eternal Springtime

M. BLUM

Rodin's *Monument to Balzac,* for instance, places the famous French author's craggy face above a flowing mass of loose robes. This depiction incensed the French **Societe des Gens de Lettres** (which commissioned the work) when it was first exhibited.

Many of the sculptures can be found outdoors in the formal garden or near the reflecting pool. The cast of *Eternal Springtime* (illustrated below, at left) is the one Rodin gave to author **Robert Louis Stevenson** in 1885. Rodin worked for 37 years on *The Gates of Hell,* a tableau of about 190 writhing, miniature bas-relief figures. Uncompleted at the time of the sculptor's death in 1917, Mastbaum made the first bronze cast of the work, which now stands at the museum entrance. ♦ Donation. Tu-Sa 10AM-5PM. N. 22nd St and the Pkwy. 763.8100

28 Ramada Inn $ The free parking and the pool make this motel a good buy, even if it's a bit dreary. Overlooking the **Rodin Museum,** the Ramada is convenient to Parkway attractions but somewhat removed from other parts of the city. The good news is that public transportation is nearby. Walk over to 21st Street to catch the 48 bus to the Society Hill area; the 32 bus will take you to City Hall and south on Broad Street. ♦ 501 N. 22nd St (at Pennsylvania Ave). 568.8300

29 Parkway House Drawing from Art Deco and the new International style, this pyramidal brick 1953 building with rounded bay windows was one of the first luxury apartment houses built after World War II. It was designed by **Gabriel Roth** and **Elizabeth Fleischer.** ♦ N. 22nd St and Pennsylvania Ave

30 Tavern on Green ★$$ A busy neighborhood restaurant with wooden floors, red Formica tables, and nature prints, Tavern looks out onto pretty Green Street. In summer, outdoor tables allow for dining alfresco. The food is not spectacular, but you can eat simply at reasonable prices. The mainstays are salads in tortilla shells or pita, hamburgers, stir-frys, and yuppie pastas. The one-pound grilled garlic rib steak and shrimp in curried cream with roasted peanuts and toasted coconut are also safe bets. ♦ Eclectic ♦ Lunch and dinner. N. 21st and Green Sts. 235.6767

31 Jack's Firehouse ★★$$$$ One of those beautiful old firehouses that has outlived its purpose now draws diners to a desolate stretch across from the old Eastern State Penitentiary. The current owner-chef, **Jack McDavid,** took over the building and established an upscale version of the down-home Southern cuisine he was known for at his place in the **Reading Terminal Market.** The dark wood interior features a brass fire pole, high ceilings, and a real Schuylkill River racing scull dangling from above. The setting alone is worth a visit, but the food is so inconsistent

you may leave feeling either cheated or genuinely satisfied. McDavid, who is said to churn his own butter, make his own ketchup, and grow his own herbs, appears to be well known in part because of good public relations and the novelty of Southern cuisine in a Northern city (although the prices are not down-home). It's best to avoid dishes that are too complicated and stick with traditional Southern choices. Some of the better selections are black-eyed pea and ham hock soup, pan-roasted lamb garnished with figs and peppers, buffalo accompanied by corn pudding, and pan-roasted trout. The cruvinet at the bar dispenses wine by the glass. ♦ American ♦ Lunch and dinner; dinner only on Saturday; Sunday brunch. 2130 Fairmount Ave (between N. 21st and N. 22nd Sts). Reservations recommended. 232.9000

32 Eastern State Penitentiary The last prisoner left Eastern State in 1972, but this Gothic Revival monument to incarceration remains a ghostly presence in the Fairmount neighborhood. Though it is considered an architectural treasure, some nearby residents rue the dark, medieval shadow it casts on the area. The massive fortress, completed in 1836, occupies 12 acres with its stone walls, crenellated towers, and radiating cellblocks. The design by **John Haviland** leans heavily on **Sir Jeremy Bentham's** 1787 radial plan for English institutions, which consisted of seven long cell blocks branching out from a central rotunda. In this case, the rotunda served as an observation tower.

Completed in 1836, Eastern State is considered one of the most influential buildings in Philadelphia and is a **National Historic Landmark:** more than 300 prisons around the world were built along Haviland's design. At the time, the prison was the largest construction project in the country's history; the fact that it came with central plumbing and heating further distinguished it. The prison was designed for repentance as well as confinement. Each prisoner was put in solitary confinement—in cells 8 feet by 12 feet, with a single skylight and a toilet—and given the chance to study the Bible and reflect on his crimes. The layout was modified over the years to include four additional two-story cellblocks and other buildings. In 1988, the structure came close to demolition—plans called for a supermarket and parking lot in its place—but preservationists rallied to save it. There are hopes of converting it into a tourist site and museum. In the meantime, the penitentiary is only occasionally open for tours, sponsored by the **Philadelphia Preservation Coalition.** ♦ Fairmount Ave and N. 21st St. 546.0531

Restaurants/Clubs: Red   **Hotels:** Blue
Shops/ ♣ Outdoors: Green   **Sights/Culture:** Black

33 London Grill ★★$$$ In back, a dining solarium with hanging potted plants and a terracotta floor looks out onto 23rd Street. Two additional low-lit dining rooms feature tiled floors and a marble bar. You can dine better elsewhere for the same price, but if you want to try out a neighborhood restaurant, this is as good as they come. The grill offers a rib-eye steak with shallot jam and a potato pancake, lamb with roasted pepper salad and couscous, and a molasses pork loin with stewed lentils. Roasted quail is stuffed with corn bread and accompanied by sweet potato chips. Changing pasta entrées are available. ◆ American ◆ Lunch and dinner; dinner only on Saturday and Sunday. 2301 Fairmount Ave (at N. 23rd St). 978.4545

Rembrandt's

34 Rembrandt's ★★$$ With a name like this, it's no surprise to find prints of the famous painter's work in the bar and rear dining room, a small library of books about him in many languages, and a dark wood interior to give the restaurant the ambience of Amsterdam. The eclectic menu achieves culinary artistry in its own right. Chicken wings, duck strudel with shiitake mushrooms, Moroccan lamb salad with couscous, and salmon steamed in parchment are some of Rembrandt's better offerings. ◆ American ◆ Lunch and dinner; dinner only on Saturday and Sunday. 741 N. 23rd St (at Aspen St). 763.2228

35 Girard College The richest man in America at the time of his death in 1831, French-born **Stephen Girard** kept his adopted country financially afloat during the War of 1812, and started the Philadelphia Savings Fund Society in 1813. He left the bulk of his $7 million estate to found Girard College (pictured below) for "poor white male orphans." Integrated since 1968, it now boards about 500 boys and girls from 1st to 12th grades. A collection of Girard's elegant furniture and household items are on display on campus in Founder's Hall, a Greek Revival temple noted for its Corinthian colonnade. Designed by **Thomas Ustick Walter,** the college was completed 16 years after Girard's death. His will stipulates that "no ecclesiastic, missionary or minister of any sect whatsoever, shall . . . be admitted for any purpose, or as a visitor, within the premises of (Girard) College." The rule is still enforced. ◆ Th 2-4PM, other times by appointment. Girard and N. Corinthian Aves. 787.2600

36 North Star Bar ★★$$ A haven for rock fans in a seedy section of Fairmount, this restaurant and club serves great bar food. Two contemporary, casual dining rooms, one with pinkish marbleized walls and sponge-painted tables and the other with a glass roof and a ceramic tile floor, provide the ambience. Skip the hamburgers and try some of the more eclectic offerings: grilled vegetable souvlaki, Chinese dumplings, and enchiladas. The live music ranges from rhythm and blues to world music and rock. ◆ Eclectic ◆ Dinner and late-night snacks. Live music W-Sa. N. 27th and Poplar Sts. 235.7827

37 Bridgid's ★★$$$ Walking down the blocks of row houses nearby, you can smell the garlic and herbs at work in this kitchen. Bridgid's has two personalities—it's a shot-and-a-beer bar up front and a Belgian bistro in the back. Classical music plays in the tiny rear dining room, with its white tablecloths and

Girard College

L.D.WARE.

candles. The menu features escargots, chicken-liver mousse, and fresh mussels. Try the crispy duck with peppercorn sauce, duck stuffed with ground veal and pistachios, or the veal sautéed with shrimp and bay scallops in a lemon sauce. The bar boasts a large selection of Belgian beers. Bridgid's wins the city's bargain lunch award hands down: a whole cold lobster with salad comes dirt cheap.
♦ Belgian ♦ Lunch and dinner; dinner only on Saturday and Sunday. 726 N. 24th St (at Meredith St). 232.3232

38 Fidelity Mutual Life Insurance Company Building Designed by **Zantzinger, Borie and Medary,** with sculpture by **Lee Lawrie,** the 1927 Fidelity Mutual Building stands as an Art Deco counterpoint to the neoclassical glories of the Parkway. At the main door, two sculpted dogs protect the company's assets. The building was renovated and renamed in 1983 by the Reliance Standard Life Insurance Company.
♦ Pennsylvania and Fairmount Aves

39 Statue of Joan of Arc **Emmanuel Drémiet's** statue was unveiled in 1890 on the Girard Avenue Bridge. ♦ Kelly Dr and N. 25th St

40 Eakins Oval If you're walking to the **Philadelphia Museum of Art,** use the crosswalk at the oval, which is named for Philadelphia painter **Thomas Eakins,** the famous 19th-century artist noted for his expressive human figures. The enormous equestrian statue of **George Washington** sits on a base in the center of the oval incorporating fountains that represent four great rivers: the Delaware, Hudson, Mississippi, and Potomac. The internationally known German sculptor **Rudolf Siemering** designed the three-tiered monument, which was unveiled in 1897 in **Fairmount Park,** and moved here in 1928. The monument of Washington and the fountains are flanked by two other fountains that memorialize **John Ericsson,** designer of the Civil War ironclad *Monitor,* and **Eli Kirk Price, Jr.,** one of the civic leaders responsible for the Parkway's construction. ♦ N. 24th St and the Pkwy

41 Philadelphia Museum of Art
The museum houses one of America's greatest public collections of art in more than one half-million square feet of space. Not only does it display a millennium of European art, it also includes masterpieces from Asia and the Near East. Philadelphia art barons were quick to grasp the future, and all the international art movements are well represented in their bequests to the museum, which holds an important work by virtually every major 20th-century artist.

Museum architect **C. Clark Zantzinger** and his colleagues, **Horace Trumbauer** and **Charles L. Borie, Jr.,** presented their three Grecian temples to the public in 1928. Lawyer **Eli Kirk**

Price led the museum effort, initiating the construction of both wings at once so that the city government could not back out of completing the project. For 30 years the museum's first director, **Fiske Kimball,** aggressively pursued great artwork, outbidding and out-hustling more established museums.

Minnesota Mankato and Kosota stone give the building a warm, golden cast; its roof is covered by four acres of blue tile and guarded by bronze griffins. The three temples are attached at right angles, with tall porticoes topped by pediments. **C. Paul Jennewein's** glazed terracotta figures on the right temple's pediment represent characters from classical mythology, with Zeus presiding. Two cascading fountains follow the stairs going down to the Parkway, now sometimes called the "Rocky steps," after the film in which **Sylvester Stallone** jogs triumphantly up them. **A. Thomas Schomberg's** statue of Stallone was placed at the top of the stairs for the filming of *Rocky III*. The statue was eventually removed to the **Spectrum,** while two bronze footprints mark the place where Stallone—the statue and the man—once stood. From the rocky bluff at the rear of the museum is a splendid view of the **Schuylkill River,** the **Waterworks,** and **Boathouse Row.** In the springtime, the **Azalea Garden** blooms down the hill just beyond the Italian Fountain.

The entrance from the car park in the rear of the museum provides far easier access to the institution via the West Foyer, but walk to the front anyway. You'll get a great view of the city and see the vision realized by the Parkway's founders.

Just beyond the first-floor entrance, the **Great Stair Hall** is dominated by **Augustus Saint-Gaudens'** 1892 statue of the nude huntress *Diana,* rescued from the demolished Madison Square Garden in New York. So sexy a piece of statuary is this that the antipornography crusader **Mary Hubbert Ellis** campaigned to prevent its relocation to Philadelphia in 1932. Directly above the entrance soars the mobile *Ghost,* by **Alexander Calder,** grandson of **Alexander Milne Calder** and son of **Alexander Stirling Calder.** "Sandy" Calder's mobile completes the trio of his family's Parkway sculptures with his grandfather's *William Penn* atop **City Hall** and his father's **Swann Memorial Fountain** in **Logan Circle.**

The museum counts among its treasures the John G. Johnson Collection of European Painting, which covers the 13th to the 19th centuries. Small but stunningly vivid is the Flemish painter **John van Eyck's** early 16th century *Saint Francis Receiving the Stigmata,* and **Rogier van der Weyden's** *Crucifixion with the Virgin and St. John* is considered one of the greatest masterpieces in American museums today.

PHILADELPHIA MUSEUM OF ART

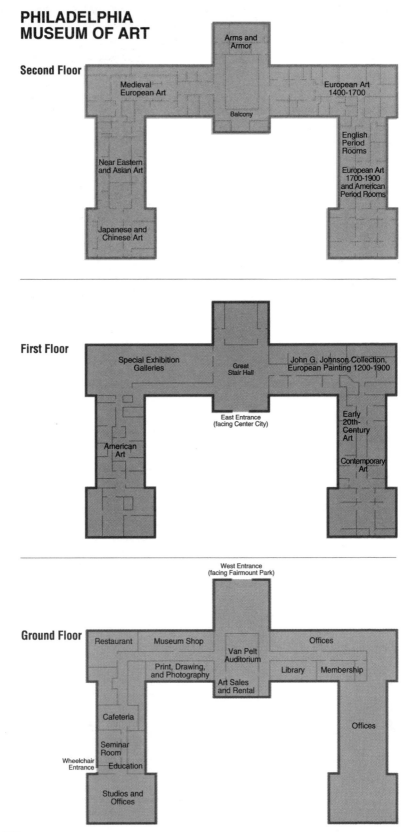

Second Floor

Arms and Armor

Medieval European Art

European Art 1400-1700

Balcony

English Period Rooms

Near Eastern and Asian Art

European Art 1700-1900 and American Period Rooms

Japanese and Chinese Art

First Floor

Special Exhibition Galleries

Great Stair Hall

John G. Johnson Collection, European Painting 1200-1900

East Entrance (facing Center City)

American Art

Early 20th-Century Art

Contemporary Art

Ground Floor

West Entrance (facing Fairmount Park)

Restaurant

Museum Shop

Van Pelt Auditorium

Offices

Print, Drawing, and Photography

Library

Membership

Art Sales and Rental

Cafeteria

Seminar Room

Wheelchair Entrance

Education

Offices

Studios and Offices

In the gloried 20th-century rooms, one of **Jasper Johns'** most important works, *Painting with Two Balls* (1968) appears near **Claes Oldenburg's** 1970 *Three-Way Plug* suspended from the ceiling (Oldenburg has so many significant pieces in Philly that you might think he was related to the Calders). The German **Anselm Kiefer** ranks among today's greatest living artists; his stark, disturbing *Nigredo* suggests the burnt wasteland that is the legacy of this century's world wars. The early modern collection is dominated by **Marcel Duchamp,** whose work here includes *Nude Descending a Staircase* and *The Bride Stripped Bare.* The latter is composed of two large glass panels severely cracked after a showing at the Brooklyn Museum in 1926-27; when the damaged work was returned to the artist, he declared that, at last, it was finished. Don't miss Duchamp's final work, *Given 1. The Waterfall 2. The Illuminating Gas,* which at first appears to be little more than a barn door set in a darkened room. Approach the door and peek through two knotholes in the wood to get the full, grisly effect of the installation. The museum has equally provocative work by **Giorgio de Chirico, Pablo Picasso, Joan Miró, Salvador Dalí,** and the largest group of sculpture by **Constantine Brancusi** outside of Paris.

Return to the Great Stair Hall and cross over to the South Wing to see the American Collections, which include Pennsylvania furniture and silver, Shaker art, and crafts. The museum has a prominent collection of work by neglected African-American artists, including **Henry Ossawa Turner** and **Horace Pippin,** whose 1943 *Mr. Prejudice* has recently received critical reappraisal. A comprehensive collection of work by **Thomas Eakins** is on display, including his 1877 painting of *William Rush Carving His Allegorical Figure of the Schuylkill River.* Rush is shown sculpting from a nude model as a chaperone looks on. In 1825 Rush, in fact, completed two sculptures, which are fittingly located in the next room (fiberglass copies have been placed atop their original home, the **Fairmount Waterworks** just below the museum, beside the Schuylkill River).

The rest of the first floor is set aside for special exhibitions, for which there is usually a separate admissions charge.

Asian and European art extend across the second floor; the confusing layout is now being remedied by a reinstallation of the museum's collection scheduled to be completed in 1995. At that time, all the European art from 1100 to 1900 will be arranged chronologically. As the project proceeds, individual galleries will be closed.

Among the upstairs treasures are masterpieces by **Rubens, Poussin, Delacroix, Ingres, Turner, Degas,** and **Toulouse-Lautrec.** Note the evolution of European painting by two great paintings in adjacent rooms, **Pierre Auguste Renoir's** Impressionist *Bathers* (1887), and a work on the same subject, but painted in 1906, heralding the bright dawn of abstract art, *The Large Bathers* by **Paul Cézanne.**

The Near Eastern, Asian, Chinese, and Japanese collections are excellent, tending toward huge reconstructions of ancient Asian sites that take up entire rooms on the second floor. The *Pillared Temple Hall* from Madura in southern India is reconstructed from three 16th-century shrines to Vishnu. Another room, artificially lit as if by daylight, is occupied by the 14th-century *Temple of the Attainment of Happiness,* from Nara, Japan.

The ground floor includes an inexpensive, cheerful cafeteria, a restaurant, and a well-stocked museum shop, as well as galleries for prints, drawings, and photographs. On Wednesday evenings, the museum offers special programs, with gallery tours, talks, and films, tied to the city's "Make It a Night!" promotion. ♦ Admission; free Sunday from 10AM to 1PM. Tu, Th-Su 10AM-5PM; W 10AM-8:45PM. N. 26th St and the Pkwy. 763.8100

42 William M. Reilly Memorial A trust fund established by the estate of a Pennsylvania National Guard general provided for this grouping of Revolutionary War heroes. The first four bronze figures, placed in the 1940s, depict European military officers who joined the colonists' cause: the Polish **General Casimir Pulaski,** the Prussian **General Friedrich von Steuben,** the French **Major General Marquis de Lafayette,** and the Irish **General Richard Montgomery.** In later decades, memorials to **John Paul Jones** and **General Nathanael Greene** were added. ♦ On the terrace behind the Museum of Art (between N. 26th St and the Pkwy)

43 Fairmount Park If you find yourself viewing any sizable patch of green in Philadelphia, chances are it's part of Fairmount Park. The park system encompasses 8,700 acres—about 10 percent of all the land in Philadelphia—and is said to be the largest urban park in the world. The claim is very arguable. The **Fairmount Park Commission** manages all that green space, including Rittenhouse Square, the Wissahickon Valley, all the green areas lining the Parkway, and even the front yard of the cathedral.

Most Philadelphians would agree that Fairmount Park proper consists of the large, contiguous expanse of green extending about four miles from behind the art museum to the **Falls Bridge** near the neighborhood of East

Falls. It's roughly the shape of South America, and the park's territory reaches eastward and westward from both sides of the river drives. The park is so vast that the park commission has had to make choices as to which sections should be given priority for upkeep. But large expanses are well maintained and Philadelphia's inhabitants consider the park their backyard. This is where they picnic, grill hamburgers, and drink beer (alcohol is permitted almost everywhere in the park), read, stroll, and play with their kids. There are playing fields, tennis courts, biking trails, children's playgrounds, outdoor sculpture, and some of the nation's finest examples of early American residences in this urban oasis of breathable air and open spaces. A map is a must if you plan to explore the land off the river drives, as the circular roads tend to take you back to where you started—that's if you're lucky. Maps are available at the Visitors Center on John F. Kennedy Boulevard in Center City West. ◆ 686.2176

44 Fairmount Waterworks "Philadelphia is most bountifully provided with fresh water, which is showered and jerked about, and turned on, and poured off everywhere. The Water Works, which are on a height near the city, are no less ornamental than useful, being tastefully laid out as a public garden, and kept in the best and neatest order." **Charles Dickens** extended this praise during a visit to Philadelphia in 1840, when the Waterworks already had completed 25 years of service. **Frederick Graff** designed the classic structures that housed steam engines, which in 1815 began pumping four million gallons of water daily to a reservoir at a site now occupied by the **Philadelphia Museum of Art.** From there, the water was fed by gravity to hydrants and residential taps. The cost of the steam engines prompted the city to dam the river and shift to hydropower in 1822, through a set of waterwheels housed in the **Old Mill House.** By 1835, further construction and extensive landscaping of the **South Garden** and the **Esplanade** drew visitors from throughout America and Europe. The architect's son **Frederick Graff, Jr.**, introduced the first turbines in 1862, which eventually replaced the waterwheels. Pollution on the Schuylkill closed the Waterworks in 1909. For 50 years the site housed an aquarium, before falling into decline. A continuing restoration project of this **National Historic Landmark** promises to turn the Waterworks into an interpretive museum and restaurant. ◆ Tours by appointment. Schuylkill River near N. 25th St. 581.5111

45 Schuylkill River Notoriously difficult to spell, Schuylkill means "hidden river" in Dutch. Stretching 100 miles from its headwaters in the anthracite belt in Schuylkill County to the Delaware River in South Philadelphia, the river is a former industrial

giant and a major reason for Philadelphia's growth in the 18th and 19th centuries. Here behind the art museum, its role is aesthetic and recreational: the centerpiece of Fairmou Park and the subject of hundreds of landsca portraits over the centuries. In the 1800s excursion boats trolled the waters. Today i famous for its scullers, who work out even i cold months. The annual **Dad Vail Regatta** May draws rowing teams from around the country and fills the bleachers along Kelly Drive. Still, one of the best activities on the banks of the Schuylkill is a sedentary one: sitting quietly, contemplating the water. ◆ Behind the Museum of Art

46 The River Drives The serpentine roadway that parallel the Schuylkill are among Philadelphia's most picturesque thoroughfares. **Kelly Drive,** formerly **East River Drive,** runs along the east side of the river from the **Museum of Art** to **Lincoln Dri** above East Falls. The **West River Drive** follows the other side of the river. For the unaccustomed motorist, the drives' sharp curves and distracting scenery can be hazardous. Contiguous pathways forming a eight-mile loop are a prime attraction for cyclists and walkers. By means of these pathways and the **Wissahickon Valley Trail** it is possible to bike from the museum to th Montgomery County line, about a 24-mile roundtrip. In the spring, fall, and summer, West River Drive is closed to car traffic for part of every weekend. ◆ West River Dr: closed to cars Sa-Su 7AM-noon Apr-Oct. Bounded by the Museum of Art and Falls Bridge

47 Boathouse Row At nighttime, you can se the outline of these delightful late 19th and early 20th century Victorian boathouses wit their turrets, gables, and coats of arms. Line with pinpoint lights, they create a fairy-tale image visible from the other side of the rive The 10 houses were built by private groups and then occupied by nine rowing clubs. Th clubs, known as the **Schuylkill Navy,** have kept the sport an important part of Philadelphia life. Number 13, the **Undine Barge Club,** was erected in 1883 by Philadelphia's famed **Frank Furness.** ◆ Kelly Dr (off Sedgely Dr)

48 Lemon Hill The nucleus of **Fairmount Pa** the site of this residence was originally occupied by financier **Robert Morris'** estate which included greenhouses stocked with lemon trees. The trees gave the mansion its name, which it kept after Morris sold it to merchant **Henry Pratt.** Like the other Fairmount Park mansions, Lemon Hill is furnished with period artifacts and is open the public. The house currently serves as a chapter headquarters of the **Colonial Dame of America.** ◆ Admission. W-Su 10AM-4:30PM. Lemon Hill Dr. 232.4337

Pedal-Pushing Philadelphia Style

Like tens of thousands of suburbanites, **Robert Montgomery Scott,** the president of the **Philadelphia Museum of Art,** takes the train to work. What makes his commute different is that Scott uses two bicycles along the way. He pedals from his home to the station, parks his bicycle, then takes the train to **30th Street Station.** There he picks up another bicycle and pedals to the art museum.

Scott's routine is still out of the ordinary in Philadelphia—a city that until recently was considered hostile terrain for cyclists. But cycling activists have succeeded in initiating changes. Visitors who now want to see the city from a two-wheeler are finding more possibilities than ever before. While Center City's streets are generally narrow and inhospitable to bike riders, cyclists can opt for a number of safe and scenic trails just beyond downtown. Both **SEPTA,** the local transit authority, and **PATCO,** New Jersey's high-speed line, allow cyclists to take their bikes on commuter trains during nonpeak hours.

The **Bicycle Coalition of the Delaware Valley,** at P.O. Box 8194, Philadelphia, Pennsylvania, 19101, has put together a comprehensive cycling map available by mail. Scenic routes are marked in green, and "recommended" routes in blue. A word of caution: some routes—Spruce and Sansom streets, to name two—are only for experienced urban cyclists. Call 215/BICYCLE for more information.

Try these scenic itineraries:

West River Drive From April to October, this road through Fairmount Park is closed to cars from 7AM to noon. Its wide flat curves and vistas of the **Schuylkill River** make for a very pleasant four-mile ride.

Museum of Art to Roxborough This 24-mile roundtrip ride begins on the paved pathway at **Kelly Drive** behind the museum. Take it past the **Falls Bridge** to **Ridge Avenue** and cross Ridge to pick up the **Wissahickon Trail,** which ends at Northwestern Avenue in Roxborough. Retrace your tire tracks to the Falls Bridge, then cross over to West River Drive for variety. You'll get a good view of **Boathouse Row** and the **Fairmount Waterworks** on your way back to the museum's front entrance.

Benjamin Franklin Bridge If you're up for a short, hilly, and spectacular trip among the rooftops of Old City, enter the bicycle path on the bridge at Sixth Street. The ride across the bridge is pretty, but once you get to the other side there's not much scenery. So turn back and check out the mesmerizing 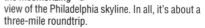 view of the Philadelphia skyline. In all, it's about a three-mile roundtrip.

Cooper River Park The 400-acre park along the Cooper River in Philadelphia's South Jersey suburbs of Cherry Hill, Haddon Township, Collingswood, and Pennsauken sports a four-mile loop. It is blessedly flat, offering a nice break from the calf-busting hills across the Delaware River.

Schuylkill River Trail Enter the **Manayunk Tow Path** at Cotton Street, taking it to the Spring Mill Train Station in Conshohocken. Follow the bike-route street signs for the next two miles until the path resumes, leading the way to Valley Forge. Distance: about 12 miles roundtrip.

Ridley Creek State Park A 4.5-mile paved loop winds through what might be Delaware County's most popular recreation area. Enter at a small parking lot at the north end of Barren Road near the bridge over Ridley Creek.

Valley Forge National Historic Park Six miles of paved biking and walking trails wend through the park's undulating terrain near **King of Prussia.** The Visitor's Center is located near the Route 23 entrance.

Washington's Crossing State Park The road along the seven-mile Delaware and Raritan Canal Feeder runs from Washington's Crossing to Lambertville in New Jersey. The unpaved canal path is bikeable.

49 Ellen Phillips Samuel Memorial The three terraces of allegorical statuary fronting the river are the gift of a Philadelphia philanthropist who died in 1913. Seeking to encourage the art form of sculpture, Phillips established a fund that sponsored three international exhibitions. These served to bring many great artists, along with great artwork, to Philadelphia. Some of the best pieces originally intended for the memorial ended up elsewhere in the city. The selection process was interrupted by financial depression and war, and it was not until 1961 that the last piece in the group was dedicated. ♦ Kelly Dr (near Brewery Hill Dr)

The grouping is called **The Emblematic History of the United States:**

South Terrace Starting where it all began is **Wheeler Williams'** *Settling of the Seaboard* (1942), celebrating the taming of the continent by Europeans and the drive for independence. *The Puritan and the Quaker* (1942) by **Henry Rosin** reminds U.S. citizens that their nation was founded by religious dissenters.

Central Terrace Conceived in the late '30s, the grouping of *The Immigrant, The Plough, The Slave,* and other heroic figures depicts the workers who built the country from muscle and sweat. The terrace is dominated by the most abstract piece in the memorial, *The Spirit of Enterprise* by **Jacques Lipchitz,** who cast the bronze in 20 separate pieces from 1950 to 1960.

North Terrace Four granite figures from the 1950s suggest that in the 20th century, America finally achieved its civilization. These tributes to *The Poet, The Preacher, The Scientist,* and *The Laborer* are all by foreign émigrés.

50 Statue of Cowboy America's romance with the Wild West was transformed into art by **Frederic Remington,** whose 1908 equestrian statue, his only large-scale bronze, perches on the rock above the drive. A dramatic apparition that continues to startle commuters, Remington's cowboy pulls the reins just as his mount is about to leap into traffic. ♦ Kelly Dr (between Brewery Hill and Fountain Green Drs)

51 Monument to Ulysses S. Grant The equestrian statue memorializing the 18th president of the United States guards the entrance to **Fountain Drive.** Designed by **Daniel Chester French** and **Edward C. Potter,** it was dedicated in 1899, with **President McKinley** in attendance. ♦ Kelly and Fountain Green Drs

52 Smith Playground For almost 100 years, kids have been visiting this old-fashioned six-acre playground and finding it to their liking. Though the equipment is now very dated, the appeal hasn't lessened in the Nintendo era. A gift from wealthy Philadelphian **Richard Smith,** who died in 1894, the playground is stocked with old-time metal swings, merry-go-rounds, and climbing equipment. A 12-foot-wide enclosed sliding board lets 10 kids slide down it at once. A mansion converted into a playhouse is specially designed for pre-schoolers, with lots of doll strollers, small cars, and a play kitchen (no video games here). The basement is home to a kiddie driving course, with pedal cars, a pretend gas pump and a working traffic signal. ♦ M-Sa 9AM-4:45PM. Near N. 33rd St and Oxford Ave

53 Mount Pleasant When **John Adams** visited **Captain John MacPherson's** home in 1775, he reported to a friend that the former privateer possessed "the most elegant Seat in Pensilvania [sic]" and "a clever Scot Wife." The central projecting pavilion, topped by an imposing pediment, and the use of stucco, makes Mount Pleasant (illustrated at right) the most distinctive

home in the park. MacPherson sold the home, a Georgian-style country house, to **Benedict Arnold.** It was confiscated before the famous traitor could move in. The house is furnished and maintained by the **Philadelphia Museum of Art.** ♦ Admission. W-Su 10AM-4:30PM. Mt Pleasant Dr. 763.8100

54 Laurel Hill (Randolph House) The Georgian brick mansion was completed by **Francis Rawle** in 1760. After he died in a hunting accident, his widow **Rebecca** married the Quaker pacifist **Samuel Shoemaker.** Their home was confiscated when Shoemaker was convicted of treason during the Revolutionary War, providing **General Joseph Reed,** president of the Supreme Council of Pennsylvania, with a summer retreat. In 1784, Rebecca Rawle Shoemaker bought back the mansion, and it later became the home of **Dr. Philip Syng Physick,** the father of American surgical practice. ♦ Admission. W-Su 10AM-4:30PM. Edgeley Dr. 235.1776

55 Public Canoe House Emulating the scullers, more or less, you can rent rowboats and canoes by the hour. ♦ Daily 11AM-6PM mid-Mar to Oct. Kelly Dr (below Strawberry Mansion Bridge). 225.3560

56 Woodford By all accounts, Fairmount Park was a hotbed of treason during the Revolutionary War. While **George Washington** and his men suffered through the winter of 1777 in **Valley Forge,** British **General William Howe** was being lavishly entertained by **Crown Agent David Franks** at Woodford. Franks' daughter **Rebecca** was the toast of the Redcoats. The oldest part of the Georgian country house dates to 1756. Its exterior brickwork is Flemish bond, and the nine-foot-high entrance doors, flanked by Tuscan columns, lead to a beautifully furnished interior. ♦ Admission. W-Su 10AM-4:30PM. Woodford Dr (off Ridge Ave). 229.6115

Mount Pleasant

57 Strawberry Mansion This stuccoed brick mansion was built in the 1790s along simple Federal lines. The Greek Revival wings added in the early 1820s converted a relatively modest country house into a massive mansion. It was owned by **Judge Joseph Hemphill,** whose son **Coleman** cultivated strawberries from roots imported from Chile. Coleman Hemphill was an optimist: he invited **Daniel Webster** to a political banquet meant to make peace between northern and southern Democrats. Webster arrived, eyed the company, offered a toast to the strawberries, and escaped out the ballroom window. A restaurant famed for its strawberries-and-cream dessert, in fact, operated here later in the century. An antique toy exhibit is displayed inside. Strawberry Mansion also is the name of the struggling neighborhood that fronts the park here. ♦ Admission. W-Su 10AM-4:30PM. Strawberry Mansion Dr (off Ridge Ave). 228.8364

58 Laurel Hill Cemetery "It's really a sculpture garden: a forest of looming obelisks, Greek-temple mausoleums, odd statues, and stone crypts festooned with doodads and decorative detail," **Ron Avery,** of the *Philadelphia Daily News,* wrote of this Victorian cemetery-cum-park. When the 99-acre, nonsectarian cemetery was created in 1836 from designs by noted architect **John Notman,** burial grounds were places of rest for the dead and recreation for the living. Elaborate monuments and sculptures marked the graves of prominent Philadelphians. Families brought picnics to this hilly serene spot above the Schuylkill. Some of the more moving sculptures include **James Thom's** *Old Mortality* (inspired by **Sir Walter Scott's** book of the same name) near the entrance and the tomb of the coal magnate and philanthropist **William Warner.** Carved by **Alexander Milne Calder,** Warner's sarcophagus is shown being opened by a draped angel to allow his winged soul to escape. For a time, Laurel Hill was such a popular place for the living that its owners were forced to control the numbers of its (temporary) visitors with tickets of admission. It still gets visits from the curious and is reachable from Center City by taking the 61 bus. Maps and guides are available, as are burial plots. ♦ Tu-Sa 9:30AM-1:30PM. 3822 Ridge Ave (Huntingdon St to Allegheny Ave). 228.8200

59 Chamounix Mansion $ Built in 1802, and an inexpensive hostel since 1964, the mansion offers elegant period furnishings on the ground floor and dormitory facilities on the second floor, with separate accommodations for men and women. Common rooms, a kitchen, laundry facilities, and free parking are available. The mansion sleeps about 25, and another 25 beds are in the 1856 Gothic Revival carriage house. The only public transportation to the remote hostel is the **Park Trolley.** ♦ Chamounix Dr. 878.3676

60 Belmont Mansion Erected in 1743, and often added to subsequently, the mansion became the home of **Judge Richard Peters,** a supporter of the Revolution and friend of George Washington. The three-story building, surrounded by a colonnade, became a cafe in its later life. It's now rented out for banquets. ♦ Belmont Mansion Dr. 878.8844

61 Belmont Plateau The Philadelphia skyline vista as seen from the top of the art museum steps is well known, but the view from Belmont Plateau is even more spectacular. You get a sweeping north-south panorama of the area from the **Philadelphia Inquirer Building** at Broad and Callowhill streets to the **Walt Whitman Bridge.** At night, when the distant city pulses with light, the view is electrifying. On warm evenings, the recently expanded parking area is well occupied. (Truth be told, not all the couples come for the view.) This also happens to be the site of busy playing fields and a kite launch. To reach the plateau from Center City, take the Schuylkill Expressway or the West River Drive to Montgomery Drive, make a right at Belmont Mansion Drive. ♦ Off Belmont Mansion Dr

62 Mann Music Center From the middle of June through July, the **Philadelphia Orchestra** plays three concerts each week under the stars; other nights through the summer are dedicated to pop concerts. ♦ George's Hill Dr (near N. 52nd St and Parkside Ave). 567.0707

63 Catholic Total Abstinence Union Fountain Designed for the centennial by **Herman Kim,** this marble monument to the temperance movement is shaped like a Maltese Cross; on each axis are statues of prominent Catholics. Looking at this dry, cracked fountain makes you yearn for a drink. ♦ N. Concourse Dr and States St

64 Japanese House and Gardens Exquisitely out of place and time, the 16th century-style teahouse is a zone of quiet contemplation—even with many visitors about. Designed by **Junzo Yoshimura** and assembled by four craftsmen imported from Japan, the house is set in a garden near a stream and surrounded by Japanese trees. A gift of the **American-Japan Society** of Tokyo, it was first exhibited in the Museum of Modern Art in New York in 1957. Age and the elements have left the house untouched. During the spring and summer, events include tea ceremonies and origami demonstrations. ♦ W-Su 11AM-4PM May to mid-Oct. Lansdowne Dr (east of Belmont Ave). 878.5097

Restaurants/Clubs: Red	Hotels: Blue
Shops/ Outdoors: Green	Sights/Culture: Black

65 Memorial Hall The only large building remaining from the Centennial Exhibition sits atop a rise in the park, its square glass-and-cast-iron dome visible for miles. **Hermann Schwartzmann** designed the Beaux Arts structure—which was conceived as an art museum for the centennial and later became the **Pennsylvania Museum of Art**—after a trip to Vienna. The three arched doorways lead to a grand central rotunda. On the dome, which is illuminated at night, *Columbia* hoists a laurel wreath. The winged horses at the entrance, **Vincent Pilz's** *Pegasus,* originally guarded the Vienna Opera House. The building, which later inspired the design of the New York Metropolitan Museum of Art as well as the German Reichstag, is now occupied by the **Fairmount Park Commission** offices. ♦ N. 42nd St and N. Concourse Dr

66 Smith Memorial Arch The two giant Doric columns with statues of **Major General George Gordon Meade** by **Daniel Chester French** and **Major General John Fulton Reynolds** by **Charles Grafly** can be seen from nearly anywhere in the park. They're on top of two triumphant arches at the entrance to the 1876 Centennial fairgrounds (though the arches weren't completed until 1912). Thirteen sculptors collaborated on the monument, which was made possible by the bequest of **Richard Smith,** a typesetter and Civil War hero. The figures, busts, and equestrian statues depict several of Pennsylvania's fighting men—and Smith himself. Don't miss the whispering bench near the memorial. If you sit at one end and whisper, a friend sitting at the opposite end can hear you. ♦ N. Concourse Dr

67 Cedar Grove The Quaker farmhouse was originally located in the **Frankford** section of Philadelphia. Inherited by the family of **Isaac** and **Sarah Morris** in 1793, five generations of Morrises lived here until it was given to the **Fairmount Park Commission,** which moved it to its present location, with many of the original furnishings intact. The kitchen is stocked with utensils, including a huge brass caldron. ♦ Admission. W-Su 10AM-4:30PM. Lansdowne Dr (near Black Rd). 763.8100

68 Sweetbriar The Federal-style country house was built by **Congressman Samuel Breck** in 1797. Breck was a gracious host to foreign visitors like **Lafayette** and **Talleyrand,** and an arts and science enthusiast. The congressman helped establish the Philadelphia school system. Inside, floor-to-ceiling windows overlook the river and the **Fairmount Waterworks.** The chandelier is from a palace owned by the **Aga Khan.** Breck's own 1834 sketch of Talleyrand shows the French diplomat in his old age. ♦ Admission. W-Su 10AM-4:30PM. Sweetbriar Hill (north of Lansdowne Dr). 222.1333

69 Letitia Street House This small dwelling i the oldest surviving brick house in America. A carpenter, **John Smart,** built the two-room, two-story house in 1713 on what is now Market Street. It was later moved to its present location, and supplied with period furnishings. The house is not open for tours. ♦ Lansdowne Dr (near W. Girard Ave)

70 Philadelphia Zoo Established in 1859, the Philadelphia Zoo is the oldest in America, as well as one of the newest given that it constantly and vigorously reconfigures itself A leader in animal conservation projects and captive breeding programs, the zoo protects more than 50 endangered species. In recent years, it has put many of its animals into ope environments meant to approximate the wild Orangutans and gibbons play, and gorillas meander among the trees and bushes of the **World of Primates**. In **Bear Country,** polar bears swim in a 200,000-gallon tank with glass walls—ideal for viewing their incongruously graceful strokes. The new **Carnivore Kingdom** is home to otters, red pandas, a jaguar, and a snow leopard, who live amid a tableau of boulders. (The rocks a fake, though; they conceal heating coils inside.) Catch a view of the otter swimming his laps.

The **Bird House,** opened in 1916 to designs **Mellor, Meigs and Howe** is one of the most unusual spots in the zoo: many of the avians fly freely among the visitors inside, without inhibitions. Goldfinches may zip past your ea a hummingbird will hover just inches in front of your face. In the **Carnivora House,** the zookeepers throw lions and tigers fresh mea a crowd-pleaser since the time of the Roman Empire. The **Reptile House** is a dark, tombli series of rooms with glass cases built into th walls. Tree frogs, swimming turtles, and ungainly boa constrictors, coiled up like fat garden hoses, call these cases home. Don't miss the alligators in the back.

The zoo operates both a small **Children's Zo** with pony rides, educational talks by zookeepers, and opportunities to pet the animals, and the **Treehouse,** designed by **Venturi, Rauch and Scott Brown.** Inside the Treehouse, small children climb and scramb over giant play sculptures of frogs, caterpillars, and other creatures. There is separate admission for the Treehouse, as well as for the aerial monorail tour (the latter is probably not worth the money). The best place to eat is at the tables alongside the **Impala Fountain,** a terrific water sculpture of exuberant, leaping impala by **Henry Mitchell**. A snack bar right inside the primate house has atrocious food; bring your own instead. If you must buy lunch, try the outdoor grill near Carnivore Kingdom.

The 18th-century mansion called **Solitude,** which stands near the flamingos, was built by **John Penn,** grandson of **William Penn**. The Victorian zoo entrance pavilions with wrought-iron gates were designed by **Frank Furness** and **George Hewitt**. ♦ Admission. Daily 9:30AM–5PM. N. 34th St and Girard Ave. 243.1100

Bests

Joan Myers Brown
Executive Director, Philadanco

I am a Philadelphia lover—born and raised in one of the ghettos here. I love giving back to this community, especially to young black kids who don't even dare to dream. . . . I'm a builder and a provider of dreams for them.

The **Painted Bride Art Center** has such diverse programs; there's always something wonderful going on.

Zanzibar Blue, where the music and food are divine.

Philadanco (my place), where a zillion kids come daily to be a part of the world of dance.

The **Rittenhouse Hotel** is tops in service and downright luxury.

Experiencing the many, many wonderful types of restaurants in Philadelphia.

Shopping all over town—I'm a shopaholic who looks for the best bargains and thinks nothing of taking all day to buy one thing.

The city's orchestra, ballet, and theater still hold magic for me. I love to lose myself in them.

Fairmount Park, a place of beauty and pleasure all year long. **West River Drive** and the boathouses.

Tea at the **Four Seasons Hotel**—A true "ladies" afternoon pleasure.

No one should miss the **Franklin Institute,** along with these must-sees—the **Philadelphia Museum of Art,** the **Philadelphia Zoo,** and the **Camden Aquarium** (across the bridge).

Jim's Steaks, Philadelphia pretzels, Breyer's Ice Cream, Dwights B-B-Q . . . and so much more.

In the 1960 presidential race, John F. Kennedy won Philadelphia by 330,000 votes. Nationally, he defeated Richard Nixon in the popular vote by only 114,000.

Kathy Dilonardo
Chief of Interpretation and Visitor Services, Independence National Historical Park

My neighborhood—**Queen Village**—a great mix of architecture, quiet streets, churches, and parks, plus **Essene's,** a great organic food store with excellent produce, grains, and spices.

Independence Hall—where freedom began for all of us—viewed from my office window. **The Second Bank Portrait Gallery,** housing portraits of our founding fathers.

The **Chinese Gate** on 10th Street in Chinatown—fascinating craftsmanship of another culture, and **Ray's Coffee Shop** on Ninth Street in Chinatown for great food.

Logan Square's **Swann Memorial Fountain** and **Rittenhouse Square,** both original parts of **William Penn's** "Greene Country Town."

Pennsbury Manor—Penn's reconstructed home, upriver from Philadelphia.

The **Italian Market** for Italian bread, cheese, olives, meat, and water ice.

Buying coffee or cookware at **Fante's Cookware** and spices at **The Spice Corner.**

South Street (especially on Halloween), when it's filled with lots of strange people. Also there, **The Book Trader, The Eyes Gallery,** and **South Street Souvlaki** (great Greek food).

The **Bond House** bed-and-breakfast inn.

Smith Playground, which has swings and slides (wow!) for children and adults, plus **Valley Green Inn** and **Devils Pool** in Fairmount Park. Also, the **Japanese House** and **Memorial Hall**—left from the 1876 Sesquicentennial.

Reading Terminal Market—great smells, lots of fresh produce, and Pennsylvania Dutch specialties, plus the **Down Home Diner.**

The junglelike atrium in **The Philadelphia Stock Exchange.**

A tour of the **Edgar Allan Poe National Historic Site** and browsing in their reading room and bookstore.

The **Phillies** at the Vet and the **Flyers** at the Spectrum—great entertainment.

Browsing at the **American Institute of Architects** bookstore just down the street from **Joseph Fox Bookstore.** (AIA has lots of Christmas ornaments and children's games and books.)

The **Bears Park** (a small playground) in the 300 block of Delancey Street.

The **Azalea Garden** off Kelly Drive is absolutely fantastic in May.

Locust Walk on the Penn campus.

Jewelers Row, where you'll find a dozen or more jewelry shops, plus merchants selling semiprecious stones—be sure to go there if you like lapidary.

Fabric galore on **South Fourth Street**—all colors, weights, and patterns—especially for quilters and anyone planning a wedding. **Marmelsteins** has all the accoutrements.

University City

Exactly as the name suggests, University City is an area dominated by college campuses and the hum of student life. Located within the neighborhood extending from the **Schuylkill River** to 45th Street are th **University of Pennsylvania** (known as **Penn**) and **Drexel University**, temporary homes to more than 30,000 students, who cram in lectures and laboratories by day, and nearby ethnic restaurants by night.

For visitors, the Penn campus holds the most interest. Founded as a small academy for men in a single brick building in 1749 by **Benjamin Franklin** and a group of fellow civic leaders, the coed campus now sprawls over 250 acres and contains one hundred academic departments. Some of Philadelphia's leading architects had a hand in shaping the university, with its juxtaposition of ivy-covered 19th-century buildings and impressive modern structures. Noteworthy architectural highlights include **Frank Furness'** 1891 **Anne and Jerome Fisher Fine Arts Building; The University Museum of Archaeology and Anthropology** building, designed by **Wilson Eyre** with **Frank Miles Day** and **Cope and Stewardson** and built in 1893 (th museum's vast galleries filled with archaeological finds from around the world are a must-see); and modern master **Louis I. Kahn's** seminal **Alfred Newton Richards Medical Research Building**, completed in 1961. Other cultural treasures on campus are the cutting-edge **Institute of Contemporar Art (ICA)**, and the three-stage **Annenberg Center**, a performing arts comple that hosts drama, music, and dance performances throughout the year.

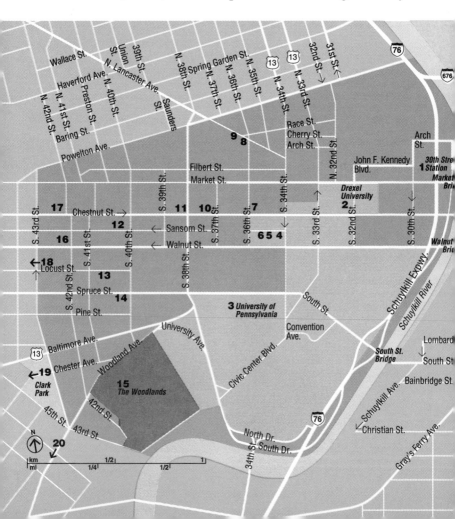

Take time out from the university and its many sights for lunch at one of the ethnic restaurants concentrated west of 38th Street; save a late afternoon for studying the Victorian tombstones at **The Woodlands**, an 18th-century estate that was converted into a park and cemetery in the 1840s; and be sure to peek into the wonderfully restored neoclassical **30th Street Station**, the second-busiest train station in the country. On the outskirts of the campuses are neighborhoods of Victorian row houses, including **Powelton Village** and **Spruce Hill**; and beyond 45th Street lie the vast stretches of working-class homes and ghettos of **West Philadelphia.**

These days it's easy to reach the area west of the Schuylkill River by car, train, subway, or foot. But in the early 1800s, the only way across the water was over the **Permanent Bridge**, a simple wood structure built in 1805 and destroyed 70 years later. The bridge received heavy use from the beginning—in a single night in 1806, some 5,000 people were said to have crossed it to fight a fire on the western side. Today bridges at Spring Garden Street, JFK Boulevard, Market Street, Walnut Street, South Street, and Gray's Ferry Avenue span the waterway—and few even notice they are crossing a major river. Still, the area seems far removed from Center City, lacking the dynamic mix of commerce, residences, hotels, and restaurants characteristic of the downtown core. It does have more than its share of busy streets, however. Traffic whips along Market, Chestnut, Walnut, and Spruce streets at a faster clip than in Center City, kicking up clouds of dust and intimidating pedestrians. Save your walking legs for the (relatively) tranquil campuses.

---

1 30th Street Station As you cross the Market Street Bridge or John F. Kennedy Boulevard leaving Center City, look for the majestic Corinthian columns of this monumental train station. You might expect such a palatial building to have a cold, impersonal interior, but 30th Street's main concourse is one of the warmest, most romantic public spaces in the city. Though less a tourist attraction than **Union Station** in Washington, DC, the station merits a visit even if you don't have to catch a train. Few who pass through here forget its beauty.

This was the country's first major station designed for electric trains, and smokeless engines made it possible to build it right over the tracks. The first section opened in 1933, and the rest was built gradually over the next 17 years. The neoclassical design is the work of the Chicago architectural firm of **Graham, Anderson, Probst, and White** (also responsible for Philadelphia's **Suburban Station**). Over the years a coat of grime obscured the stone columns, gilt ceilings, and classical sculptures, but a recent $100 million restoration has uncovered the original beauty.

Though a hub of **Amtrak's** northeast corridor and of regional commuter rail lines, 30th Street Station rarely feels crowded. The main concourse is so cavernous that pigeons fly about beneath the 10-story coffered ceiling. (Note the ceiling's orange and red detailing.) Roman travertine stone walls and low-lit bronze and glass fixtures give the concourse—featured in the movies *Witness* and *Blow Out*—a lovely aura. The *Pennsylvania Railroad War Memorial,* a bronze winged angel holding the limp body of a soldier, commands the east end of the room. American artist **Walter Hancock** created the 39-foot monument, installed in 1950 as a tribute to the 1,300 railroad employees killed in World War II. Viennese artist **Karl Bitter's** *Progress of Transportation,* a bas-relief completed in 1895 and moved from the city's old Broad Street Station in the 1930s, adds drama to a waiting area beside the Amtrak ticket counters. The piece is an ode to different modes of transportation: oxen and wagon, steam locomotive, steamboat, and airplane.

If you're in the neighborhood at lunchtime, the south side of the station is a pleasant place for a quick meal. The original storefronts have been spruced up and occupied by new tenants, most of them selling food. There's also a candy store, bookstore, and flower stall. ♦ Open daily 24 hours. 30th and Market Sts. Amtrak 824.1600

Within 30th Street Station:

Salumeria $ Pasta with sweet and hot sausages and fresh asparagus in a garlic-anchovy sauce are available to eat in the station or take home. ♦ Italian deli ♦ M-F 8AM-7PM; Sa-Su 9AM-6PM. 222.7444

John Yi $ This stand proffers salmon burgers, a crab-cake platter, and Cajun mussel salad to enjoy on the premises, as well as fresh fish to take home and cook yourself. ♦ Seafood ♦ M-Sa 7AM-7PM; Su 10AM-6PM. 386.3449. Also at: Reading Terminal Market. 923.0487

Sheila's Muffins $ Grab a banana, carrot, blueberry, applesauce raisin, or chocolate muffin to nibble on a long train ride. ♦ Bakery ♦ M-Sa 6AM-7PM; Su 7AM-7PM. 222.4444

2 Drexel University In 1891 financier **Anthony J. Drexel** founded the **Drexel Institute** as a technical school for working-class young people. The school became Drexel University in 1970 and is now the city's third-largest university, with 11,000 students in six colleges. Drexel excels in engineering, business, and computer studies, and it has one of the oldest cooperative education programs in the country (most undergraduates must alternate their studies with full-time work). It was also the first university to require all students to have a personal computer. The **Main Building,** completed in 1890 to designs by **The Wilson Brothers,** has one of the city's finest interior spaces, a skylit atrium of red tile, pink marble, white enameled brick, and wrought-iron balustrades. ♦ S. 32nd and Chestnut Sts. 895.2000

PENN

3 University of Pennsylvania "It has long been regretted as a misfortune to the youth of this province that we have no academy in which they might receive the accomplishment of a regular education," **Benjamin Franklin** lamented in 1749 after playing a leading role in an ill-fated earlier effort to start one. A few months later he and some of his friends formed the **Academy** in the brick Charity School building on Fourth Street. The group included 10 signers of the Declaration of Independence, seven signers of the Constitution, and 21 members of the Continental Congress.

Franklin became the first president of the board of trustees, and created a core curriculum of mathematics, geography, history, logic, and science. The Academy established the country's first medical school in 1765, and became the University of Pennsylvania—known today simply as **Penn**—in 1792. The university grew rapidly, opening the country's first law school, first teaching hospital, and the **Wharton School of Finance and Commerce;** it moved to larger quarters at Ninth and Chestnut streets in 1829. Early pioneers of science associated with the university included astronomer **David Rittenhouse,** naturalist **Joseph Leidy,** and **Alexander Dallas Bache,** a professor of chemistry who

119

directed the Coast and Geodetic Survey. Architect **Paul Philippe Cret,** who designed Rittenhouse Square and the Rodin Museum in Philadelphia, brought prestige to the university's school of architecture.

In 1872 Penn's trustees decided to relocate the university to an open space west of the Schuylkill River, a quiet setting that quickly became a congested urban area. Until 1940 it was mainly a regional school, with students and faculty commuting from the Philadelphia area. This changed dramatically with the end of World War II and the beginning of education benefits for former GI's. Today the university, which includes a hundred academic departments and 12 graduate schools, occupies 250 acres and has 20,000 students.

During the 1960s the campus was altered and enlarged as part of the **"University City"** redevelopment project, undertaken by both the University of Pennsylvania and **Drexel University,** with help from the **Philadelphia Redevelopment Authority.** The Authority provided the funds to tear down many old structures between the river and 44th Street and replace them with new buildings. Streets bisecting the Penn campus were closed and surface trolley cars replaced by a subway line. The changes gave the school a small college green and a more cohesive setting.

Though it's not a grassy, idyllic campus, Penn has a series of garden courtyards that link a number of beautiful buildings representing an extraordinary range of architectural styles. There are some unpopular buildings as well, such as the formidable-looking dormitory towers (known as **Superblock**). ◆ Bounded roughly by S. 33rd and S. 40th Sts, and Chestnut and Spruce Sts

On the University of Pennsylvania campus:

Franklin Field Named for the university's well-known founder, Franklin Field possesses all the charm missing from **Veterans Stadium.** The architectural firm of **Frank Miles Day** gave the stadium a distinctly Philadelphian brick exterior and a U-shape that puts you close to the action no matter where you sit. The athletic facility opened in 1895 with tennis courts, running tracks, and playing fields, and was enlarged for collegiate football in 1922, in time for the Penn-Navy game attended by **President Harding.** The **Philadelphia Eagles,** who played their home games here until the Vet opened in 1971, won their last National Football League championship at Franklin Field, defeating **Vince Lombardi's Green Bay Packers** 17-13 in 1960. It's still the home of Penn football and the **Penn Relays** track meet held every April. The quarter-mile track opens to the public when athletic practice permits; call for the schedule. ◆ S. 33rd and Spruce Sts. Box office M-F 9AM-4:30PM. 898.6151

The University Museum of Archaeology and Anthropology When this museum opened in 1887, the fields of archaeology and anthropology were in their infancy. Though they've since become widely familiar through books and television documentaries, the museum's vast galleries, filled with exotica, still capture that original excitement. Archaeological finds from ancient Egypt, Mesopotamia, Mesoamerica, Asia, Greece, and Rome and from native cultures in Africa, Polynesia, and North and South America are showcased in the 30-plus galleries of this world-class museum. Two 17th-century cloisonné lions flank the entrance to the **Chinese Rotunda,** which also houses one of the largest crystal balls in existence. (Experts believe the 55-pound crystal ball belonged to **Empress Dowager of China.**) In the **Lower Egyptian Gallery** you can see a 12-ton granite *Sphinx of Ramesses II,* circa 1293-1185 BC, as well as attention-grabbing Egyptian mummies. Elsewhere in the building are samples of the oldest writing in the world, and histories in stone of the ancient Maya of Guatemala.

In contrast to other major museums of the period, such as the palatial Metropolitan Museum of Art in New York, The University Museum is on a more human scale. Visitors enter the museum building via an exotic torii-style wrought-iron gate and then pass through a lovely courtyard with a reflecting pool. Inspired by the medieval brick architecture of Northern Italy, Italian-born architect **Wilson Eyre,** who started *House and Garden* magazine, modeled the building's main section (completed in 1893) in part after the **Church of San Stefano** in Bologna, with Romanesque and Byzantine arches, a Mediterranean tile roof, and mosaic tiles beneath the cornice. The brick is cast with a rough mortar and pebbles, giving it more texture and a less refined look. The capitals and columns in the courtyard at the South Street entrance came from Roman ruins in Amman, Jordan, and were donated by the **Kingdom of Jordan. Alexander Stirling Calder,** Philadelphia's premier early 20th-century sculptor, made the four statues, which represent American Indian, African, Asian, and Oceanic cultures.

Inside, the museum's extraordinary rotunda—measuring 90 feet high and 90 feet in diameter—is composed of concentric circles of overlapping Mercer tiles without any supporting beams. **Mitchell/Giurgola** designed the modern glass-and-reinforced-concrete addition to the museum, which was completed in 1971.

Many of the more than one million objects housed here are the bounty of archaeological expeditions sponsored by the museum and the university. Renowned archaeologists such as **Leonard Woolley,** who excavated the 4,500-year-old **Royal Tombs of Ur** in what is now Iraq, and **William Farabie,** who from 1913 to 1916 investigated little-known South American tribes, were affiliated with the university. The elaborate jewelry and decorative pieces Woolley extracted from the Tombs of Ur in the 1920s—many fashioned from delicately shaped hammered sheets of gold— are on the second floor. ◆ Admission. Tu-Sa 10AM-4:30PM; Su 1-5PM. 3260 South St (between 32nd and 33rd Sts). 898.4000

Within The University Museum of Archaeology and Anthropology:

Museum Cafe ★$ Dine in a room with floor-to-ceiling windows looking onto both the new and old facades of the museum. This is just a cafeteria, but the simple sandwiches, pizzas, and soups make a decent lunch. The daily special might be a pasta dish with tomatoes, shrimp, and feta cheese.
◆ American ◆ Lunch and snacks. 898.4000

Museum Shop The sort of knickknacks you might collect at souvenir shops in more exotic locales are found here, including Nubian bookmarks, Egyptian appliqués, Mayan rulers, jewelry, and assorted pottery. ◆ Tu-Sa 10AM-4:30PM; Su 1-5PM. 898.4000

Penn Tower Hotel $$ Even with The University Museum of Archaeology and Anthropology next door, the location remains somewhat lacking given the traffic on 34th Street. Owned by the **University of Pennsylvania,** the hotel is popular with those visiting the campus (only a block away) or patients at one of the hospitals across the street. The lobby has a '70s look, with a round tiled fountain and potted palms, but it's bright and comfortable. Choose from 200 spacious and fully equipped rooms or 10 suites. Day care is available to guests at the **Penn Children's Center.** ◆ Civic Center Blvd (at S. 34th St). 387.8333, 800/356.7366; fax 386.8306

Irvine Auditorium **Horace Trumbauer** (architect of the Free Library and several local hospitals and hotels) designed this auditorium to resemble a medieval French cathedral, with a steeply sloping roof, spires, turrets, and gargoyles. Colorful Gothic designs adorn the interior, which houses one of the largest pipe organs in the world. Construction was completed in 1929. ◆ S. 34th and Spruce Sts

Anne and Jerome Fisher Fine Arts Building Usually referred to simply as the **Furness Building,** this is one of the great masterpieces of **Frank Furness,** the architect who adorned Philadelphia with his idiosyncratic Victorian designs. Housing the library of Penn's Graduate School of Fine Arts, the Furness Building (illustrated below) is an energetic, unforgettable structure, "both serene and hysterical," as described by **Paul Goldberger,** architecture critic for the *New York Times.* The building was almost torn down in the 1950s, when it was very much out of fashion, but is now here to stay, having recently undergone a $16.5 million restoration under the direction of the renowned Philadelphia firm of **Venturi, Scott Brown and Associates.**

Completed in 1891 as the university's main library, the building has a coarsely textured, deep red facade of brick, fieldstone, and terracotta. The north side looks ecclesiastical, with a semicircular churchlike apse; the south side, where you'll find the library stacks, looks somewhat like a train shed (not surprising given the architect's many railroad commissions). Furness intended to make the stacks expandable.

The building's most dramatic space is the four-story reading room, which resembles an exterior courtyard or a railroad waiting room with skylights, gargoyles, and exposed iron beams overhead. The reading room's brick and limestone walls have two-story terracotta arches above squat stone columns that seem about to spring upward. On the west wall is a massive stone fireplace with a tile roof, arched dormer, and steel-faced clock. As you tour the Furness Building, look for the epigrammatic inscriptions on the leaded-glass windows: "Talkers are no great doers," "Men should be what they seem," and "Self love is not so vile a sin as self-neglecting." ◆ M-F 9AM-5PM. S. 34th St (facing the College Green). 898.8325

Within the Anne and Jerome Fisher Fine Arts Building:

Arthur Ross Gallery This intimate gallery with parquet floors specializes in one-of-a-kind exhibits on art history and ethnography. Women in ancient Egypt, Guatemalan textiles, and the restoration of the Parthenon, with architectural renderings of work by Greek architect **Manolis Korres,** have been featured.

Furness Building

Retrospectives of works by faculty, including the semiabstract figures of **Maurice Lowe**, occasionally take place. ♦ Free. Tu-F 10AM-5PM; Sa-Su noon-5PM. 898.4401

College Hall An example of what is commonly referred to as Collegiate Gothic architecture, this is quintessential Ivy League. College Hall, the first building on Penn's West Philadelphia campus, housed lecture halls when it opened in 1872. Now the university's administrative offices are located here. The exterior, topped by a French mansard roof, is made of serpentine rock quarried outside Philadelphia in Chester County. The building originally had towers at each end. Adjacent to College Hall is **Logan Hall,** the second building on campus (completed in 1874) and initially the home of the university's medical department. Philadelphia architect **Thomas W. Richards** designed both buildings. ♦ Locust Walk (between S. 34th and S. 36th Sts)

Benjamin Franklin Statue One of three statues of the university's founder on the Penn campus, this 1899 bronze of a wizened Franklin seated on a granite base is the work of **John J. Boyle,** a prominent turn-of-the-century Philadelphia sculptor. (The other Ben Franklin statues are on 33rd Street near Spruce Street and on a bench off the western end of Locust Walk.) ♦ Locust Walk (in front of College Hall)

Split Button Sculpture Inspired by the thought that **John J. Boyle's** paunchy *Benjamin Franklin* across Locust Walk might pop a button, sculptor **Claes Oldenburg** and artist **Coosje van Bruggen** created this four-foot-high painted aluminum button in 1981. The artists deemed the button "society's most disregarded object." ♦ Locust Walk (in front of the Van Pelt Library)

Locust Walk Streetcars used to run right through campus on **Woodland Avenue,** which intersected the former Locust Street on what is now the **College Green.** Both this portion of Locust Street and Woodland Avenue were closed to traffic by 1960 and now serve as the main pedestrian way through the campus. ♦ Bounded by Walnut and Spruce Sts, and S. 34th and S. 38th Sts

The Quadrangle They just don't make dorms like this anymore. Archways, gargoyles, bay windows, sculptures, and gables surprise and delight throughout this rambling complex, reminiscent of the college buildings at Cambridge and Oxford. **Cope and Stewardson,** the firm that planned similar Jacobean Revival buildings at Princeton University and other American colleges, is responsible for the redbrick and white limestone design. One of the first dormitory complexes on such a grand scale in the country, the four-story "quad" is actually a collection of 39 contiguous buildings enclosing a large quadrangle and smaller courtyards. Construction began in 1895, when a small number of out-of-town students were gravitating to the university, and the last building was completed in the 1950s. Students used to decorate the oak-paneled rooms with Persian rugs, drapery, and elegant furniture of their own. The style today—as you'll notice if you peek through the windows—is more spartan. ♦ Spruce St (between S. 36th and S. 38th Sts)

Alfred Newton Richards Medical Research Building When constructed in 1961, this laboratory building became a seminal structure of the late 20th century, establishing **Louis I. Kahn** as one of the century's most influential architects. Kahn was a Penn professor, a genius known for breathing new life into modern architecture. In contrast to the glass and steel of prevailing skyscrapers, the Richards Building and the adjoining **Goddard Laboratories** (built a short time later) are geometric designs constructed of heavy masonry. The engineering was extremely novel: the frames of both buildings are of rigid reinforced concrete with "post-tensioned" beams held in place by steel cables, a design that eliminates the need for interior structural columns. Elevators, stairs, and heating ducts—what Kahn referred to as the "servant areas"—are in separate brick towers alongside the labs, lit naturally through large geometric windows. (Notice that the scientists within have covered up many of these windows to protect either their privacy or their experiments from exposure and heat.) The brick and concrete facades and adjoining stair towers ingeniously reflect the brick and stone chimneys and turrets of the 19th-century dormitory buildings across the walkway. Behind the laboratories is a small botanical garden with a pond and pathways. ♦ 37th St and Hamilton Walk

Annenberg Center Walter Annenberg, newspaper publisher, philanthropist, and former ambassador to Great Britain, donated the money for construction of this brick performing arts center on the Penn campus. Drama, music, and dance performances are held in the center's three theaters: the 970-seat proscenium **Zellerbach Theatre;** the intimate 200-seat **Harold Prince Theatre;** and the 120-seat **Studio Theatre.** The **Philadelphia Drama Guild, Philadelphia Festival Theater for New Plays,** and **Philadelphia Dance Company** all perform here. Events throughout the year include an annual series of avant-garde music and a dance series that features nationally known groups, such as the **Mark Morris Dance Group** and the **Paul Taylor Dance Company.**

The **Annenberg Center Theatre Series** presents a variety of classical and new plays (a local production of South African playwright Athol Fugard's *My Children! My Africa!* and Shakespeare's *The Tempest* with actors from the **Royal Shakespeare Company** have been among them). Come May, the **Philadelphia International Theater Festival for Children,** a five-day event with puppeteers, storytellers, singers, and jugglers from around the world, takes center stage. ♦ Box office M-F noon-6PM; noon-9:30PM on performance days. 3680 Walnut St (between S. 36th St and the S. 37th St Walkway). 898.6791

Institute of Contemporary Art (ICA)
Founded in 1963, ICA is a major exhibitor of avant-garde art. It was the first museum to show the work of **Andy Warhol** in 1965 and introduced performance artist **Laurie Anderson** and painter **David Salle** in 1986. ICA also organized the traveling exhibit of **Robert Mapplethorpe's** sexually explicit photographs, which caused a storm of protest as it traveled the country. In 1991 the museum moved from cramped quarters elsewhere on campus into this sleek geometric building designed by **Adele Santos,** a former architecture instructor at the University of Pennsylvania. A bright gallery on each floor, with ceilings peaking at 32 feet, comprise the main exhibition spaces. ♦ Admission. W 10AM-7PM; Th-Su 10AM-5PM. S. 36th and Sansom Sts. 898.7108

Superblock The largest construction project undertaken by the university, this $41 million high-rise dorm complex provides accommodations for 3,500 undergraduates. The aloof, fortresslike buildings include a dining hall and parking garage. ♦ Bounded by S. 38th and Spruce Sts, and S. 40th and Walnut Sts

On 13 May 1985, the city of Philadelphia dropped a bomb on a house occupied by MOVE, a cult group known for its rejection of modern life, its threats to neighborhood residents, and its bizarre habits (members bred rats and ate only raw food). Eleven people were killed and 63 West Philadelphia row houses were destroyed in the attack.

Restaurants/Clubs: Red   Hotels: Blue
Shops/ 🌳 Outdoors: Green   Sights/Culture: Black

Ben Franklin: Philadelphia's Resident Genius

Typically caricatured as a balding fellow with half-moon glasses and a kite string in his hand, **Benjamin Franklin** is one of the most beloved and revered of the country's early founders. In 1706, at the age of 17, Franklin arrived in Philadelphia seeking work as a printer. Forty years later, Philadelphia might well have been named Franklinville or Franklintown, so pervasive was the influence of this single man.

In his lifetime Franklin made many civic improvements, having installed the first streetlights and founded the first fire brigade, the first militia, the first life insurance company, and the first hospital. Testing his principles of electricity with a kite tied to a key, Franklin invented the lightning rod, which ultimately spared thousands of buildings destruction by fire. He also invented bifocal glasses and the Franklin stove.

Initially, however, Franklin went into business as a printer—he published the *Pennsylvania Gazette*—and made enough money to retire at the age of 42. He then devoted his life to science, politics, and other interests, establishing the **Library Company of Philadelphia,** which served as the Library of Congress from 1774 to 1800; the **American Philosophical Society,** a distinguished organization that survives to this day; and, with others, the **University of Pennsylvania.** A prominent member of the **Pennsylvania Assembly,** he played a crucial role in the Revolutionary government, helping to draft the **Declaration of Independence.** His famous homespun essays extolling hard work and thrift were compiled in the *Poor Richard's Almanack* and his famous *Autobiography.* Among the many aphorisms attributed to him: "Early to bed and early to rise make a man healthy, wealthy, and wise."

As a young man, Franklin viewed the British empire as enlightened. But like other key colonial figures, his attitude soured when British control became tyrannical. In 1776, the Revolutionary government sent Franklin to France as a diplomat, seeking support for the colonies' struggle against England. In 1778, after the British defeat at Saratoga, the French threw their support behind the colonists, largely in response to Franklin's encouragement.

Franklin returned to the newly independent nation in 1785. Though 79 years old and in poor health, he managed to attend daily sessions of the **Constitutional Convention** in the summer of 1787. His political stature and his ability to forge compromise helped keep the convention together. He had reservations about parts of the document but signed it anyway because he believed in the principles it embodied. In so doing, he heeded the advice he had given to the delegates, urging each of them to "doubt a little of his own infallibility."

As you walk the streets of Philadelphia, look for tributes to this historical figure, a man who helped shape a colony into a nation. The national memorial to Franklin is the rotunda of the **Franklin Institute.**

123

4 Le Bus ★$ For years this restaurant operated out of an actual bus parked at the corner of 35th and Sansom streets. Now a cafeteria in two row houses, Le Bus fuels hordes of college students at breakfast, lunch, and dinner. The sandwiches—chicken salad, ham, roast beef—are large and sometimes hastily thrown together. Salads, daily entrée specials (often including a decent vegetarian lasagna), and homemade soups provide variety. The main attractions, however, are the breads, pastries, and muffins. ♦ American ♦ Breakfast, lunch, and dinner. 3402 Sansom St (between S. 34th and S. 36th Sts). 387.3800

5 White Dog Cafe ★★$$$ **Madame Helena Blatavasky,** a Russian noblewoman who founded the **Theosophical Society** and lived in this row house more than a hundred years ago, is the inspiration behind the enormously popular restaurant that now occupies the site. Influenced by Eastern religions, the society believed in a "universal brotherhood without distinction of race, creed, sex, caste, or color," embraced reincarnation, and eschewed religious dogma.

Current owner **Judy Wicks** aspires to a higher ground as well, opening her restaurant to forums on such political issues as crime in the city, the Middle East peace talks, and the murder of Martin Luther King, Jr. Nevertheless, most people come for the food and the homey atmosphere. Pictures of white dogs predominate (the restaurant is named after a white pooch that played a mystical role in Blatavasky's life), and lace curtains, antique oak tables and chairs, and gingham table-cloths decorate the dining rooms. Attempts at novelty sometimes overwhelm the eclectic food, but the dishes are generally satisfying. Standards include a pan-seared duck breast with cider thyme sauce, roasted pork chop filled with walnuts and Gorgonzola, and baked salmon with a sourdough Dijon crust and a creamy dill sauce. At lunch, try mussels in a Thai curry, falafel, or smoked trout. The homemade breads are made from organic grains. Chocolate pudding cake with cinnamon ice cream or the peanut nougat and chocolate pie are musts for dessert. Light

food and local beers are served at the bar. ♦ Eclectic ♦ Lunch and dinner; brunch on Sunday. 3420 Sansom St (between S. 34th and S. 36th Sts). 386.9224

6 The Black Cat White Dog Cafe owner **Judy Wicks** also runs this "alternative gift store" adjoining the restaurant. The offbeat collection of house-wares and knickknacks includes everything from copper cookie cutters and paper lamp shades to chairs made of twisted twigs and iron lamp stands, plus jewelry and men's ties. ♦ M, Su 11AM-9PM; Tu-Th 11AM-11PM; F-Sa 11AM-midnight. 3424 Sansom St (between S. 34th and S. 36th Sts). 386.6664

7 Sheraton University City $$$ Located two blocks from the Penn campus, the 20-story Sheraton has 377 sunny, recently renovated rooms. There's also an outdoor pool and reasonably priced overnight parking. ♦ S. 36th and Chestnut Sts. 387.8000, 800/325.3535; fax 387.7920

Within the Sheraton University City:

Smart Alex $$ The standard repertoire of chain hotel restaurant food is served: potato skins, hamburgers, baked half chicken, and prime rib. ♦ American ♦ Breakfast, lunch, and dinner. 386.5556

36th St. Deli $ Turkey, roast beef, and corned beef sandwiches make this a serviceable pit stop. **Bassetts** ice cream is also available. ♦ Deli ♦ Breakfast and lunch. 387.7920

8 Zocalo ★★★$$$ Pinpoint lights frame the large first-floor windows and Mexican art decorates the walls of the handsome dining rooms in this restaurant that creates delicious contemporary Mexican cuisine. Try the sautéed mushrooms with chiles and greens in a cilantro vinaigrette or the *sope* sampler, followed by grilled swordfish in warm corn tortillas with grilled vegetables and a tangy green salsa. The menu also offers vegetarian dishes. Sit on the dining terrace when weather permits. ♦ Mexican ♦ Lunch and dinner; dinner only on Saturday and Sunday. 3600 Lancaster Ave (at N. 36th St). Reservations recommended. 895.0139

In the 1700s, John Bartram ("The Father of Botany") traded seeds and roots from his farm on the Schuylkill River with fellow gardeners in England. His garden, located at 54th Street and Lindbergh Boulevard in West Philadelphia, is planted with samples he took as he traveled through the American wilderness.

9 Lemon Grass ★★$$$ A cut above the average Thai restaurant in the city, Lemon Grass has a steady following. Start out with the traditional *mieng cum*—toasted coconut chips, lime, ginger, and peanuts served on lettuce with a plum sauce. Then move on to a Thai salad of grilled beef, dried red peppers, onions, lime juice, and basil, or "Young Girl on Fire," a roasted Cornish game hen stuffed with pineapple and raisins and flamed with Thai whiskey. The large vegetarian menu includes Musaman Curry, bean curd with mixed veggies in a red curry peanut sauce with coconut milk, onions, and potatoes. Mango with sticky rice and sesame seeds makes a fine ending. ♦ Thai ♦ Lunch and dinner. 3626 Lancaster Ave (between N. 36th and N. 37th Sts). Reservations recommended. 222.8042

10 International House $ This impressive concrete high rise, designed by **Bower and Fradley** in 1970, is a residence for international students, a cultural center, and a hotel for visiting academics. If you have "an academic affiliation"—perhaps you're attending a conference or visiting a university—you can stay in one of the 379 dormitorylike rooms, most of which come with single beds, a desk, a chair, and a dresser, at bargain-basement prices. Exterior and interior walls are a brownish gray concrete, and the bathrooms are communal. More than 400 students from 50 or so countries live here, some staying for several years and others for just a few weeks. Founded in 1918, this nonprofit corporation is affiliated with 12 other "International Houses" around the world. ♦ 3701 Chestnut St (between S. 37th and S. 38th Sts). 387.5125

Within the International House:

THE BAZAAR SHOP

The Bazaar Shop If you're looking for jewelry, toys, musical instruments, and crafts from around the world, this lobby shop sells hand-painted Ukrainian eggs, Israeli ceramics, and much more. ♦ M-F 10AM-8PM; Sa 1-7PM; Su 1-6PM. 895.6560

11 Chestnut Cabaret Six nights a week, big-name and up-and-coming musicians perform at the Chestnut Cabaret, a club that features an eclectic mix of rock, world music, country, rhythm and blues, and alternative rock. Sit at the cocktail tables for the less popular shows, or stand when a group such as **The Hooters** is scheduled. ♦ Cover. 3801 Chestnut St (at S. 38th St). 382.1201

12 Tandoor India ★$ One of four Indian restaurants in the neighborhood, Tandoor India is distinguished by its pleasant interior. Hanging plants, skylights, traditional Indian art, and cases filled with currency from around the world serve as decor. *Naan* (unleavened bread) from the large *tandoor* (Indian clay oven) comes with each meal. A buffet is usually available, with selections that vary daily, plus these staples: red-skinned tandoori chicken marinated in homemade yogurt and freshly ground herbs; *saag paneer,* minced spinach cooked with homemade fried cheese in spices and a light cream sauce; and *gulab jamun,* soft milk balls dipped in honey syrup. ♦ Indian ♦ Lunch and dinner. 106 S. 40th St (near Sansom St). 222.7122

13 Boccie ★$ Located in a warehouse also occupied by a branch of **Urban Outfitters** (a source of trendy housewares and clothes), this contemporary pizzeria turns out impressive pies from a wood-burning oven. In a bid to seem authentically Italian, the restaurant is named after its boccie court, a sand-filled rectangle intended for the Italian game. Boccie is popular in South Philadelphia but not necessarily with the pizzeria's crowd of students and young couples, who let their children toss around the leaden balls. Cramped and noisy, the restaurant has small tables, neon accents, and a dining balcony overlooking the boccie court. The pizza fluctuates between fabulous and so-so. When they're on, the crust is flavorful and chewy. Toppings include fresh mozzarella; spinach and prosciutto; scallops, bacon, and mozzarella; and barbecue sauce and spicy Italian sausage. Try the Moroccan: yogurt sauce, grilled lamb, scallions, and fresh coriander. ♦ Italian ♦ Lunch and dinner; dinner only on Sunday. 4040 Locust St (between S. 40th and S. 41st Sts). 386.5500

14 Genji ★★$$ Fine sushi is prepared in this basement restaurant with a tatami (sit-on-the-floor) area and blond-wood tables, popular with both locals and the university crowd. Order your sushi à la carte—the best way to go—or choose from an assortment of Japanese appetizers and dinner entrées. Salmon broiled in teriyaki sauce, noodles with shrimp, vegetable tempura, and tofu with assorted vegetables are all prepared at your table. ♦ Japanese ♦ Lunch and dinner; dinner only on Saturday and Sunday. 4002 Spruce St (at S. 40th St). 387.1583

In 1896, the University of Pennsylvania brought African-American educator and writer W.E.B. Du Bois to Philadelphia to study the city's blacks. His book, *The Philadelphia Negro,* became a classic sociological study.

15 The Woodlands Originally the splendid estate of **William Hamilton,** grandson of lawyer **Andrew Hamilton,** who designed Independence Hall, today The Woodlands is both a park and a historically significant—and still operating—cemetery. Hamilton, a country gentleman who fully indulged his interests in architecture and botany, cultivated one of the most extensive gardens in colonial America. (**Thomas Jefferson** and **George Washington** were said to have visited the grounds.) His mansion, a **National Historic Landmark** currently undergoing restoration, reportedly served as an inspiration to Jefferson when he was building **Monticello.**

Completed in 1790, the Federal-style house is noteworthy for its novel layout: the first floor has rooms of five distinct geometrical forms, including two large ovals. Secret passages honeycombed throughout the house allowed the servants to circulate in and out of sight. After Hamilton's death the property was acquired by the **Woodlands Cemetery Company,** which offered the 78 acres of grounds for "removing the dead from the midst of the dense population of our cities, and placing them in operation with the beautiful works of nature." The cemetery boasts a fascinating collection of Victorian tombstones, many of them imposing obelisks. Among those buried here are artists **Thomas Eakins** and **Rembrandt Peale,** 1812 Naval hero **Commodore David Porter,** millionaire **Anthony Drexel,** noted Philadelphia Beaux Arts architect **Paul Philippe Cret,** and local financier **Francis M. Drexel.** Today the cemetery is run by a nonprofit group. The **Woodlands Heritage National Recreation Trail,** operated by the National Park Service, wends its way through the now somewhat scraggly cemetery grounds. Only the ballroom of the house is open to visitors. ♦ Free. Cemetery daily 8AM-4PM. House ballroom M-F 8AM-4PM. S. 40th St and Woodland Ave. 386.2181

16 The Restaurant School ★★$$ Help the chefs of tomorrow learn their trade by dining at the restaurant of this culinary school, the alma mater of a number of notable chefs. Students not only cook the meals but also design the changing menu and wait on tables. The result: excellent service and trial-and-error food. Nothing is served that fails completely, however, and you'll generally find the dishes commendable—and the bill

affordable. Choices border on elegant, ranging from lobster bisque to salmon encased in pastry and served with lentils. The lovely atrium room of an 1856 mansion provides a pleasant setting. ♦ Eclectic ♦ Dinner. Closed Sunday and Monday. 4207 Walnut St (between S. 42nd and S. 43rd Sts). Reservations recommended. 222.4200

17 American Diner ★$ This stainless-steel dining car, built in 1947 by **Paramount Motor Cars,** was resurrected in 1989, just in time for the retro diner movement. Part diner and part souvenir (with the requisite jukebox and cake in glass cases), American Diner specializes in hearty dishes such as meat loaf with mashed potatoes, sautéed catfish fillet with pecan butter sauce and rice pilaf, grilled rib-eye steak with appealingly greasy onion rings, and roast leg of lamb with potatoes. Side dishes include macaroni and cheese and fried plantains. And a diner wouldn't be a diner without ice-cream sodas and mountainous cakes and pies. ♦ American ♦ Breakfast, lunch, and dinner. 4201 Chestnut St (between S. 42nd and S. 43rd Sts). 387.1451. Also at: 435 Spring Garden St. 592.8838

18 The Red Sea ★$ Have a glass of water ready and waiting before you dig into the food at this Ethiopian restaurant, where you're in for one of the hottest meals of your life. Scoop up spicy stews with *injera,* the moist Ethiopian flat bread. Order the Shefensen Special, a sampling of every major item on the menu, and you'll have traveled along Ethiopia's culinary road map: you'll get *key wat,* beef chunks with garlic, pepper, and onion; *timt'mo,* a mixture of lentils and herbs that will make your nose burn; *doro wat,* chicken braised with pepper, onions, tomato, and garlic, served under a hard-boiled egg; and *hamli,* sautéed onion with broccoli leaves and collard greens. The restaurant occupies two row houses. ♦ Ethiopian ♦ Lunch and dinner. 229 S. 45th St (at Locust St). 387.2424

19 Gables $ This redbrick Victorian mansion (pictured above) with a wraparound porch and a garden provides homey, reasonably priced rooms (16 in all) and morning muffins with coffee. ♦ 4520 Chester Ave (at S. 46th St). 349.7764

20 John Bartram House and Gardens
 Carolus Linnaeus, the renowned Swedish botanist, once called **John Bartram,** who lived from 1699 to 1777, "the greatest natural botanist in the world." He is certainly recognized as the New World's first botanist, and his botanical garden here on 44 serene acres was one of the first in the country. Bartram traveled throughout the American wilderness collecting plant samples, sending many of them to Europe, and is credited with introducing more than 200 plants to European gardeners, including the sugar maple. Some of his handiwork still flourishes here, including pawpaws, ginkgo, persimmons, and oaks. His 18th-century Pennsylvania stone house (pictured above)—a **National Historic Landmark**—was recently restored. ♦ Free; admission for guided tour of both house and garden. M-F noon-5PM; Sa-Su noon-4PM. S. 54th St and Lindbergh Blvd. 729.5281

Bests

George E. Thomas, Ph.D.
Frank Furness scholar, Author of *Frank Furness: the Complete Works*

Frank Furness (1839-1912) returned Philadelphia architecture to its characteristic red brick while pushing design to express function in a way that determined the nature of modern architecture. Furness' pupils included **Louis Sullivan,** in turn the teacher of **Frank Lloyd Wright.** His best buildings have a visceral vitality similar to the force of the works of his great contemporaries, Mark Twain and Thomas Eakins. Though half of his 600-plus commissions have been demolished, remarkable Furness buildings still remain, including:

Best Restoration: The **Venturi, Scott Brown and Associates'** redo of the **Anne and Jerome Fisher Fine Arts Building** (constructed from 1888 to 1891), a railroad-stationlike building with a rust-red exterior. The great skylighted reading room is a renewed treasure. When Frank Lloyd Wright saw the library in the 1950s, he exclaimed, "It is the work of an artist!" Penn's **Architectural Archives,** with its treasure of **Louis I. Kahn** material, is located in the basement.

Best Early Work: Furness and Hewitt's **Pennsylvania Academy of the Fine Arts** (constructed from 1871 to 1876; restored 1973 to 1976 by **Studio Four**). The masterpiece of the Centennial year, the academy building shrieks for attention with a French Second Empire facade overlaid by multicolored English Gothic detail. The interior is a symphony of light leading the visitor through a brilliant, skylighted stairhall to naturally lighted galleries. Displayed here is one of the chief collections of American painting.

Best Surviving Bank: The **Centennial Bank** (constructed in 1876) at 32nd and Market streets. Its bold, three-sided facade is a billboard for three converging streets and revels in the requirements of commerce. Other surviving banks include the classical building occupied by **Mellon Bank** (completed in 1907) at Broad and Chestnut streets, and the **Northern Savings Fund Society** (built in 1872) at Sixth and Spring Garden streets.

Best City Houses: The boldly assertive forms of the **Thomas Hockley House** (constructed in 1876) at 235 South 21st Street represent the various interior spaces, while the floral ornament over the entrance pays tribute to nature as celebrated by Furness' family friend **Ralph Waldo Emerson.** (The adjacent houses to the south at 237-41 South 21st Street are also the work of the Furness office in 1883.) The **Robert Lewis House** (completed in 1886) at 123 South 22nd Street marks the more sculptural and plastic phase of Furness' maturity; **Susan Maxman** restored it for her architectural offices.

Best Small Gem: The **Undine Barge Club** (built in 1823) on Kelly Drive in Boathouse Row—a taut, tough composition.

Best Country House: The 1881 **William F. Rhawn House** at Rhawn Street and Verree Road is closed, but the mansion's clifflike mass and pyramidal roof make it worth the long trip from the city center.

Best Railroad Station: Furness designed nearly 200 stations for the Reading, the Pennsylvania, and the Baltimore and Ohio railroads, of which perhaps a dozen survive. Fortunately, the most remarkable of the small stations was restored recently by the **Chestnut Hill Community Association.** The soaring leap of the passenger porch, the stunning confrontation of trackside and streetside, and the powerful asymmetry around forms derived from the railroad engines it served make **Gravers Lane Station** (completed in 1883) one of the 19th century's most incredible buildings.

Best Church: Though much denatured by later alterations, the **First Unitarian Church** (which Furness completed in 1886 for the parish his father had served for 50 years) still proves its worth because of the interior. Skylights (now covered) down the building's center lighted a low, trussed space that celebrated Unitarian theology. Furness-designed pulpits and a large leaded-glass window on the east transept honor nature. The church is located at Van Pelt and Chestnut streets.

Restaurants/Clubs: Red	**Hotels:** Blue
Shops/ Outdoors: Green	**Sights/Culture:** Black

1/2 1
mi 1/4 1/2
N

56 *Morris Arboretum*

Germantown Pike

Hillcrest Ave.

55

54

53

Ridge Pike

Barren Hill Rd.

Manor Rd.

57 *Andorra Natural Area*

Northwestern Ave.

Bells Mill Rd.

Wissahickon Ave.

Oldline Rd.

Henry Ave.

Manatawna Ave.

Spring Ln.

58

Hagy's Mill Rd.

Port Royal Ave.

Summit Ave.

Shawmont Ave.

Wise's Mill Rd.

Wigard Ave.

Fairmount Park

Wissahickon Creek

Hampton Rd.

Crefeld Ave.

Norwood Ave.

Germantown Ave.

Stenton Ave.

Bethlehem Pike

Paper Mill Rd.

422

CHESTNUT HILL

Pastorius Park

Seminole Ave.

Willow Grove Ave.

Hartwell Ln.

St. Martins Ln.

Huron St.

Mermaid Ln.

Valley Green Rd.

15

Cherokee St.

McCallum St.

Allens Ln.

Wissahickon Ave.

For nos. 16-5
see pg. 136

Ridge Ave.

Livezey St.

Silverwood St.

Domino Ln.

Umbria St.

Parker Ave.

Fountain St.

Gorgas Park

Leverington Ave.

Wilde St.

Manayunk Ave.

Green Ln.

Shurs Ln.

Main St.

Fairmount Park

Walnut Ln.

Wissahickon Dr.

Hollow Rd.

76

23

Conshohocken State Rd.

N. Woodbine Ave.

Manayunk Rd.

Rock Hill Rd.

Belmont Ave.

Schuylkill River

Ridge Ave.

MANAYUNK

For nos. 59-82,
see pg. 143

Northwest

Magical as it seems in the midst of such a congested urban area, Northwest Philadelphia is home to 1,400 rugged acres of undeveloped land known as the **Wissahickon Valley.** The name "Wissahickon" (derived from the American Indian expressions for "catfish stream" and "muddied waters") is particularly suited to the valley's wending roads, craggy cliffs, stone bridges, and waterfalls. The valley is thickly forested and steep, with the **Wissahickon Creek** flowing between Precambrian rock from one of the earth's oldest rock formations. Houses nearby are made from "Wissahickon schist," a stone that bears a distinct glimmer. In 1700, mystic **Johann Kelpius** chose the valley, now part of **Fairmount Park,** as the place where he and his followers would await the end of the world. And **Edgar Allan Poe** spent time here memorializing it in his poem *The Elk.* As you walk the wooded pathway along the creek, you'll happen across benches purchased by the relatives of deceased Philadelphians. "He loved the Wissahickon," reads the tiny plaque nailed to one.

Colonists first ventured into Northwest Philadelphia in the 1700s, setting up paper mills, farms, and country retreats not far from the Wissahickon Creek. Later, as the railroads connected the area with the original city, separate communities emerged. Today, such towns as **Chestnut Hill, Manayunk,** and **Germantown** retain their own indelible personalities. Easily reached by car, bus, or train, they offer a wealth of interesting shops, restaurants, and historic sites.

The **Battle of Germantown,** a pivotal event in the Revolutionary War, was fought on a Germantown estate, and you can still see the actual pockmarks patriot cannon fire made in **Cliveden,** the mansion of

Pennsylvania's then chief justice **Benjamin Chew** (he was a loyalist). **George Washington** set up his temporary offices at what is now known as the **Deshler-Morris House** during the summer of 1792 to escape the yellow fever epidemic in Philadelphia. Later, starting in the 1840s, middle-class families built picturesque villas and Victorian mansions in the town. Two streets—**Tulpehocken Street** and **Walnut Lane**—are particularly vivid examples of this period. SEPTA train routes R8 and R1 run from Center City to Germantown, stopping at Tulpehocken Street, Queen Lane, and Chelten Avenue.

In contrast, Chestnut Hill emerged as a significant community only after the railroad moved farther out in the 1850s, quickly becoming a fashionable address. Today the entire community, noted for its mix of residential architecture, is on the **National Historic Register.** On its shady streets, scented by boxwood in the summer, you'll find English cottages, Italianate villas, and Tudor mansions alongside modern designs by such famous architects as **Louis I. Kahn** and **Robert Venturi.** The neighborhood also has modest row houses, parks, and sidewalks, making it more inviting to visitors than the exclusive communities of Philadelphia's **Main Line.** The Chestnut Hill portion of **Germantown Avenue,** the long cobblestone road that starts in Germantown and comprises Chestnut Hill's main retail district, has taken off in recent years. Though old-time Chestnut Hillers disdain the arrival of chain stores such as **Banana Republic** and **The Gap,** the street's revival has also attracted a high concentration of good restaurants and the sort of shops you won't find at the mall. SEPTA runs commuter trains to the station at the top of the hill on Germantown Avenue.

Abutting the **Schuylkill River,** Manayunk (pronounced man-ee-YUNK) had very different origins. Its position on the river and the construction of the Schuylkill Navigation canal system led to its emergence as a textile manufacturing town in the early 1800s. Blue-collar families have long resided in the row houses that seem to tumble down the community's steep hills. Having lost its industrial base, the town has found a new identity. Manayunk's **Main Street** is now wildly popular for its artsy mixture of restaurants, galleries, and shops. People like to say this is what **South Street** could have been before it became gimmicky. Indeed, the street is refreshingly devoid of slickness and commercial hype. Main Street gets much of its charm from the fact that it evolved spontaneously, without the interference of large developers and big-shot planners. In the small row houses on each side of the street are shops selling secondhand jeans, designer shoes, '50s mementos, hand-painted mirrors, and avant-garde furniture. SEPTA runs trains to Manayunk on the Norristown line, but the bus is the best way to go. SEPTA's No. 61 runs from Center City to Main Street.

---

1 Lincoln Drive One of Philadelphia's most scenic roadways links **Germantown, Mount Airy,** and **Chestnut Hill** with the rest of the city. The eastern portion of the road—formerly known as **Wissahickon Drive**—winds along Wissahickon Creek and its rocky ravines. In the words of *Inquirer* columnist **Clark DeLeon:** "It was a road that resembled its name, with a curve for every syllable. If your car tires had ink on them they could almost spell Wissahickon in cursive just by traveling the route." The upper part of the road, which leads to Mount Airy and Chestnut Hill, was called Lincoln Drive. In 1984 the city renamed the entire highway Lincoln Drive so that the road would be more easily identified under one name. The speed limit in the old Wissahickon Drive section is 25 miles per hour, and though Philadelphians are notorious for disregarding it, you'd be wise to take it easy. ♦ Bounded by Kelly Dr and Allens Ln

Restaurants/Clubs: Red   **Hotels:** Blue

Shops/ 🌳 Outdoors: Green   **Sights/Culture:** Black

2 RittenhouseTown Right off Lincoln Drive in a pretty, woodsy niche of **Fairmount Park** is the site of the first paper mill in the Western Hemisphere. Seven 18th-century houses that were grouped around the mill still stand. **Wilhelm Rittenhausen** came to the U.S. from Holland in 1688 and built a mill here on the **Monoshone Creek,** a tributary of the Wissahickon. It manufactured fine white paper and remained one of this country's most important paper mills for one hundred years. The recently opened visitor's center has a working model of a colonial paper mill, and a studio offers papermaking workshops by local artists. Don't try to enter Rittenhouse Town from Lincoln Drive. Turn right off Lincoln Drive onto Rittenhouse Street, then left onto Wissahickon Avenue. After crossing Lincoln Drive, enter the first driveway on the left. ♦ Admission. Sa-Su noon-4PM. Groups: W-F by appointment. 206 Lincoln Dr (at Wissahickon Ave). 438.5711

3 Stenton The country seat of **James Logan,** one of the early Pennsylvania colony's greatest intellects and civic leaders, is named after the Scottish village where Logan's father was born. Logan was an Irish Quaker who came to Pennsylvania as **William Penn's** secretary. When Penn returned to England, Logan managed the colony until after Penn's death. During the fledgling years of the colony, he served as secretary of the province, president of the Pennsylvania Provincial Council, and chief justice, among other things. He spoke the language of the Lenni Lenape and was Penn's Indian negotiator; made the first translation of Cicero's *Cato* published in America; and was an amateur astronomer and botanist in his spare time. Today his extensive library is housed in the Library Company of Philadelphia (illustrated above). The somewhat austere 1728 Georgian brick building (a **National Historic Landmark**) resembles a small Irish manor house with a formal symmetrical facade. It's furnished with pieces dating from 1730 to 1830. ♦ Admission. Tu-Sa 1-4PM Mar-Dec. 18th St and Windrim Ave. 329.7312

4 Grumblethorpe Wine importer **John Wister,** a German immigrant, made this his summer home from 1744 until his death in 1781. A British general used the house as his headquarters and died here from wounds suffered in the Battle of Germantown in 1777.

During the 18th century the three-story house was known simply as "Wister's Big House." Note that there are two front doors—a typical feature of early Pennsylvania German architecture. Wister's grandson, **Charles Jones Wister,** was a scientist and inventor who also lived in the house and observed the movement of the planets from his observatory on top of his smokehouse on the property. Wister's descendants occupied the house until 1940. ♦ Admission. Tu, Sa-Su 1-4PM or by appointment. 5267 Germantown Ave (at Bringhurst Ave). 843.4820

5 Deshler-Morris House The women volunteers who staff this **National Park Service** building like to call it "the oldest standing White House in America." In the summer of 1792, **President George Washington** came to Germantown to escape Philadelphia's yellow fever epidemic and carried on the country's business from this house. **Thomas Jefferson, Alexander Hamilton,** and **Henry Knox** attended cabinet meetings here. Aside from its historic importance, this is a notable example of 18th-century Georgian architecture. The original structure, built between 1750 and 1772, consisted of just two rooms; a substantial enlargement in 1770 added a spacious dining room, a living room, and more bedrooms. With low ceilings and wooden floors, it is typical of small English manors from the same era. The Chippendale camelback sofa in the living room is the only piece authentic to the house (the others are antiques from the period). A large, tranquil garden behind the house has pachysandra, a ginkgo tree that dates back to Washington's time, and a small herb garden. ♦ Nominal admission. Tu-Su 1-4PM Apr-Dec. 5442 Germantown Ave (between Coulter St and School House Ln). 596.1748

6 Germantown In 1683 **William Penn** deeded a tract of land to 13 German families led by **Francis Daniel Pastorius.** They established Germantown, which was an independent community long before it became part of Philadelphia. The town was laid out along both sides of an Indian trail, now **Germantown Avenue,** and the early German settlers made it a center of papermaking and printing.

As far back as the 1700s, the community was a refuge from the city for such wealthy British colonists as **James Logan** and **Benjamin Chew,** whose estate, **Cliveden,** was the site of the **Battle of Germantown** during the Revolutionary War. The yellow fever epidemics of 1793, 1794, and 1797, which killed one-seventh of the city's population, sent more Philadelphians to Germantown to escape the plague.

In the early 19th century Germantown began its growth as a major textile manufacturing center. Railroad lines connected it with

Philadelphia in the 1840s, making it a full-fledged suburb, and in 1854 it was officially incorporated into the city. As early as the 1930s, Germantown began to suffer from urban problems, and by the 1950s its middle-class and affluent families started to leave for the suburbs. Though it still contains pockets of poverty, Germantown's historical war sites and mansions are national treasures, and the community boasts an outstanding collection of Victorian residential architecture. Many of the historic sites are closed from October to April and have limited hours during the open season. The best way to tour Germantown is by car. Germantown Avenue is cobblestoned, so be prepared for a bumpy ride. ♦ Bounded by Johnson St and Roberts, Wissahickon, and Chew Aves

7 Ellen Rose ★$$$ From the frayed wall-to-wall carpets to the bay windows and table linens in varying shades of purple and lavender, this restaurant in a large Victorian house is old-fashioned and charming. Many of the diners are neighborhood regulars who don't seem to mind the occasionally erratic service. Try the broiled mushrooms with herbed cheese and apple slices as an appetizer. Recommended entrées include spicy Thai chicken breast in coconut milk and peanut curry; roast Cornish hen with honey orange sauce and wild rice; and scallops with water chestnuts, baby corn, straw mushrooms, red pepper, and candied ginger. On weeknights lighter fare is available, such as hamburgers, crab cakes, quesadillas, and popcorn shrimp (tiny rock shrimp dipped in a spicy batter and fried). In warm weather, dine outdoors in the backyard. ♦ Eclectic ♦ Lunch and dinner; dinner only on Saturday and Sunday. 5920 Greene St (at Haines St). Reservations recommended. 843.1525

Ebenezer Maxwell Mansion

8 West Walnut Lane Heading west from **Wyck,** this lovely street of eclectic residential architecture dates to the second half of the 19th century. The ornate European-style houses with facades of stone or stucco tell of the aspirations of the modestly affluent families who lived here. Built in 1864, **No. 11** has a Palladian window and eyebrow window on the roof. **No. 125** is a combination of Flemish bond brick and Tudor half-timbering with a Flemish gable. **No. 143,** constructed in 1856, was renovated in the 1880s for the **Button** family, which owned steam-powered mills. The stone English Gothic-style house at **No. 200,** with its steeply pitched gable roof, blue trim, and crenellated tower, was the home of **Joseph G. Mitchell,** a founder of the Presbyterian Church at Greene and Tulpehocken streets. ♦ Between Germantown and Wayne Aves

9 Wyck One of the oldest houses in Philadelphia, Wyck is situated on an estate purchased in 1689 by **Hans Millan,** a Swiss Mennonite. His son-in-law built a house that later was absorbed into the existing building. Wyck was used as a hospital by the British army during the occupation of Germantown 1777. In the 1800s the estate was owned by the Haines family; in 1824 **Reuben Haines** engaged architect **William Strickland** to unify the additions to the house, and in 1825, when the **Marquis de Lafayette** visited during his tour of the U.S., it looked much as it does today. It was occupied by the Haines family until it was given to the Germantown Historical Society in 1973.

Haines was a founder of the Pennsylvania Horticulture Society, and his wife, **Jane,** planted the box-bordered rose garden, which today has 37 varieties of antique roses and is one of the oldest gardens in the country still growing according to its original plan. ♦ Admission. Tu, Th, Sa 1-4PM or by appointment Apr-Dec. 6206 Germantown Av (at Walnut Ln). 848.1690

10 Ebenezer Maxwell Mansion Thirty years ago, this Victorian house was on the verge of destruction, with plans to convert the lot into gas station. But neighborhood residents couldn't bear to see it torn down and rallied to save it. Over the years, volunteers have spent thousands of hours renovating the building, which was in an extreme state of decay. The result is a delightful example of 19th-century residential architecture and interior design. If you're at all into Victorian wallpaper, furniture, marbling, or wall stenciling, this is a great place to visit. Displays explain the styles of the period and how the renovation was accomplished.

The stone house was built in 1859 to the designs of **J.C. Hoxie** by **Ebenezer Maxwell,** a textile merchant and real-estate speculator. It was enlarged in the 1870s by its second owners. The eclectic exterior has an Italianate tower, Flemish gables, French steep mansard roof, and Gothic embellishments. The building is full of faux decorative details, providing a classic example of how middle-class home owners of the period tried to imitate the dwellings of the very rich. The wallpaper in the entranceway was made to look like marble; the mustard-and-magenta linoleum floor (linoleum was invented in 1859) imitates mosaic tiles; and a fine grain is painted on the cheap door frames. A sand-encrusted paint was applied to the exterior window frames to make them look like stone.

Except for a marble-topped table, which belonged to one of the owners, all the furniture was donated and is authentic to the period. Note the ornate brass gaslit chandelier in the dining room with tiny foxes reaching for bunches of grapes beneath its globes. One of the house's best features is the ceiling stenciling in the second-floor bedrooms, which are being restored. ♦ Admission. Th-Su 1-4PM Apr-Dec. 200 W. Tulpehocken St (at Greene St). 438.1861

11 West Tulpehocken Street Once a family farm, Tulpehocken Street was developed into a road of stately mansions during the late 1800s. Many of the homes, with their gingerbread woodwork, varied trellises, and towers, have remained intact. The Victorian Gothic house at **No. 9** and the house across the street at **No. 20** are known respectively as the **Queen's House** and the **Ladies in Waiting House.** They were built as a refuge for **Queen Maria Cristina** of Spain in case she was forced to leave her country due to political upheaval. The Italianate houses at **Nos. 112, 120,** and **128,** built in 1858, were culled from an architect's design book with individual features added to differentiate them. **No. 240** is an eclectic villa in pink stucco and brick designed by the noted architect **Frank Miles Day** in 1893. ♦ Between Germantown and Wayne Aves

Philadelphia's heaviest snowfall, 21.3 inches, occurred on 11 February 1983. The runner-up was the storm on 5 April 1919, when 21 inches covered the city. The average snowfall for the entire winter season is 21.6 inches.

12 Cliveden **Benjamin Chew,** a leading figure in the early history of the Pennsylvania colony and prominent lawyer who became chief justice of the Supreme Court of Pennsylvania in 1774, purchased 11 acres here in 1763 and constructed a stone country estate (shown above) of simple grandeur. On 4 October 1777, when Chew's home stood empty, British soldiers under the command of **General William Howe** took over the house and fended off an attack of patriots during the **Battle of Germantown.** Within an hour of the start of the battle, 75 American patriots are said to have lain dead on Cliveden's front lawn. **George Washington's** troops were unsuccessful in routing the British from the house, which they occupied for about a week. (Though the colonists lost the infamous battle, French observers at the scene were so impressed by their fighting skills that they returned home and convinced **King Louis XVI** to sponsor the Revolutionary War.) You can still see the scars made by cannons in the building's facade, damaged statuary on the front lawn, and a bullet hole inside Chew's first-floor office.

Cliveden's symmetrical exterior has a stately center pavilion and pedimented front door. A belt course divides the first and second stories of the stone facade, and five limestone urns on brick pedestals crown the roof. Inside, Tuscan columns stand in the large entrance hall. The estate contains an outstanding collection of early American furniture, including a mahogany camelback sofa crafted by the famous Chippendale furniture maker **Thomas Affleck** and covered in yellow damask. The sofa was purchased by Chew from **William Penn's** family in 1760. Affleck also made the elegant chest-on-chest in the second-floor back bedroom. Other interior highlights include the immense carved wood mirrors made by **James Reynolds** in the 1700s, and, in the dining room, mahogany knife cases purchased by **Benjamin Chew, Jr.**, in London in 1789. A Louis Vuitton trunk made in 1868 sits in the second-floor hallway. Legend has it that the trunk spared a Chew family member from the *Titanic* disaster because it arrived late at the port, postponing her departure.

In a back study on the first floor are a collection of Chew's English law books and a map depicting the Mason-Dixon line in 1767, a boundary that Chew adjudicated. After the Revolutionary War, Chew, who did not favor military rebellion, escaped the harsh treatment accorded to other loyalists and was appointed presiding judge of the state's high court of appeals. Seven generations of Chews lived in the house, which is a **National Historic Landmark.** A gift shop is on the premises. ♦ Admission. Tu-Sa 10AM-4PM; Su 1-4PM. Closed Jan-Mar. 6401 Germantown Ave (at Cliveden St). 848.1777

13 Upsala Built in 1798 out of Wissahickon schist, this Federal mansion was the estate of **John Johnson,** great-grandson of an early German settler and a leading Germantown citizen in the early 19th century. It was here that **George Washington's** troops camped during the **Battle of Germantown** when staging their assault on British troops occupying **Cliveden** across the street. The dignified house has a square facade with a marble belt and marble lintels above the windows. The library is decorated in beautiful shades of peach, mustard, and maroon, and has a mantel carved with swags, rosettes, and shields.

Some of the furniture was owned by the Johnson family, and there are many notable 18th- and 19th-century antiques, including a walnut tall-case clock made by Philadelphia clockmaker **John Wood, Jr.,** and a maple high-post bed by cabinetmaker **Jacob Super.** As with other historic houses in Germantown, Upsala narrowly avoided destruction in the 1940s. ♦ Admission. Tu, Th 1-4PM or by appointment Apr-Dec. 6430 Germantown Ave (between Johnson and Upsal Sts). 842.1798

Some of early Philadelphia's favorite dishes: pepper pot (a thick soup of meat, vegetables, pepper, and other seasonings, said to have been created during the winter of 1777-78, when George Washington's army was down to tripe, peppercorns, and various scraps of other food), scrapple (a Pennsylvania Dutch dish made of finely chopped scraps of pork mixed with cornmeal, broth, and seasonings, and cooked as a loaf), cinnamon buns, and homemade ice cream.

14 Umbria ★★$$$ Run by the mother-daughter team of **Donna** and **Lisa Consorto,** this tiny, narrow storefront is one of the best finds in Mount Airy. The dining room is dressed up with textured and mirrored walls, large goblets at each table, and a plush purple rug. In addition to serving consistently good food, the restaurant allows guests to bring their own wine. Start with grilled sweet Italian sausage in a spicy fig sauce or mushrooms baked in phyllo with pureed yellow bell peppers. Entrées include sweetbreads with marsala wine and shiitake mushrooms; crisp roasted duck with a brandy-orange sauce; and fillet of salmon in sourdough. Look for the long list of nightly specials on the blackboard. ♦ Eclectic/Italian ♦ Dinner. Closed Monday. 7131 Germantown Ave (at Mt. Airy Ave). Reservations recommended. 242.6470

15 Wissahickon Valley While it runs along the spine of densely populated neighbor-hoods—Germantown, Roxborough, Mount Airy, and Chestnut Hill—the Wissahickon is virtually cut off from urban life. Most of the valley's 1,400 acres are part of **Fairmount Park** and comprise one of its most popular sections. The valley's five-mile gravel and dirt path, known as both **Forbidden Drive** and **Wissahickon Drive,** is a haven for joggers, cyclists, walkers, and horseback riders. (It's closed to automobiles—hence the name Forbidden Drive.) This is a great place to stroll in any season. On the hottest days of summer it's relatively cool, and after a snowstorm, the woods are enchanting.

Forbidden Drive wends along the creek in a gorge, passing waterfalls, an old covered bridge, an inn, massive cliffs, and secluded benches. The busiest area is in the vicinity of the **Valley Green Inn,** where ever-vigilant ducks in the creek feed on most anything that is tossed to them. Forbidden Drive can get congested on weekends, but the park has dozens of trails off the well-beaten path. Trail maps are sold at several locations, including the Valley Green Inn; the **Andorra Natural Area,** off Northwestern Avenue; **O'Donnell's Stationery,** 8335 Germantown Avenue, in Chestnut Hill; **Way to Go,** 4363 Main Street, Manayunk; and the **Rand McNally Map and Travel Store,** One Liberty Place, Center City.

Parking is available on the Chestnut Hill side of the creek on Valley Green Road, which forks off the western end of Springfield Avenue, and off Bell's Mill Road, between Ridge and Germantown avenues. About three fourths of a mile south of Bell's Mill is the only covered bridge in a U.S. city, and to the north is the serene Andorra Natural Area. At the southern end of the valley, the drive meets a two-mile paved pathway that parallels the creek as it hooks hard toward the Schuylkill. It's a pleasant, less crowded alternative for a bike ride, especially recommended during the fall foliage season for its striking panoramas. The only drawback here is the noise of traffic from Lincoln Drive. ♦ Bounded by Lincoln Dr and Northwestern Ave, with parking areas on southbound Lincoln Dr, Valley Green Rd, and Bell's Mill Rd. 686.2176

Within the Wissahickon Valley:

Valley Green Inn ★$$$ Legend dates this inn to the 1600s, but it probably wasn't built until the 1850s, sometime after the advent of Wissahickon Drive, the gravel path running right out front. The green-shuttered building provides a lovely setting for a meal. The porch overlooks the creek and a stone bridge, and the three homey dining rooms display old photos, antique clocks, and cooking utensils. People have always come here more for the surroundings than the food, which has grown fancier in recent years. Try the duck breast salad with Roquefort, the filet mignon with shallots and port wine, or the veal and shrimp piccata. ♦ Eclectic ♦ Lunch and dinner. Wissahickon Dr (at Springfield Ave and the Wissahickon Creek). 247.1730

16 **Chestnut Hill** Until the commuter railroad was extended to Chestnut Hill in the 1850s, this was a modest village of farmers, millworkers, and shopkeepers. Once it was linked to the city, **Henry Howard Houston,** a director of the Pennsylvania Railroad, exploited Chestnut Hill's scenic setting along the Wissahickon Valley to create a fashionable suburb. Houston commissioned the architects **George** and **William Hewitt** to help him build an enormous inn and church, constructed nearly a hundred houses (including his own), and donated land for the **Philadelphia Cricket Club,** the country's first.

Houston's son-in-law, **George Woodward,** continued development of the western section of the community into the 1930s. Between 1890 and 1905 the population of Poffrabia, a village in Northern Italy, dropped from 2,200 to 1,000 when its stoneworkers left for Chestnut Hill to build its stone estates. The eclectic architecture represents the work of nearly every significant late 19th- and early 20th-century Philadelphia architect, and the entire community is now a **National Historic District.**

Chestnut Hill is the highest elevation point in Philadelphia, rising from 294 feet at Mermaid Lane to 446 feet at Summit Street. German-town Avenue, the cobblestone former Indian trail that also runs through Germantown, is the neighborhood's principal street. One of the great things about visiting Chestnut Hill is the parking. The local merchants' association had a brilliant idea when they decided to open little lots and staff them with friendly retirees. The attendants will give you a ticket, which you must have stamped wherever you eat or shop. The lots are located off Germantown

Avenue on Southampton Avenue, Highland Avenue, and Bethlehem Pike. ♦ Bounded by Lincoln Dr, Northwestern, Stenton, and Ridge Aves

17 **Druim Moir** Named after the Gaelic phrase for "great crag," this stone structure was built for developer **Henry Houston** in 1886 to look like a Scottish baronial castle. It was designed by **George** and **William Hewitt,** the architects responsible for most of Houston's buildings. In the 1940s alterations removed turrets and gables, leaving the house much less elaborate than it once was. The mansion overlooks a magnificent walled garden designed by **Robert Rhodes McGoodwin** after World War I. Druim Moir was made into three attached houses, each with its own lot. Next door is the privately owned **Brinkwood,** a stone and cedar-shingled house built by Houston for his son in 1887. ♦ West end of Willow Grove Ave

18 **Chestnut Hill Academy** This rambling castlelike structure was once the **Wissahickon Inn,** a vacation spot for city dwellers. It was designed with rich exterior woodwork, corner bay windows, and half-timbered dormers by the **Hewitt Brothers** in 1884. The inn had 250 rooms and was situated on a so-called lake, created by the damming of a nearby creek. It didn't last long as a resort and became a prestigious prep school in 1898. ♦ Willow Grove Ave and Huron St

19 **St. Martin-in-the-Fields Episcopal Church** Henry Houston commissioned the Hewitt Brothers to build this lovely stone Gothic church with arches and a four-story tower, completed in 1888. Situated next to the playing fields of the **Philadelphia Cricket Club** and across the street from the prestigious **Chestnut Hill Academy,** the church adds to the picturesque English setting. The beautiful west window was crafted by **Louis C. Tiffany.** ♦ Willow Grove Ave and St. Martin's Ln

A Quaker from the time he was a young man, William Penn brought his philosophy of religious tolerance to the colony of Philadelphia (which drew Lutherans, Anglicans, Presbyterians, and Baptists). By 1700 Quakers accounted for only 40 percent of the population, and by 1880 less than one percent of the city's population was Quaker.

Riots broke out on the streets of Philadelphia in 1844 as a result of fighting between Catholics and Protestants. Irish Catholics had come to the city in large numbers during the potato famine of the 1840s, and many Protestants wished to restrict their numbers. More than 20 people were killed and two Catholic churches burned to the ground during the riots.

Restaurants/Clubs: Red   Hotels: Blue
Shops/ 🌳 Outdoors: Green   **Sights/Culture:** Black

CHESTNUT HILL

For nos. 1-15 and 53-82, see pg. 128

29 Pastorius Park

Fairmount Park

20 Yu Hsiang Garden ★$$ Popular because it's the only Chinese restaurant in Chestnut Hill, this restaurant decorated with Oriental screens has decent spareribs and scallion pancakes. ◆ Chinese ◆ Lunch and dinner. 7630 Germantown Ave. 248.4929

21 Italian Oven $ The craze for Italian cuisine and wood-burning ovens has been reduced to a formula in this chain restaurant with bottles of olive oil and peppers on display, grottolike walls, black-and-white tiles, and a cheerful atmosphere. The pizzas from the wood-fired oven and large selection of pasta are decent; and the pan sautéed fish with pasta, grilled chicken sandwich, and Italian vegetable soup are all good for the price. An inexpensive children's menu comes with crayons and dried noodles to keep the little ones busy. ◆ Italian ◆ Lunch and dinner. 7700 Germantown Ave (between Cresheim Valley D and Mermaid Ln). 242.4450

The General Mail Facility at Chestnut and 30th streets in Philadelphia handles more than 8 million pieces of mail daily.

22 The Night Kitchen
★$ The rich, crumbly chocolate shortbread cookies, caramely cinnamon buns loaded with nuts, and cakes topped with real frosting set this bakery apart from other bake shops that tend to go heavy on fluffy white icing. The breads, scones, muffins, soups, and small pizzas are also good. ♦ Bakery ♦ Tu-F 7:30AM-5:30PM; Sa 8AM-5PM; Su 8AM-noon. 7725 Germantown Ave (between Mermaid Ln and Moreland Ave). 248.9235

23 Windfall Gallery Folk art from around the world is artfully displayed in this boutique near the bottom of the hill. The jewelry is varied and interesting, as is the selection of carved animals from Africa, Southwestern pottery and tiles, decorative mirrors, and picture frames. ♦ M-Tu, Th, Sa 10AM-5PM; W 10AM-8PM; F 10AM-6PM; Su noon-4PM. 7944 Germantown Ave (at Willow Grove Ave). 247.6303

24 The Little Nook Handmade earrings in silver, brass, and gold in simple feminine styles are sold in this small, unpretentious storefront. Silk scarves and neckties by artist **Michelle Marcusa**, decorative tiles, perfume bottles, and whimsical glass flowers are also available. ♦ M-Sa 10AM-5PM. 8005 Germantown Ave (at Willow Grove Ave). 242.1878

25 Sulgrave Manor "The adulation of things colonial and Revolutionary blended at times into out-and-out Anglophilia, a worship of English roots that seems on its face unfaithful to the intent of the American Revolution," Temple Professor **Morris J. Vogel** has written of Philadelphia culture. He noted this house, built in 1926 for the city's Sesquicentennial Celebration, as a prime example. With its steep slate roof and stone facade, it was meant to be a replica of an English manor once occupied by **George Washington's** ancestors. Believe it or not, it was moved from the Sesquicentennial fairgrounds in South Philadelphia to this idyllic spot. ♦ 200 W. Willow Grove Ave (between Lincoln Dr and St. Martin's Ln)

26 Houston-Sauveur House Henry Houston built this house in 1885 in the Queen Anne style, characterized here by an exuberantly busy exterior of half-timbered gables, dormers, porches, odd-shaped windows, a steeply pitched roof, and railings. The house was designed by Houston's principle architects, the **Hewitt Brothers**. ♦ 8205 Seminole Ave

27 Vanna Venturi House Unfortunately, you can barely make out the striking geometry of this famous house (shown above) in the summertime, when the view is obscured by trees. The house, designed in 1962 by **Venturi and Rauch** for **Robert Venturi's** mother, is considered a classic of postmodern design. The most striking feature is the sloping gabled roof divided by a deep recess with an arched window. ♦ 8330 Millman St (at Sunrise Ln)

28 Margaret Esherick House The elegant simplicity of this house designed in 1960 by famous modern architect **Louis I. Kahn,** who was a professor at the University of Pennsylvania, blends in well with the lush, leafy neighborhood. The structure is essentially two stuccoed concrete blocks with vertical and horizontal windows, a narrow chimney shaft, and natural cedar shutters. Its simple lines benefit by contrast with Chestnut Hill's more sumptuous houses. ♦ 204 Sunrise Ln (at Millman St)

29 Pastorius Park No fancy ball fields, playgrounds, or tennis courts can be found in this charming park, just green meadows, large shade trees, benches, and lots of quiet. It's a great place for a picnic. ♦ Bounded by Lincoln Dr, Abington Ave, and Roanoke St

30 Under the Blue Moon ★★★$$$ Almost two decades have passed since the graduates of the first class of the **Philadelphia Restaurant School** went out on their own. **Gene** and **Phyllis Gosfield**, a husband and wife team, were among them. The Gosfields leased this former toy store with long bay windows, hung handmade banners of blue moons out front, and covered the tables with batik cloths. At the time, it was all pretty radical. Through the years and varying trends, their restaurant has endured with a multicultural menu that has changed remarkably little. You can't go wrong with some of the standbys: lobster rangoon (a fried wonton filled with lobster, garlic, and cheese and served with apricot chutney), shrimp Westphalian (beer-batter shrimp wrapped in ham), or Donald's Chinese Duck (half a duck, roasted with Chinese herbs and then deep fried, served on spicy noodles with a pungent dipping sauce). Lamb Turkestan is sautéed with cherry tomatoes, onions, and oregano and comes with a sauce of yogurt, cucumber, and garlic. Try the homemade ice cream for dessert. ♦ Eclectic ♦ Dinner. Closed Monday and Sunday. 8042 Germantown Ave (at Abington Ave). 247.1100

31 Bredenbeck's Bakery and Ice Cream Parlor ★$ Skip the baked goods here and have a cone topped with Bassetts or Häagen-Dazs ice cream. There's no place to sit, but after walking around Chestnut Hill, ice cream sure tastes refreshing. ♦ Bakery ♦ M-Th 11AM-10PM; F-Sa 11AM-11PM; Su 10AM-10PM. 8126 Germantown Ave (between Abington Ave and Hartwell Ln). 247.7374

32 Flying Fish ★★★$$$ Fresh fish prepared inventively without fuss or formality is the strength of this restaurant, one of three in Chestnut Hill owned by **Paul Roller.** Roller was serving mahimahi and orange roughy before they became standards at Center City restaurants. Try the grilled tuna with fried peppers and rosemary; the shrimp and sausage with fennel, tomatoes, and onion served on polenta; or the seafood stew with mussels, shrimp, clams, scallops, monkfish, and lobster tail. The crab cakes are meaty and rich. Veal and chicken dishes are also on the menu. Lemon tart, fruit pie, and chocolate cakes are excellent choices for dessert. The tiered dining area, noisy on a busy night, is casual with blond woods, white walls, ceiling fans, and picture windows. ♦ Seafood ♦ Lunch and dinner; dinner only on Monday. Closed Sunday. Reservations recommended. 8142 Germantown Ave (at Hartwell Ln). 247.0707

33 Everything Beatrix Peter Rabbit appears on virtually everything—quilts, baby jumpers, toddlers' sweaters, baby cups, and bowls—in this overwhelmingly pastel boutique. ♦ M-Tu, Th-F 10AM-5:30PM; W 10AM-8PM; Sa 10AM-5:30PM. 8139 Germantown Ave (at E. Hartwell Ln). 248.9522

"The Sound of Philadelphia" is an expression that refers to the smooth, orchestrated style of soul music pioneered by producers Kenny Gamble and Leon Huff, who currently run Philadelphia International Records on Broad Street. The Sound (often identified as a precursor to disco) became enormously popular in the early 1970s, inspiring the O'Jay's "Love Train" and Elton John's "Philadelphia Freedom," two hits recorded in the city.

Restaurants/Clubs: Red   **Hotels:** Blue
Shops/ 🌳 **Outdoors:** Green   **Sights/Culture:** Black

34 The Secret Garden Pass through the opening in the ivy-covered stone wall and a lovely miniature garden to find an ample selection of children's books, games, puzzles, stuffed animals, and greeting cards. Toys are provided for the kids to play with while you shop. ♦ M-Sa 10AM-5PM. 12 E. Hartwell Ln (at Germantown Ave). 247.1410

35 A Slice of Heaven ★★$$ With floral prints and antique brass chandeliers, this contemporary tearoom started out primarily as a dessert place, and it remains a good source for Key lime pie, lemon tart, angel food cake, and something called Chocolate Death (three layers of chocolate mousse cake filled with chocolate cream and truffles). But today fine lunches and dinners are also offered in a small dining area with floral tablecloths and sprigs of fresh flowers. The menu includes a prime rib steak seared with brandy; roasted salmon with orange-honey glaze; fettuccine tossed with shiitake, porcini, and button mushrooms; and an old-fashioned chicken potpie. ♦ Eclectic ♦ Breakfast, lunch, and dinner. 8225 Germantown Ave (between Hartwell and Southampton Aves). 248.3388

🍍 **Chestnut Hill Hotel** 🍍

36 Chestnut Hill Hotel and the Centre at Chestnut Hill $$ If you want to stay overnight in Chestnut Hill, this is your only option. The 28-room hotel shares a large 19th-century building with two restaurants and various shops. The small rooms are not luxurious but are neatly furnished with four-poster beds and homey antiques. The restaurants and shops that comprise the Centre at Chestnut Hill are not affiliated with the hotel. ♦ 8229 Germantown Ave (at Southampton Ave). 242.5905, 800/628.9744

Within Chestnut Hill Hotel and the Centre at Chestnut Hill:

Nana Ltd. Grandparents will find lots of adorable, and pricey, outfits—from frilly party dresses to baby bonnets to nautical windbreakers. ♦ M-Sa 10AM-5:30PM; Su noon-4PM. 8229 Germantown Ave (between Southampton Ave and Hartwell Ln). 247.6467

J.B Winberie $$ Fajitas, stir-frys, pasta, and burgers are the mainstays of this grottolike restaurant in the Chestnut Hill Hotel building. The first floor contains a noisy bar, and the white-stucco cellar downstairs is the main dining area. In warm weather, the large front porch of the hotel is popular among those who want to sit outside at little round tables with umbrellas. Winberie may be the last restaurant in the city serving fondue, a rich cheddar beer mix served with crusty bread and sliced apples. ♦ Eclectic ♦ Lunch and dinner. 247.6710

Pollo Rosso ★$$ With warm textured walls and a huge papier-maché chicken, this stylish trattoria was instantly popular when it opened in 1993. On the second floor of the Chestnut Hill Hotel building, the main dining area has large windows overlooking Germantown Avenue, where trolleys clatter constantly on their journeys up and down Chestnut Hill. The rear dining area has a bar and is more chic. Pizzas come from a wood-fired oven. Try Pizza Slautare, which resembles the pizza served in some parts of Italy, with no cheese, just artichoke hearts, roasted peppers, sun-dried tomatoes, garlic, and fresh herbs. Chicken is marinated in olive oil and thyme, then spun on the rotisserie and served with two vegetables. Other good bets are lamb on skewers, grilled steak, and rotisserie duckling. Along with a kid's menu, children are supplied with crayons and a place mat for coloring. ♦ Italian ♦ Dinner. 248.9338

Victoria and Company Conservative wedding gifts and decorative pieces for the tasteful home are sold in this sunny boutique. **Portmeirion** ceramics, **Pimpernel** place mats, painted mailboxes, and a small, unusual selection of wall mirrors are among the highlights. ♦ Tu, Th-F 10AM-6PM; W 10AM-8PM; Su noon-5PM. 248.4040

Chestnut Hill Farmers Market More than a dozen vendors sell produce, flowers, fresh coffee beans, pasta, meats, and fish in a shedlike building behind the Chestnut Hill Hotel. It's a good place to stop for a cup of coffee and a sweet roll in the morning. However, there are no tables for sitting. ♦ Th-F 9AM-6PM; Sa 8AM-4PM. No phone

37 **Noodles** ★$ Two bright dining rooms with blond wood benches and Formica-topped tables offer salads, pasta, and light entrées. The service is erratic, and overall the place is not as well-managed as the other restaurants owned by **Paul Roller**. But it's popular for

pancakes and French toast on Sunday. The ice cream is homemade. ♦ American ♦ Breakfast, lunch, and dinner. Closed Monday. 8341 Germantown Ave (at Gravers Ln). 247.7715

38 **Gravers Lane Station** This small railroad station built in 1883 seems fairly uninteresting when you pull up front. But walk around to the tracks and you'll see the signature details of architect **Frank Furness,** beloved for his use of Victorian ornament. The cone-shaped ticket tower and the complex of dormers, heavy brackets, and trusses in the shed that overhangs the outside waiting area are quintessential Furness. ♦ Gravers Ln and Anderson St

39 **Intermission** Devotees of the performing arts stock up on books about Woody Allen and Marlon Brando, movie scripts, librettos, Broadway CDs, film posters, and children's puppets here. ♦ M-Tu, Th-F 11AM-5PM; W 10AM-8PM; Sa 10AM-5PM; Su noon-5PM. 8405 Germantown Ave (between Gravers Ln and Highland Ave). 242.8515

40 **El Quetzal** Women's peasant clothing from India, Ecuador, and Indonesia; carved animals from Kenya; hand-painted trays and figurines from Mexico; and T-shirts sporting aboriginal Australian designs fill the racks and baskets in this Third World boutique. ♦ M-F 10AM-6PM; Sa 10AM-5PM. 8427 Germantown Ave (between Gravers Ln and Highland Ave). 247.1840

41 **2 Susans** Loose-fitting women's clothes in natural silks, knits, and linens are available in this lunchbox-size boutique that also offers a nice selection of ceramics and costume jewelry. Designer **Eileen Fisher** is responsible for much of the clothing. Look for the beautiful—and expensive—oversize sweaters in arresting colors. ♦ M-Sa 10AM-5PM. 8428 Germantown Ave (between Gravers Ln and Highland Ave). 242.0533

42 **The Wooden Train** All the toys of yester-year, including the **Brio, Ravensburger,** and **Playmobil** lines, are sold here—at much higher prices than when Grandpa used to make them. The decent selection of children's books has such classics as **Robert McCloskey's** *Make Way for Ducklings.* ♦ M-Sa 10AM-5PM. 8437 Germantown Ave (between Gravers Ln and Highland Ave). 242.5660

42 **The Philadelphia Print Shop** This is a wonderful place to browse through old prints. In addition to affordable works by lesser-known artists are bird prints by **John James Audubon,** botanicals by **Thorton** and **Redoute,** caricatures from magazines such as *Harpers Bazaar,* scenes of Philadelphia, and military drawings. ♦ M-Sa 10AM-5PM. 8441 Germantown Ave (at Highland Ave). 242.4750

The Crying Game: Sports Losers and Legends

True, they once booed Santa Claus. And yes, in 1989, **Mayor Edward Rendell** paid a fellow football fan to throw a snowball at a visiting player. But forgive Philadelphia fans their trespasses, for they have endured some of the most forgettable moments in sports history. In the 1972-73 National Basketball Association season, the **Philadelphia 76ers** finished with a record of 9-73. That's 9 wins and 73 losses. As for the **Philadelphia Phillies** baseball team, they lost 23 games in a row in 1961, a record that stands to this day. While they were heading for the 1993 World Series, they were constantly reminded of their 1964 collapse. That year, the team held first place by 6 1/2 games in the National League pennant race with just 12 games to go, then proceeded to lose 10 in a row, handing the pennant to the **St. Louis Cardinals.**

Disregarding Philadelphia's "City of Losers" stigma, the city's fans remain intensely loyal (or, at the very least, masochistic). In good years and bad, **Philadelphia Eagles** football games sell out **Veterans Stadium,** while the Phillies draw two million spectators minimum. Despite the occasional run of *very* bad luck, the city has produced some genuine sports legends. **Joe Frazier,** who won the heavyweight championship by unanimous decision over **Muhammad Ali** in March 1971, typified the

Philadelphia fighting style: keep coming, keep punching, and take two to land one (which "Rocky, the Philadelphia prizefighter that Hollywood create immortalized). **Bobby Clarke,** a diabetic, set a standard for heart and tenacity in the National Hockey League during his inspiring career with the **Philadelphia Flyers.** He led the Flyers to successive Stanley Cups in the '73-'74 and '74-'75 seasons.

Wilt "The Stilt" Chamberlain, of the 76ers, one of the NBA's all-time greats, once scored 100 points i a single game. Any true basketball fan would find that a greater accomplishment than his boast that he's slept with 20,000 women.

In 1980, the Phillies, led by third-baseman **Mike Schmidt** and pitcher **Steve Carlton,** won their first and only world championship. When relief pitcher **Tug McGraw** struck out **Willie Wilson** of the Kansas City Royals for the last out of the sixth game, Mike Schmidt leaped into McGraw's arms— an indication of how that victory would also affect the city's fans. Knowing there were Philadelphians in the stands, the Kansas City authorities took no chances. With the Phillies leading the Royals late i the game, contingents of policemen on horseback and guard dogs lined up to "remind" the rowdy crowd to keep their celebration low-key, as befits visitors from the City of Brotherly Love.

---

43 Robertson Florists Though essentially a flower shop (and one of the best in the region), the wonderful glass conservatory in the back, with ivy-covered walls, fountains, and pampered flowering plants, is worth walking through even if you're not in the market for greenery. Garden-related knickknacks are on display throughout the store. ♦ M-F 9AM-6PM; W 9AM-8PM; Sa 9AM-5PM; Su noon-4PM. 8501 Germantown Ave (at Highland Ave). 242.6000

44 Baggage Room Wedding gifts abound, including crystal, fancy porcelains and ceramics, and needlepoint pillows. ♦ M-Sa 9:30AM-5PM. 9 W. Highland Ave. 247.1446

45 The Candle Shop
Traditional tapers in a variety of colors, novelty candles, Israeli menorahs, and other wax wares are included in the ample candle collection. ♦ M-Sa 9:30AM-5PM. 15 W. Highland Ave. 248.1459

46 Chestnut Hill Cheese Shop The scent of ripe cheese and fresh coffee beans lingers outside the door of this cheese shop with fairly steep prices but an exceptionally knowledge-able staff and a first-rate selection. ♦ M-Th, Sa 9AM-5PM; F 9AM-6PM; Su noon-4PM. 8509

Germantown Ave (between Highland and Evergreen Aves). 242.2211

46 8515 Depot ★$$ Railroad ties were used t build the interior of this family-oriented restaurant dedicated to trains and the lore of the iron horse. Among the interesting feature inside are a large collection of old-time ticket pictures of some of the greatest trains to run the nation's rails, and a glass-covered floor that serves as a ceiling for the antique toy trains that run below. One of the three dining areas is a wooden caboose. The conservative menu features prime rib every night. Good be are veal barbison (veal medaillons with slices of lobster meat, brie, seedless tomatoes, and herbs in a butter sauce) and flounder Imperia (a baked or broiled fillet with crabmeat and a lemon-herb sauce). All dinners come with salad, vegetables, and a choice of potatoes. Cold sandwiches, entrée-size salads, and pas are also available. ♦ American ♦ Lunch and dinner. 8515 Germantown Ave (between Highland and Evergreen Aves). 247.6700

47 Antique Gallery Though it all looks expensive, some of the wonderful estate jewelry here is quite affordable. There's a larg selection of Scottish agate jewelry, as well as Art Deco and Art Nouveau decorative pieces i porcelain, bronze, and pottery. ♦ Tu-Sa 10AM 5PM. 8523 Germantown Ave (at Evergreen Ave). 248.1700

Anglecot

48 Anglecot The whimsical sundial above the front entrance and the eyelid dormer in the attic are some of the delightful details in this house designed by **Wilson Eyre,** who was born in Italy and moved to Philadelphia in 1877, and is known for energizing the city's suburban architecture. This delightful structure, built in 1883, represents Eyre's use of the Queen Anne style, characterized here by a complexity of gables and odd-shaped windows. The brick and wood building and the carriage house out back were recently restored and converted into condominiums. ♦ Evergreen and Prospect Aves

49 The Post Light American country lighting fixtures in wrought iron, wood, and brass fill this small store. The cut-paper shades and traditional country furniture are particularly nice. ♦ M-Tu, Th-Sa 10AM-5PM; W 10AM-8PM. 8611 Germantown Ave (between Evergreen Ave and Bethlehem Pike). 242.3810

50 Watson House "Cottages and villas, surrounded by neat grounds, trees, shrubbery, and flowers, many of them costly and handsome, all comfortable and pretty. . . . The same spectacle is to be seen on every lane near Germantown all the way up to Chestnut Hill. . . . They are the results of the railroads which enable anyone to enjoy the pleasures of the country life and at the same time attend to business in town." So wrote **Sidney George Fisher,** a chronicler of events in the area in the latter half of the 19th century. This was one of the first grand houses in Chestnut Hill. Built in 1856, the stucco house, now in a state of disrepair, looks like an Italian villa with a tower. And though the architect is unknown, it shows the influence of Philadelphia architect **Samuel Sloan,** who brought Italianate design to Chestnut Hill. ♦ 100 Summit Ave

51 Price House Reminiscent of an Italian villa, this cream-colored mansion built in 1854 with flat roofs and arched windows has an elegant central bell tower. As you walk or drive through the area, you'll notice quite a few other palazzolike mansions that were constructed around the same period. ♦ 129 Bethlehem Pike (between Stenton and Germantown Aves)

52 Roller's ★★$$ A fiercely loyal clientele frequents owner/chef **Paul Roller's** bright cafe tucked in a corner of a low-slung shopping center off Germantown Avenue. A former ice cream parlor, the restaurant has terracotta floors, cafe chairs and blond wood tables, and large windows with half-curtains. It's better suited to lunch or brunch than dinner, when the tight quarters seem less agreeable. The nouvelle American cuisine is simply prepared using fresh seasonal produce. Try the Parmesan-coated flounder; chicken with goat cheese, basil, and sun-dried tomatoes; roast pork loin stuffed with dried fruits and cider-mustard-cream sauce; or broiled bluefish with horseradish sour cream. Several fish specials are also usually available. On Sunday, excellent pancakes and French toast are served for brunch. All desserts are homemade, and standouts include the pecan pie, chocolate cake, and lemon soufflé tart. ◆ American ◆ Lunch and dinner; Sunday brunch. Closed Monday. In Top of the Hill Plaza, 8705 Germantown Ave (at Bethlehem Pike). 242.1771

52 Roller's Market Buy the desserts available at **Roller's** restaurant next door, as well as take-out pasta, salads, and entrées. ◆ Tu-Sa 11AM-7PM. 8705 Germantown Ave (at Bethlehem Pike). 248.5510

53 Pepper House Rough Wissahickon stone, a simple tower, and an austere facade make this one of many houses in Chestnut Hill that blend seamlessly into the area's natural setting. The English country-style house was designed by **Willing and Syms,** a prominent Philadelphia firm of the 1920s and 1930s, and built in 1920. ◆ 9120 Crefeld Ave (at Hampton Rd)

54 High Hollow Only a veteran voyeur can make out anything but the cobblestone courtyard and steeply pitched roofs of this private stone mansion overlooking Fairmount Park. Hidden by trees and located at the end of a descending driveway, the house was designed in 1914 by and for **George Howe** (noted architect of the PSFS Building in Center City) in the evocative style that Howe called Wall Street Pastoral, based on traditional English and French houses. High Hollow is considered by critics a minor masterpiece of American domestic architecture. ◆ 101 W. Hampton Rd (at Crefeld Ave)

55 Woodmere Art Museum Charles Knox **Smith** worked his way up from humble beginnings as a grocer's boy in the **Kensington** section of the city to become the owner of his own oil company. During the late 1800s he amassed a large collection of European and American paintings, porcelains from around the world, carved ivories, laces, and Oriental art. In his will, he specified that his Victorian mansion be converted into a museum. The doors of Woodmere first opened in 1940. Eight galleries and salons display Smith's collection, along with contemporary works by regional artists. **Benjamin West's** dramatic oil painting *The Fatal Wounding of Sir Philip Sydney* is part of the permanent collection, as are **Frederick Church's** *Sunset in the Berkshire Hills* and 19th-century oils by

Jasper Cropsey. Several rooms are decorate with Smith's furnishings, including Oriental rugs and a large Meissen chandelier and mirror frame. The **Helen Millard Gallery** exhibits art for children created by children. Woodmere also hosts art classes, an annual members' exhibition, and a juried show for regional artists. ◆ Donation requested. Tu-S 10AM-5PM; Su 2-5PM. 9201 Germantown Ave (between Bells Mill Rd and Hillcrest Ave 247.0476

56 Morris Arboretum of the University of Pennsylvania Few pleasures in Philadelph are as wonderful as a stroll through these 9: acres, which include meadows, sculpture, a English rose garden, stunning Asian trees, a pond with Royal swans, a Tuscan love temp and rolling hills. The estate of brother and sister **John** and **Lydia Morris,** built in 1887 a known as **Compton,** was given to the university in 1932. The Morrises—from a wealthy Quaker family—had traveled the wo collecting plant specimens that would thrive the area's temperate climate. The university was charged with converting their beautiful exotic garden into a public facility and resea center. Over the years the university, which tore down the Morris mansion in the 1960s, has augmented the family's plant collection, making trips to China, Korea, and Taiwan. Today more than 6,000 trees and shrubs fro around the world flourish on the grounds, among them a spectacular Katsura tree, a Japanese camellia, a purple European beech a Chinese elm, a weeping hemlock, witch hazels, hollies, pines, and hundreds of rhododendrons and azaleas. A long majestic alley of towering oak trees was demolished a tornado in 1991.

The Morrises drew on various periods and styles in creating their gardens, though the overall landscape resembles an informal English garden. The statue of *Mercury* in a loggia on the northern end of the arboretum typical of Victorian English landscaping. The **Hill and Cloud Garden,** on the north side of the pond, is a miniature Oriental garden with small hills and valleys that typify those foun in Japan and China. The formal **Rose Garde** a collection of old and new species surroun by a stone wall, blooms from May to Octobe Winners of the **All America Rose Selection** are displayed in the garden before they are introduced to the public in commercial catalogs. (These new varieties are to the left the circular stone steps at the entrance of th Rose Garden.)

In 1983 the arboretum's board of managers agreed to gradually acquire a fine arts collection, and a number of modern sculptu are scattered throughout the grounds. While many of these pieces are striking, they have altered the character of the gardens, making them more precious and museumlike. One the most impressive sculptures is *Two Lines*, by American artist **George Rickey.** Marking the spot of the demolished Morris mansion, it consists of two scissorlike stainless-steel arms, each 30 feet long, which rotate at the top of a 32-foot rod according to the movements of the wind. ♦ Admission. M-F 10AM-4PM; Sa-Su 10AM-5PM. Guided tours: Sa-Su 2PM. 100 Northwestern Ave (between Germantown and Stenton Aves). 247.5777

57 Andorra Natural Area
This 210-acre preserve of steep rocky paths and native forest continues Fairmount Park's greenway along Wissahickon Creek. Follow the rocky path from the parking area to the **Tree House,** a 100-year-old wooden house that serves as the preserve's headquarters and contains displays on wildlife, plants, and local history. A naturalist is usually on hand to talk about the valley or lead walking tours along some of the more than five miles of trails. Trail maps and program calendars are kept on the porch.

The preserve is the former site of the **Andorra Nursery,** which left behind some unusual plantings, including Japanese scholar trees and bigleaf magnolias. Native trees include tulip poplar, black cherry, and white oak.
♦ Trails: daily dawn to dusk. Tree house hours vary; call for schedule. Northwestern Ave (off Ridge Pike). 685.9285

58 Schuylkill Center for Environmental Education Located at the extreme northwestern edge of the city, this is one of Philadelphia's quieter hiking areas, with 40 acres of rolling hills, woodlands, ponds, walking trails, and a native animal population that includes deer and fox. The center has an excellent bookstore and gift shop where you can buy the latest field guides on insects, climate, geology, and botany; an exhibit area for children; a library; and a vast collection of local insect specimens. Educational programs for preschoolers to adults are also conducted here. If you visit between May and September, be sure to wear long pants on the hiking trails, where Lyme disease, transmitted by infinitesimal deer ticks, has been contracted. ♦ Admission. M-Sa 8:30AM-5PM; Su 1-5PM. 8480 Hagys Mill Rd (at Spring Ln). 482.7300

59 Manayunk It's been called a workingman's San Francisco, and though the analogy is a bit of a stretch, Manayunk's steep hills overlooking the Schuylkill River and row houses that ascend like stairs do seem familiar. Called **Flat Rock** by the English settlers who first came to this area in 1683, it remained a small village until 1822, when the Manayunk section of the **Schuylkill Canal** was built. The canal made this portion of the river, characterized by churning rapids, navigable, and greatly enhanced the village's economic fortunes. After being renamed Manayunk, an Indian expression for "place to drink," the town became a textile manufacturing center,

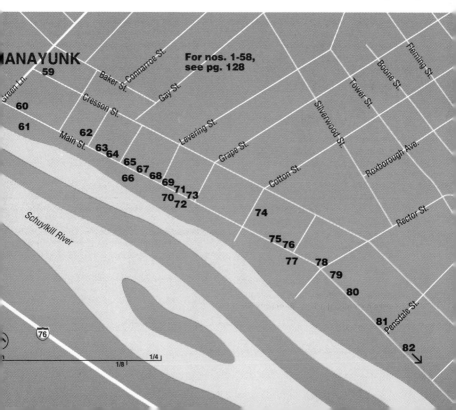

and English, Irish, German, Italian, and Polish immigrants built row houses up the narrow streets on the hills along the river.

Boom times hit in the 1880s, and Manayunk was flush with mills and commerce. **Main Street,** which runs parallel to the river, was lined with stores, hotels, restaurants, and banks. A few factories remain, but Manayunk is no longer a symbol of industrial might. In the late 1970s, a towpath and boardwalk were built along the old canal, and in 1983 Main Street became a **National Historic District.** Today Main Street flourishes once again, attracting people to its wealth of shops, restaurants, and art galleries. ♦ Bounded by Green Ln and Ridge Ave

60 U.S. Hotel Bar and Grill ★$$ In 1903 the U.S. Hotel was granted a permit to construct a bar next door. Eleven years later, when the hotel was ripped down and a movie theater took its place, the bar was spared. The long, narrow saloon retains much of its original interior, including the lovely green and white tiles, a tin ceiling, and a cherry bar with shelves and glass fronts. The dining area is a cramped row of tables that lines the long wall opposite the bar. Steaks, barbecued baby back ribs, a fish of the day, and coconut shrimp served with a tangy orange sauce are highlights of the brief menu, and nightly specials are posted on a blackboard. The crab corn chowder is not to be missed. A raw bar with clams, shrimp, and oysters is located in the rear. ♦ American ♦ Lunch and dinner; dinner only on Sunday. 4439 Main St (off the E. Green Ln Bridge). 483.9222

61 Wear It Again Sam Contemporary and vintage clothing sold here includes Pendleton shirts, jeans, some great old handbags, and lots of black. ♦ M-F 11AM-6PM; Sa noon-5PM. 4430 Main St. 487.0525

62 Grasshopper ★★$$$ As if to defy the traditional red of other Chinese restaurants, this elegant storefront is awash in apricot. Flickering votive candles and fresh flowers adorn each table, and fanned linen napkins are splayed in the wine glasses. Owner/chef **Philip Tang** has created a small menu that culls from the cuisines of China and Europe. You can get hot and sour soup or chicken corn chowder, dumplings made of steamed veal and leeks, or fried squid with a honey sauce. Filet mignon comes in black bean sauce and veal cutlets in dill cream sauce. ♦ Chinese/European ♦ Dinner. Closed Monday and Sunday. 4427 Main St (between Connaroe and Carson Sts). 483.1888

63 Siamese Princess ★$$ Contemporary Thai food is served in generous portions in this warm dining room with black lacquer chairs and deep burgundy wallpaper. Try the well-seasoned Thai dumplings, stuffed with minced shrimp, pork, and seaweed. Lemongrass, lime juice, and tender chicken strips heighten the flavor of *tom ka gai,* a Thai chicken coconut soup. Mildly hot *phad thai* consists of shrimp, bean sprouts, rice noodles, and ground peanuts, and the very spicy *yun nuea* combines rare sirloin slices, chile peppers, raw onion, coriander, and mint. Vegetarian dishes are available, too. ♦ Thai ♦ Dinner. 4421 Main St. 483.5335

64 People People Appealing casualwear for men and women comes in all-natural fibers in this triple-tiered store that also sells jewelry and shoes. You'll find great men's ties with bold geometric patterns, an interesting assortment of women's hats, and simple, well-cut dresses and blouses. ♦ M-Th 11AM-6PM; F-Sa 11AM-11PM; Su noon-6PM. 4419 Main St (between Connaroe and Gay Sts). 487.2139

65 Sonoma ★★★$$ The noise in this sophisticated restaurant filled with skylights and contemporary art can be unbearable when the place is jammed—as it always is on weekend nights—but it's a small price to pay for the excellent, reasonably priced food. Owner/chef **Derek Davis'** Cal-Ital, or California/Italian, cooking shines in such entrées as roast chicken with rosemary; grilled turkey fillets with pesto; and garlic rib-eye steak. Entrées come with roasted potatoes, dense, crusty bread, and salad or Italian greens in oil. Pizzas are made with a wonderful thin, flaky crust in a wood-burning oven. One pie is topped with grilled rock shrimp, tomatoes, hot peppers, leeks, fontina cheese, and basil. Upstairs, a Russian vodka bar serves caviar, smoked salmon, and oysters in cream and vodka. ♦ Italian ♦ Lunch and dinner. 4411 Main St (at Gay St). Reservations recommended. 483.9400

Restaurants/Clubs: Red   **Hotels:** Blue

Shops/ ♣ **Outdoors:** Green   **Sights/Culture:** Black

main**ly**
shoes

66 Mainly Shoes Cork platforms, tooled leather boots, suede pumps, and classical calf flats are sold in one of the city's better shoe stores. Designer brands include **Clergerie, Larry Stuart, Vittoria Ricci,** and **Claude Montana.** ♦ M-F 10AM-6PM; Sa 10AM-9PM; Su 10AM-5PM. 4410 Main St. 483.8000

67 Beans Beauty Supply Those expensive shampoos and conditioners you usually find in hair salons are available here at reasonable prices. ♦ M-Tu 10AM-6PM; W-Sa 10AM-9PM; Su noon-5PM. 4405 Main St (between Levering and Gay Sts). 487.3333

68 Charles Tiles One of the larger and more handsome storefronts on Main Street displays a large selection of imported tiles for floors and walls. Spanish and Portuguese wall tiles, French limestone floor tiles, Mexican terracottas, and bas-reliefs are laid out in this lovely space with large windows and decorative woodwork. ♦ Tu-Sa 10AM-5PM. 4401 Main St (at Levering St). 482.8440

69 Turtledove Beautiful dyed silks are among the wares sold at this expensive women's boutique. Silkscreening and the Japanese method of shibori are used by "fiber artists" to create wonderful pieces of "art to wear." You won't find these scarves, dresses, and blouses in a department store. ♦ M-Th 11AM-6PM; F 11AM-10PM; Sa 11AM-5PM; Su noon-5PM. 4373 Main St (at Levering St). 487.7350

J**ake's**

69 Jake's ★★★$$$ It's hard to miss this popular restaurant: a humorous piece of pop art—a dinner table and wine bottle splashing its contents into a glass—juts from the building's facade at the second story. Eschewing the white-wall minimalism of many of its contemporaries, Jake's has textured green walls with rainbow lighting and a clever collection of modern artwork and sculpture. The kitchen smokes its own fish, and a different hickory-smoked fish appetizer is available daily. Try the smoked duck salad with strawberries and a balsamic vinegar dressing, or the smoked chicken with arugula and angel hair pasta in a sun-dried tomato vinaigrette. Entrée offerings range from a simple grilled beef fillet with potato puree to barbecued salmon in a sauce of apple cider, soy, and garlic, served with fried yams. Crab cakes are a house specialty: the jumbo lump crabmeat is prepared in a shrimp mousse. The wine list is extensive. ♦ American ♦ Lunch and dinner; dinner only on Saturday and Sunday. 4365 Main St (between Levering and Grape Sts). Reservations recommended. 483.0444

69 Way to Go Travel Books and Accessories Everything from formulaic travel guides to collections of literary writing on foreign lands is sold in this tiny but comprehensive store. ♦ M-Tu, Th 10AM-6PM; W 10AM-9PM; F-Sa 10AM-11PM; Su noon-5PM. 4363 Main St (between Levering and Grape Sts). 483.7387

70 Somethings Different The offbeat collection of women's clothing for party, work, and play includes faux motorcycle jackets of appliquéd black wool and trim blazers with Southwestern beading. Also in stock are unusual silk prints and a belt collection that includes hand-painted leathers, wrought metal, and rhinestone-encrusted pieces. ♦ Tu, Th, Sa 10:30AM-6PM; W, F 10:30AM-8PM; Su noon-4PM. 4358 Main St (between Levering and Grape Sts). 487.0508

70 Mickey's of Manayunk If you need a cocktail table that resembles a huge leather-bound stack of books or a stars-and-stripes lamp, you'll find them in this eclectic store that seems like a parody of Ralph Lauren's home furnishings boutiques. Overstuffed pillows, potpourri, cotton throws, an **Heirloom** onyx chair, and a **Gainsborough** redwood chair are among the other items for sale. ♦ M-Sa 11AM-6PM; Su noon-5PM. 4358 Main St (between Levering and Grape Sts). 487.3003

71 Pat King's The range of women's clothes in this new boutique includes silk floral dresses you could wear to a wedding and odd fringed vests that resemble upholstery. ♦ M-F 11AM-6PM; Sa 11AM-9PM; Su noon-5PM. 4357 Main St (between Levering and Grape Sts). 487.7890

71 Pacific Rim Dark, torturously carved woods from faraway lands line the walls of this shop. Among the other exotica: a wooden puppet from Java, traditional Southeast gamelons, assorted ceremonial swords, Indonesian masks, water buffalo bells, Thai gongs, and a carved wooden banana tree. They'll ship purchases anywhere. ♦ Tu-Th 11AM-7PM; F 11AM-10PM; Sa 11AM-11PM; Su noon-5PM. 4351 Main St (between Levering and Grape Sts). 482.0498

"The King of the Country where I live hath given me great Province; but I desire to enjoy it with your Love and Consent, that we may always live together as Neighbors and friends."

—**William Penn in a letter to the Lenni Lenape Indians**

Principles and Pacifism: Philadelphia's Quaker Roots

When **William Penn** arrived in Philadelphia in 1682, he brought with him the fiercely idealistic and principled brand of Christianity known as **Quakerism.** Today more than 13,000 Quakers live in Philadelphia, the largest assemblage in the world (hence nicknames such as "Quaker City" and "City of Brotherly Love," the latter of which refers to the credo of tolerance Quakers live by). Once recognizable by their drab, gray attire and their manner of addressing one another as "thee" or "thou," Quakers no longer distinguish themselves by how they dress. They gather in meetinghouses for services that are very different from those that take place in most churches—typically sans ministers, sermons, and music. The group observes a period of silence during which a few may be moved to speak.

Although many religious groups populated the Pennsylvania colony in the 1700s, Quakers became the earliest leaders. Penn had espoused Quakerism as a young man after he met **George Fox,** founder of the **Religious Society of Friends,** the official name of the Quaker religion. Fox believed that the faithful should rely on God's "inward light" rather than on creeds and church rituals; he adhered to principles of democracy, religious tolerance, and egalitarianism, all of which drew the ire of the Church of England and the monarchy. "When the Lord sent me into the world, he forbade me to put off my hat to any high or low," said Fox. "And I was required to 'thee' and 'thou' all men and women, without respect to rich or poor, great or small." (The term "Quaker" is said to derive from Fox's comment to an English judge that he should quake only at the word of God. The Quakers' use of "friend" is a reference to the words of Jesus in the Gospel according to John: "You are my friends if you do what I command you.")

Seeking refuge from persecution, Quakers came to Philadelphia and established a colony based on their keen sense of morality. Swearing, lying, playing cards or dice, and holding stage plays were all prohibited under Pennsylvania's legal code because of the Quakers. Their principles of egalitarianism and tolerance also influenced not just local laws but the **U.S. Constitution,** which was written in Philadelphia. In contrast, the Quakers have had little direct influence over the city's government since the **French and Indian War,** when the Quaker members of the Pennsylvania colonial assembly resigned en masse rather than compromise their pacifism and support military action.

Quakers, once Philadelphia's wealthiest and most powerful citizens, are best known today for their liberal activism. During the past 50 years, they've been outspoken proponents of disarmament and civil rights. The **American Friends Service Committee,** started by Quakers in 1917 as a pacifist organization, has its headquarters at 15th and Cherry streets. The group, which runs programs promoting world peace and aiding the poor, won the Nobel Peace Prize in 1947. Though their numbers have dwindled steadily over the years, the Quakers have successfully adapted their 300-year-old religion to the 20th century. As for the future, Philadelphia will remain, at least in a small way, a Quaker city.

71 Owen Patrick Gallery This contemporary art gallery sells paintings, jewelry, sculpture, furniture, and ceramics made by artists from the U.S. and abroad. **Susan** and **Steven Kemenyffy's** raku-fired ceramic wall sculptures and photographer **Catherine Jansen's** snapshots of Italy superimposed on paintings or architectural pieces have been on display. ♦ Tu-W 11AM-6PM; F-Sa 11AM-9PM; Su noon-5PM. 4345 Main St (between Levering and Grape Sts). 482.9395

71 Family Chen $$ A low-lit box of a restaurant with large tables and fastidious service offers unmemorable Szechuan food. The huge pu-pu platter is a sampler of heavy fried dough and the noodle dishes come with syrupy sauces. ♦ Szechuan ♦ 4341 Main St (between Levering and Grape Sts). 483.2050

72 Ma Jolie Atelier A handsome 1912 bank building with a mezzanine, 12-foot-tall windows, and a recessed ceiling with ornamental moldings and a lovely sky mural the glamorous showroom for moderately expensive women's clothing in subdued, casually hip designs. A third of the inventory is produced on the premises. ♦ M-Tu 11AM-6PM; W-Th 11AM-9PM; F-Sa 11AM-11PM; Su noon-6PM. 4340 Main St (between Levering and Grape Sts). 483.8850

73 Best Friends Earthy, feminine clothing is sold in a room decorated in a Southwestern motif. Lace-topped T-shirts with little satin flowers, silk blouses, antique dresses, and straw hats are just part of the collection. ♦ M 11AM-5PM; Tu 9:30AM-5:30PM; W-Th 9:30AM-9PM; F 9:30AM-10PM; Sa 9:30AM-11PM; Su noon-5PM. 4329 Main St (between Levering and Grape Sts). 487.1250

73 Two by Four Collectibles Old Popeye dolls, vintage commercial signs and lunch boxes, '50s costume jewelry, framed *Colliers* covers, and other kitschy collectibles are here for the asking. Anybody need a set of **Three Stooges** dolls for $175 or a used Hamilton Beach milk shake machine for $195? ♦ M-Sa 11AM-6PM; Su 11AM-5PM. 4323 Main St (between Levering and Grape Sts). 482.9494

Above Two by Four Collectibles:

Antique Marketplace of Manayunk
Reproductions are banned at this antiques showroom, which displays the wares of 80 dealers. ♦ M-Sa 11AM-6PM; Su 11AM-5:30PM. 482.4499

74 Casa Mexicana ★$$ Pink linens, green arc lights, and a staff that is eager to please brighten the dining room of this restaurant that serves traditional Mexican and Mexican/American entrées. Try the spicy chicken breast in mole sauce, beef fajitas, or the Nacho Grande appetizer, a dam-those-arteries extravaganza layered with frijoles, beef or chicken, cheese, and sour cream. ♦ Mexican ♦ Lunch and dinner. Closed Monday. 111 Cotton St (between Cresson and Main Sts). 487.1009

75 La Petite Gourmet ★$ Homemade brownies, cupcakes, and cookies—the kind you don't even get at home anymore—are served in a small coffee shop with a counter and outdoor seating. Cappuccino and espresso and some cold salads, sandwiches, and take-out dishes are also available. ♦ Coffee shop ♦ M-Th 7AM-9PM; F 7AM-10PM; Sa 8AM-10PM; Su 8AM-4PM. 4311 Main St (between Cotton St and Roxborough Ave). 487.7461

76 American Pie Contemporary Crafts
Contemporary folk art, such as wood mirrors painted in bright greens and pinks, hand-painted ceramic tiles, and Czechoslovakian glass earrings, fill this boutique. ♦ M-Tu, Th 11AM-8PM; W 11AM-9PM; F-Sa 11AM-10PM; Su 11AM-6PM. 4303 Main St (at Roxborough Ave). 487.0226

77 Le Bus Main Street ★$ A cavernous dining room with a stone wall, wooden beams, and enormous windows offers a great setting to while away an hour. The casual menu is promising, but the quality vacillates. Try the peppers stuffed with rice, sun-dried tomatoes, feta and cheddar cheese, and sunflower seeds or the grilled Jamaican jerked chicken (an entire chicken cut up and marinated with allspice, clove, rosemary, garlic, scallions, and olive oil, and served with a mixture of ketchup and bananas). Appetizers include a decent *hummus,* and the homemade breads are good.

♦ Eclectic ♦ Breakfast, lunch, and dinner; dinner only on Saturday and Sunday. 4266 Main St (between Cotton and Rector Sts). 487.2663

78 Main-ly Desserts ★★$ Decorated with floral swags and china teapots, this storefront serves cappuccino and some decent treats, particularly a strawberry shortcake with white chocolate and a triple chocolate mousse cake. Bassetts ice cream is served alone or on top of brownies with chocolate sauce. The restaurant also makes sandwiches, salads, and home-made soup for lunch. ♦ American ♦ Lunch, desserts, and coffee. 4249 Main St (at Rector St). 487.1325

79 Bananahand Everything for the well-dressed but not too preppy child is sold at top price here. The selection is particularly good for little girls who like to wear floral prints, straw hats, and party shoes. ♦ M-Th 11AM-6PM; F-Sa 11AM-8PM; Su noon-5:30PM. 4245 Main St (between Rector and Pensdale Sts). 483.3301

80 Catherine Starr Gallery Colorful figurative and primitive paintings, sculpture, and ceramics are sold here. Owner **Catherine Starr** likes to call it "a happy collection." ♦ Tu-Sa 11AM-6PM; Su 1-5PM. 4235 Main St (between Rector and Pensdale Sts). 482.7755

81 Thomas' ★$$$ The wood and marble bar offers a glimpse of what a Manayunk taproom looked like at the turn of the century. It's better to dine on the second floor, in the quieter, dressy high-ceilinged room. The steaks, including steak au poivre and filet mignon with herb butter and mushrooms, are the best offerings on the fairly pricey menu. There's also crab cakes with rémoulade, veal sautéed with sun-dried tomatoes and goat cheese, and roast duck with a plum sauce. For an appetizer, sample the mushroom tart, a flaky pastry filled with mushrooms, Parmesan, Bermuda onions, and tomatoes. ♦ Continental ♦ Lunch and dinner; dinner only on Saturday and Sunday. 4201 Main St (at Pensdale St). 483.9075

82 The River Deck Cafe and Dance Club $$ A former mill with a rough stone facade has been converted into a "multiconcept facility." You can dance to Top 40 tunes in the nightclub, dine in a dim publike room with a jukebox and '70s decor, or, in the warm months, enjoy drinks and light food on a deck overlooking the river. Dress must be "casual but fashionable," and brutish bouncers occasionally enforce the requirement at their whim. Broiled steaks and seafood dominate the menu. The crowd is generally twenty- and thirtysomething. ♦ American ♦ Cover on Friday and Saturday. Lunch, dinner, and snacks; Sunday brunch. DJ: W-Su nights. Live jazz: Su 5-9PM in warm months. 4100 Main St (at Shurs Ln). 483.4100

Don Matzkin
President of Friday Architects/Planners, Inc.

Bicycle, run, or walk the eight-mile circuit along the **Schuylkill River** from the **Philadelphia Museum of Art** to the **Falls Bridge** and back to the other side of the river.

The walking tours offered by the **Foundation for Architecture.**

Driving trips along former Indian trails and colonial roads: Ridge Avenue, Passyunk Avenue, Lancaster Avenue, Roosevelt Boulevard (Route 1), Germantown Avenue, and their extensions into the near suburbs.

On even the hottest nights you can find a breeze around the fountain between the **Society Hill Towers.** Depending on the kindness of the on-duty doorman and your own sense of self, you might even be able to dangle your hot tootsies in the water.

Performances (in season) at the **Painted Bridge,** the **CEC,** and the **Point Breeze Performing Arts Center.**

Rittenhouse Square at lunchtime on a warm, sunny day.

Barbecue from the **Rib Crib** in Germantown.

Greens in oil and other Italian fare at **Ralph's** in South Philly.

Seafood at **Seafood Unlimited** in Center City.

Crabs at **Byrnes' Tavern** in Port Richmond.

Lemon Grass, a Thai restaurant on Lancaster Avenue in Powelton Village.

The view and the "Wasp-American" food at **Williamson's** atop the GSB Building on City Avenue.

The West Philly branch of the **American Diner.**

John Dowlin
Designer/Writer/Consultant/Editor,
(Bicycle) Network News

Philadelphia has 3,000-plus restaurants, some of which let you BYO (bring your own ale, porter, lager, and wine). Here are a few of my favorites:

In East Philly:

Dmitri's serves possibly the best Greek seafood (and lamb) on the East Coast. They don't take reservations, so shoot some pool across the street while you wait for a table—or hang out on a sidewalk bench.

Osteria dell' Artista is run by retired soccer players **Giuseppe Rosselli** and **Salvatore Arena,** two guys who know their pasta, garlic, chicken, and seafood. No reservations, no credit cards, no bullshit, just come on in and enjoy one of Philly's best Italian restaurants. "If you bring a bottle of wine," says Giuseppe, "bring a good one, so I can have a glass, too."

Van's Garden, now in the shadow of the new Convention Center. Let's hope this little Vietnamese place can hold on and hold out! There's nothing better than a bowl of steamy *pho* (rice noodle soup) on a rainy day or Van's lemongrass chicken any evening. No frills. If **Reading Terminal Market** is t bustling for you, Van's is the place.

In West Philly:

Tandoor India, one of more than a half dozen India restaurants near the University of Pennsylvania campus, is a delight: nicely decorated, very clean, loving service, and the food—like the Taj Mahal itself—is "a song on air." Should you forget to BYC the owner just might have a bottle of wine for you! (Think about it . . . instead of paying $30,000-plus a Philadelphia liquor license, the restaurateur who "tries harder" can easily offer wine and beer to deserving customers free of charge—for years—a still stay in business.)

For devotees of Thai cuisine, **Manus' Place** is the "faculty club" where students are welcome. Feel a cold coming on? Forget vitamin C; just order any o their red or green curry dishes—medium to very spicy. No virus can withstand the right amount of curry. To start off, the chicken lemongrass cocon soup will ease you into the promised land. **Univers Beverage** on the opposite corner provides "vitami Y" by the case (or by the six-pack at nearby **Welsh's**). That's Y for **Yuengling,** brewers of Chesterfield ale, which is very, very good for you. To have it prechilled, call Jim at 387.BEER.

Dahlak, a superb Ethiopian-Eritrean restaurant, wi take you back a century or two! Spicy, delicious dishes served with lentils and collard greens are spread over a large platter of *injera,* a spongy crep that's the only utensil here. Try their tips of beef or lamb, and ask **Neghisti** for plenty of ice water. She and her husband are the managers and couldn't be more accommodating. At **Asmara,** another Ethiopi place, they let you bring your bicycle inside and yo kids can bring their own hamburgers and fries. Yes there's a new world order, and it starts at home, ri here in Philly!

Giuseppe Rosselli
Chef/Owner, Trattoria dell'Artista and Osteria dell'Artista

The **Italian Market** in South Philly, where nothing has changed in 90 years.

The **Philadelphia Museum of Art,** where you can s everything from Picasso to Van Gogh.

First Friday art tours of **Old City,** when the gallerie stay open late.

The **Benjamin Franklin Bridge** at night.

The **Betsy Ross House.**

The **Trattoria dell'Artista** and the **Osteria dell' Artista,** of course! Winners of many awards and th most inexpensive restaurants in the city.

The **Capitol** (the first one).

South Street.

The people who live here, always friendly and carin

.C. Staab
ice President/Communications, Philadelphia
onvention & Visitors Bureau

he walkway on the **Benjamin Franklin Bridge**
a great place to jog above the traffic, with a
rrific view.

irst Fridays in Old City, when the art galleries stay
pen late.

"he Gross Clinic" at the **Eakins Gallery** at **Thomas
efferson University** is a wonderful discovery
r visitors. See the finest American paintings—
eriod—in an out-of-the-way location.

uesday night Mummers concerts in the summer at
e **Mummers Museum**—the 1950s reincarnated.

aribou Cafe, for attitude and hot chocolate.

lfred E. Schuyler
useum Curator/Botanist, Academy of Natural
ciences

wann Memorial Fountain in Logan Square is a
culpture of a man, a woman, and a young girl
presenting Philadelphia's three rivers. It's a
onderful combination of art and water by
lexander Stirling Calder.

odin Museum, where there's an outdoor sculpture
The Thinker. Rodin's masterpiece uses the human
dy as a vital portion of human thought.

e **Washington Monument,** a sculpture of George
ashington on horseback, is an outstanding
semblage of associated works, including four
untains symbolizing the Delaware, Potomac,
udson, and Mississippi rivers. The animals and
ative Americans around the fountains are very
alistic.

e series of statues of revolutionary heroes
Revolutionary Row") between the **Philadelphia
useum of Art** and **Boathouse Row.** My favorite is
athaniel Greene with his words "We fight, get beat,
se up, and fight again."

ansom Street Oyster House, an unobtrusive
afood restaurant that is among the best anywhere.

ock Street Brewing Company has good food with
op-of-the-line" beers brewed on the premises.

rders Book Shop & Espresso Bar for a compre-
nsive selection of all kinds of books along with good
rgains. And **Bookhaven** has an excellent selection
diverse secondhand books at bargain prices.

eading Terminal Market, an indoor market with
astronomic treats to satisfy every appetite.

e outstanding habitat dioramas from all parts of
e world at the **Academy of Natural Sciences**—a
id-20th century effort that probably will never be
plicated.

alea Garden—along Kelly Drive between the
iladelphia Museum of Art and Boathouse Row—
spectacular in May and worth a visit throughout
e spring and summer. The **Franklin Tree** blooms in
ly and August.

E. Digby Baltzell
Emeritus Professor of Sociology, University of
Pennsylvania

Walking in **Fairmount Park,** especially along the
Wissahickon Creek in Chestnut Hill, and lunching at
Valley Green Inn.

Dining at the **Tree Tops** restaurant in the Rittenhouse
Hotel, and looking out over Rittenhouse Square.

People-watching from a park bench in **Rittenhouse
Square.**

Browsing in secondhand bookstores, particularly
William H. Allen's, the **Booktrader,** and the **Book
Barn** (on Route 100, near West Chester).

Watching Penn football on **Franklin Field,** the finest
stadium in America.

Walking four miles down **Broad Street** to watch the
Phillies, returning home by subway—nonstop to **The
Bellevue** in eight minutes.

Shopping on Saturday at **Reading Terminal Market,**
especially among the Amish farmers.

Walking around the **Belmont Mansion** area, the best
site for viewing the city at sunset or at night when it's
lit up.

Jack H. McDavid
Chef/Owner, Jack's Firehouse

The **Philadelphia Museum of Art** is a fabulous piece
of architecture filled with masterpieces from
throughout time.

Schuylkill River at night, when it's magnificently lit,
and the sun in the early morning casts a wonderful
hue over all the boathouses.

Reading Terminal Market, which is filled with
farmers and fishmongers; lunch at the **Down Home
Diner.**

The **Liberty Bell** in front of Constitution Hall, where
the Declaration of Independence was signed.

Foods from neighborhood restaurants, especially
fish at **Dmitri's,** pizza at **Tacconellis,** Chinese food
incomparably prepared by **Susanna Foo,** or
aggressively French cuisine at **Le Bec-Fin.**

Accommodations at the **Four Seasons Hotel** and
brunch at **The Swann Lounge.**

Eastern State Penitentiary, the first prison to have
separate cells.

As early as the 1700s, locals complained that
Philadelphia was not the world's most intellectual
city. An early colonist lamented: "There are no
bookbinders here . . . nothing counts but
chopping, digging, planting, plowing, reaping."
But others saw it as a bastion of civilization. In
1811, architect Benjamin Henry Latrobe said,
"The days of Greece might be revived in the
woods of America, and Philadelphia become the
Athens of the Western World."

Day Trips

Philadelphia's cultural and historical breadth extends far beyond the Liberty Bell and Independence Hall, into the rolling green hills of the countryside. A host of must-see attractions are within a 90-minute drive in any direction from downtown.

To the south lie the rolling hills and horse farms of the **Brandywine Valley,** a suburb both of Philadelphia and **Wilmington, Delaware.** The valley's genteel estates, mannered country gardens, and subtle natural beauty inspired many of the paintings of **N.C., Andrew,** and **Jamie Wyeth.** The world-famous **du Pont** family also left its mark on the area: their formal **Longwood Gardens** rival those of Versailles, and their collection of 18th- and 19th-century American furnishings at **Winterthur** mansion is among the foremost in the country.

To the north, the wooded seclusion of **Bucks County** offers escape from the hectic pace of both Philadelphia and New York City. Once the favorite country getaway of **Oscar Hammerstein,** the Algonquin's roundtable gang, and many other famous names in the arts, the county's chic country-politan atmosphere still attracts the literati. Towns such as **New Hope** and **Lambertville** successfully blend lovely riverside settings with fine dining and deluxe bed-and-breakfast inns. Bucks is a great place to gallery hop, and the country nightlife is just as hip as in the big city. For the kids, the county offers **Sesame Place,** the world's only amusement park inspired by educational television.

Head east for the glitter and pizzazz of **Atlantic City,** the Las Vegas of the East Coast and a real hoot whether you're a gambler or just an admirer of over-the-top kitsch. This New Jersey resort town bops 24 hours a day and it's never too early or late for a champagne cocktail or a roll of the dice. Big-name stars perform in the nightclubs, and virtually everyone strolls on the boardwalk, which at dawn can seem as crowded as Calcutta. In addition to the casino life, the seaside city has some of the country's broadest sand beaches and excellent ocean swimming. And if you'd rather not take your chances with Lady Luck, consider a peaceful weekend unwinding in **Cape May,** a windswept resort town known for its lacy Victorian architecture.

West of Philadelphia is the famous **Main Line,** more a way of life than a tourist attraction. Upscale incomes support the area's beautiful homes, fine boutiques, new-concept retail stores, and the largest mall on the East Coast. A cultural highlight is the notoriously eccentric **Barnes Foundation,** which holds one of the world's largest private collections of Impressionist paintings. The Main Line is of particular interest to history buffs as well: it was from here that **George Washington's** spies monitored British activity in Philadelphia while the Revolutionary army was encamped at **Valley Forge.** Today, the quiet **Valley Forge National Historical Park**—marked by statues, memorials, and open fields where visitors are free to roam—is one of the region's most popular recreation areas.

Northwest of Philadelphia are **Lancaster County** and nearby **Reading,** a shopaholic's idea of bliss with 300-plus discount outlet stores. Lancaster offers much more than a change of scenery—almost a change of century, with Amish and Mennonite farm families dressed in traditional garb and living without electricity or indoor plumbing. Amish country provides a rare chance to examine an iconoclastic culture in the backyard of a big city.

tlantic City

e first U.S. city outside Nevada to legalize casino
mbling, Atlantic City, New Jersey, entered the big
gues in 1978 with the opening of **Resorts,** the first
today's dozen glitzy gaming palaces. It's an easy
ve from central Philadelphia to what the locals call
nply "A.C." Just take Interstate 95 and the
njamin Franklin Bridge or the Walt Whitman Bridge
o New Jersey, then pick up the Atlantic City
pressway, which is well marked. In about an hour
u'll find yourself in this exciting city by the sea.
tually all the casino-hotels offer free indoor park-
, provided you bring your receipt to the gambling
or for a validation stamp (you don't have to gam-
, though). If you are among the thousands of
itors who prefer to use public transportation, take
casino-underwritten bus services that stop daily
most Philadelphia neighborhoods. The fee is about
5 round-trip, but the casinos usually give passen-
rs more than that amount in coupons for free food
d quarters for gambling. Consult Philadelphia
wspaper ads or call a casino directly for bus
edules. You can also reach Atlantic City by conve-
nt **Amtrak** trains (800/872.7245); they depart
veral times a day from 30th Street Station for the

Atlantic City Rail Terminal, four blocks from the main
casino strip.

Perhaps the town's most endearing feature is the
Boardwalk (which actually extends through the
neighboring town of **Ventnor**), a six-mile elevated
walkway flanked by casinos, hotels, and shops on
one side and wide sandy beaches on the other. Made
of wooden planks laid out in a herringbone pattern
and supported by a steel structure, today's
Boardwalk had its genesis in 1870, when the city
council wanted to find a way to keep visitors from
tracking sand into hotels and railway cars.

Before 10AM, cyclists and joggers enjoying the
ocean breeze dominate the Boardwalk. By noon,
however, pedestrian traffic is thick with visitors
strolling from casino to casino. On fair summer days,
this is people-watching heaven, as high-rolling New
Yorkers, foreign tourists, and charter bus groups
from as far away as Kentucky mingle with one another and stop by dozens of essentially identical video
arcades and junk souvenir shops.

Favorite Boardwalk snacks include the many flavors
of saltwater taffy from **James'** or **Fralinger's,** both of
which have several shops along the casino trail.
While James' taffy will give your jaw a challenging
workout, Fralinger's melts in your mouth. Also
recommended are **Steel's Fudge,** corn dogs, and

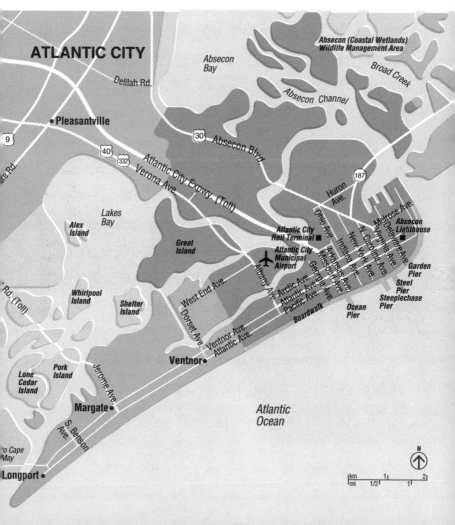

excellent fresh lemonade served at the stands along the Boardwalk.

Each of the 10 Boardwalk casino-hotels has more than 500 guest rooms and vast, carpeted gambling areas where guests can play their favorite games of chance 24 hours a day. The smoky gambling floors have no clocks or windows, which can lead you to lose track of time.

While all the casinos claim to outdo one another in deluxe accommodations, they are actually quite similar. Interior design runs toward rococo gilded moldings and crystal chandeliers. All have overpriced luxury restaurants, 24-hour coffee shops, and much ballyhooed all-you-can-eat buffets. If you prefer to dine away from the casinos, try one of the city's popular traditional restaurants. **The Knife and Fork Inn** (★★$$$$; Atlantic and Pacific Aves, 609/344.1133), in a striking white stucco building, serves fine seafood worthy of its price. **Abe's Oyster House** (★★$$$; 2031 Atlantic Ave, 609/344.7701) is a more moderately priced seafood restaurant with an excellent raw bar, and a simple white-tiled interior. **The White House Sub Shop** (★★$; 2301 Arctic Ave, 609/345.1564) is great for cheap eats and a sense of history. Autographed celebrity photos sing the praises of White House sandwiches. Cheesesteaks and hoagies are even better here than in Philly because of the wonderfully chewy Italian rolls.

The casinos also offer lots of live entertainment, much of it free with a two-drink minimum. These complimentary "lounge show" acts range from sultry female jazz vocalists to '50s rock 'n' roll cover bands to the occasional stand-up comedian. Quality varies significantly, too, but if you wander from lounge to lounge you'll likely discover at least one act that you would happily pay to see again. If you're willing to pay top dollar ($30 and up), you can catch major headliners in any of the casinos' big theaters, where such stars as **Liza Minnelli, Jerry Seinfeld,** and **Cher** regularly perform. Call individual casinos or consult Philadelphia newspapers to find out who's playing.

Hotel-casinos located on the Boardwalk include:

Bally's Grand ($$; Boston Ave, 609/340.7111), classy as far as casinos go and tops for serious gambling, as it tends to be less hectic and distracting than the other large casinos a few blocks away.

TropWorld ($$; Brighton Ave, 609/340.4000), which in addition to the usual trappings, features **Tivoli Pier,** a small indoor amusement park with kiddie rides and carnival games.

Trump Plaza ($$; Mississippi Ave, 609/441.6000), now one of tycoon **Donald Trump's** three Atlantic City casinos, though originally built for **Playboy Enterprises, Inc.** Wags have speculated that the peculiar architecture—a sleek glass tower with a wider, knoblike top—is intentionally phallic. Another oddity: Despite the Trump divorce, the casino's exorbitantly priced French restaurant is still called **Ivana's** (★★$$$).

Caesars ($$; Arkansas Ave, 609/348.4411), a sister hotel of **Caesars Palace** in Las Vegas. Glutted with pink marble and oversize reproductions of classic sculpture (Michelangelo's *David* weighs in at 17 tons), it's truly a faux Roman monstrosity.

Bally's Park Place ($$; Park Pl, 609/340.2000), which, in addition to having mercifully spare modern decor, is worth noting for **The Spa,** a well-equipped gym where daytrippers are welcome to pay a small fee to work out, sit in the whirlpool, or get a massage.

The Claridge ($$; Indiana Ave, 609/340.3400), a luxury hotel back in Atlantic City's precasino heyday that retains a genuinely elegant exterior and lobby area. The casino is as gaudy as those of its neighbors, but because it's divided into

M. BLUM

ree levels it seems more intimate and less verwhelming than most.

he Sands ($$; Indiana Ave, 609/441.4000), which as a high-tech skywalk called the People Mover that lides you over a courtyard between the Boardwalk nd the hotel past a memorabilia display from old- me Atlantic City.

lerv Griffin's Resorts ($$; North Carolina Ave,)9/344.6000), a hotel-casino with the ambience of n antiquated mansion, although the facilities are tate of the art. A few times a year, Merv himself hows up here with his backup singers, **The abulous Mervtones,** giving audiences a classic amp experience.

rump Taj Mahal ($$; Virginia Ave, 609/449.1000), e biggest, most ostentatious casino in town, pped with onion domes and minarets. Staffers ear turbans and caftans, and exotic place names re used with abandon (**The New Delhi Deli,** for stance). The facility's **Mark Etess Area** is the rgest casino-owned hall and hosts major pop con- erts and championship boxing matches.

he Showboat ($$; Delaware Ave, 609/343.4000), ith Disneyesque decor that has turned the large bby area into a New Orleans-style town square. But hat really sets the Showboat apart is an amazing)-lane bowling alley with Day-Glo balls in red, range, green, blue, and yellow.

addition to the casino-hotels, a Boardwalk trek ads past **Convention Hall** (Georgia Ave), where the liss America Pageant has been held annually since 940, and **Ocean One** (Missouri Ave), a three-story tall designed to look like a cruise ship, which juts to the Atlantic like a pier. The mall offers spectacu- r views and ocean breezes on its outdoor bservation decks. During the busy summer season ou can see amusing demonstrations of kitchen gad- ts, juicers, and other merchandise advertised on te-night TV.

tlantic City has two other casino-hotels, **Harrah's** 6$; 1725 Brigantine Blvd, 609/441.5000) and **rump's Castle** ($$; Huron Ave and Brigantine Blvd,)9/441.8300), both situated by the calm waters of bsecon inlet a couple of miles from the Boardwalk. hese hotels share a sense of serenity and relaxation way from the constant hustle, and are highly recom- ended for those serious about gambling or looking r a more tasteful ambience.

tlantic City's post-midnight hot spot is **Studio VI** (12 outh Mt. Vernon St, 609/348.0192), a high-energy isco that attracts a comfortable mix of gays and traights who dance until dawn, along with the casi- o workers, musicians, and occasional celebrity ntertainers who come here to unwind after their vening's work.

The only space on Parker Brothers' Monopoly board that doesn't correspond to a real Atlantic City site is Marvin Gardens, which is actually in nearby Margate and is correctly spelled Marven Gardens.

If you're visiting Atlantic City in summer and are inter- ested in the beach as much as the casinos, drive a few miles south to the communities of **Ventnor, Margate,** and **Longport,** where many Philadelphians have sec- ond homes. The beaches here are cleaner than those in Atlantic City, attracting a family-oriented crowd. After you settle in, beach patrols will approach and ask for a few dollars per person for a pin-on "beach badge." This small usage fee covers the costs of maintenance and professional lifeguards.

While in Margate, don't miss **Lucy The Margate Elephant** (9200 Atlantic Ave, 609/823.6473), a **National Historic Landmark** and excellent example of whimsical Victorian architecture. Built in the 1880s to lure prospective land buyers to the shore, Lucy is a two-story, metal-clad wooden structure in the shape of an elephant. Lucy eventually fell into weathered disrepair and was scheduled for destruction in the late 1960s, but local housewife **Josephine Harron** began a "Save Lucy" campaign, which led to the splendid restoration of the unusual edifice you see today. For a nominal fee, you can explore Lucy inside and out.

Across the street from the pachyderm is **Ventura's Greenhouse** (★★$$; 106 S. Benson Ave, Margate, 609/822.0140), a casual restaurant and bar known for its garlicky white pizza and spacious outside deck overlooking the beach. Crowded every summer after- noon with sun worshipers sipping daiquiris and cold beers, Ventura's deck is the place to be seen in Margate in the daytime.

Once you've had your fill of the excitement in Atlantic City, venture south to **Cape May**—the perfect anti- dote to the clanging racket of hundreds of slot machines. Treat yourself to a few nights in one of the sumptuously restored Victorian bed-and-breakfasts, and spend the day puttering around the antique shops or taking long walks along the beach. The 19th-centu- ry architecture of this tiny resort town is inspiration enough to carry a camera around at all times; the bright-colored shingles, white picket fences, and other ornate details beg to be captured on film.

Brandywine Valley

Painter **N.C. Wyeth** once described his home turf in the Brandywine Valley as a place of "succulent mead- ows" and "big, sad trees." This sweeping sun-dappled valley of horse farms, country estates, and rolling hillsides runs alongside the Brandywine River for about 30 miles starting south of Philadelphia and ending just below Wilmington, Delaware. Rich in history and filled with visitor attractions, yet surpris- ingly underutilized by Philadelphians, the Brandywine Valley is still dominated by Wilmington's industrial dynasty, the **du Ponts,** Huguenots who came to this country more than 200 years ago.

The most popular Brandywine sights, particularly the several du Pont estates, are huge, so allow plenty of time to explore them by focusing on only a few of the major attractions. Also, consider packing a picnic to enjoy in one of the area's many gardens rather than using up a chunk of the day in a restaurant.

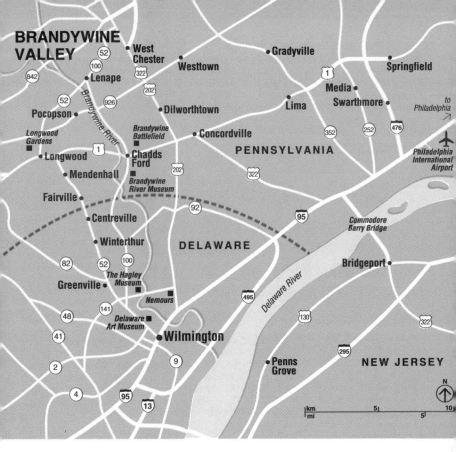

BRANDYWINE VALLEY

Although **Amtrak** provides service to and from downtown Wilmington several times a day, virtually every place you'll want to hit is outside the city proper, making a car the best way to take in the terrain. From Philadelphia, drive about 25 miles south on Interstate 95, then exit according to your specific itinerary. All the major sights in the valley are close together, despite the fact that you'll be crossing the Pennsylvania border and going into Delaware in some instances.

Without question, Brandywine Valley's one must-see attraction is **Longwood Gardens,** 30 miles from Philadelphia (admission; daily 10AM-5PM, some evenings in summer and around Christmas; U.S. 1, Kennett Sq, 388.6741). Internationally regarded as the country's foremost horticultural institution, Longwood is laid out to encourage leisurely walking and observation. You'll feel shortchanged if you allot less than two hours for a visit.

Once the country residence of **Pierre S. du Pont,** the thousand-acre Longwood estate has 11,000 plant species in its fertile soil. The five-acre **Fountain Garden** was completed in 1931, inspired by a similar display at the Chicago World's Fair in 1893. Several evenings each summer, classical concerts synchronized with the fountains and colored lights are held here. **The Terrace Restaurant** (★★$), a lovely lunch spot, serves very good salads.

While outdoor displays vary according to season (April and May offer the widest profusion of blooms, rose gardens highlight the summer months, and chrysanthemums as wide as Frisbees are among fall favorites), the gardens' greenhouse conservatories grow orchids and other tropical plants year-round. At Christmastime the greenhouses are festooned with colored lights and poinsettias. Another indoor highlight, opened in 1992, is the **Cascade Garden,** where waterfalls and Brazilian foliage evoke the homeland of designer **Roberto Burle Marx.**

The du Ponts set the tone for much of Brandywine Valley life, but **William Penn's** Quakers also left an important historical legacy. Near the entrance gates to Longwood Gardens is the **Brandywine Valley Tourist Information Center** (388.2900), housed in

a simple clapboard structure that served as a Quaker meetinghouse until 1940. The house of worship

was also a gathering point for the area's active slavery abolition movement. The valley became a hotbed of abolitionist activity in 1786, as Quaker merchants and farmers participated in the "underground railroad," which helped southern slaves escape to the North. In support of the cause, local Quakers hosted such speakers as **Susan B. Anthony** and **Sojourner Truth.**

If you'd like to add a bit of spice to your visit to Longwood, drive a few miles north to the **Chadds Ford Winery** (free tasting and self-guided tour Tu-Sa 10AM-5:30PM, Su noon-5PM; $5 guided tour Sa-Su 12:30PM; U.S. 1, Chadds Ford, 388.6221). Run by **Eric** and **Lee Miller,** this operation has been producing wine since 1983. Eric's expertise in wine-making is showcased on the weekend tours, when he guides visitors through the crushing, fermenting, aging, and bottling processes. This 45-minute wine-making lesson is as good as any you'll get in the United States outside of California. Tastings after the tour let you sample the winery's fine table reds and whites before purchasing some to take home. A popular novelty is Chadds Ford's Apple-Spice wine, a great autumn drink when served warm.

Brandywine River Museum

Nearby, the **Brandywine River Museum** (admission; daily 9:30AM-4:30PM; U.S. 1 and Rte 100, Chadds Ford, 388.2700), which opened in 1971, is as notable for its building as for its art holdings. The museum is a project of **The Brandywine Conservancy,** a local interest group involved in shaping policies for water resources and historic preservation. It's housed in a converted Civil War grist mill, where the original rough-hewn beams and wide wooden floorboards enhance the ambience of the exhibit galleries. The second-floor lobby features a curved, cobblestone floor that leads to dramatic bowed glass walls, where you can look down through the trees for a spectacular view of the Brandywine River. Antique stables in front of the building are used for crafts fairs and occasional live entertainment.

Focusing on local artistic heritage, the museum holds an impressive collection of paintings by three generations of the **Wyeth** family: **N.C., Andrew,** and **Jamie.** While the works on display are changed regularly, visitors can count on seeing some of N.C.'s classic book illustrations, Jamie's popular pig paintings, and many of Andrew's most famous works (the controversial *Helga* series is the major lure). **Maxfield Parrish, Rockwell Kent,** and **Horace Pippin** are among the other significant American artists whose works are shown here. After touring the galleries, be sure to step out behind the museum, where there is a small wildflower garden and a pleasant walking trail along the riverbank.

Also along U.S. 1 is the **Brandywine Battlefield** (nominal admission; Tu-Sa 9AM-5PM, Su noon-5PM; U.S. 1, Chadds Ford, 459.3342), which, unlike Valley Forge, saw actual fighting during the Revolution. It was here that Washington's army was handed a defeat by the troops of British **General William Howe** in a raging battle that proved a turning point in the war (French **General Lafayette** was so impressed with the rebels' tenacity that he decided to join forces with Washington). On the battlefield are a visitors' center and two restored Quaker farmhouses that served as headquarters for Washington and Lafayette.

With a history that predates the Revolution, it's not surprising that the Brandywine Valley is an antique collector's paradise. Many of the best shops and stalls—some of the greatest finds pop up at sporadic, flea market-style weekend events—can be found in and around **West Chester.** This charming town of less than 20,000 is a major beneficiary of America's mid-19th-century fascination with Greek Revival architecture. The **Chester County Tourist Bureau** (117 West Gay St, 344.6365) is housed in an Athenian building designed by the style's foremost advocate, **Thomas U. Walter.** The bureau's courteous staff will point you to further examples of Walter's work and to the current hot spots for antiques, among them **Herbert Schiffer Antiques** (1469 Morstein Rd, 696.1521), a seemingly perpetual mother lode for early American furniture located on a working dairy farm just outside of town.

After the Battle of Brandywine, rowdy Redcoats caused serious damage to the **Dilworthtown Inn** (★★★$$$; Old Wilmington Pike and Brinton's Bridge Rd, Dilworthtown, 399.1390), constructed in 1758. Now restored to its handsome original state, the inn serves a fine, fancy supper. Vegetables and herbs used in the cooking are grown in the house gardens; local pheasant, quail, and partridge are featured entrées.

Winterthur

Winterthur (admission; Tu-Sa 9:30AM-5PM, Su noon-5PM; Rte 52 N, exit 7, Winterthur, 302/888.4713), once the estate of **Henry Francis du Pont,** is both a testament to the skills of early American artisans and an example of obsessive collecting. In 1927 du Pont began to redecorate his nine-story mansion—originally built in 1839—with antique mantels and moldings from old homes along the East Coast. From domestic woodwork, du Pont moved on to collect examples of all the American interior-decorative arts, eventually incorporating items produced during the historically sweeping period of 1650 to 1850. Not one for eclectic decor, du Pont arranged his finds in complete period room settings.

Today the museum's 196 rooms are fully decorated with more than 89,000 objects made or used in early America and the colonies. Furniture, needlework, clocks, and porcelain are kept in remarkable condition. Silver pieces by **Paul Revere** are a highlight, along with original Chippendale furniture and the oft-photographed **Montmorenci** staircase. The museum opened to the public in 1951, and in 1992, a 35,000-square-foot exhibition center was opened to showcase even more acquisitions.

Winterthur also features a 200-acre naturalistic garden, which is best seen—particularly if you are flowered-out from a visit to Longwood—via a relaxing 45-minute guided ride on the **Garden Tram.** After your tours, the **Pavilion** (★★★$$) restaurant is worth a stop; if you're not hungry for a meal, you can enjoy high tea in this genteel setting. All tours of Winterthur are guided, and small children are not encouraged to participate.

If your visit inspires you to start up a little Winterthur of your own, drive down the road a piece to **David Stockwell, Inc., Antiquarians** (3701 Kennett Pike, 302/655.4466), where nothing dates later than 1830. The glorious period home furnishings here routinely sell for tens of thousands of dollars.

Winterthur and other places throughout the Brandywine Valley play host to an exciting series of equestrian events from April to November, generally open to the public at no charge. The valley's horsey set kicks off early spring with point-to-point and steeplechase races, in which horses and riders must ford streams, jump fences, and climb steep hills before crossing the finish line. Throughout summer and fall, fox chases and polo matches draw up to a hundred participants and 15,000 spectators. Picnics and tailgate parties are part of the fun, and the sporting events are often accompanied by carriage rides and exhibitions of antique cars. To find out whether your visit will coincide with any of these festivities, call the Brandywine Valley Tourist Information Center at 388.2900.

Were it located elsewhere, **Rockwood** (admission; Tu-Sa 11AM-4PM; 610 Shipley Rd, Wilmington, 302/658.2400) would be notable for its 70 acres of bucolic gardens. But in the Brandywine Valley these are little more than a footnote to the du Pont holdings. Still, the manor house, designed in 1851 by English architect **George Williams** for banker **Joseph Shipley,** is an outstanding example of Rural Gothic architecture, with charming gables and gingerbread beamwork, and antique Irish and English furnishings.

Nemours (admission; Tu-Sa 9AM-3PM, Su 11AM-3PM May-Nov; Rockland Rd, Wilmington; reservations required, 302/651.6912), another du Pont family estate, offers a soft, European charm. The 102-room mansion, fashioned in the style of a Louis XVI chateau, was designed by the New York architectural firm of **Carrere and Hastings,** and built between 1909 and 1910 by **Smyth and Son** of Wilmington. The home's furnishings reflect **Alfred I. du Pont's** pride in his family's French heritage. Nemours also makes a clear statement about the du Ponts' view of themselves as one of the world's greatest family empires: In addition to the French finery—including chandeliers and a hall clock once owned by **Marie Antoinette**—other dynasties are represented at either side of the property. On one end are the tremendous garden gates built in 1488 for Wimbledon Manor in England, and at the other are the elaborate ironwork gates that stood guard over the palace of **Catherine the Great** in St. Petersburg. The gardens themselves, inspired by Versailles, show a much more formal sense of discipline and symmetry than those of Longwood or Winterthur. Because Nemours sees less tourist traffic than

Winterthur, there is an exceptional sense of intimacy and personal attention on the tours here, which include a guided walk through rooms on three floors of the mansion and a bus ride through the gardens. Tours run just over two hours.

While visiting all the lush du Pont gardens and estates, you'll undoubtedly wonder how the family came to wield such wealth and prominence in the Brandywine Valley. Though plenty of the du Ponts' fortune came with them from Europe, the family was charged with entrepreneurial spirit, and a visit to **The Hagley Museum** (admission; daily 9:30AM-4:30PM Mar-Dec; M-F 1:30PM (one tour only), Sa-Su 9:30AM-4:30PM Jan-Mar; Rte 141, between Rte 100 and U.S. 202, 302/658.2400) illustrates how the du Ponts continued to prosper in America. It was on this site that the postcolonial industrialization of the Wilmington area began, as the du Ponts opened black gunpowder mills that eventually evolved into the family's chemical and textile businesses. Visitors are escorted around the 230-acre grounds by jitney and permitted to explore refurbished mills, machine shops, and workers' quarters. Guides in period dress provide demonstrations of domestic arts and discuss the home life of mill workers in the 1800s. The Brandywine River was the main source of power for the Hagley employees, and working waterwheels, steam engines, and water turbines represent the high tech of yesteryear.

Eleutherian Mills, the du Ponts' original Georgian-style family residence, is located on the Hagley grounds. The home was built near the dangerously combustible powder mill as a gesture of the du Ponts' solidarity with their laborers. Explosions were serious enough, however, to cause the family to vacate the house until the early 20th century, when industry had moved elsewhere.

Given the international stature of the Philadelphia Museum of Art, the **Delaware Art Museum** (free; Tu 10AM-9PM, W-Sa 10AM-5PM, Su noon-5PM; 2301 Kentmere Pkwy, Wilmington, 302/571.9590) is frequently passed over by visitors to the area, although this smaller museum has some significant holdings. **The Bancroft Collection** of English Pre-Raphaelite art is the largest of its kind in the United States. Displayed in dramatic Victorian-style galleries and augmented by an unparalleled scholarly archive, the collection includes works by **Dante Gabriel Rossetti, Edward Burne-Jones, William Holman Hunt, Marie Spartali Stillman,** and **John Everett Millais.** Also of note is an extensive collection of early 20th-century American illustrations, with more than 50 works by Brandywine artist **Howard Pyle** and dozens more by his students, including **N.C. Wyeth, Frank Schoonover,** and **Maxfield Parrish.** Finally, the museum boasts a novel **Children's Participatory Gallery,** which features a variety of hands-on art projects, most notably a wall-length pegboard that becomes an ever-changing mosaic as kids add and remove colorful shaped tiles.

With all the Brandywine region's high-toned attractions, it may come as a surprise that the area is also the country's fungus capital. Commercial mushroom

rowing in the United States was started in the 1890s
y **J.B. Swayne** of **Kennett Square.** Today, the
randywine Valley is the top mushroom growing
gion in the country, and mushrooms are
ennsylvania's largest cash crop. **Phillips
lushroom Place** (Rte 1, a half mile south of
ongwood Gardens, 388.6082) is a gift shop full of
ushroomabilia that boasts an adjacent "mushroom
useum." Don't bother: It costs a buck and a half to
into the musty walk-in closet of a museum with an
dequate diorama and a miserable video circa 1980.
nis is not the only dark side of the region's mush-
oom business: Kennett Square's cash crop is grown
nd harvested in dark, damp breeding houses where
atino and Asian immigrants complain of poor pay
nd conditions. The mushroom workers' grievances
nd efforts at unionization have stirred up some of
e Brandywine Valley's most negative publicity in
cent years.

fungi-free natural history is more your speed,
sit the **Delaware Museum of Natural History**
dmission; M-Sa 9:30AM-4:30PM, Su
oon-5PM; 5 miles west of Wilmington on Rte 52,
02/652.7600). While small, the museum offers
omprehensive collections of birds and seashells.
isplays such as the world's largest bird egg and a
00-pound clam delight kids.

onsider ending your day (or staying overnight) in
owntown **Wilmington.** The single must-see here is
e **Hotel du Pont** ($$$; 11th and Market Sts,
02/594.3100), a magnificent hostelry built in 1913
y **Pierre du Pont.** Lavish beyond any of Philadel-
hia's first-class hotels, this 12-story palace features
lded ceilings, richly carved paneling, and enough
arble to have emptied an entire quarry. Many of the
uest rooms are appointed with antiques and original
t. Even if you're not staying the night, consider an
egant dinner or Sunday brunch in the hotel's **Green
oom** (★★★★$$$$), which offers fine service and
ench cuisine in a stunning room lit by dramatic
ystal chandeliers. Many Philadelphians make the
alf-hour drive south to celebrate special occasions
this setting.

If you'd like to stay but not to
splurge, a good bet for its
extremely convenient location
is the **Brandywine Valley Inn**
($$; 1807 Concord Pike,
800/537.7772), which offers
special packages including tick-
s to Longwood and Winterthur.

hose who are spending the evening in town should
e what's playing at **The Grand Opera House** (818
arket Street Mall, 302/658.7598). Built in 1871, this
e example of cast-iron architecture is full of
ctorian decorative touches. Serving as Delaware's
erforming Arts Center, the Opera House hosts a
road spectrum of events, from symphony
erformances to pre-Broadway tryouts of major
usicals. Architectural tours of the premises are
ailable by appointment.

owntown Wilmington hardly ranks with Fifth
venue as a shopper's paradise, but do consider

making Delaware your souvenir central while visiting
the Philadelphia area: the Diamond State has no
sales taxes.

Bucks County

From historical sights to towns with a bohemian
bent to amusement parks for children, Bucks County
has a great variety of attractions. It's an easy 90-
minute drive up Interstate 95 from Philadelphia. If
you prefer to take public transportation, SEPTA
commuter trains to Doylestown leave downtown
Philly at least once an hour during the daytime;
phone 215/580.7800 for train schedules.

Bucks County's main points of interest are in the
scenic Delaware River Valley. The river itself played a
significant role in the county's economic life a century ago in terms of inland shipping, and today in
terms of tourism.

In spring and summer, the waters of the Delaware
are most inviting, especially for "tubing," which in
recent years has become the warm-weather craze in
the Philadelphia area. The stretch of the Delaware
commandeered by the folks at **Point Pleasant Canoe
& Tube** (reservations requested at least one week in
advance; daily 9AM-5PM April-Nov; Byram Rd off
Rte 32, 10 miles north of New Hope, 215/297.8823)
is the sport's *de facto* capital. Patrons of Point
Pleasant pay a modest fee to rent bright-colored,
reinforced inner tubes, then are driven upriver, where
they enter the Delaware's brisk current for a leisurely
three- or four-hour float back to home base. The ride
is picturesque, and the 80° water is virtually pollu-
tion-free, as Point Pleasant is both a preservation
society and an amusement vendor. Point Pleasant
also offers boating and rafting.

The 60-mile **Delaware Canal** system was built in
1840 to provide easy transportation of heavy goods,
from produce to limestone. Canal traffic reached its
peak in the 1860s, when as many as 3,000 boats and
barges a day used this now calm, quiet waterway.
Declared a **National Historic Corridor** in 1988, the
canal and towpath are kept in pristine condition by
both government and private agencies, including the
New Hope Mule Barge Company (admission; call
for times; New and S. Main Sts, New Hope,
215/862.2842), which offers one-hour mule-towed
barge rides on the canal from New Hope between
April and mid-November. Passing by secluded inns,
colonial buildings, and shady woodlands, these relaxing journeys have special appeal for history buffs,
romantics, and families. All barge rides include a
brief history lesson, and some provide banjo music.

If you simply enjoy scenic drives, **River Road** parallels the towpath for the length of the canal and can be
accessed at many points throughout the county.

A stroll through **Doylestown,** the county seat, will
give you a good idea of Bucks County's general fla-
vor. Simple one- and two-story buildings dating back
to the 19th century, a main street called Main Street,
and an ingenuous friendliness mark the town's character. But mixed in with Doylestown's small-town
atmosphere are plenty of hip, big-city offerings.

Consider the block of State Street just east of Main. Right across from the conservative wicker pieces and garden supplies at **Poor Richard's** (26 E. State St, 215/348.4655) is a bona fide New Age concession, **Earth Energy** (21 E. State St, 215/348.4451), which carries the latest in crystals and meditation audiotapes. According to a sign in the window, there's even "Aromatherapy by Appointment."

The same block features the snazzy blue and yellow Deco exterior of **The County Theater** (20 E. State St, 215/348.3456). In early 1993, the failing commercial cinema was taken over by a nonprofit group of local film aficionados, and the theater now screens foreign and art films. "You don't have to drive to Philadelphia or New York!" proclaims a sign heralding the new management.

Still, for urban escapees, Doylestown's small-town qualities are its biggest charms. It's doubtful that anything will strike you as more perfectly American, more Jimmy Stewart, than a good, cheap meal at **Eat Your "HART" Out: Robin & Beth's Hometown Luncheonette** (★★★$; breakfast and lunch, closed Saturday and Sunday; 24 N. Main St, 215/345.8873). Located in the wedge-shaped Hart Building, this bustling little establishment offers fresh club sandwiches, homemade soups, and super lemon poppyseed muffins. Robin and Beth know what their regular customers want before they even order, and all the customers seem to know each other.

What would a small town be without its resident eccentric? Doylestown's all-time oddball genius, **Henry Chapman Mercer**, left quite a legacy. A self-styled Renaissance man and an accomplished archaeologist, Mercer had his greatest find close to

his home in 1897, when he discovered some pre-1850 iron farm implements and began collecting them. Predicting that they would prove invaluable t future archaeologists, he expanded his collection to more than 50,000 pieces, representing the tools of some 60 early American trades plus an excellent assembly of period children's items.

The highly original museum Mercer built to house these items is part of a one-man construction boom that led to four buildings along what is today know as **Mercer Mile.** The **Mercer Museum,** the **Moravia Tile Works,** and Mercer's home, **Fonthill,** with its neighboring carriage house, were built by unskilled local laborers who worked without blueprints (admission to all three sites; M-Sa 10AM-5PM, Su noon-5PM; Rte 313 and E. Court St, 215/348.9461 Constructed entirely of reinforced concrete, Fonthil and the museum branch off into weird nooks and crannies, and the little tan carriage house looks like giant sandcastle. Cold and clammy inside, these buildings are rumored to have occasional condensation showers during winter.

Mercer's fancy for ceramic tile led him to open a ful fledged factory (now in scaled-back operation) on h property. The Moravian Tile Works produced mosaics that grace not only the walls of Fonthill and the museum, but Pennsylvania's state capital, the palace of Monte Carlo, and other buildings around the world. A tour and slide show about the tile work are part of a visit to the Mercer Mile.

Across the street from the Mercer Museum is the **James A. Michener Art Museum** (nominal admission; Tu-F 10AM-4:30PM, Sa-Su 10AM-5PM 138 S. Pine St, 215/340.9800), the well-known

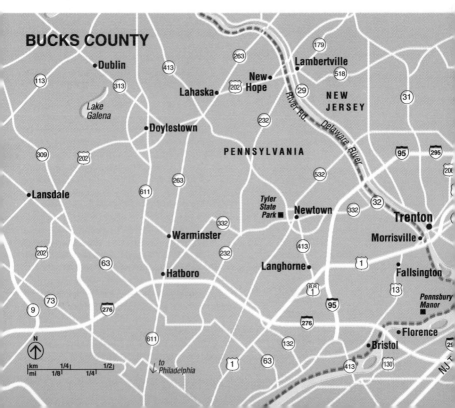

BUCKS COUNTY

thor's lasting contribution to his hometown. In
cent years, Michener's largesse has led to ongoing
ultimillion-dollar expansions of both the physical
ant and the permanent collections of the museum.
It even as the facilities expand, the Michener
useum keeps a tight focus on 19th- and 20th-cen-
ry American art, with a special eye toward native
cks County painters and sculptors. A quilt festival
featured each winter. Michener fans might also
joy seeing one of the writer's first desks. While the
useum's holdings are modest, the main building is
finitely worth a good look: it was once the **Bucks
unty Jailhouse.**

st north of Doylestown is **Green Hills Farm**
dmission; guided tours Tu-Sa 10:30AM, 1:30PM,
30PM, and Su 1:30PM, 2:30PM; closed January
d February; 520 Dublin Rd, Dublin, 215/249.0100),
e 60-acre homestead of another famous American
iter, **Pearl S. Buck.** The only woman ever to win
th the Nobel and Pulitzer prizes, Buck wrote more
an a hundred books here—novels, nonfiction, and
ildren's stories. The 1835 stone farmhouse was
me to Buck and her international family of adopted
ildren for 38 years, beginning in 1934. A mix of
nnsylvaniana and Orientalism, the house is evoca-
e of the two worlds that inspired the China-born
thor. See the handsomely carved Chinese
rdwood desk where Buck wrote *The Good Earth*
uminated by lamps fashioned from Pennsylvania
ockery jugs. The volunteer tour guides are
tremely well-versed in Buck's life and work. The
ro agencies Buck founded to aid international adop-
ns and help displaced Amerasian children continue
operate out of Green Hills today. Buck is buried
der a towering ash tree on the property that she
lled "the root of my American life."

ddler's Village (M-Th 10AM-5:30PM, F 10AM-
PM, Sa 10AM-6PM, Su noon-5:30PM;
5/794.4000), in Lahaska, between Doylestown and
w Hope, is one of those love-it-or-hate-it tourist
tractions that's all bric-a-brac, cobblestones, and
ctorian Revival whimsy. More than 70 boutiques
d restaurants with cute names like **Knobs 'N'
ockers** and **Auntie Em's Cookies** fill little stone
ildings set along winding brick paths. The spring-
ne flowers are honestly impressive, and at
ristmas, the "Village" is a twinkly sight to behold.
en naysayers may be charmed by the small
rousel Museum, with its collection of carved
ooden figures, circus memorabilia, and a working
tique merry-go-round.

arby is the old-fashioned
arry Valley Farm (admission;
ily 10AM-5PM; Street Rd,
haska, 215/794.5882),
sically a children's pet-
g zoo. Guides escort
milies around this onetime lime-
one quarry, permitting
ildren to shout and jump in a
yloft and introducing them
various critters, including a
0-pound pig and Cocoa, the
etland pony. Timid kids are

encouraged to feed corn to some particularly docile
sheep, and the barn full of "please touch" farm implements will get the imaginations going.

Central to any day in Bucks County should be a visit
to **New Hope,** the funky art-filled village on the banks
of the Delaware. With only four major streets—Main,
Bridge, Ferry, and Mechanic—the town encourages
strolling through galleries and eccentric boutiques
that lack the cloying quality of Peddler's Village.
Though New Hope has become a real tourist draw, it
has fended off overtures by the Gaps and Benettons
of the world and retained a real personality of its own.
It's a favorite weekend haunt of young Philadelphians
and New Yorkers, and you'll find a diverse crowd
enjoying the riverside foliage and wandering ducks.

Some New Hope favorites include:

Atlanta Annie's Art Deco (95 S. Main
St, 215/862.9565), a shop that isn't
altogether true to its name. You'll
find some items as recent as early
'90s Phillippe Starck furniture.
Owners **Jules Smith** and **Dave Hunt**
have a great eye, though, and their collection, while
small, is always impressive.

Farley's Book Shop (44 S. Main St, 215/862.2452),
which keeps up to date in an impressively wide range
of subjects.

Now and Then Shop (15 E. Bridge St, 215/862.5777)
leans very much toward "Then," with its authentic
'70s headshop decor, including lava lamps, Hendrix
posters, and Deadhead paraphernalia.

Hot Plates (40 S. Main St, 215/862.3220), **Andy
Popkin's** unique shrine to good old-fashioned restaurant dinnerware. Popkin scours warehouses
nationwide for glossy, wide-rimmed plates, hefty
soup bowls, and dreamy cream pitchers. For diner
fanatics, this place is a must.

Both sides of Main Street are lined with outdoor
porch bars, all of which offer reasonably priced drinks
and bar food. **Martine's, Karla's,** and **Havana** will
suit you fine.

If you're looking for ice cream rather than cocktails,
hit **Gerenser's** (22 S. Main St, 215/862.2050) for
unusual flavors like African Violet.

Wildflowers (★★★$$; 8 Mechanic St,
215/862.2241), an indoor/outdoor cafe beside the
canal, overlooking the sculpture garden of the **Now
Voyager** gallery next door, serving excellent midget
sandwiches and $7.50 dinner specials.

For dinner, don't miss **Mother's** (★★★$$; 34 N.
Main St, 215/862.9354), with a casual atmosphere
and creative cooking. If you like sweet but sophisticated tastes, this kitchen does wonders with fruit, like
kiwi-orange salmon, or duck stuffed with lemon
pound cake and glazed with blueberries.

Evening entertainment options include New York-
quality cabaret at nearby **Odette's** (S. River Rd,
215/862.2432), **John and Peter's Place** (96 S. Main
St, 215/862.5981) for cold brews and local rock, or
the mammoth dance floor at **The Cartwheel**
(215/862.0880) on Route 202 just outside of town.

159

BUCKS COUNTY PLAYHOUSE

Recommended to connoisseurs of camp is the **Bucks County Playhouse** (Main St, 215/862.2041), where the summer-stock season of musicals and comedies features TV celebrities such as **Loretta Swit,** game show host **Gene Rayburn,** and perennial New Hope thespian **William Shatner.**

While in New Hope, don't forget to cross the Bridge Street Bridge to **Lambertville, New Jersey,** another artsy town with a smattering of slightly higher-brow shops. Your best bet is the **Antique Center at the People's Store** (28 N. Union St, 609/397.9808), where more than 30 dealers of fine furniture, housewares, and Oriental rugs oversee joint display areas that have an open flow usually not found in multidealer operations.

Another Lambertville showcase for a number of collector-dealers is **The 5 & Dime** (40 N. Union St, 609/397.4957), with a sleekly enticing display of toys from the '50s and '60s, including Howdy Doody puppets and Scooby Doo alarm clocks. If you're a baby boomer, you're virtually guaranteed to find old favorites here.

On Saturdays and Sundays from early morning until about 3PM, more than 200 outdoor tables and 43 permanent buildings are used for the **Golden Nugget Antique and Flea Market,** a fine display of both treasure and junk (located 1½ miles south of Lambertville on Rte 29, 609/397.9424).

If you're spending the night, it's wise to choose the quieter streets of Lambertville over New Hope. Right on the river is the modern, well-appointed **Inn at Lambertville Station** ($$; 11 Bridge St, 609/397.4400), ideal weekend headquarters for couples and families.

Back in Pennsylvania, just south of New Hope, is **Washington Crossing Historic Park** (nominal fee for building tours; M-Sa 9AM-5PM, Su noon-5PM; Rtes 532 and 32, 215/493.4076), which features an annual Christmas reenactment of the historic crossing of the Revolutionary Army from Pennsylvania en route to Trenton. The park's **Taylor Mansion,** a faithfully restored 19th-century house, and the **McConkey Ferry Inn,** where **George Washington** and his men had Christmas dinner in 1776, are also open to the public. A wildflower preserve, watchtower, and commemorative statuary round out this excellent picnic spot.

Farther south and essential for hard-core history lovers are two pre-Revolutionary haunts of colony founder **William Penn.** His country plantation, **Pennsbury Manor** (admission; Tu-Sa 9AM-5PM, Su noon-5PM; 400 Pennsbury Memorial Rd, Morrisville, 215/946.0400), where he lived on the Delaware River for only two years, has a main manor plus 21 outbuildings, including a bakery and an ice house. Guides in period dress lead informative tours.

Perhaps the most interesting feature of the estate is the main house's fine collection of original 17th-century furniture, predating by a hundred years or more the colonial pieces found in most Philadelphia-area historic sights.

In nearby **Fallsington,** the Quaker village where Penn came to worship, the pioneer life of Pennsylvania's first settlers can be seen in the barebones furnishing and primitive straw sleeping mats marking the restored domestic interiors. The **Fallsington Historical Society** offers a slide show and guided tour (nominal fee; call ahead to arrange visits; 4 Yardley Ave, Fallsington, 215/295.6567), or you can take a self-guided walking tour.

Bucks County's single biggest tourist attraction is **Sesame Place** (admission; varying hours, May-early October; off Rte 1, Langhorne, 215/752.7070), a highly interactive theme park geared toward children between the ages of 3 and 10. The playground keeps kids physically and mentally active while entertaining them with the familiar characters from TV's "Sesame Street." Water rides include waterslide flumes, the tamer **Rubber Duckie Rapids,** and **Ernie's Waterworks,** a slippery maze of colorful pipes and fountains. New as of 1993 is **Twiddlebug Land,** where kids feel as small as Bert and Ernie's insect friends, surrounded by giant flowers, huge marbles, and an enormous spoon that serves as a slide. **Sesame Studio** provides high-tech adventures as children learn about color, light, and motion by concocting their own special effects extravaganza. Life-size Muppet characters stroll about and perform several shows daily. This is a great warm-weather experience for children as long as parents are content to sit patiently on the sidelines. Call ahead to check the park's capacity status; there are occasional admission cut-offs in high season.

If it's raining the day of your planned trip to Sesame Place, check out nearby **Sportland America** (daily 10AM-midnight; 9 Cabot Blvd, Langhorne, 215/547.7766), an entirely indoor facility that includes miniature golf, bumper cars, batting cages, roller skating, and, of course, a video arcade. Many a soggy afternoon has been salvaged here.

Since the opening of Sesame Place in 1980, the Bucks County lodging industry has changed a bit. Motels have been built to handle the region's newly won family trade, and adults-only rules have been loosened up at many of the wonderful inns and bed-and-breakfasts. **The Bucks County Tourist Commission** (215/345.4552) lists several dozen historic lodgings and can provide guidance based on your requirements. Be sure to ask about minimum lengths of stay, as some of these inns require two-night commitments on weekends.

Celebrated residents of Bucks County have included lyricist Oscar Hammerstein, anthropologist Margaret Mead, novelist Pearl Buck, playwright George Kaufman, and painter Edward Hicks, famous for his *Peaceable Kingdom.*

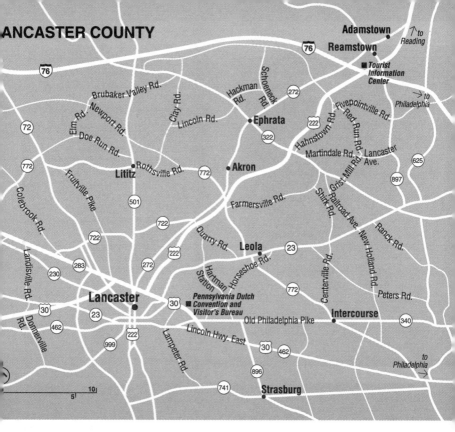

among the better choices is **Oscar Hammerstein's Highland Farms** ($$$; 70 East Rd, Doylestown, 215/340.1354), which has four guest rooms on five acres. The most popular tourist attractions are nearby, but you may prefer to hide out in this intimate inn over the weekend. The famed lyricist's stone and stucco country home boasts high ceilings, a secondstory wraparound porch, a swimming pool, and a tennis court. **Henry Fonda** was married on the grounds, and **Stephen Sondheim** was a guest. A full breakfast is included with your stay.

To the north a bit, on River Road in **Erwinna,** are the **Isaac Stover House** ($$$; 294.8044) and **Evermay on the Delaware** ($$; 294.9100). These comfortably refurbished antique-filled 19th-century hostels include breakfast and afternoon refreshments in their room rates. On weekends only, Evermay prides itself on its gourmet dining room (★★★$$$), which features an elaborate six-course prix fixe meal and is open to guests and the public. The Stover House is owned by television personality **Sally Jessy Raphael.**

Lancaster County

A 90-minute drive west from Philadelphia up Interstate 76 and the Pennsylvania Turnpike will lead you straight to the heart of Amish country. The hypnotic winding of even the major highways draws you into the Lancaster area, where the air is farm-country fresh and Amish girls in mesh bonnets ride Lawnboys over the lush pastures. Please note that the district's most traditional factions consider having their photographs taken a sin. **Always ask permission.**

To begin your tour of the Pennsylvania Dutch country, take Turnpike exit 21 and follow the signs for about a mile to **Zinn's Diner** (★★$; 215/267.2210) at the Route 272 junction. With its adjacent

miniature golf course and batting cages, Zinn's certainly looks like a tourist trap, but a glance at the menu and your fellow diners will verify the authenticity of the place. If a platter of "beef heart mit filling," "chicken und waffles," or "stuffed pig stomach" is not to your liking, try a sandwich or one of the more straightforward specials like hearty, dumpling-packed stews.

The tourist center next to Zinn's is staffed with friendly locals who make reliable recommendations after listening to your interests. Rather than part-timing teens, Lancaster's information centers are generally staffed with sharp, no-nonsense seniors. If you don't make it to Zinn's, hit the area's largest tourist station, the **Pennsylvania Dutch Convention and Visitor's Bureau** (daily 9AM-5PM in winter, daily 8AM-6PM in summer; 501 Greenfield Rd just off Rte 30 by the city of Lancaster, 717/299.8901), where a multi-screen slide show, "There Is A Season," provides a well-rounded overview of local attractions.

For answers to serious questions about the Amish religion and lifestyle, stop at **The Mennonite Information Center** (daily 9AM-5PM; 2209 Millstream Rd, Lancaster, 717/299.0954). If you call several weeks ahead, the center can help arrange one of the most rewarding Lancaster experiences available: for a modest fee, several dozen devout Mennonite families welcome visitors to their home dinner tables a couple of nights a week. These intimate visits provide true cultural exchanges.

Stick to Route 272 to pack as much variety as possible into your one-day outing. One mile north of the turnpike, stop in **Adamstown** to tour the award-winning **Stoudt's Brewery** complex (free; M-Sa 9AM-11PM, Su 9AM-5PM; 215/484.4385). About 10 small-batch brews are created throughout the year and sold fresh in champagne-style bottles. A pasteurized version of one golden variety is sold region-wide in conventional 12-ounce bottles. Summer weekends feature German brauhaus music and tastings plus dancing in an Oktoberfest-style beer hall. For lunch and dinner, the Stoudt family also operates the **Black Angus** (★★★$$) restaurant on-site, where all the beers and an amazing selection of wines are served with locally raised steaks.

Heading south on Route 272, you can't miss **Doll Express** (free; M, Th-Su 8AM-6PM; 215/267.2414) in Reamstown, a cooperative of more than a hundred dealers of collectible dolls, dollhouses, and miniatures who display their wares in dozens of actual freight train cars.

Train enthusiasts should derail from Route 272 to the town of **Strasburg,** off Route 741, an original hub of the **Pennsylvania Railroad** and home to the **Pennsylvania Railroad Museum** (717/787.8268),

the national headquarters of the **Toy Train Collectors' Association** (717/687.8976), and a number of other railroad-related shops and exhibits.

The Green Dragon Farmers Market and Auction (free; F 9AM-10PM; 955 N. State St, 717/738.1117), off Route 272 in Ephrata, is a town-size combination of flea market, farmer's market, and livestock sale and auction. It's a great place to browse through and nibble on local foods, and a good reason to schedule your Lancaster trip for a Friday, the only day the Green Dragon is open. More than 10 varieties of local bologna—sweet, savory, and not remotely like the supermarket kind—are sold here. You'll also find every imaginable cut and cooked variety of beef and pork, and some you won't want to imagine. One local favorite is tongue souse, best described as a cross between olive loaf and Jell-O.

Other Green Dragon highlights are:

Listening to the mile-a-minute auctioneers hollering prices of farm equipment; browsing through stalls of books written in the Pennsylvania German language; tasting **Michael's Breads** (cloud-soft and flecked with onion or cinnamon); and cooling off with a cone at **Lapp's Ice Cream**—the bonneted Amish women who serve you also milked dairy cows earlier in the week.

Going Dutch: A Glimpse of the Amish

Chances are you'll encounter the Amish (also referred to as the **Pennsylvania Dutch**) on a visit to the Philadelphia area; if you visit **Lancaster County,** about an hour and a half west of the city, you're bound to see them riding in their anachronistic horse-drawn buggies. More than 15,000 Amish, members of an Anabaptist sect that originated in 17th-century Germany and Switzerland when it separated from the Mennonites, live in the rural county.

Named after **Jacob Amman,** a Swiss Mennonite bishop, the Amish—who believed that true Christians should not bear arms, use force, or hold public office—left their homelands because of war and persecution, arriving in Philadelphia in 1737. The agrarian group found the fertile soil of Lancaster County, now home to the nation's largest Amish community, particularly attractive and well-suited to their lifestyle. The Amish live simply and dress modestly. Women wear bonnets and long dresses with aprons and shawls; married men and those over 40 are required to grow untrimmed ear-to-ear beards with the upper lip shaven, and wear black hats and suspenders. Belts are forbidden. And sect members are also expected to intermingle only among themselves.

The Amish don't own cars; eschew modern farm machinery and electricity; and tend to avoid contact with the non-Amish, except in matters of commerce. Their farm products—fresh vegetables,

poultry, jellies, preserves, and relishes—are immensely popular with Pennsylvanians and tourists, as are their patchwork quilts. (The quilt plays two important roles in Amish life, decorative and functional; it is assembled communally from scraps.)

Though the Amish maintain an uneasy relationship with modernity, that hasn't kept them from prospering. One reason for their good fortune is their birthrate: The average family has 6.6 children, most of whom remain in the community. Approximately 90,000 Amish live in North America.

While Lancaster County's gently rolling farmland has been good to the sect, it hardly provides a sanctuary. The Amish have been a constant source of curiosity for tourists, journalists, and Sunday drivers, and in the 1980s suffered the ultimate invasion when the **Pennsylvania Bureau of Motion Pictures and TV Development** (yes, there is such a thing) persuaded Hollywood to shoot its movie about the Amish, starring **Harrison Ford,** in Lancaster County. The filming of *Witness* stirred deep controversy among members of the religious group, who not only shun publicity, but likewise oppose film and photography. Infuriated Amish leaders actually threatened to uproot the community and move elsewhere. Ultimately, the state commerce department reached an agreement with them, pledging to never again promote the group as a feature film subject.

Nearby is the **Ephrata Cloister** (free; M-Sa 9AM-PM, Su noon-5PM; 632 W. Main St, Ephrata, 717/733.6600), a compelling historical site with 20 buildings (including the Academy, pictured above) that housed one of America's earliest communal societies. Founded by German Pietist **Conrad Biessel** in 1732, the group reached its peak population of about 300 in 1750. Spare and severely self-disciplined, the Cloister community is notable for having been both coed and celibate. A fascinating tour and slide show focuses on the group's haunting original music and medieval Germanic architecture.

If you're planning to stay overnight in Amish country, consider **Doneckers** ($$; 100 N. State St, 717/738.9501), Ephrata's village-within-a-town. Given the rural surroundings, this is a surprisingly upscale complex

of art galleries, fashion boutiques, and restaurants housed in finely refurbished turn-of-the-century buildings. Lodging prices are reasonable, especially given the antique-furnished rooms with Jacuzzis and other modern amenities. If you're tired of snacking and want some serious cuisine, try **The Restaurant at Doneckers** (★★★$$$), where the prices at lunch are especially reasonable.

Branch off to the northwest at Route 772 and drive about five miles to the town of **Lititz,** home of **Julius Sturgis Pretzels** since 1861. Here you can take a guided tour of the small factory and even do a little pretzel twisting of your own (nominal admission; M-Sa 9AM-4:30PM; 219 E. Main St, 717/626.4354). Many of Sturgis' pretzels are handmade, and you can watch the Amish women braiding dough. Sturgis cranks out an impressive variety of pretzels, from delicious honey-mustard crumbles to their horse-and-buggy-shaped Amish tribute.

"Pennsylvania Dutch" is a somewhat misleading name for the Amish and Mennonites who make their home in Lancaster County; these groups are actually descendants of Swiss and German immigrants. "Dutch" is a mangling of the German "Deutsch" (which means German).

Heading south again on 272, switch to Route 772 South to venture deep into farm country, the location of such towns as **Akron** and **Leola.** Watch for local families in the traditional Amish dress of dark suits and broad-brimmed hats for men and modest, apron-draped dresses for women. Children, dressed much the same as the adults, play outside one-room schoolhouses and in family yards (many Amish are firm advocates of home schooling). The Mennonites shun modern technology, and many homes don't have electricity or telephone service. In the fields, some farms do use tractors, but many farmers can be seen working the fields with seven-mule teams hooked to their plows.

Teenagers love T-shirts from **Intercourse, Pennsylvania,** and yours will probably want one, too. But this charming Amish town will appeal to the whole family. Among the spots to visit is **People's Place** (free; M-Sa 8:30AM-5PM; Rte 772, 717/768.7171), which features a first-rate free film and slide introduction to the Amish and Mennonite people and their faith. Also here is a hands-on children's exhibition called **Amish World,** where kids can try on traditional garb and play with simple farm equipment.

With so much to explore, you may want to spend an additional day in Lancaster County. A good, centrally located family hostelry with movie theaters and a swimming pool is the **Best Western Eden Resort Inn** ($$; Rtes 30 and 272, 717/569.6444) in the city of Lancaster. Couples may prefer **King's Cottage** ($$; 1049 E. King St, 717/397.1017), a deluxe mansion converted to a bed-and-breakfast. Located five minutes from downtown Lancaster, they serve an excellent high tea.

Main Line

Like L.A.'s Bel-Air and Cleveland's Shaker Heights, Main Line is American suburbia at its most luxurious. Posh modern homes and "George Washington Slept Here" estates share the quiet, tree-shaded streets of this 20-mile stretch just west of the city.

The Main Line is so-named because of its location along what was once "the main line" of the **Pennsylvania Railroad.** Today, SEPTA runs the trains on what remains one of the busiest segments of commuter railroad in the country. Known officially as the Paoli Local, the Main Line train can be boarded in Philadelphia at the **Market East Station** (11th and Filbert streets), **Suburban Station** (15th Street and JFK Boulevard), or the stately, refurbished **30th Street Station** (30th and Market streets). The Paoli Local generally runs twice an hour both into and out of town. Call 215/580.7800 for specific schedules.

For decades an old-fashioned mnemonic device has been used for the names of the communities (and train stations) that make up the Main Line: The first letter of each word in "**O**ld **M**aids (substitute **M**en if this offends) **N**ever **W**ed **A**nd **H**ave **B**abies. **P**eriod" corresponds to the towns of **O**verbrook, **M**erion, **N**arberth, **W**ynnewood, **A**rdmore, **H**averford, **B**ryn Mawr, and **P**aoli. (Nowadays, some trains make a few additional stops.)

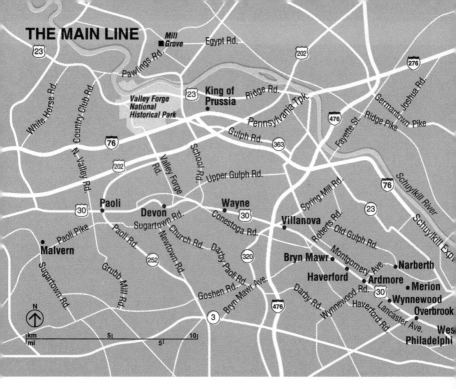

THE MAIN LINE

Because of its location close to Philadelphia, the Main Line differs from the more far-flung wealthy suburbs of other metropolitan areas. This proximity has kept "old" money near the center of the city, helping Philadelphia maintain a thriving urban core and keeping charity funds flowing to Center City cultural institutions. (Main Line communications mogul **Walter Annenberg** has endowed a graduate school at the University of Pennsylvania, a research institute downtown, and a gallery at the Philadelphia Museum of Art.)

The Main Line is relatively light on tourist attractions per se. In fact, the area's biggest draw was never intended to be open to the public. **The Barnes Foundation** (300 N. Latches Ln, Merion, 667.0290), a five-minute walk from the Merion train station (turn right on Merion Road at the station, then left on Latches Lane), was the private art collection of the late **Dr. Albert C. Barnes,** an eccentric man who amassed his fortune by inventing an eyewash. Housed in a building designed by **Paul Philippe Cret,** more than a thousand major works by artists such as Renoir, Cézanne, Matisse, and Van Gogh make this one of the world's finest displays of 19th- and 20th-century painting. Barnes wanted to keep his masterpieces from the eyes of critics and the public, so he permitted only a select group of students to view his collection. But in 1961, a court order claiming that tax breaks were given to the foundation as an educational institution led the way to limited public access. Reservations are still required, except on Fridays to Sundays, when about a hundred visitors are allowed in without reservations. In 1993 the foundation's board of directors broke with many of Barnes' time-honored idiosyncrasies and sent the highlights of the collection on a two-year tour of international museums. When the paintings return and the Foundation reopens to the public in late 1995, increased attention will undoubtedly make the Barnes more popular than ever. Call ahead for a schedule and reopening date.

While the Barnes galleries are closed, **The Arboretum of the Barnes Foundation** (M-F 9:30AM-4:30PM), which surrounds the main building, remains open to all. A remarkable 12-acre collection of more than 290 types of plants, the arboretum was designed in 1930 by University of Pennsylvania Professor of Landscape Architecture **Frank Schrepfer.** It's particularly notable for its Asian specimens, including the Korean boxwood, the paperbark maple, and the rare handkerchief tree. Radios and sports equipment are forbidden in the gardens.

About a mile away, on a busy commercial thoroughfare, you'll find the **General Wayne Inn** ($$$; 625 Montgomery Ave, 664.5125), a rustic tavern dating back to 1704 and a daily reminder to harried passersby that they live in the midst of history. **Benjamin Franklin** and Wayne himself were among the inn's colonial-era visitors. In 1843 **Edgar Allen Poe** drank and composed portions of "The Raven" here. Follow Poe's lead and stick to drinking at the inn's heavy wooden bar.

Next door is the pale yellow **Merion Meeting House** (Su 11AM; no telephone), a 1695 structure once attended by colony founder **William Penn.** Quaker worship is still held weekly and is open to the public.

A few stops beyond Merion, the view from the **Bryn Mawr Station** platform will give you a general idea e Main Line lifestyle. Bryn Mawr, along with the ther towns on the Paoli Local line, is not marked by e generic suburban sprawl that characterizes so uch of America; it's more like a small village, with a ntral civic and business area surrounded by outly- g residential areas. The station overlooks a little een public square that's home to a dentist's office, service station, a bank, and an excellent public rary.

ter a stroll through town, stop for lunch or dinner the **Central Bar and Grille** (★★★$$; 39 Morris ve, 215/236.8725), directly across from the train ation. Once a baggage depot, this chic, moderately iced watering hole was ingeniously revamped in 91 by architect **Edwin Bronstein** with witty tributes the Main Line's railway history. The handsome, egularly shaped new front wall uses corrugated uminum and red neon highlights to hint of heavy achinery, while small, regularly spaced windows er the booths suggest dining in private train com- rtments. Through these trackside windows you n watch trains whiz by as you dine. The interior is odern, with mauves, pinks, and checkerboards mplementing the excellent California-style salads d light entrées with a touch of Thai seasoning. The rseshoe-shaped bar is a favorite spot for young ofessionals. (In fact, this is the very neighborhood here TV's "thirtysomething" was set.)

you're venturing out to the Main Line by car, take ute 76 West from downtown Philadelphia to Route South, then head east on Route 23 East (Lancaster venue), which runs parallel to the rail line.

ue to the area's high standard of living, the Main ne has lately become a testing ground for new con- pts in upscale retail marketing. Three particularly novative shops can be found along Lancaster venue. First is **Zany Brainy: A Zillion Neat Things r Kids** (270 E. Lancaster Ave, Wynnewood, 2.2050). Bright confetti-patterned carpeting, a free ini-movie theater, and themed displays make edu- tional toys, books, games, and software virtually esistible to th children d parents. ke a cross tween

A.O. Schwartz and public television, Zany Brainy gularly features free activities, from art lessons to ience talks.

ext, head up Lancaster Avenue to **Borders Books & usic** (Rosemont Sq, Rosemont, 527.1500). This tional chain's first multimedia store has more than ,000 square feet filled with books and the Main ne's most comprehensive selection of CDs. While p is well stocked, locals flock to the store for its tensive catalog of jazz, classical, and international usic. Borders also has an espresso bar and two vent" spaces—for children and adults—where thors and musicians present free programs several nes a week.

nally, don't miss the magnificent **Anthropologie** 01 W. Lancaster Ave, Wayne, 687.4141), the flag- ip of what will eventually become a national chain of eclectic emporiums. The brainchild of local entrepreneur **Dick Hayne,** creator of the **Urban Outfitters** stores, this stunning Art Deco boutique is housed in a former auto dealership and is decorated with wood planks, granite slabs, and terracotta tiles. Coins tossed in the bubbling mosaic fountain are donated to the Women's Resource Center. Displays include beds in unusual shapes stacked high with pillows, and chic, politically correct housewares, candles, picture frames, and women's clothing. Spend as little as $3 for a cake of rainbow-hued soap or thousands for some of the most elaborate dried-flower arrangements you'll ever see. This is one of the few stores in the Philadelphia area that New Yorkers actually come down to visit.

If you're hungry and tired after your visit to Anthropologie, treat yourself to a gourmet lunch or dinner at **Restaurant Taquet** (★★★$$$; 139 E. Lancaster St, Wayne, 687.5005). Fine French cuisine is served at this brasserie in the awning-festooned **Wayne Hotel** ($$$), and in warm weather you can dine alfresco.

As you drive back to town, take note of the many educational institutions along Lancaster Avenue. **Villanova University, Haverford College,** and **Bryn Mawr College,** with its **Louis Kahn**-designed **Erdman Hall Dormitory** (1960-65), can be seen along the way.

Reading

Once a boomtown at the terminus of the leg-endary **Reading Railroad,** the city of Reading began a serious economic decline in the 1950s as man-ufacturing moved overseas and train travel became nostalgia rather than necessity. Located in Berks County just northeast of Lancaster, Reading was made virtually obsolete by modern highway sys-tems and air travel.

Local boosters proved resilient, however, offering favorable lease terms and attractive incentives to draw retailers and manufacturers into the Reading area to open discount stores. As name-brand com-panies from **Wrangler** to **Fieldcrest** and **Ralph Lauren** took Reading's bait, the discount phenomenon snowballed, pulling in tourists from far away and bargain hunters from nearby. Now billing itself as the "Outlet Capital of the World," rather than riding the rails, Reading is riding the sales.

If you want to shop Reading's 300-plus discount emporiums, tack a few hours onto a visit to Lancaster County rather than making a special trip. Unless you're a shopaholic, Reading can't be consid-ered a full-day event. Still, since the country drive from Philadelphia on Interstate 76 and Route 422 is a pleasant one and won't take more than 90 minutes, Reading is surely worth a look.

You can cover more ground on weekdays, but weekends are not unbearably crowded. For children—or anyone else who doesn't share a love of shopping—the many video arcades and coffee shops make the wait easier.

When you drive into Reading, head up **Skyline Drive** to **The Pagoda** (M-F noon-5PM, summer until 8PM; Sa-Su noon-6PM, summer until 9PM; Skyline Dr, 372.0553), a blue Japanese-style structure that is astoundingly incongruous in its surroundings and a good indication of the lengths this once-sagging area went to increase its tourist trade. Climb to the top of the seven-story building, however, and you'll be rewarded with a perfect panorama of the city and surrounding farmland.

To shop most efficiently, hit the outlet malls, which feature a half dozen to several dozen retailers under one roof. Keep in mind that virtually every piece of

clothing for sale in these stores is an overrun, a discontinued item, or an irregular. Don't worry, though. Overruns are in perfectly good condition; manufacturer just overestimated conventional retailers' orders. Discontinued items are also in fine shape, just be aware that you won't be this season fashion plate if you wear them. Irregulars, which a labeled as such, demand a sharp eye—a practical invisible crooked stitch is considered irregular, but so is something as important as a missing buttonhole. Then again, in a bakery company's out let, cookies were once deemed irregular because they had too *many* chocolate chips!

VF Factory Outlet

Start your conspicuous consumption at the very largest discount complex, the **VF Factory Outlet**

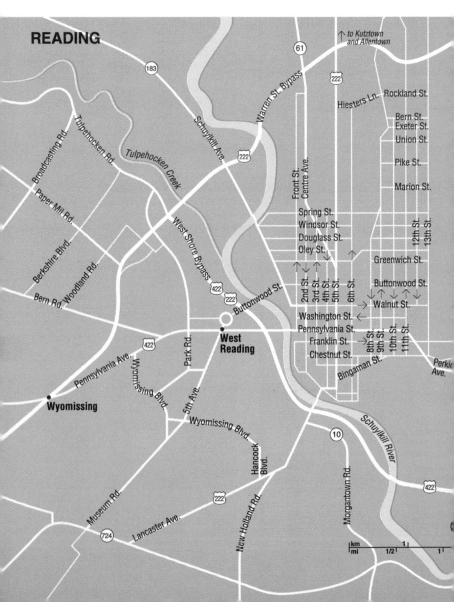

F 9AM-9PM, Sa 9AM-6PM, Su 11AM-5PM; Park
and Hill Ave, Wyomissing, 378.0408), owned by
parent corporation of apparel companies as di-
se as **Vanity Fair, Wrangler, Jantzen,** and
sport. Almost all merchandise here is priced at a
50 percent off recommended retail. The VF outlet's
nphlets, available at virtually every Reading and
caster County visitor's center, include a certificate
$5 off any combined purchase of more than $50
n mall stores. Adjacent to the VF stores are **Bass**
e and **Black & Decker** discount operations.

t, head downtown to **The Reading Outlet Center**
-Th 9:30AM-6PM, F-Sa 9:30AM-8PM, Su noon-
M; 801 N. Ninth St, 373.5495) for **Corningware,**
ch leather goods, **Farah** slacks, **Ralph Lauren's**
o sportswear, and rain gear by **London Fog** (some
y good buys here).

en downtown, hit the **Reading Station Designer
tlet Center** (M-Sa 10AM-9PM, Su 10AM-7PM;
N. Sixth St, 373.2600), where the ambience is
h-toned even though the prices remain low. While
area's other outlets cut their costs through bare-
es displays and minimal decor, the Station wins
nts for charm, with its Victorian-style buildings
rounding a pleasant, well-groomed courtyard. The
t buys on brand names here include **Brooks**
thers and **Cole-Haan** shoes.

ke every effort to eat at the deservedly famous
's Restaurant (★★★$$$; Seventh and Laurel
373.6794)—though that means sticking around
l evening, as lunch is not served here. Owner
k Czarnecki is one of the country's experts on
d mushrooms, and his family collects an
ndance of morels and other forest morsels daily
se in the cooking. Joe's also has an impressive
ction of California wines and waiters.

ne brands have nothing to do with the shopping at
nningers Antique & Farmers Market (Sa 8:30AM-
M; 740 Noble St, Kutztown, 683.6848), in nearby
ztown. Considered one of the top
markets in the world, this

indoor-outdoor
extravaganza draws up to
1,200 dealers from 42 states
on peak summer Saturdays.
ending on one's perspective, wandering through
nningers is like falling into a treasure chest or
ing into your weird uncle's junk drawer. One day's
wsing brought home some medieval armor, a
h-baked shoo-fly pie, and a handful of World War
signia pins. Beer can collectors, Shaker furniture
lers, and booksellers all compete for your dollar

here. Don't be afraid to haggle; many of the vendors
don't hesitate to overcharge.

Also of note in Kutztown is the **Rodale Research
Center** (call for information; 611 Siegfriedale Rd,
683.6383). A major publisher of magazines, such as
Men's Health and *Prevention,* and books on garden-
ing and alternative health, Rodale maintains this
facility to explore and develop the fields of organic
farming and gardening. Guided tours are free and
very informative.

Reading is one of the few towns where a minor
league baseball club plays right near its big league
affiliate. The **Reading Phillies** are the AA farm team
of the Philadelphia Phillies, so they benefit doubly
from the locals' home-team spirit. **Municipal
Stadium** (Rte 671 South, by Rte 222, 375.8469) has
great sight lines and an intimate feel. Also, because
tickets cost a fraction of big league prices ($2 to $5),
this is a great place to take children to their first
ball game.

To move from the all-American game of baseball to
something altogether different, consider one of
Reading's least publicized features: **Stone Man
Willy.** An unidentified criminal who attacked a nun in
the late 1800s, "Willy" hung himself in Reading's
central jail. When no relatives claimed the body,
funeral director **Theodor Auman** received permission
from the state to try a new embalming fluid on the
corpse. The formula literally petrified the body,
which—having browned in color—is still in good
form at the **Theodor Auman Funeral Home** today
(247 Penn St, 370.0200). Photographs are forbidden
and tours are not offered, but if you must, Willy *does*
receive guests by appointment.

If you're staying overnight, **The Inn at Reading** ($;
1040 Park Rd, Wyomissing, 372.7811) is a good bet.
It's modern, well located, and has a tourist informa-
tion center on the premises.

Valley Forge

Located just 18
miles from
downtown
Philadelphia, the
**Valley Forge
National Historical
Park** offers a challenge to
the imaginations of tourists and amateur historians
alike. During the famed winter encampment of 1777-
78, Washington's Continental Army of 12,000 used
virtually all of the 3,500 acres for entrenchments,
livestock pens, parade grounds, and a thousand log
cabins. Today, the area is a vast, rolling blanket of
green; the Visitor's Center and a handful of simple
monuments are the only hints of that momentous
revolutionary winter. Valley Forge tourism peaks in
the summer months, when weather conditions are
least similar to those faced by Washington's men.

For visitors who want a break from the colonial histo-
ry of downtown Philadelphia, the wide vistas and
fields of Valley Forge provide a welcome opportunity
for relaxation and play. Kite-flying, sunbathing,

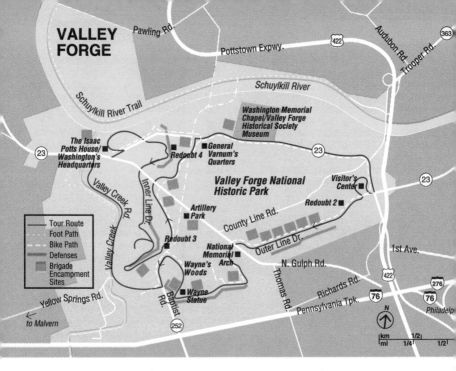

Frisbee, and touch football are common activities here, so don't hesitate to bring along your sporting equipment. The National Park Service has even created special jogging and biking paths, used much more by natives than tourists.

The best way to reach the park is by car. Take the Schuylkill Expressway (Interstate 76) west from Philadelphia and watch for the signs. Exit 26B will put you on North Gulph Road for 1½ miles, leading to the Visitor's Center. Valley Forge can also be reached by SEPTA bus 125, which departs from 16th Street and JFK Boulevard; however, with stops and a transfer, the trip can take close to two hours. Call 215/580.7800 for bus information.

The **Visitor's Center** (783.1077), a contemporary building that reflects the grassy landscape, includes a modest display of colonial artifacts, a ranger station, and an excellent traveler's reference desk with detailed maps and information on attractions and special events throughout the Philadelphia area. The materials here are updated frequently, so check them for antique shows, auctions, or art festivals that coincide with your visit.

The center's 15-minute film presentation, *Valley Forge: A Winter Encampment,* shows the vast expanse of the park in winter and describes the failing health of Washington's poorly clothed and fed troops. The film is especially useful if you are trying to explain the historical significance of Valley Forge to children.

For every Continental soldier killed in combat during the American Revolution, three died of disease. Nearly one-sixth of the 12,000 men who encamped at Valley Forge perished as a result of illness during the course of the winter.

A self-guided 10-mile driving loop whisks you around the park's memorial sites, including equestr an statuary; the **National Memorial Arch,** a handsome, quote-covered tribute to the revolutionary soldiers; the re-created huts of the **Muhlenberg Brigade;** and **Wayne's Woods,** a stand of tall pines retrofitted with tables and benches for picnicking. The **Isaac Potts House,** built in 1774 and still standing in its original form, was converted from farm use to serve as Washington's headquarters during the war. There is a $2 fee for a brief tour of the interior, which is furnished with period reproductions.

The final stop on the route is the **Valley Forge Historical Society Museum** (nominal admission; M-Sa 9:30AM-4:30PM, Su 1-4:30PM, 783.0535), which houses 4,000 pieces of memorabilia in four themed collections that symbolize patriotism: Washingtoniana, military equipment, colonial artifacts, and Valley Forge.

Adjacent to the museum is the **Washington Memorial Chapel,** where free carillon concerts are held on Sundays at 2PM. In warm-weather months, visitors' imaginations get a boost from occasional costumed reenactments of army training procedure by local historical groups (call the Visitor's Center fo the schedule).

Two miles from Valley Forge is **Mill Grove** (free; museum Tu-Sa 10AM-4PM, Su 1-4PM. Grounds Tu-Su dawn-dusk; Audubon and Pawlings Rds, 666.5593), a small museum and wildlife preserve o the 130-acre estate of famed colonial-era naturalist **John James Audubon.** More than 175 species of birds have been identified here. Audubon's informal naturalistic drawing style—which broke with traditionally formal wildlife art—grew from his observations of birds from the front porch of his house, now the site of the museum.

Another artist's homestead worth visiting is the **Wharton Esherick Museum** (guided tours only; nominal admission; Sa 10AM-5PM, Su 1-5PM, closed January and February; off Diamond Hill Rd; reservations required, 644.5822), which comprises the 20th-century master's former studio and stone farmhouse. Although formally trained as a painter in Philadelphia, Esherick drew inspiration from his woodland surroundings, first carving elaborate frames for his pictures, then moving on to sculpt the dramatically contoured wooden furniture that made him famous. Located on the Horseshoe Trail, two miles west of Valley Forge, Esherick's studio is preserved as it was during his lifetime, with no signs or plaques to detract from the moving sense of the artist at work.

For those in need of a history break, the East Coast's largest shopping center, **The Court and The Plaza** at King of Prussia (M-Sa 10AM-9:30PM, Su 11AM-5PM; Rte 202 and N. Gulph Rd, 265.5727), is just 10 minutes away. Anchored by **Macy's, Bloomingdale's, Sears,** and the Philadelphia-based **John Wanamaker** and **Strawbridge & Clothier** department-store chains, and including more than

350 additional specialty shops and restaurants, you'd think this mall had it all. "Not so" say its ambitious developers, who in 1993 began an expansion project that will add a **Lord & Taylor,** a **Nordstrom,** and 135 more boutiques by 1996. This is not the neck of the woods for culinary adventuring: stick to familiar chains in the mall (**Houlihan's, Friday's,** etc.) and save your gastronomic curiosity for downtown Philly.

If you have lingered in the Valley Forge area until evening, consider attending some top-drawer live entertainment. The **Valley Forge Music Fair** (Rte 202, Devon, 644.5000), which began as a summertime tent theater in the early 1970s, proved so popular that it was converted to a year-round 3,000-seat indoor arena featuring major nightclub acts, from **Rosemary Clooney** to local heroine **Patti Labelle.** Call ahead for the schedule.

For more serious entertainment in a lovely rustic setting, try the nationally recognized and critically acclaimed **People's Light and Theatre Company** (39 Conestoga Rd, Malvern, 644.3500), which presents an impressive array of drama, from the classics to the cutting edge.

Bests

Mark H. Biddle, Esquire
Attorney/President, Independence Hall Association

The Assembly Room at **Independence Hall; Carpenters Hall;** and **Christ Church** never cease to fill me with wonder. These buildings, so small by modern standards, reflect simply and well the monumental principles that have inspired, and today continue to inspire, people around the world.

Lunch or dinner at the original **Carolina's** restaurant off Rittenhouse Square and at the new Carolina's in Radnor.

A drive through the superb countryside along the **Brandywine.**

Boathouse Row—for the views, the rowing, and other sports in **Fairmount Park.**

The **Bassetts Ice Cream** counter and other stands at **Reading Terminal Market,** which has been an authentic food market for years, not just another created "festival marketplace." Real Philadelphians eat ice cream.

John Higgins
Executive Director, Foundation for Architecture

The main stairway at the **Pennsylvania Academy of the Fine Arts** is worthy of comparison with the Renaissance stairways by Michelangelo. The architect, **Frank Furness,** was trying to develop a distinctly American architectural style. See for yourself whether he succeeded in the design of this splendidly eccentric building.

Designed in 1915 by **Paul Philippe Cret,** the consummate architect, **Rittenhouse Square** is

supremely elegant and understated. It is the most beautiful and best kept of the five Philadelphia squares originally laid out by **William Penn** in 1682.

The two great rooms inside **Independence Hall,** where American independence was debated and declared, are infused with the most remarkable aura of history and majesty.

The gardens of **Winterthur** in the Brandywine Valley are a perfectly maintained example of classic English landscape design—you'll think you're in the Cotswolds. Fabulous azalea and peony gardens as well.

The first row of any balcony at the **Academy of Music,** which was modeled after La Scala in Milan. Lean over to take in one of the most magnificent neobaroque interiors in the country while you listen to great music.

The 19th-century boathouses on the **Schuylkill River** are charming Victorian buildings outlined at night with thousands of tiny lights, the whole reflected in the stillness of the water just above a weir.

The view of Philadelphia from the east terrace of the **Philadelphia Museum of Art.** Look down the Benjamin Franklin Parkway, Philadelphia's Champs-Elysées, toward City Hall and the Center City skyline.

The view from the top of **City Hall;** the tower here is the only accessible spot overlooking the entire city.

The **Italian Market,** though less refined than the Reading Terminal Market, is one of the last open-air markets in the country that hasn't been gentrified. It feels like a working-class market in Rome. You will see the most amazing cross section of Philadelphians jostling each other to get the attention of the vendors.

Index

A

au bon pain ★$ **54**
Azalea ★★$$$ **18**

B

H

I

J

W

Y

Z

Restaurants

Only restaurants with star ratings are listed below. All restaurants are listed alphabetically in the main (preceding) index. Always call in advance to ensure a restaurant has not closed, changed its hours, or booked its tables for a private party. The restaurant price ratings are based on the average cost of an entrée for one person, excluding tax or tip.

★★★★ An Extraordinary Experience
★★★ Excellent
★★ Very Good
★ Good

$$$$ Big Bucks ($35 and up)
$$$ Expensive ($20-$35)
$$ Reasonable ($12-$20)
$ The Price is Right (less than $12)

★★★★

★★★

★★

Hotels

The hotels listed below and at right are grouped according to their price ratings; they are also listed in the main index. The hotel price ratings reflect the base price of a standard room for two people for one night during the peak season.

$$$$ Big Bucks ($175 and up)
$$$ Expensive ($125-$175)
$$ Reasonable ($75-$125)
$ The Price Is Right
(less than $75)

$$$$

$$$

$$

$

Features

Bests

Maps

Page	Entry #	Notes

Page	Entry #	Notes

ACCESS® Travel Diary

Page	Entry #	Notes

Page	Entry #	Notes

Credits

Writers/Researchers
Laura Quinn
Old Philadelphia
Center City East
Broad Street/South
  Philadelphia
Center City West
Parkway/Fairmount Park
University City

Tom Moon
  Orientation
  South Street/Waterfront

Jim Gladstone
  Day Trips

Other Contributors
Susan Jensen
Ken Kalfur
Christina Long
Howard Shapiro
Anthony Wood

ACCESS®PRESS

Managing Editor
Linda Weber

Project Editor
Lisa Zuniga

Staff Editor
Karin Mullen

Assistant Editor
Erika Lenkert

Editorial Assistant
Karen Decker

Contributing Editors
Leslie Plummer Clagett
Charlotte Knabel
Jean Linsteadt
Antonia Moore

Editorial Consultant
Rebecca Forée

Proofreaders
Jeff Campbell
Susan Charles
Elizabeth Ferguson
Julie Powell

Word Processor
Jerry Stanton

Design/Production Manager
Cherylonda Fitzgerald

Designers
Barbara Bahning Chin
Carrē Furukawa
Claudia Goulette

Maps
Michael Blum
Kitti Homme
Scott Summers

Special Thanks
Jim Andrews
Mark H. Biddle
Mark Brokering
Michael Copeland
**Foundation for
  Architecture**
Greta Greenberger
Mike Hardy
Maria Hjelm
James Nelson Kise
Mark Frazier Lloyd
Tom McNichol
Steve Peterson
Tredyffrin Public Library
**University of Pennsylvania,
  Architectural Archives**

Cover Design ©
**The Understanding
  Business**

Cover Photograph ©
**Andrea Pistolesi/
  The Image Bank**

Printing and Otabind
Webcom Limited

ACCESS®PRESS does not solicit individuals, organizations, or businesses for inclusion in our books, nor do we accept payment for inclusion. We welcome, however, information from our readers, including comments, criticisms, and new listings.

The publishers and authors assume no legal responsibility for the completeness or accuracy of the contents of this book, nor any legal responsibility for the appreciation or depreciation in the value of any premises, commercial or otherwise, by reason of inclusion or exclusion from this book. All contents are based on information available at the time of publication. Some of the maps are diagrammatic and may be selective of street inclusion.

Independence Hall Association

Independence Hall Association was founded in 1942 by public-spirited citizens and business leaders, led by Judge Edwin O. Lewis. The group's objective was to safeguard historic structures in Old Philadelphia and to improve their surroundings. This led to the federal establishment of what is today Independence National Historical Park. The Independence Hall Association, whose current President is Mark H. Biddle, is headquartered in Carpenters' Hall, 320 Chestnut Street. Members of the Association include leaders of Philadelphia's civic, business, professional, and philanthropic communities.

Printed in Canada